FREEDOM IN ECONOMICS

The importance of freedom as a value in political philosophy has long been challenged by the concept of welfare in theories of distributive justice and economic equity. In recent scholarship it has regained its central position, and progress is now being made by philosophers and economists to re-establish its importance. Recent theories of justice emphasize the value of individual choice, freedom and responsibility, while economic models now analyse how opportunity sets can be ranked by individuals interested in flexibility and freedom, how individual rights and basic liberties can be modelled in the theory of social choice, and how equitable allocations of opportunities can be defined.

This book presents a range of articles by philosophers and economists, debating the most crucial aspects of the subject: the definition and value of freedom; the valuation of opportunity sets; the modelling of rights in social choice theory; the opposition between outcome-oriented and opportunity-oriented theories of justice; the economic analysis of individual responsibility and the applications of theories of equal opportunities; the empirical acceptance of moral principles laid down by theorists. The book provides a substantial contribution to the fruitful dialogue between the philosophy and economics in this area. Each chapter is integrated, being followed by comments which explore the underlying debates.

Jean-François Laslier is a researcher at the Centre National de la Recherche Scientifique, and **Marc Fleurbaey**, **Nicolas Gravel** and **Alain Trannoy** are, respectively, associate professor, assistant professor and full professor of economics at the Université de Cergy-Pontoise.

Routledge Studies in Social and Political Thought

FREEDOM IN ECONOMICS

New Perspectives in Normative Analysis

Edited by Jean-François Laslier, Marc Fleurbaey, Nicolas Gravel and Alain Trannoy

Routledge
Taylor & Francis Group

LONDON AND NEW YORK

First published 1998
by Routledge
2 Park Square, Milton Park, Abingdon, Oxfordshire OX14 4RN

Simultaneously published in the USA and Canada
by Routledge
711 Third Avenue, New York, NY 10017

First issued in paperback 2014
Routledge is an imprint of the Taylor & Francis Group, an informa business

Typeset in Times by
BC Typesetting, Bristol

British Library Cataloguing in Publication Data
A catalogue record for this book is available from the British Library

Library of Congress Cataloguing in Publication Data
Freedom in economics: new perspectives in normative analysis/Jean
-François Laslier [et al.].
p. cm.
Includes bibliographical references and index.
1. Social choice. 2. Social justice. 3. Welfare economics.
4. Liberty. I. Laslier, Jean-Francois.
HB846.8.F73 1998
330.1–DC21 97-7493

ISBN 978-0-415-15468-0 (hbk)
ISBN 978-1-138-00704-8 (pbk)

CONTENTS

v

CONTENTS

Part II Rights

Part III Opportunities

CONTENTS

CONTRIBUTORS

Richard Arneson Department of Philosophy, University of California, San Diego, USA.

Walter Bossert Department of Economics, University of Waterloo, Waterloo, Canada.

Anne Brunel Centre de Recherches en Economie Mathématique et Econométrie, Université de Caen, Caen, France.

Kurt Devooght Katholieke Universiteit Leuven, Leuven, Belgium.

Marc Fleurbaey THEMA, Department of Economics, Université de Cergy-Pontoise, Cergy-Pontoise, France.

Louis Gevers Facultés Universitaires Notre Dame de la Paix, Namur, Belgium.

Nicolas Gravel THEMA, Department of Economics, Université de Cergy-Pontoise, Cergy-Pontoise, France.

Peter J. Hammond Department of Economics, Stanford University, California, USA.

Daniel M. Hausman Department of Philosophy, University of Wisconsin-Madison, USA.

Serge-Christophe Kolm Ecole des Hautes Etudes en Sciences Sociales, Paris, France.

Jean-François Laslier THEMA, Université de Cergy-Pontoise, and CNRS, Cergy-Pontoise, France.

Bezalel Peleg Department of Economics, Cornell University, Ithaca, New York, USA.

Emmanuel Picavet UFR de Philosophie, Université Paris I (Panthéon-Sorbonne).

CONTRIBUTORS

Clemens Puppe Institut für Wirtschaftswissenschaften, University of Vienna, Austria.

John E. Roemer Department of Economics, University of California, Davis, USA.

Maurice Salles Centre de Recherches en Economie Mathématique et Econométrie, Université de Caen, Caen, France.

Erik Schokkaert Katholieke Universiteit Leuven, Leuven, Belgium.

Alain Trannoy THEMA, Department of Economics, Université de Cergy-Pontoise, Cergy-Pontoise, France.

Dirk Van de Gaer Katholieke Universiteit Leuven, Leuven, Belgium.

Philippe Van Parijs IRES, Université Catholique de Louvain, Louvain-la-Neuve, France.

Antonio Villar Department of Economics, University of Alicante, Alicante, Spain.

INTRODUCTION AND OVERVIEW

Marc Fleurbaey, Nicolas Gravel,
Jean-François Laslier and Alain Trannoy

This volume contains a sample of papers presented at the conference '*Ethics and Economics of Liberty*' which took place at Université de Cergy-Pontoise on June 20–21, 1995. The purpose of the conference was to give economists and philosophers the opportunity to meet and exchange their ideas on the role of freedom as a normative criterion for appraising alternative states of affairs.

A priori, freedom seems to be at the heart of economics. Economists constantly refer to freedom of choice, free exchange, free entrepreneurship, free trade, free markets and so on. And, as a matter of fact, before the end of the nineteenth century, the use by economists of freedom as a normative criterion to evaluate alternative states of affairs was common. Hicks [33] has recalled to our attention the fact that, for classical economists of the nineteenth century, 'the contention that economic freedom made for economic efficiency was no more than a secondary support' (p. 138). J. S. Mill [43], for instance, when he writes that 'Restrictions on trade or on production for purposes of trade are indeed restraints; and all restraint qua restraint is an evil' (p. 91) uses freedom as the only criterion to compare alternative policies. So do Marx and Engels [17] (despite what the tradition that their work inspired may suggest) when they defend their ideal of a communist society on the basis that it would bring 'the conditions for the free development and activity of human under their own control' (p. 22) and that it would

> make it possible for me to do one thing to-day and another tomorrow, to hunt in the morning, fish in the afternoon, rear cattle in the evening and criticize after dinner, just as I have in mind, without even becoming hunter, fisherman, shepherd or critic.
>
> (p. 22)

Yet, from the end of the nineteenth century to very recently, freedom as such has virtually disappeared from the conceptual framework of economists except, as in M. Friedman [24], as an instrumental means of improving welfare and efficiency.

1

The reason for this should come as no surprise to historians of economi
thought. The end of the nineteenth century is associated with the take-ove
of economics by the so-called marginalist revolution. The focus of Jevons
Menger, Walras, Edgeworth and, after them, Marshall and Pigou on indi
vidual subjective preferences to explain prices had indeed an obvious
counterpart in the normative branch of the discipline: namely that individual subjective preferences should also be the natural criterion to assess
the 'social goodness' of alternative states of affairs. This approach, which
became known as *welfarism*, still dominates mainstream economics. Until
the last two decades, and with isolated, although vivid, exceptions like
Hayek [30], Hicks [32] and Buchanan [7], it remained unchallenged as *the*
theoretical foundation of normative economics.

It would take the talent of better historians of recent economic thought
than us to give a full explanation for the recent (and still timorous) altera-
tion of this hegemony and the reappearance of freedom as a criterion of
intrinsic importance in normative economics to which this book echoes.
Yet, from observing the trend of mainstream research in normative economics in the last two decades or so, it is possible to locate three areas in
which concepts and notions directly relevant for understanding freedom
were forged. Two of these areas are rooted in economics. The third stems
from philosophy, and more specifically from John Rawls's [50] seminal
contribution.

First there is the theory of rights whose introduction in economics was
made by Sen [53] under the attractive banner of a paradox. It is indeed
common in the political sphere to conceive freedom as being embodied in
a set of rights, and it is usual to treat 'human rights' and 'basic liberties'
as being more or less the same. And, quite clearly, the problem of defining
an adequate system of individual territories – or individual rights – within
which individual liberties can be exercised compatibly is of crucial importance for implementing the ideal of a society of free individuals. For this
reason, the proof made by Sen that the existence of individual rights can
conflict with economists' sacrosanct Pareto-optimality sparked an impress-
ive literature which quickly revealed that the very way by which rights are
modelled can itself be a matter of controversy. Sen's original formalization
of an individual right was framed in terms of the social choice theoretic
notion of *decisiveness*. Mary has the right to paint her bedroom walls any
colour she likes if Mary is decisive – or is a dictator – in any (social) decision
involving exclusively the choice of colour of her bedroom. To this formalism, authors like Gardenfors [25] and Gaertner, Pattanaik and Suzumura
[64] have opposed that of *games forms*. In the game form approach, there
is an explicit modelling of the actions – or strategies – available to individuals as well as of the final outcomes – or social states – that result
from alternative combinations of individual actions. Within such an
approach, an individual right is modelled as a particular combination of

2

sets of admissible individual strategies. For instance, Mary's right to choose the colour of her bedroom wall would be interpreted as meaning both that Mary can choose any strategy that leads to a social state involving her room painted in any conceivable colour *and* that other individuals can *not* choose strategies that prevent such social states from occurring. Hence the modern theory of rights appears to be in a state of infancy, with quite a sizeable prospect for future developments.

Whichever modelling representation is chosen, rights are typically conceived in terms of negative freedom (using the standard distinction introduced by I. Berlin [3]). That is, a right to do a particular thing is typically understood as a freedom from not being prevented to do this thing, rather than as freedom to actually do the thing. As such, rights correspond to a notion of freedom which, for many authors, is the only acceptable one. For instance, Buchanan [8] claims that 'an individual is at liberty or free to carry on an activity if he or she is not coerced from so doing by someone else, be this an individual or a group' (p. 10), and argues that positive freedom is an altogether different notion. F. von Hayek [30] also defends this viewpoint: 'Whether or not I am my own master and can follow my own choice and whether the possibilities from which I choose are many or few are two entirely different questions' (p. 17). Yet, there are also many authors, like A. Sen [57], P. van Parijs [44], and before them F. Knight [37], who hold the view that the relevant practical question is that of actual power or opportunity rather than negative freedom.

The desire to account for both negative and positive freedom has motivated a recent interest for the notion of freedom of choice as a property of the individual's *opportunity set*, that is, the set of all options that are available for choice to an individual at a given instant. This is the second area where normative economics is currently integrating the concept of liberty. To the best of our knowledge, the first paper that examines the notion of freedom of choice by considering properties of a ranking of opportunity sets is Jones and Sugden [35], although some questions relative to freedom as flexibility had already been explored by Kreps [42]. This topic reappeared in Sen's Dewey [56] and Marshall [57] lectures and gave rise to Suppes's [62] and Pattanaik and Xu's [45] axiomatic characterizations of the ranking of opportunity sets based on the comparison of their cardinality. From these results originate a growing literature (see, e.g., Arrow [2], Bossert [5], Bossert, Pattanaik and Xu [4], Foster [23], Gravel ([27], [28]), Klemisch-Ahlert [36], Pattanaik and Xu [46], Puppe ([48], [49]) and Sen ([58], [59], [60])) which tries to decipher the various reasons for which individuals may value freedom of choice and to explore alternative rankings of opportunity sets induced by these reasons. A focal point of this literature is the difficulty of combining the *instrumental* value of freedom – that is, the extent to which it allows satisfaction of preferences over options – with its *intrinsic* value – that is, its value for its own sake, irrespective of any other consequence it may entail for the decision-maker. The two streams of literature just mentioned are concerned with defining and implementing individual freedom. The literature on ranking opportunity sets on the basis of freedom of choice is concerned with the definition of individual freedom. The literature on rights is interested in the problem of making the individual freedoms mutually compatible. This leaves open the question of how to allocate more 'justly' or more 'equally' the individual freedoms, which is precisely the object of the third area of research which has led to the recent interest of economists for freedom. As mentioned, this literature has its origins in philosophy. In conventional welfare economics, concerns for equality and/or fairness are addressed in terms of individual welfare. When individual welfare is not assumed to be interpersonally comparable,[1] the typical concept used to reflect these concerns is that of 'no-envy' (introduced by Foley [22], Kolm [38], Pazner and Schmeidler [47], and Varian [63]). When individual welfare is assumed to be interpersonally comparable, inequality aversion is handled by imposing appropriate assumptions on the social welfare function. The first decisive attack against individual welfare as the appropriate *equalisandum* came from John Rawls [50] who proposed replacing welfare by an index of 'primary goods'. Rawls work was followed by Dworkin [16] and, more recently, by Arneson [1], Cohen [11], Sen [55] and Van Parijs [44]. The problem covered by this literature is clear enough. Given a notion of freedom embodied in a particular ranking of opportunity sets, a natural egalitarian and freedom respectful normative objective would seem to consist in equalizing as much as desired the individual opportunity sets and, once this level of equalization is achieved, in letting the individuals choose from their opportunity sets their best option according to whatever objective they may pursue. This, in substance, is the programme exposed by Dworkin [16]. While this approach is correct in principle, it is not immediately implementable in practice. The huge diversity of individuals in health, productive and consumptive capacities, etc. makes the prospect of getting anywhere close to an appropriate level of equalization of opportunity sets deeply impossible. Individuals with heart disease do not have the option to run a marathon available in their opportunity set. Nor do individuals with poor manual dexterity have the option of playing piano like Horrowitz. Arneson [1] has proposed a way out of this problem. He suggests that the objects to equalize (or to be reallocated more 'justly') should not be individual sets of options but, instead, individual sets of utilities associated by each individual to the options. Another metric of opportunity sets is proposed by Cohen [11]. This philosophical discussion on the choice of the appropriate metric of opportunity set with respect to an egalitarian objective has motivated a new stream of research that tries to cast this discussion in terms of more formal economic models. Representative pieces of this literature are Bossert

4

INTRODUCTION

[5], Bossert and Fleurbaey [6], Fleurbaey (18], 19]), Fleurbaey and Maniquet ([20], [21]), Herrero [31], Iturbe and Nieto [34], Kranich ([40], [41]), Roemer ([51], [52]) and Van de Gaer [13]. Essentially, this literature addresses the problem of equalizing individuals' opportunity sets under the constraints that only physical resources are transferable between individuals. To achieve this task, this literature assumes that individual characteristics (preferences, consumptive and productive abilities, initial endowments in terms of physical goods, etc.) can be partitioned in two categories. In the first category are characteristics that are assumed to be morally irrelevant (or arbitrary) in the sense that the individual can not be assumed to bear responsibility for the specific value taken by these characteristics. To the contrary, the second category comprises characteristics for which the individual is assumed to be responsible and, for this reason, that are assumed to be morally relevant. Given such a partition, the allocating mechanisms considered in the literature tend to exhibit a conflict between two categories of principles: principles of *compensation* and of *natural reward*. The first principle, egalitarian in spirit, requires that interindividual differences in morally irrelevant characteristics be more or less compensated by redistribution of physical resources. The second principle, which reflects a concern for individual freedom, requires that no transfers take place between individuals which differ only by the value of their morally relevant characteristic.

The contributions presented in this volume are grouped into the three broad sections corresponding to these three recent lines of research. Part I contains papers which attempt to make more precise the notion of freedom in the spirit of the literature on ranking opportunity sets. What, exactly, do we mean when we say that an individual is (more or less) free? Why, after all, do we attach so much importance to this notion? These basic, albeit important, questions are addressed in the first section from both a philosophical and axiomatic view point. Part II focuses on the theory of rights, re-examining the social choice approach and exploring new developments of the game form approach, as well as related issues such as the exchange of rights. Finally, while Parts I and II are interested primarily in defining and implementing individual freedom, the contributions grouped in Part III are more concerned with the problem of 'justly' or 'equally' distributing individual freedom and opportunities, in line with the third area of research sketched above. Each chapter is followed by a comment from another contributor to the volume or, in some cases, from some other scholar who has contributed to the field. It is our hope that this method of presenting the contributions to this volume will highlight the controversial features of the task of defining and implementing such a difficult notion as that of liberty which contribute for no small part to the interest of the enterprise.

In the opening paper of Part I, Serge-Christophe Kolm proposes a thorough answer to the definitional questions and explores some consequences of his answer for the broader issue of defining and implementing distributive

5

justice. Kolm defines freedom as a structure of causality relating the 'individual will' (as the cause) and an action of this individual (as the effect). In Kolm's view therefore, freedom is an attribute of an action. An action is free if it is caused by the will and is more free than another if it is more caused by the will than the latter. Pursuing an idea proposed in his earlier work [39], he argues that the reasons for attaching normative importance to the structure of causality embodied in his conception of freedom are 'ontological'. That is, we value freedom simply because we respect the individual whose 'will' is the source of freedom. For Kolm not attaching importance to freedom would amount to denying the individual agency in a deep sense. Kolm's view is discussed by D. Hausman.

Chapters 3 and 5 are less ambitious in scope and refer to a somewhat different, although compatible, notion of freedom: that of freedom of choice. They belong to the growing literature mentioned above that aim at making sense of the statement 'offers at least as much freedom of choice as' applied to the alternative individual opportunity sets. Although this approach conceives freedom as an attribute of an opportunity set (and not as an attribute of an action), it does not conflict with Kolm's view. An opportunity set is typically viewed as the collection of objects (or 'actions', in Kolm's terminology) over which the individual, driven by her 'will', will exert her freedom (in Kolm's sense). The basic question addressed in this literature are: What does it mean for an individual to have more opportunity for choices (i.e. to have more 'freedom of choice')? Why would an individual value the fact of having more 'freedom of choice'?

In Chapter 3, Clemens Puppe, following Foster [23], Kreps [42] and Arrow [2], proposes a particular answer to these questions. More specifically, he starts from a particular answer to the second question and uses it to address the first question. The answer given to the second question is quite compelling. An individual values an enlargement of her opportunity set because she does not know in advance what preferences she will have at the time she will choose from the set. Accordingly, a ranking of opportunity sets based on freedom must refer to some set of possible preferences that the individual may have when making a choice. Using this notion of freedom, Puppe draws a formal analogy between the classical problem of social choice – which deals with the aggregation of different individual preferences over social states into one social ranking – and the problem of ranking opportunity sets – which in Puppe's approach amounts to aggregating the various preference orderings that one individual can have into one ranking of opportunity sets. He then uses this formal analogy, as well as a representation theorem due to Kreps [42], to axiomatically characterize two rules for ranking alternative opportunity sets: a 'unanimity rule' (a change of opportunities is freedom improving if it is beneficial for every possible preference that the individual can have) and a 'modified majority rule' (a change of opportunities increases freedom if it is beneficial for a majority

6

of possible preferences). Clemens Puppe's essay is commented on by Nicolas Gravel, Jean-François Laslier and Alain Trannoy, principally with respect to its interpretation of Kreps's representation theorem and to the definition of freedom in terms of possible future preferences.

In Chapter 5, Nicolas Gravel, Jean-François Laslier and Alain Trannoy do not address the question of why an individual may value an enhancement of her freedom of choice. Taking this valuation for granted, they explore the properties that a ranking of opportunity sets based on their freedom of choice could plausibly satisfy. In this respect, their essay is very much in the spirit of Pattanaik and Xu [45], Suppes [62], Klemisch-Ahlert [36] and Puppe [49], among others. The main contribution of their paper is to propose an axiom which recognizes explicitly the social context in which individual freedom of choice is assessed. This axiom, which they call reallocation independence, states that if the same ranking of opportunity sets is used to evaluate every individual's freedom of choice, then a mere reallocation of the objects of choice among a given number of individuals cannot lead to a unanimous improvement in individual freedoms. The main result of this paper is that this axiom characterizes the class of all rankings of opportunity set that admit an additive numerical representation. The famous cardinality ranking characterized by Pattanaik and Xu [45] and Suppes [62] (a set offers more freedom than another when and only when it contains more elements) is a particular case of this class. This paper is commented on by Clemens Puppe who, among other things, questions the assumption for the ranking of individuals opportunity sets to be the same for all individuals.

Part II of the book examines, conceptually and practically, some issues related to the definition of an appropriate system of rights. Chapter 7, written by Maurice Salles and Anne Brunel, consists in a re-examination of Sen's [53] approach for studying systems of individual rights and of some aspects of the literature that have followed this seminal contribution. Among other things, Brunel and Salles stress some interpretative difficulties with Sen's classical formalism in terms of decisiveness and suggest some possible ways out of these difficulties. Their suggestions are carefully examined by Peter Hammond in Chapter 8.

In Chapter 9, Bezalel Peleg develops a particular formalism of rights within the general approach of game forms as advocated by several authors (Gardenfors [25], Gaertner, Pattanaik and Suzumura [64] in particular). His model is based on the notion of an effectivity function originally proposed by Gardenfors [25] and later by Deb [14]. In this approach, granting a right means that a subset of social states is guaranteed to the right-bearer. The author defines a *constitution* as a set of rights, each of them being assigned to some agents or groups of agents, and giving them the guarantee of related subsets of social states. The problem considered by Peleg is to devise a legal game which enforces all these guarantees in the sense that, for every right, it provides each right-bearer with a strategy that always leads to the subset of social states defined by the right. In this rich framework, Peleg gives a general theorem of existence of a game compatible with a given constitution, and proposes an illuminating discussion of some paradoxes, such as Sen's [53] and Gibbard's [26]. This paper is commented on by E. Picavet from a rather philosophical standpoint.

Peter J. Hammond has contributed much to the conceptual debate on the appropriate formalization of rights. Yet, in Chapter 11, he considers a somewhat more 'applied' issue, namely, the possibility for individuals to freely exchange their rights in an economic environment. Some time ago Coase [10] suggested that allowing for a free exchange of many rights is likely to eliminate many inefficiencies arising from conflicting exercises of rights (a situation called by economists 'externalities'). Hammond's essay examines Coase's conjecture in the context of a general equilibrium framework with a continuum of agents. More specifically, Hammond's model deals with what he calls 'widespread externalities'. Widespread externalities are effects of the exercise of some right by some agent which, roughly, affects all agents. Hammond's main finding is that when quotas are inefficiently given to the agents, free exchange of rights may not be Pareto-improving because it may affect the global amount of externalities. Pareto-improvement is generally guaranteed only when originally unused quotas are confiscated. Peter Hammond's essay is commented on by A. Villar.

Finally, Part III of the book deals with the distribution of liberties in the spirit of the philosophical and economic literature mentioned above. In Chapter 13, Richard Arneson first examines various ways to compare opportunity sets, and stresses the contrast between the approaches based on counting options and those concerned with the likely value of the chosen option. He looks for a way to retain the best part of each kind of approach in a coherent mixed view. To some extent this part of his essay is close to the topic studied in Part I, and like Gravel, Laslier and Trannoy, he explicitly relates this discussion with the project of using this evaluative device in distributional issues. The second part of this paper comes back to the basic question of whether distributive justice should really be concerned only with the freedom or opportunity to lead a good life, and yields a qualified negative answer, based on the idea that even though freedom has a lot of value for a human life, it need not take moral precedence over the value of life itself in the formulation of social goals.

Philippe van Parijs' rejoinder tries to defend the view that justice has to do with resources or opportunities rather than with final outcomes. He restates the basic intuition for theories of justice as equal opportunity and tries to answer Arneson's basic arguments. He argues first that freedom is not the object of any fetishism in these theories because it is possible to distinguish between what matters for individuals – that is final welfare – and what matters for social justice – that is the 'means' of achieving final welfare. He then

8

goes on in re-examining the problem of 'bad choosers'. Van Parijs argues that opportunity-oriented justice can deal with the problem of bad choices adequately, although he admits that outcome-oriented criteria are likely to have less severe consequences for individuals who tend to mistake their own interest.

Chapters 15, 17 and 19 are more closely connected to the economic literature discussed above that tries to implement the ideal of equality of opportunities in economic environments when only physical resources can be transferred between individuals. In Chapter 15 Marc Fleurbaey provides a survey of this economic literature and proposes a few concepts that enable one to interpret the various solutions proposed and discussed in this literature. In particular, he reviews the general incompatibility exhibited in this literature between the principle of compensation and that of natural reward discussed above. Marc Fleurbaey's survey is commented on by Louis Gevers.

In Chapter 17 John Roemer pursues further his own solution (proposed in Roemer [51] in particular) to the problem of implementing the ideal of equal opportunities in a tractable way. Given any partition of the individual characteristics between characteristics over which individuals bear responsibility and those with respect to which the individual can not be held responsible, John Roemer's proposal is based on a particular 'statistical' method for measuring the degree of individual responsibility in her final outcome. This method amounts to consider the distribution of outcomes *within* a class of individual characteristics with respect to which individuals are not responsible to be the result of the sole responsibility of the individuals. Accordingly, John Roemer's solution would recommend that no transfers be performed between individuals within a same class of characteristics with respect to which they bear no responsibility. However, the solution will recommend that transfers be made between individuals who, in their respective *distinct* class of 'irrelevant characteristics', occupy the same statistical position in the distribution of outcomes. According to Roemer, the transfers should then be made in a way that maximizes a particular social welfare function. Applying his solution to a problem of optimal taxation, he shows that the tax scheme obtained with his solution lies somewhat in between a scheme that would be obtained by applying a standard utilitarian social welfare function and one that would result from using a maximin criterion. John Roemer's paper is commented on by Dirk Van de Gaer who, in his doctoral dissertation [13], has proposed a related, although different, solution to the problem of implementing the ideal of equalizing opportunities.

In Chapter 19 Erik Schokkaert and Kurt Devooght present results of opinion surveys dealing with axioms and solutions studied by Bossert and Fleurbaey (1996) [6]. They show that respondents easily accept both the notion of 'compensation' and that of 'natural reward' but that they tend to prefer the first one when the two axioms are incompatible. They also show that the answers are sensitive to the context, and in particular, when redistribution of income is at stake, the principles are rejected in a way that suggests that respondents are eager to encourage effort and willing to reward inherited talent. The results of their experiments are discussed by Walter Bossert.

In our view, there are a few lessons that can be drawn from this volume. First, freedom is now a vivid field of research in the economic theory of the nineties. The number and the quality of the contributions presented at the conference, including those which were not included in the current volume, illustrates eloquently this state of affairs.

Second, current research on liberty makes use of various techniques and languages, ranging from standard economic analysis and philosophical reflection to axiomatic reasoning and experimental methods. This plurality is a good thing but, in our view, more remains to be done. In particular, disciplines such as law and psychology which should have a lot to say about the meaning and the social implementation of freedom have not yet appeared on the scene.

Freedom is, undoubtedly, a complex and rich notion. For this reason, it should not be surprising that the recent attempts at formalizing and implementing freedom echoed in this volume have left unexplored many dimensions of this concept. One of these unexplored dimensions concerns the formalization of the interactive aspect of individual choices and consequences. When an individual chooses an action from an opportunity set, such a choice is mapped to a consequence via an interaction with the choices made by other individuals. For the most part, current reflection upon freedom seems to ignore this crucial difference between an *action* – whose choice is made by the individual- and a *consequence* of this action – which is the result of a simultaneous choice of actions by all individuals in the considered society. This distinction, which is well-known to game theorists, needs to be more explicitly taken into consideration in the exercise of modelling and defining individual freedom. Although the game form approach to the problem of defining rights provides a step in this direction, much more remains to be done.

ACKNOWLEDGEMENTS

We gratefully acknowledge the financial support of the following institutions: Ecole des Hautes Etudes en Sciences Sociales, Conseil Général du Val d'Oise, Syndicat de l'Agglomération Nouvelle de Cergy-Pontoise, Université de Cergy-Pontoise and the Ministère de la Recherche et de l'Enseignement Supérieur.

INTRODUCTION

NOTE

1 Rigorous statements of alternative definitions of measurability and interpersonnal comparability of individual welfare can be found in [9], [12], [15], [29], [61] and [54], among others.

REFERENCES

[1] R. J. Arneson (1989) Equality and equal opportunity for welfare. *Philosophical Studies*, 56: 77–93.
[2] K. J. Arrow (1995) A note on freedom and flexibility. In P. P. K. Basu and K. Suzumura (eds), *Choice, Welfare and Development: A Festschrift in Honour of Amartya K. Sen*, chapter 1, pages 7–15. Oxford University Press, Oxford.
[3] I. Berlin (1969) *Four Essays on Liberty*. Oxford University Press, Oxford.
[4] P. P. K. Bossert, W. and Y. Xu (1994) Ranking opportunity sets: An axiomatic approach. *Journal of Economic Theory*, 63: 326–345.
[5] W. Bossert (1995) Redistribution mechanisms based on individual character-istics. *Mathematical Social Sciences*, 29: 1–17.
[6] W. Bossert and M. Fleurbaey (1996) Redistribution and compensation. *Social Choice and Welfare*, 13: 343–355.
[7] J. M. Buchanan (1975) *The Limits of Liberty*. University of Chicago Press, Chicago.
[8] J. M. Buchanan (1986) *Liberty, Market and the State*. Wheatsheaf Books, Brighton.
[9] D. D. C. Blackorby and J. A. Weymark (1984) Social choice with interpersonal utility comparisons: A diagrammatic introduction. *International Journal of Economics*, 25: 327–356.
[10] R. Coase (1960) The problem of social cost. *Journal of Law and Economics*, 3: 1–44.
[11] G. A. Cohen (1989) On the currency of egalitarian justice. *Ethics*, 99: 906–944.
[12] C. D'Aspremont and L. Gevers (1977) Equity and the informational basis of social choice. *Review of Economic Studies*, 46: p. 199–210.
[13] D. V. de Gaer (1993) *Equality of Opportunity and Investment in Human Capital*. PhD thesis, K. University, Leuven.
[14] R. Deb (1994) Waiver, effectivity and rights as game forms. *Economica*, 61: 167–178.
[15] R. Deschamps and L. Gevers (1978) Leximin and Utilitarian rules: A joint characterization. *Journal of Economic Theory*, 17: 143–163.
[16] R. Dworkin (1981) What is equality? part I: Equality of welfare, part 2: Equal-ity of resources. *Philosophy and Public Affairs*, 10: 185–246.
[17] F. Engels and K. Marx (1844) *The German Ideology*. International Publishers, New York. English Translation 1947.
[18] M. Fleurbaey (1994) On fair compensation. *Theory and Decision*, 36: 277–307.
[19] M. Fleurbaey (1995) Three solutions to the compensation problem. *Journal of Economic Theory*, 65: 505–521.
[20] M. Fleurbaey and F. Maniquet (1994) Fair allocation with unequal production skills: The solidarity approach to compensation. Technical Report 9419, THEMA.
[21] M. Fleurbaey and F. Maniquet (1996) Fair allocation with unequal production skills: The no-envy approach to compensation. *Mathematical Social Sciences*, 32: 71–93.

11

[22] D. K. Foley (1967) Ressource allocation and the public sector. *Yale Economic Essays*, 7.
[23] J. Foster (1993) Notes on effective freedom. Mimeo, Vanderbilt University.
[24] M. Friedman (1962) *Capitalism and Freedom*. The University of Chicago Press, Chicago.
[25] P. Gardenfors (1981) Rights, games and social choice. *Nous*, 15: 341–356.
[26] A. Gibbard (1974) A pareto-consistent liberal claim. *Journal of Economic Theory*, 7: 388–410.
[27] N. Gravel (1994) Can a ranking of opportunity sets attach intrinsic importance to freedom of choice? *American Economic Review: Papers and Proceedings*, 84: 454–458.
[28] N. Gravel (1998) Ranking opportunity sets on the basis of their freedom of choice and their ability to satisfy preferences: A difficulty. *Social Choice and Welfare*, forthcoming.
[29] P. J. Hammond (1976) Equity, Arrow's conditions and Rawls's difference principle. *Econometrica*, 44: 793–803.
[30] F. V. Hayek (1960) *The Constitution of Liberty*. Routledge, London.
[31] C. Herrero (1996) Capabilities and utilities. *Economic Design*, 2: 69–88.
[32] J. R. Hicks (1959) *Essays in World Economics*. Clarendon Press, Oxford.
[33] J. R. Hicks (1981) A manifesto. In *Wealth and Welfare: Collected Essays in Economic Theory* Vol. 1. Blackwell, Oxford.
[34] I. Iturbe-Ormaetxe and J. Nieto (1995) On fair allocations and monetary compensations. *Economic Theory*, 7: 125–138.
[35] P. Jones and R. Sugden (1982) Evaluating choices. *International Journal of Law and Economics*, 2: 47–65.
[36] M. Klemisch-Ahlert (1993) Freedom of choice: A comparison of different rankings of opportunity sets. *Social Choice and Welfare*, 10: 189–207.
[37] F. H. Knight (1947) *Freedom and Reform: Essays in Economics and Social Philosophy*. Harper, New York.
[38] S. C. Kolm (1972) *Justice et Equité*. Editions du CNRS, Paris.
[39] S. C. Kolm (1982) *Le Bonheur-Liberté: Boudhisme Profond et Modernité*. Presses Universitaires de France, Paris.
[40] L. Kranich (1996) Equitable opportunities: an axiomatic approach. *Journal of Economic Theory*.
[41] L. Kranich (1996) Equitable opportunities in economic environments. *Social Choice and Welfare*.
[42] D. M. Kreps (1979) A representation theorem for 'preference for flexibility'. *Econometrica*, 47: 565–577.
[43] J. S. Mill (1974) *On Liberty*. Harmondsworth, Penguin, London. First publication, 1859.
[44] P. V. Parijs (1995) *Real Freedom for All. What (if Anything) can Justify Capitalism?* Clarendon Press, Oxford.
[45] P. K. Pattanaik and Y. Xu (1990) On ranking opportunity sets in terms of freedom of choice. *Récherches Economiques de Louvain*, 56: 383–390.
[46] P. K. Pattanaik and Y. Xu (1995) On freedom and preferences. Mimeo, University of California, Riverside.
[47] E. Pazner and D. Schmeidler (1974) A difficulty in the concept of fairness. *Review of Economic Studies*, 41: 441–443.
[48] C. Puppe. Freedom of choice and rational decisions (1995) *Social Choice and Welfare*, 12: 137–154.
[49] C. Puppe (1996) An axiomatic approach for 'preferences for freedom of choice'. *Journal of Economic Theory*, 68: 174–199.

[50] J. Rawls (1971) *A Theory of Justice*. Berknap Press of Harvard University Press, Cambridge, Massachusetts.

[51] J. E. Roemer (1993) A pragmatic theory of responsibility for the egalitarian planner. *Philosophy and Public Affairs*, 22: 146–166.

[52] J. E. Roemer (1996) *Theories of Justice*. Harvard University Press, Cambridge Massachusetts.

[53] A. K. Sen (1970) The impossibility of a Paretian liberal. *Journal of Political Economy*, 78: 152–157.

[54] A. K. Sen (1977) Non-linear social welfare functions: A reply to Professor Harsanyi. In R. Butts and J. Hintikka (eds), *Foundational Problems in the Special Sciences*, pages 297–302. D. Reidel, Dordrecht.

[55] A. K. Sen (1985) *Commodities and Capabilities*. North-Holland, Amsterdam.

[56] A. K. Sen (1985) Well-being, agency and freedom: The Dewey lectures 1984. *Journal of Philosophy*, 82: 169–221.

[57] A. K. Sen (1988) Freedom of choice: Concept and content. *European Economic Review*, 32: 269–294.

[58] A. K. Sen (1990) Welfare, freedom and social choice. *Recherches Economiques de Louvain*, 56: 451–486.

[59] A. K. Sen (1991) Welfare, preferences and freedom. *Journal of Econometrics*, 50: 15–29.

[60] A. K. Sen (1993) Markets and freedoms: Achievements and limitations of the market mechanism in promoting individual freedoms. *Oxford Economic Papers*, 45: 519–541.

[61] S. L. Strasnick (1975) *Preference Priority and the Maximization of Social Welfare*. PhD thesis, Harvard University.

[62] P. Suppes (1987) Maximizing freedom of decision: An axiomatic approach. In G. Feiwel (ed.), *Arrow and the Foundations of the Theory of Economic Policy*, pages 243–254. New York University Press.

[63] H. Varian (1974) Equity, envy and efficiency. *Journal of Economic Theory*, 9: 63–91.

[64] P. P. W. Gaerner and K. Suzumura (1992) Individual rights revisited. *Economica*, 59: 161–177.

Part I
LIBERTY

1

THE VALUES OF FREEDOM

*Serge-Christophe Kolm**

ABSTRACT

This chapter presents the definition of liberty, the reason why equal liberty in a broad sense is the necessary basic structure of modern social ethics, the various relevant characteristics and types of freedom, and the dozen reasons to value it that lead to the actual construction of justice in society. This is applied to the determination of distributive justice in showing the relevant distinction of liberties, the resulting polar cases and the efficient resolution of their conflicts. The use of liberty in social contracts, merit, desert and responsibility is also noted.

INTRODUCTION AND SUMMARY

In all societies, what is just or right is essentially defined in terms of freedoms, rights, powers, means, and the correlative duties and obligations. These items are liberties, or can generally be expressed in terms or with concepts of liberty in the broad sense.[1] The social ethic of modernity consists of a specification of these liberties, which excludes inequalities based on family status, and will be presented later. Note that incomes, goods, welfare and the like appear as particular or limiting cases: income is purchasing power, one is free to consume, use, exchange, etc., the goods one possesses, and there can be rights to have certain goods or a certain level of welfare (the relations between agents' ends and means will be further considered below). The other items are more explicitly rights, powers or liberties.

But if liberty is so essential, we had better know what we talk about when we utter this term. Impression, intuition or alleged evidence are of no help, since we know, as scientists, that everything is determined, irrespective of our knowledge or ignorance of the specific causal influences.[2] The answer will turn out to be that liberty is a type of structure of causality: freedom is more caused by the will, or by reason (or by other specific parts of the agent). But why should we value a structure of causality? The dozen types of reasons to value freedom that one can observe will be

17

presented. This will include the two polar clusters of liberty as a means of satisfaction (possibly happiness), and of the existential (ontological) value of liberty as a condition for agency (and hence dignity, responsibility, creativity, etc.). These reasons take into account the reasons to shun freedom, and their relevance depends on a number of characteristics of the considered liberty, which will be pointed out.

This analysis of liberty will permit us to determine the social optimum and in particular global justice, or macrojustice (different from the multifarious cases of microjustice, or local justice). In summary, the relevant classification of liberties will distinguish act-freedom, its extension into process-freedom, and means-freedom, which makes precise Marx's intuitive opposition between formal freedom and real freedom ('positive freedom' is a totally different thing, considered in the conclusion along with 'negative freedom'). Macrojustice that focuses on individuals' situations ('individualistic') and takes as end values individuals' items that these individuals desire ('respectful') is built up on a triad of priorities consisting of:

1 the respect of basic rights which are act-freedom and have *de facto* legal priority in liberal-democratic states;
2 the satisfaction of basic needs; and
3 Pareto-efficiency (possibly with 'laundered' preferences).

The priority of basic rights and basic needs is grounded in their existential value. A certain respect of cultures also has priority. Then distributive justice necessarily has the form of a moral polyarchy whose main problem is the imputation of human assets and liabilities in dividing human capacities into those whose benefits are equalized by sharing the product (for productive capacities) or by compensation, and those whose 'natural' or 'spontaneous' allocation is endorsed and respected, or, in other words, in defining the domains of equal means-freedom and of process-freedom. The three polar cases consist of:

1 the ideal equalization of the benefits from all resources, including human capacities which include consumptive capacities, transformed for efficiency into 'Practical Justice' or leximin in interpersonally comparable and ordinal 'fundamental preferences', which is relevant notably when basic needs are not all satisfied or for the alleviation of deep sufferings;
2 at the extreme opposite, full process-freedom which requires a notable public sector to remedy market or exchange failures according to 'liberal social contracts';
3 the endorsement of the 'natural' allocation of preferences only, which implies equality in consumption goods replaced, for Pareto-efficiency, by the limitations in income inequalities defined by the multidimensional

maximin of 'efficient super-equity' and by 'fixed duration income equalization'.

The distributive optimum results from a mix of these three polar principles in proportions which depend on the state of society but which are rather clearly defined for each stage and type of development.

Thus, the equality of liberty and its extensions, rather than the sum of utilities and 'social welfare', constitutes the rational individualistic way to define what is just or right in society. This view has characterized the modern world for the last two centuries, outside a relatively tiny group of people, all scholars in English-language philosophy and academic economics, misled by Bentham's purely contingent and political anti-rights ideology.[3]

This chapter is organized as follows. The following section will explain why rationality requires the basic structure of justice to be prima facie equal liberty. This will require the provision of minimal indications about the definition of liberty. The various characteristics, distinctions and types of liberty that are relevant and essential for the social ethical evaluation will then be presented, followed by the problem of valuing liberty, and the dozen or so broad types of reasons for valuing freedom. It will then be shown how the necessary principle of equal liberty determines justice, and particularly macrojustice, in society. The chapter will successively consider the classification of freedoms most relevant to the theory of justice, the priorities of act-freedoms, basic rights and basic needs, distributive justice determined by the assignment of capacities to the ethical ends of means- or process-freedoms, its three polar cases, the answers to their inefficiencies, and their optimum mix. Finally, the chapter will discuss two other families of concepts of justice based on process-freedom: social contracts, fundamental insurance and original positions; and merit, desert and responsibility.

Before the presentation of these questions, a few preliminary remarks may help the reader to situate their necessity and their scope. The value of liberty is considered the essential issue in ethics and in social ethics by many people and by almost all non-communitarian traditions (and not only in the West).[4] Analysis of specific and particular aspects of this question can consider relevant concepts, problems and possible importance only by beginning with the question of liberty. An operational and non-superficial view of freedom necessarily begins, after the consideration of the nature and definition of liberty, with the distinction of the basic characteristics and aspects of freedom and of the reasons to value it; here, the alternative to distinction is confusion. This paper draws from this analysis a principal conclusion that lacks neither focus nor importance, since this is the solution to the question of macrojustice and in particular of distributive justice in society. Finally, nobody who has ever *thought* about freedom

has found it an easy topic; its difficulty is matched only by its importance
Yet I hope to show that it is not a necessarily mysterious and intractable
topic, and that minimal reflection in this field can yield major practical
conclusions for social ethics.

THE REASON FOR EQUAL FREEDOM

Equal liberty

This chapter was written in France, a country theoretically ruled by the
principle 'Liberty, Equality, Fraternity' and whose 200-year-old republican
constitution begins with and gives precedence to the Declaration of the
Rights of Man and of the Citizen: 'Men are free and equal in rights'.
Indeed, this constitutes the basis of all modern liberal states of law. More
generally, liberties and rights have always been the material of the definition of social order and the issues of political and social struggles, settle-
ments, claims and ideals; the modern novelty is, rather, the extension of
claims of equality to all persons, irrespective of ascribed or birth status.
It should be noted that utilitarianism was made the dominant ethic of
English political philosophy by Bentham for the exclusively political purpose of fighting the revolutionary American and French rights- and
freedom-based principles on the ideological battleground. Bentham himself
thought that adding pleasures of different persons makes no sense. Utilitarianism later seduced academic economists, who turned it into 'social
welfare'. It was never taken up beyond these two very limited scholarly cir-
cles (the principle 'choose A rather than B because individual 1 prefers A
to B more than individual 2 prefers B to A' is an occasional criterion of
local and partial allocation which generally does not imply differences or
additions in utilities).[5] Yet, the lack of meaning of the concept of 'aggregate happiness or satisfaction' affects the importance neither of individual
happiness (the American Declaration guarantees the right to 'the pursuit
of happiness'), nor of Pareto-efficiency: the preamble of the 1789 Declaration asserts that claims based on these rights promote the happiness of all.
Rights should in particular determine the distribution. After stating the
basic rights which actualize act freedom (see below), in its first sixteen
articles, the 1789 Declaration confronted the distributional issue in its
seventeenth and last article. After much hesitation between the right to
assistance and the respect of properties (different from the respect for
unspecified property of article 2), the deputies chose the latter, that is,
full process-freedom (see below) and free exchange. The whole text is
thus tilted toward protective and 'formal' freedom and away from 'real'
freedom. However, a right to the satisfaction of basic needs (assistance)
was introduced at the beginning of the ensuing constitution and in the
later revolutionary declarations (plus, in the end, at Condorcet's insti-

20

;ation, the right to free education). These debates have framed very neatly he issues of the political and social debates and struggles over the course)f the following two centuries (at least).

In the triple motto, fraternity can resolve conflicts between liberty and equality in inducing voluntary transfers or restraints. Yet the main relation between liberty and equality is that the principle is an equality of liberty. This, however, can mean very different things, such as equal freedom to keep or exchange unequal properties, or equal *real* freedoms constituted by material means of action and in particular of consumption. Then, since this principle can be interpreted in so many different and opposed ways, it can solve the social ethical question only if one begins by answering the questions: why equality, and why liberty?

Equality constitutes the easy part. Rationality in its normal sense of 'for a reason' implies an 'equal treatment of equals in the relevant characteristics', given that this reason should also select a single solution among mutually exclusive alternatives. Indeed, an unequal treatment of such equals can have no basis to be chosen rather than a permutation of these treatments among these individuals (notice that selection by lottery should justify the chosen probabilities – such as equal ones – and it does not really constitute a relevant reason and hence it can only be a second-best device in case of indivisibilities). If, moreover, the 'treatment' of an individual is deemed not to depend on other individuals' relevant characteristics or treatments, the direct application of a 'reason' onto relevantly identical individuals provides identical 'treatments'.[6]

But why value liberty? Indeed, if, as scientists, we believe in causality and determination, one might argue that liberty just does not exist. In particular, in 'oeconomia' an individual's 'choice' is determined by his preferences and his domain of possibilities. The impression of freedom of the will that we may experience merely rests on an ignorance of certain of our internal causal determinations. Full knowledge of these determinations is impossible, because the *conoscendum* is part of the knower, it has the same degree of complexity, and it is influenced by the information acquired. But this does not prevent us from knowing that we are determined, that our acts, thoughts, tastes, desires, preferences, choices, intentions or projects are determined, as everything else is. Then, can one value ignorance *per se*? Is liberty diminished by a better knowledge of physiology, psychology or psychoanalysis? At any rate, the *impression* of liberty neither is liberty nor proves that it exists (see, for instance, the case of gods, spirits or transcendental 'selves'). What, then, *is* liberty?

Defining liberty

This question turns out to be an 'easy' one: liberty is a structure of causality. The age-old and much-discussed dilemma between liberty and

21

determinism turns out to be an elementary misconception. 'Free' is an instance of 'caused by', and 'freer' is an instance of 'more caused by'. It remains to specify the relevant causes and effects. In the core concept of liberty, the effect is an act or an action of an individual, and the cause is this individual's will or reason. An action is a set of acts with an intention and a meaning. Since reason needs the will in order to implement its conclusions into acts or actions, reason-freedom implies will-freedom and covers a more restricted set of instances. Certain relevant causal influences can be indirect and pass through other parts of the individual (such as in training) or through parts of the external world (such as in toolmaking, investment, or commitment), in providing means, conditions, or constraints that are among the causes of the manifestation of later acts. Our present purpose does not involve extending the concept of liberty to acts that are impulsive, compulsive, reflex or akratic (from *akrasia*, weakness of the will), or caused by the nervous system. We also disregard metaphorical uses of the word 'free' that are not specific to humans (such as 'this tree is free to grow in this direction'). Of course, the intention of an action can be, for example, to train, to obey a norm, or to rest in staying quiet and undisturbed, and acts include communication-acts, speech-acts, thought-acts, and so on. From this definition of liberty for acts, actions and individuals, one can define liberty for other social entities such as societies, countries or markets, by reference to individuals' acts or by analogy.

With will-freedom, the free acts are the wilful or voluntary acts. With reason-freedom, liberty results from rationality (the use of reason) and free action is rational action (in this sense).

Reason-freedom implies the various classical aspects of 'autonomy', that is, one's choice of one's principles of choice, whether this is Rousseau's definition that 'to be free is to obey a rule chosen by oneself', Kant's interpretation that this rule is rational duty opposing one's 'inclinations', the Stoic choice of one's preferences, or the Buddhist control of one's desires. In the extreme form, all spiritualities and philosophies of life enjoin one to accept the irremovable constraints and sometimes to 'want' them (for Rousseau, 'the free man wants what he can and does what he wants', but accepting one's chains does not require one to 'cover them with flowers').

The word 'choice' implies a minimum of comparative rationality for selecting among the alternatives. The concept of 'free choice' consists of a dichotomy of the causes of the (chosen) action between a certain internal process and the rest that constitutes the 'constraints' and defines the 'domain of choice'. The internal process may be epitomized by a structure of 'preferences'. I have analysed in other studies the relations between transitivity or acyclicity and rationality in the normal sense of the term, and the question of the wilful shaping of one's own preferences.[7]

Valuing liberty

Freedom, therefore, is without ontological mystery (if not without questions): liberty is a structure of causality. But, then, why should one value a structure of causality? An answer that makes liberty rather close to an end value has the form of: by respect for the beings endowed with the entity whose consequences on acts define their freedom, notably with reason; that is to say, by respect for the agents who, by definition, choose and perform the actions. This means that the causal chains from the crucial entity (e.g., reason) should be interfered with as little as possible, or, in other words, that the agents should have as effective means of action as possible. However, two aspects intervene here: the multiplicity of agents and of types of means. The multiplicity of agents and the various scarcities may render these agents rivals among themselves. Whatever the solution chosen to share this scarcity, end-valuing freedom or agency implies that the practical social ethical end values have to be in the nature of individuals' means, and from a previous remark (rational) justice requires the individual means chosen as end values of justice to be ideally equal among individuals endowed with identical relevant characteristics. However, one cannot have equality jointly for all types of means. For instance, there can be equally full rights to earn income for all, but this is inconsistent with equal incomes for all if individuals' capacities differ. This choice of equalizands provides the various possible criteria, principles and systems of justice. Certain types of means are chosen as end values, others are discarded, and adjustments among those that are retained have to be chosen when the corresponding ideal and prima facie equalities are not all equally possible. These adjustments can be of a number of types (priorities, compromises, and so on),[8] with the corresponding 'second-best egalitarianisms'. These means can be, for example, freedoms to act, incomes, opportunities, primary resources, information or education, and even capacities to appreciate consumption or life with an equalization in the form of compensation.

In one extreme and limiting case, all the means are considered globally relevant for justice, including all human capacities (human resources) with possible transfers of products of productive capacities and compensations for different consumptive capacities or capacities to be satisfied. Satisfaction refers to individuals' ends. The corresponding ideal is an equal level of satisfaction. Yet, for application in any large society, this has practically to be replaced by the second-best egalitarian criterion of leximin or maximin in satisfaction, because equal satisfaction is either impossible or is dominated by states with satisfactions that are higher for all but unequal (this priority to Pareto-efficiency is discussed below). These are the principles of Justice and Practical Justice in *Justice and Equity* (Kolm 1971). The interpersonal comparison of satisfaction is based on the theory of 'fundamental preferences' (ibid.; Kolm 1994b, 1966a, 1996e, 1997a), and it is made easier by the exclusive focus on the least satisfied or most miserable in the maximin.[9] Practically, this maximin is relevant when certain *basic needs* are not satisfied (and are not only vicarious needs), or in cases of deep suffering that can sufficiently be relieved.

In the other and opposite extreme case, the means consist of process-freedoms (see below) and the corresponding social ethic is full process liberalism if there is a priority of basic rights (ibid.), and full neo-libertarianism if there is no such *a priori* moral requirement.[10]

One can also start from a more modest and direct conception of justice, with the same result, and in the end with the same moral assumption. Justice, indeed, can be seen more directly as the adjustment among individuals' competing claims. Individuals' claims are for means to pursue their ends, with the ends themselves being the particular limiting case as just noted. Means can be called freedoms in a broad sense of the term (they can be rights, power, etc.). Then justice necessarily concerns the allocation of liberties, as a matter of fact rather than by ethical choice. However, the choice to solve the problem in taking certain of these items as moral end values is an ethical choice, which manifests or constitutes respect for agency, and leads to their ideal equalities as a requirement of rationality (as noted above).

At any rate, the rational theory of respectful justice consists of the selection of these specific prima facie equalizands, and of the adjustments and second-best egalitarianisms when an equality is not possible, or is not jointly possible with other relevant criteria which can be other equalities. This choice results essentially from an analysis of the value of the various liberties (including here powers, rights, means, etc.). These values depend in turn on the characteristics of freedom and on the types of liberties that they define.

THE ESSENTIAL CHARACTERISTICS, DISTINCTIONS AND TYPES OF LIBERTIES

These characteristics of liberty are the following, which refer respectively to the questions of cause, agent, nature, extent, constraint, value, action, use and conditions:

1 The type of the *mental or physiological process or structure* that defines the freedom of the act in causing it: reason, the will, choice, desires, preferences, tastes, certain nervous processes, etc., and possibly more specific ones that consider particular influences.

2 The type of the free *person* or agent.

3 The *nature of the acts or of the domain* of choice or action.

24

The *extent* of this domain. Note that when a liberty of a new type is added to other ones without suppressing certain of their possibilities, this is both a further complexity of the nature of the alternatives and a type of extension of domain.

5 The *nature and origin of the limits* or constraints that delineate this domain. In particular, these limits may be set by other agents' wills, or they may not be: this is *dependency* versus *independence*. The limits may also be set by institutions (themselves possibly set by wills, but endowed with a certain stability and predictability). The effects of an agent's past acts may constrain his present acts, and this may or may not have been purposeful. In 'self-restraint', an agent voluntarily limits certain of his acts; this can manifest an external constraint, as when this restraint aims to meet an external threat, but this self-restraint may also constitute a higher liberty, when it is more caused by the intra-individual entity that defines freedom, such as the will or reason, in the corresponding self-control. The set of constraints, and a given constraint, can have causes of various types.

6 The *reasons* for valuing freedom, or on the contrary for preferring it to be more restricted. These reasons are analysed in the next section. A rough dichotomy distinguishes between instrumental and existential liberty.

7 The situation of the considered liberty in the process of *action*. An action consists of *acts* using *means* for an *aim*. This provides three types of freedom, the distinction of which is essential both for the foundation and structure of basic rights and for the question of economic distributive justice (see below, and the following uses of these concepts).

8 The *use* to which this freedom is put. In particular, the free agent can use this liberty in an individual choice, or he can use it in agreement with other agents, possibly in exchange for something else.

9 The *defeasibility, alienability* and *prescriptibility* of a liberty – that is, can it be suppressed or transferred, or is it specified for a limited duration? If this is not the case, under what conditions do these properties hold? These properties can result from the nature of the freedom considered, or from social agreements or conventions, from an ethical choice, etc.

THE VALUES OF LIBERTY

The problems of valuing freedom

Liberty is a condition and a means for doing things, and in its most common conception, which is of greatest relevance here, for the achievement of the aim of the action that uses it.

Now 'liberty or death' is a motto with which many people died and which changed the world. It expresses an unconditional preference for death over a life devoid of liberty of a certain kind. Yet a dead person does not enjoy this liberty either. And among the other things that a living person can enjoy, there certainly are some which make life preferable to death. Hence this motto is irrational – unless there is some other reason for valuing freedom, or certain freedoms.

Alexis de Tocqueville (1836) was peremptory: 'He who wants freedom for anything but itself does not deserve it and will soon lose it.' This trenchant sentence rules out liberty-as-a-means from values and from possibilities: it has to be understood as a borderline case for the most basic of liberties.

One country took as its motto and anthem 'let us prefer liberty in poverty to plenty in slavery'.[11] Choosing between liberty and welfare is a standard topic of moral tales. In La Fontaine's fable *The Dog and the Wolf*, the hungry but free wolf pities the dog who is well fed, yet bears the mark of a collar. A most vivid illustration is René Clair's film, *A nous la liberté*, where a wealthy manager prefers the liberty of poverty. Buddhist wisdom enjoins abandoning material wealth so as to free oneself from 'attachments'. The general upshot is that liberty is not always valued only as a means for what it enables one to obtain by one's actions.

But is this rational, or even reasonable? Liberty is by nature a means, a possibility of action. Can one sensibly take a means as an end value? This is indeed possible for a means of individuals and an end value of a conception of justice, as a mere sharing of responsibility between the individuals and the policy that implements redistributions or that respects or protects the 'spontaneous' allocation. However, the above remarks suggest that liberty can also be valued in its own right by the concerned individuals, who attribute to it an intrinsic, final or end value,[12] sometimes with priority over other values, and this might be a reason for a theory of justice to value this freedom. But the value of a means is *a priori* only derived from what is done with it, and is thus subordinate to its use. Attributing an end value to a means is thus alienated hypostasis, fetishism. Even if individuals and cultures fall into such irrational illusions (as they commonly do with respect to selves or gods), should rational social ethics follow them on this ground?

Indeed, from its definition, liberty is a structure of causality. Now, causality is a matter of fact which *a priori* lacks the intrinsic desirability or the transcendence on which values can be based.

Furthermore, although individuals often like and desire freedom, they also commonly dislike and shun it. They have a number of possible reasons for doing so. One is constituted by the various costs of choosing, such as obtaining information, considering all of the alternatives and reasons, weighing and comparing them, and deciding. A second reason is the deeper 'anguish of choice', analysed, for instance, by Kierkegaard and particularly by Sartre, which can be a deeply disagreeable sentiment, sometimes a paralysing one. A third reason relates to responsibility, which is sometimes valued and desired but which is also sometimes disliked and shunned, and which can be an important cause of the anguish of choice. One can feel oppressed by a situation of having to choose or (and) by a sentiment of responsibility, as much as by a sentiment of helplessness and impotence elicited by the opposite absence of possible options. Moreover, an individual may prefer not to have to choose, in order to avoid others' judgement concerning his choice (this may be related to responsibility). An individual may also prefer to leave a choice to someone else whom, he assumes, has more information or wisdom. And so forth.

The attribution of an intrinsic or end value to such an undesired liberty is directly against individuals' 'welfare', in a broad sense of the term. These reasons for preferring less liberty, however, should hardly register when the reasons in favour of the considered freedom rest on the basic entities of existence, being, or indeed often dignity, to be presented shortly.

These various aspects and values of liberty should therefore first of all be disentangled.

The various reasons for valuing freedom

We now consider the various reasons why a liberty can be valuable for an individual (in his own view, in the view of other persons, or in a conception of social ethics or justice). We first note, as we shall see again below, that the unavoidable word 'means' can have various extensions and can thus be ambiguous. The following various reasons for valuing freedom begin by going, in a sense, from the most commonly manifest to the deepest.

1 Liberty is a means to obtain the desired consequences of the act it permits, in the most direct and restricted sense.

2 Liberty is a means for exercising one's capacities for movement, action, choice, reason, decision or willpower, as training for future action.

3 Liberty is a necessary condition for exercising one's capacities for action and choice for any motive, including for no further purpose. This has the value of actualizing the existence of these capacities. Liberty thus permits activity, which Aristotle, for instance, sees as the most necessary condition for *eudaemonia* – flourishing or deep happiness.

4 In its most common conception, which is most relevant here, liberty is choice and (intentional) action. Indeed, first, liberty permits choice and choice requires liberty. But liberty also requires choice which constitutes its actualization, when choice is understood in a broad sense including choosing 'inaction' and letting other persons or chance choose. Second, liberty is also *a priori* necessary for (intentional) action

27

since a coincidence of intention with a strict external necessity would be fortuitous (or would be the particular spiritual attitude of wilful acceptance). And liberty also requires action sufficiently broadly understood (including resting quietly and delegating action). An 'agent' is a purposeful actor. Hence, liberty is necessary for choice and agency, and therefore for the existence of man as chooser and agent.

5 Indeed liberty strictly defined by reason and intention which can be elaborate is characteristic of man. A deep philosophical tradition even makes it the essence of man (for example, 'my freedom is not an added quality or a *property* of my nature: it exactly is the matter of my being . . . freedom is the being of man'[13] – this tradition includes Rousseau, Kant, Hegel, the philosophies of existence, and others). In classical terms, liberty, the essenceless existence, is the essence of man's existence.[14] Unfreedom thus is denial of humanity and reduction of the person to a thing, or reification (since the emphasis is on the acting and choosing being rather than on the sentient being). This constitutes the basis of the essential and ontological values of liberty. It is the first level of these values, the second being self-creation, which will be considered shortly. Then, since freedom requires choice (in the broad sense), it is responsible for this predicament of man, who is inherently 'forced to be free' and has no other choice but to choose. Yet certain freedoms are more important than others in this respect (they are basic rights and the opportunities provided by the satisfaction of basic needs).

6 Liberty makes the chooser's will and the agent's capacities take their place among the causes of the world. It thus makes man a creator. This in turn makes him accountable for a part of what exists – it makes him 'count for something'. It also possibly makes him responsible for it.

7 In particular, liberty makes man choose and in part cause his own acts and situation. He can also in this way train and modify or create his own capacities of all kinds. In particular, at the deep level of moral and mental freedom, he can choose or change his own end values (choice of a morals and in particular Rousseau's and Kant's autonomy), desires (Buddhism) or tastes (Hellenistic philosophies). In all these respects and in all possible degrees, liberty is self-choice, self-determination, self-causation and self-creation. This is often seen as the deepest essence of man, his basic ontology.

8 Being a condition for existence, choice, action and responsibility, liberty is also a condition for awareness, respect and esteem of oneself, for dignity and for pride.

9 For the same reasons, liberty is a major condition for counting in others' eyes, for eliciting their consideration in the form of expectations and interest, appreciation, respect or esteem, or on the contrary fear, hostility, contempt or hatred, in any case for having social existence.

28

10 The various types of liberty provide particular important reasons for valuing it. The first distinctions among liberties refer to the nature of that which is chosen and of the constraints. With respect to the nature of that which is chosen, the existential-ontological value is the reason for the unconditional priority of the respect of basic rights and the satisfaction of basic needs. As regards the constraints, a main distinction concerns whether they are chosen by some other person's will, or not. In the former case, unfreedom is dependency, and the corresponding liberty, non-dependency, is independence when it is sufficiently wide. Dependency can be mutual or unilateral, balanced or unbalanced. Excessive unilateral or unbalanced dependency may be particularly detrimental to dignity and personhood (although in other cases dependency provides the 'honour of serving') – in addition to the common unpredictability of the other individual's acts, wishes or whims, and hence of the constraint. As Rousseau remarked, 'it is not the nature of things that enrages us, but only bad will'. Extensive domination is subjection when implemented by threat or force (with the limit case of slavery, when the whole domain is submitted to the will of one or several individuals). Particular values are thus attached to non-dependency and independence.

11 Liberty and its various effects elicit a spectrum of varied sentiments which entail various preferences. These sentiments can be of the free person or of other persons. Preferences concerning the aims that freedom allows one to obtain go without saying. However, one can also enjoy liberty *per se*, the activity it permits, the exercise of choice, or the consequences of liberty with respect to responsibility, importance, sense of existence, dignity, self-respect, others' views of one's choices and actions, independence, mastery of oneself, and so on. The lack of these benefits elicits opposite sentiments. Certain of these sentiments are very direct. Feeling free, being free, the pure sentiment of liberty, can produce serenity, joy, exhilaration or elation. Unfreedom can produce, on the contrary, painful sentiments of helplessness, unimportance, frustration, alienation or oppression. Furthermore, the same aspect or consequence of liberty can produce both positive and negative sentiments, alternatively and even jointly: choice can provide excitement and a sense of importance, or embarrassment, complication and anguish; responsibility can be a burden or a dignity.

Priorities and happiness

These reasons for valuing liberty constitute a rather complex set. Two major groups of reasons stand out, however. They are, respectively, freedom as a means to obtain the result of the chosen acts, and freedom as a condition for human existence and being, that is, the instrumental and the ontological-existential values of liberty, or freedom for having and freedom for being.

By its existential-ontological value, liberty is a condition for human existence, and, for this reason, it has often been seen as having priority over other values, including other reasons for freedom, and 'welfare'. This is what is expressed by the positions noted above, such as Tocqueville's indictment and the other examples. The cry 'liberty or death', for instance, manifests this transcendence: it could not be uttered for a liberty that would only be a means for some extra enjoyment of life. Freedom as a condition for human existence has 'a value but no price', or, in Kant's terms, 'dignity' and no price. This applies particularly to the specific 'basic liberties', that is, the essential Rights of Man and of the Citizen stated in the first sixteen articles of the 1789 Declaration, whose priority is implied by their being declared 'inalienable'.

Finally, respectful justice can *a priori* be based on two types of individuals' values: those in the category of liberty and those of the family of happiness. These two groups have a number of relations between themselves. First of all, the comparison of happiness appears formally as the limiting and borderline case of the comparison of liberties – where comparison means that an individual has as much or more than another – when all means are jointly included in the comparison, including the capacity for being satisfied. More straightforwardly, all the above mentioned reasons to value liberty can elicit the satisfaction or the happiness of the freer individual. We have, truly, also noted various reasons why an individual could be unhappy with liberty or with more liberty and would prefer to be less free. However, the anguish of choice and the fear of responsibility tend to vanish when more freedom in the category of mental liberty is obtained.[15] Therefore, freer practically implies happier if the scope of the increased freedom is sufficiently broad. Conversely, the individual would normally like his dissatisfaction, pain or unhappiness to be repelled or removed; the existence of these sentiments thus constitutes for him a binding constraint; hence, the alleviation of these feelings constitutes a liberation. Moreover, certain mental states such as satisfaction, happiness, and in particular the resulting serenity, are common necessary conditions for conscious free actions, in freeing the individual from more or less obsessional desires, dissatisfactions, tensions or pains,[16] just as, on the contrary, a certain dissatisfaction or unhappinesss may act as the spur for rational and wilful action. To conclude, one cannot *a priori* and in general oppose an ethic of happiness and an ethic of liberty, eudemonism (or, perhaps, 'welfarism'[17]) and eleutherism. Both values are inextricably tied by many links. The distinction can only refer to particular liberties, means or problems.

LIBERTIES AND JUSTICE

The three types of liberty with regard to action

Liberty, indeed, can be of many types, of many things, and can have many actual, specific manifestations. However, the modern theory of justice is first of all structured by the following action-centred classification of liberties in the broad sense.

An action can be seen as a set of acts using means for an aim. The acts, the aim and the relation from the former to the latter constitute the process.

The means considered here can be:

- *capacities*, which are by definition part of the agent;
- tools;
- *social power*, that is, a possibility to influence other agents' acts by force or inducement (i.e., against their will or thanks to it);
- in particular, *income* or *wealth* which are purchasing power – that is, power to induce without persuading – which can obtain voluntary services or transfers from other agents through exchange;
- other property.

An action always uses some means since the agent's will can influence the world only through certain capacities of the agent (to begin with, his willpower, and others). The aim can in particular be a product or output.[18]

The constraints on an action can therefore bear either on the availability of the means; or on the acts given the means; or on the aim given the acts and means, that is, either on the aim or product itself, or on its relation to the acts or to the means that cause it. Looser or fewer constraints of these types are respectively more means-freedom or just means, more act-freedom and more aim-freedom. Note that the understanding of 'means' is restricted here so as not to include act-freedoms (and aim-freedoms). The corresponding act-freedom and aim-freedom together constitute process-freedom.

A social ethic that advocates a liberty is by definition a 'liberalism'. Hence, there are act-liberalism, aim-liberalism, process-liberalism which is both of the former, and means-liberalism.[19]

These concepts underlie the central structure of the theory of global justice as follows: full act-freedom, justified by the existential value of liberty, leads to the human and civil rights (basic rights or liberties) and to their priority; then distributive justice is determined by choices and balances between process-freedom and equal means-freedom. This process-freedom, however, is limited by others' basic liberties for a moral reason (forbidding direct violence and the effective threat of it).

31

Basic rights and basic needs

The existential value of liberty demands act-freedom which materialize into the classical basic Rights of Man and of the Citizen (those stated in the first sixteen articles of the 1789 Declaration, thus excluding the seventeenth and last article on 'properties', which demands full process freedom). Any rivalry between acts, whatever their nature and actors, can be attributed to the means they use. Hence naked basic rights defined by the corresponding act-freedom are essentially non-rival (a qualifying discussion would be in order for certain cases of free expression).[20] These basic rights can thus be held at satiety. The statement that they should be equal for all and maximal (expressed by Rousseau, the 1789 Declaration, J.S. Mills, Rawls, and others) is therefore a bizarre and awkward expression which amounts to this full respect. It may be observed that if these rights were defined as including some means so as to make them 'real', rather than merely 'formal', this classical formulation could not hold *per se*, since there is no *a priori* limit to the amount of goods that can improve the use of these rights, and it would raise a number of questions and would have to be modified.[21] Thus, these rights being respected fully and with priority amount to the same, and this is required by the existential value of liberty.

In addition to this 'formal' requirement, the existential value demands the 'real' liberty of a minimal means-freedom in the satisfaction of basic needs. These needs are largely defined by culture (a 'decent meal' costs many times the lowest possible cost for its nutritional content), and they include means for various social relations. These basic needs also depend on the means of society, and there often is more or less a rough consensus concerning what they are in any given balanced society.[22]

Equal liberties and distributive justice

We have already seen that respectful justice consists of the selection of types of individuals' means whose allocation is ideally equalized among individuals equal in the relevant characteristics, by sharing of output, by compensatory transfers or assistance or by sharing of other resources. 'Ideally' or 'prima facie' means in the absence of an overpowering reason, and when such reasons exist, for instance when several such ideals are not co-possible, ways of adjustment and the corresponding second-best egalitarianisms have to be provided.[23] The equalizing policy concerning a means (in the restricted sense) violates a corresponding process-freedom, for instance by a redistributive taxation. In the domains that are not directly affected by this policy, process-freedom prevails. Process-freedom corresponds to what Hayek calls a 'spontaneous order', or to what the classical contractarian vocabulary would label the 'natural' allocation of a human resource (that is, each individual is entitled to the usufruct of his own capacity). The two extreme and limiting cases have been pointed out. On the one hand, full process-freedom precludes all justice-motivated supra-individual intervention in the distribution. On the other hand, end-justice considers jointly the benefits from all resources, including satisfaction capacities, as the ideal equalizand (using transfers and compensations). A third conspicuous polar case endorses the natural allocation

Table 1.1 The three polar cases of distributive justice

Capacities	Allocation		
Consumptive	Natural	Natural	Equalize
Productive	Natural	Equalize	Equalize
End value equalizand	*Process-freedom*	*Income, consumption*	*Satisfaction*
Principle	Full process-liberalism	Equal consumption or income	Needs or ends full justice
Cause of inefficiency	Market failures	(1) Multidimensional equality (2) Disincentive	Equality
Solution for efficiency	*Liberal Social Contract*, liberal public economics (Kolm 1985)	(1) *Efficient super-equity* (multidimensional maximin, Kolm 1973, 91, 93) (2) *Fixed-duration income equalization* (Kolm 1966, 91, 93)	*Basic needs* in *Practical Justice* (leximin in fundamental satisfaction, Kolm 1971)
Incomplete or irrational theories	Private full process liberalism: • Locke (1689) • The 1789 Declaration • Classical 'political economy' • Nozick (1974)	Equalizand as: (1) Consumption goods (Tobin 1970) (2) Spheres of justice (Weber and Walzer 1983) (3) Primary goods (Rawls 1971) (4) Resources (Dworkin 1981)	Utilitarianism, 'social welfare'
Omissions	Market failures	• The inefficiency of multidimensional equality: (1), (2) • Exchange capacities: (2), (3), (4) • The ethical value of prices: (2), (3)	The rationality of equality

of consumptive and satisfaction capacities, and it throws all the other resources in the equalizand pool (including individuals' productive capacities or the benefits from them). Table 1.1 shows these three polar cases, the solution to their difficulties with Pareto-efficiency, their classical but incomplete or erroneous formulations, and the omissions that cause these imperfections.

In explaining this table, two preliminary remarks are in order. First, the human resources raise almost all of the global distributional problem in modern societies. Indeed, labour income constitutes a very large part of social income, even almost all of it if one allocates capital income to the primary resources (labour and non-human natural resources), these non-human natural resources are initially allocated by processes using other resources (collective agreement, first occupancy, and reference to needs, productive capacities, and mere existence in equal sharing), and, last but not least, consumptive and satisfaction capacities are also human resources. Then, since process freedom amounts to self-usufruct and is the opposite of the equalization of the benefits from the corresponding capacities, it appears clearly that the question of distributive justice consists essentially of the allocation of the various types of capacities between these two types of liberty.

Second, respectful individualistic justice should certainly give priority to Pareto-efficiency because it represents collective freedom from the various possible causes of its failure and collective rationality (unanimity is a case of equal power), possibly with individual preferences cleaned ('laundered', 'ironed') for eliminating certain of their immoral elements such as malevolence or strong envy.[24]

The three polar cases endorse respectively the 'natural' allocation of all capacities, of all consumptive capacities and only these, or of no capacity. All three entail Pareto-inefficiency, and the corresponding efficient second-best solutions have been proposed.

Full process liberalism constitutes the classical essential justification of free markets and capitalism (along with their relative virtue of efficiency). This is the ideal of Locke, of the 1789 Declaration including its last article, of what was called 'political economy' in the nineteenth century, including by Marx, although the same principle is also what he calls, after Blanqui, socialism (since this is the straightforward interpretation of 'to each according to his work' – the basic difference, for Marx, is that the labour supply of propertyless proletarians is not really free); in recent times, this view is restated by Nozick (1974) in the framework of the American debate in political philosophy, and its rational axiomatic construction is presented in Kolm (1985). Except for this last reference, these authors limit themselves to 'private' full process freedom, which is marred by market and agreement 'failures' (such as non-excludable public goods, externalities or transaction costs) which entail Pareto-inefficiency in comparison with other possible organizations. This produces the duty to implement what these process-free exchanges or agreements would have produced in the absence of the causes of these 'failures', and this implementation is essentially performed by a 'process-liberal' public sector. Hence these public interventions basically implement the corresponding process-freedom rather than interfering with it. Each such case constitutes a 'liberal social contract' and their set is the Liberal Social Contract (see Kolm 1985, 1987a and b, 1991d). Thus completed, the theory constitutes complete full process liberalism.

The intermediate case where the natural allocation of consumptive capacities (preferences, tastes, and so on), and only of these, is endorsed, is the locus of a number of theories which advocate the ideal equalization of consumption goods (Tobin 1970), of 'primary goods' (Rawls 1971), of resources (Dworkin 1981), or within 'spheres of justice' (Max Weber, and Walzer 1983). These theories face a number of problems. Pareto-efficiency is generally violated by the multidimensional equalities in consumption goods (and, more partially, within the defined 'spheres of justice'). Dworkin's allocation of resources which are exchanged and transformed, and to a lesser degree Rawls' and Walzer's allocation of incomes (they constitute one 'primary good' and one ˅sphere of justice') which are spent, endorse the 'natural' allocation of capacities to exchange, bargain or deal on markets; these capacities can make an important difference in the final outcome; but they are not consumptive capacities, and hence their natural allocation constitutes an inconsistency for these theories. Finally, the theories that consider incomes should justify the ethical legitimacy of the corresponding prices.

The solution to these problems begins with the remark that removing preferences from the classical economic process (from productive resources to income, then to consumption goods and finally to satisfaction) leaves the consumption goods as ethical end-values. Hence the ideal equality is that of the individual bundles of these goods. But this is generally not Pareto-efficient. One then resorts to the corresponding egalitarian second-best of a multidimensional maximin (see Kolm 1977, 1987d, 1991c, 1996b) that leads to 'super-equity' (ibid., Kolm 1973a). Efficient super-equity then turns out to impose limits on the discrepancies in incomes (reckoned with efficiency prices), but these limits are much less stringent than strict income equality. This permits one to satisfy the principle of justice in avoiding the classical disincentive and inefficiency-generating effect of the redistribution of earned income.

Moreover, ethical views commonly stand somewhere in between this case and full process liberalism, that is, they hold that only part of the proceeds of productive capacities should be redistributed. One corresponding fiscal structure avoids the disincentive and inefficiency-generating effect of taxing (and subsidizing) earned income, due to the adjustment in labour duration. This is fixed-duration income equalization, which consists of the full equalization of incomes earned during a given duration, whereas the other income that the individuals choose to earn (in a free labour market) is untaxed.[25] For example, the actual income redistribution in present-day western developed countries corresponds approximately to a full equalizing redistribution of the incomes earned during the first ten to eighteen working hours of the week (but, of course, the actual fiscal structure is different and wasteful). Such a redistributive fiscal structure implies a guaranteed minimum income equal to the average wage earned during this period which can cater for basic needs. This fiscal structure ought to be adopted for reasons of efficiency, but, at any rate, its notional consideration constitutes the relevant parameter to discuss the central ethical redistributive choice in a society. The place of process-freedom and self-usufruct, measured by the time out of this duration, is here for a moral reason, rather than for the instrumental reason of the efficiency of free exchange, as is the case, for instance, for a utilitarian objective for Pareto (and the ensuing economic tradition) or with Rawls' 'difference principle'. This period defines the limit between process freedom, on the one hand, and means-freedom equalized by redistribution on the other. It describes the degree of solidarity and its actual choice will be influenced by the sense of community in the considered society. For modern nation-states in charge of most of the fiscal redistribution, the realistic levels are between one fourth and one half of the working time. Further discussion of the optimal and possible level of this parameter is presented in Kolm (1997b).

SOCIAL CONTRACTS, FUNDAMENTAL INSURANCE, MERIT, RESPONSIBILITY

Free choice is also the key valuing concept of other principles of justice, which play a role in the refinements of the preceding general classification (and which have sometimes been considered as the general solution of the problem of justice).

If freedom is ethically valued as producing good or legitimate outcomes rather than for the free choice itself, but the free choice fails to materialize because of some impediment, there is a case for implementing by other means what the free act would have produced in the absence of the impediment. This implementation may well constrain the actual act of the 'free' individual, for instance if the impediment is ignorance, or the lack of possibilities to communicate or to commit oneself that induces inefficient strategic situations (for instance of the prisoner's dilemma type). Then, as Rousseau says specifically for the latter kind of situation, 'they must be forced to be free'. This justifies both standard public regulation

36

or the protection of the imperfectly informed consumer and the most famous type of political theory, the social contract.

A social contract is a putative, hypothetical agreement that justifies a certain public organization or action. It justifies political constraint by individuals' 'free' choice. Proposed by the Stoics and rediscovered during the Renaissance, it was, during the seventeenth and eighteenth centuries, the political theory of all scholars who did not merely rely on tradition and God's will (apart from Montesquieu).[26] Recent works have used the concept differently.[27] In 'liberal social contracts'[28] the impediments to free exchanges or agreements are 'market failures' or more general 'agreement failures', and this provides the consistent completion of full process liberalism to these cases. One particular and extreme type of liberal social contract occurs when the impediment to an exchange is individuals' inability to insure against the risk of being poorly endowed with some personal characteristic, because they receive this endowment at birth or in childhood. This can cover physical or mental characteristics, such as poor health and productive capacities in low demand, education or motivation received in the family, and so on. The correction of this kind of 'market failure' consists of transfers of the would-be insurance compensation from the would-be payers of the insurance premia; these payers are the individuals well endowed with the relevant characteristic, if the insurance is a mutual insurance against this 'risk'. This is a *fundamental* insurance, studied in *The Liberal Social Contract* (Kolm 1985) as one possible consequence of valuing process-freedom. A similar scheme was proposed by Dworkin (1981), but this does not seem consistent with his basic principle, which is *resourcism*, that is, an ideal equality of resources, possibly including the considered human resource. Indeed, fundamental insurance is, on the contrary, a process liberalism, based on the moral assumption of the value of process-freedom; it leads to different levels of the capacity plus compensation for it for different individuals; and it does not provide the abstraction from preferences that Dworkin seeks to obtain.

What may be wrong (or right) with process-freedom is the implicit endorsement of the 'spontaneous' allocation of the individuals' means, and in particular of the natural allocation of the human resources. In the case of a fundamental insurance, this is the endorsement of the natural allocation of capacities or handicaps that are not at stake in the insurance. This objection disappears in an extended fundamental insurance where the individuals putatively insure for everything that differentiates among them. This is the theory of the original position, named and analysed by Rawls (1971), used by Harsanyi (1953), and suggested by Vickrey (1945). Identical individuals 'in the original position' choose the rules or the allocation before they know what actual individuals they will be and in considering (for Rawls) only their self-interest. Hence they will choose a bad outcome for certain actual individuals if this permits them to make sufficiently many other actual individuals sufficiently well off or well endowed. Thi would be unjust for the sacrificed actual individuals. And these actual indi viduals can hardly be held responsible for this choice of the original indi viduals. Indeed these original individuals first, are a myth, and second have no selves that differentiate them from their competitors in the alloca tion of resources and would transmit to specific actual individuals (if thes« original individuals have a self at all). Hence a theory of the original posi tion cannot be a theory of justice. This is confirmed by the fact that the mental process of choosing justly among opposed interests, and its con clusions, is very different from an individual's self-interested choice in un certainty (the choice concerned with justice is led by the rationality of equality recalled above). Therefore, disagreements about what specific criterion this theory leads to have no importance.[29]

In other major liberty-based concepts of distributive justice, the con straint constituted by the link between the action and its consequence for the actor is the instrument of justice. Then distributive justice is reduced not only to commutative justice (as with process-freedom or, implicitly, social contracts), but more specifically to retributive justice. The notions are those of merit or deservingness, and responsibility. Responsibility for one's own situation has been the key concept of the opponents to social insurance, and it is now emphasized in order to justify a certain restraint from egalitarian end-justice by scholars such as Cohen, Arneson, Roemer, Fleurbaey and Maniquet. Responsibility is ascription according to cause by the will and hence by freedom, a causation which can be by omission or by commission. But all the considered items have joint causes, and hence causation by a will generally does not suffice *per se* to determine the assignment. Thus responsibility entails a large part of ethical choice only submitted to a necessary condition of causation. Hence reference to responsibility denotes a type of ethical solution rather than a specific solu tion determined *a priori*. Historically, the notion of self-responsibility has played for the liberal right a role symmetrical to that played by needs for the left. But responsibility is a wider concept that extends beyond oneself, especially since responsibility can be by omission as well as by commission. Responsibility is indeed the basis of the notions of duty and of agents' liability toward the world. For this reason, it constitutes the core of major philosophies of solidarity and engagement (Sartre, Jonas, and formerly Bouglé and Braunschwig). In particular, more important than the fact that I am or am not responsible for my ends and tastes is the idea that I may be responsible for the satisfaction of my fellow men's basic needs.

CONCLUSION

Equality of liberty, broadly understood, thus constitutes the basic principle of justice, with various forms and necessary adjustments, and including the limiting cases of welfare and happiness. This holds for macrojustice, including global distributive justice, which combines a handful of criteria, for the open-ended list of multifarious issues of microjustice and its much larger list of criteria, and for mesojustice which deals with issues that are specific but very important and widespread (notably general policies concerning human capital, such as education). Therefore, the determination of the social optimum and of justice in society rests essentially on two bases, one moral and one logical. The moral basis consists of the values of liberty, based on the characteristics of liberty. The logical basis consists of a number of formal properties, concepts and results which characterize equal freedoms in various circumstances, permit adjustment among various criteria, and in particular provide the corresponding second-best freedom egalitarianisms. These properties include those that have provided the solution for macrojustice. But the most basic are the equivalence between equal independent liberty and equity in the sense that no individual prefers another's allocation to his own,[30] the extension of this property to the definition of 'no less free' and 'freer' and to the case of interdependent liberties, and the resulting definition of the efficient maximins or leximins in freedom for the cases where equal liberty and Pareto-efficiency are incompatible.[31]

The distinction of liberties that is relevant for justice, which has been used here, has more or less precise precedents. In particular, Marx's 'formal liberties' cover act-freedom and basic rights, and more generally process-freedom, whereas his 'real liberties' are means-freedom. Yet this distinction has been used to justify the suppression of basic rights. By contrast, this opposition differs completely from the famous distinction between negative freedom and positive freedom emphasized by Isaiah Berlin (after Benjamin Constant and many others), notwithstanding certain economists' misunderstanding of positive freedom. Berlin describes negative freedom as act-freedom, extended to process-freedom (he refers to 'economic liberties'), where the constraints result from other people's will (his weak point, here, is an absence of discussion of agreements or exchanges and of strategic interactions).[32] But Berlin's 'positive freedom' has nothing to do with means-freedom. Positive freedom is described by Berlin as 'being one's own master', valued for the existential reason, interpreted as the spiritual or mental freedom of choosing one's aims as with the Rousseau-Kant 'autonomy' and indeed often in the name of reason, then as choosing as one's 'true' self the reference to a group (state, nation, race, church, class), and finally as imposing people's behaviour in the name of the 'higher' or 'truer' freedom so defined. Examples of this tyranny in the name of liberty include references to 'people's will', including in Rousseauan social contracts. They would certainly also include the 'sense of history' of Hegel, for whom the freest man is the Prussian soldier marching in step, as he embodies the State. Berlin's implicit aiming at various modern ideologies is obvious. Indeed, Martin Heidegger, in his famous (or infamous) 'rectorate discourse', derives – from the Rousseau-Kant-like principle that 'to give law to oneself is the highest freedom' – that 'the highly touted "academic freedom" is being banished from the German university: being merely negative, this freedom was spurious; it meant indifference, arbitrariness of goals and inclinations, actions without restraint'. But, of course, the rule was not to be provided by pure reason but by the *Volk*'s destiny. What Berlin implicitly attacks by his criticism of positive freedom is certainly not the democratic welfare state.

Finally, the question of liberty is almost co-extensive to the question of man and of society. Hence attempts to understand or to judge man or society should necessarily consider liberty, but liberty has no reason to be less twisted a fact than the wood of which man is made according to Kant. Partial studies of specific cases and aspects of liberty necessarily have a role in this understanding, but only by starting from the overall view can they situate and appraise their contribution and ascertain that they analyse relevant and important questions.

NOTES

* I wish to thank Daniel Hausman whose comments induced me to state more explicitly and clearly a number of properties and who helped correct the English of the text. I am fully responsible for any remaining mistakes.

1 An obligation is 'no freedom not to', and so on.
2 It seems relevant here to stop short of the discussion of the general concept of causality, which will be fully understood only when the nature of time is fully understood.
3 See Kolm (1991b, 1993a, c, 1994a, 1995b, c, 1996a, b, d, e).
4 See Kolm (1982).
5 This structure is, however, valid in these cases if preferences are sufficiently weak (see Kolm 1996e, chapter 14).
6 The most elaborate presentation of the rationality of equality is in the foreword of Kolm (1997a).
7 See Kolm (1982, 1986, 1987c).
8 A full analysis of these structures is provided in Kolm (1990).
9 Note that the concept of fundamental preferences is completely different from that of 'extended sympathy' (Arrow and others), in spite of the formal similarity of the result. 'Extended sympathy' has been basically rightfully objected to by D. Hausman, J. Broome, M. Kaneko, and others.
10 That is, the theory of M. Rothbart, D. Friedman, etc. The prefix 'neo-' aims to distinguish this school from the older classical libertarians or left-anarchists.
11 This country (Sékou Touré's Guinea) soon had both extreme poverty and a bloody tyranny.
12 The analysis and the logic of this intrinsic value of liberty for individuals is explored in the book *Happiness-Freedom* (Kolm 1982).
13 Jean-Paul Sartre, *Being and Nothingness*, IV-1-1.

14 Note that liberty, the pure existence (and also *a priori* void) *has* no essence but *is* essence – of man's existence.

15 See the analysis in *Happiness-Freedom* (Kolm 1982, pp. 256–65).

16 The relations between freedom and happiness, and their causes, structures and consequences, constitute a notable part of the book *Happiness-Freedom* (Kolm 1982).

17 The term coined by Hicks (1959).

18 We have noted that the aim can be intermediate or final for the agent. It can also be more or less inherent in the act, as with the sensation provided by an activity, or with following a norm or obeying a duty (the aim can then also be seen consequentially as the fact of having followed the norm or obeyed the duty).

19 'Liberalism' is thus used here in its etymological sense of based on liberty. Note that the current English use of this term is at odds with its use in the *last* century in English and with its present and past use in all other European languages. Italian scholars have coined the felicitous neologism 'liberism' for process liberalism.

20 See Kolm (1996e, chapter 4).

21 See the discussion in Kolm (1985, part V).

22 See Kolm (1977b).

23 The various types of these adjustments are analysed in Kolm (1990).

24 A general view on laundering preferences is provided by Goodin (1986). The specific, technical application to the case of envy is presented in Kolm (1991a, 1995a).

25 This amounts to a 'concentration' (a uniform concentration toward the mean) of the 'total incomes' defined as the wage rates multiplied by total time (see Kolm 1966b).

26 A general theory of social contracts can be found in Kolm (1985, chapter 23).

27 Original position theories are considered below. Buchanan's social contract (1975) consists of the truce manifested by the respect of the actual rules of society (these rules constitute the 'constitution' which can be written, explicit, or tacit or revealed by social behaviour).

28 Kolm (1985) (also 1987a and b).

29 Rawls argues that there exists a possible ignorance in the original position (a 'veil of ignorance') with which the choice will be that the most badly treated individual will be treated as well as possible (the 'difference principle'). But why assume this ignorance? Since the issue is to allocate according to the characteristics of the individuals, it seems that the only ignorance justifiable by the theory concerns the allocation of these characteristics to the individuals, but that this ignorance should be complete. This is the 'thin veil of ignorance', considered by Harsanyi, which leads to a utilitarian form (and is one case which implies the mentioned injustice).

30 See Kolm (1971, 1973a, 1993b, 1994c, 1995a, 1996b, 1996c, 1996e).

31 See Kolm (1993d).

32 The distinction between 'freedom from' and 'freedom to' is also rich in possible confusions.

REFERENCES AND BIBLIOGRAPHY

Arneson, R. 1989. 'Equality and equal opportunity for welfare', *Philosophical Studies*, 56: 77–93.

—— 1990. 'Liberalism, distributive subjectivism and equal opportunity for welfare', *Philosophy and Public Affairs*, 19: 158–194.

Arrow, K.J. 1977. 'Extended sympathy and the possibility of social choice', *American Economic Review*, 67(1): 219–225.

Barry, B. 1989. *A treatise on social justice, volume 1: Theories of justice*, Harvester-Wheatsheaf, Hemel Hempstead.

Battifol, H. 1979. *Problèmes de base de la philosophie du droit*, LGDJ, Paris.

Benn, S. 1988. *A theory of freedom*, Cambridge University Press, Cambridge.

Bentham, J. 1789. *An introduction to the principles of morals and of legislation*, T. Payne, London, and 1970, J.M. Burns and H.L.A. Hart (eds), Athlone Press, London.

—— 1843. *The works of Jeremy Bentham*, Bowring, J. (ed.), William Tait, Edinburgh.

Berlin, I. 1958. *Two concepts of freedom*, Clarendon Press, Oxford.

—— 1969. *Four essays on liberty*, Oxford University Press, Oxford.

Buchanan, J.M. 1975. *The limits of liberty*, The University of Chicago Press, Chicago.

Cohen, G.A. 1989. 'On the currency of egalitarian justice', *Ethics*, 99: 906–944.

Del Vecchio. 1955. *La justice*, LGDJ, Paris.

Dworkin, R. 1981. 'What is equality? Part I: equality of welfare; Part II: equality of resources', *Philosophy and Public Affairs*, 10: 185–246 and 283–345.

Fauré, C. 1988. *Les déclarations des droits de l'homme de 1789*, Payot, Paris.

Feinberg, J. 1970. *Doing and deserving: essays in the theory of responsibility*, Princeton University Press, Princeton.

—— 1980. *Rights, justice and the bounds of liberty*, Princeton University Press, Princeton.

Finnis, J. 1979. *Natural law and natural rights*, Clarendon Press, Oxford.

Flathman, R.E. 1987. *The philosophy and politics of freedom*, The University of Chicago Press, Chicago.

Fleurbaey, M. 1995a. 'Equal opportunity or equal social outcome', *Economics and Philosophy*, 11: 25–55.

—— 1995b. 'The requisites of equal opportunity'. In Barnett, W.A. *et al.* (eds), *Advances in social choice theory*, Cambridge University Press, Cambridge.

—— 1995c. 'Equality and responsibility', *European Economic Review*, 39: 683–689.

—— 1996. *Les théories économiques de la justice*, Editions Economica, Paris.

Friedman, D. 1978. *The machinery of freedom*, 2nd edn, Open Court Press, La Salle, Ill.

Gewirth, A. 1982. *Human rights: Essays on justification and applications*, University of Chicago Press, Chicago.

Goodin, R.E. 1985. *Protecting the vulnerable*, Chicago University Press, Chicago.

—— 1986. 'Laundering preferences'. In Elster, J. and A. Hylland (eds), *Foundation of social choice theory*, Cambridge University Press, Cambridge.

Grzegorcyzk, C. 1982. *La théorie générale des valeurs et le droit*, LGDJ, Paris.

Hammond, P. 1976. 'Equity, Arrow's conditions, and Rawls's difference principles', *Econometrica*, 44: 793–804.

Hare, R.M. 1963. *Freedom and reason*, Oxford University Press, Oxford.

Harsanyi, J.C. 1953. 'Cardinal utility in welfare economics and the theory of risk-taking', *Journal of Political Economy*, 61: 434–435.

THE VALUES OF FREEDOM

Hart, H.L.A. 1982. *Punishment and responsibility*, Oxford University Press, Oxford.

Hayek, F. 1976. *Law, legislation, and liberty*, Routledge & Kegan Paul, London; The University of Chicago Press, Chicago.

Hicks, J. 1959. *Essays in world economy: preface*, Basil Blackwell, Oxford, reprinted as 'A manifesto', *Wealth and welfare*, 1981, Basil Blackwell, Oxford, 135–141.

Hoffe, O. 1985. *Introduction à la philosophie pratique de Kant*, Castella, Fribourg.

Kant, I. 1785. *Fundamental principles of the metaphysics of morals*, Wolff, R. (ed.), Bobbs-Merrill, Indianapolis.

Kolm, S.-Ch. 1966a. 'The optimal production of social justice', International Economic Association Conference on Public Economics, Biarritz (proceedings: Guitton, H. and J. Margolis (eds), *Economie publique*, CNRS, Paris, 1968, 109–173, and *Public economics*, Macmillan, London, 1969, 145–201).

—— 1966b. *Les choix financiers et monétaires*, Editions Dunod, Paris.

—— 1971. *Justice et équité*, CEPREMAP, Paris; reprinted: CNRS, Paris, 1972.

—— 1973a. 'Super-équité', *Kyklos*, XXVI(4): 841–843.

—— 1973b. 'More equal distribution of bundles of commodities', CEPREMAP.

—— 1977a. 'Multidimensional egalitarianism', *Quarterly Journal of Economics*, 91: 1–13.

—— 1977b. *La transition socialiste*, Editions du Cerf, Paris.

—— 1978. *Les élections sont-elles la démocratie?*, Editions du Cerf, Paris.

—— 1982. *Le bonheur-liberté*. Presses Universitaires de France, Paris (augmented edition: 1994).

—— 1985. *Le contrat social libéral*, Presses Universitaires de France, Paris.

—— 1986. *La philosophie de l'économie*, Editions du Seuil, Paris.

—— 1987a. Public economics. In Eatwell, J. *et al.* (eds), *New Palgrave Dictionary in Economics*, Macmillan, London, 1047–1055.

—— 1987b. 'The freedom and consensus normative theory of the state: the liberal social contract'. In Koslowski, P. (ed.), *Individual liberty and democratic decision-making (the ethics, economics and politics of democracy)*, J.C.B. Mohr (Paul Siebeck), Tübingen, 97–127.

—— 1987c. *L'homme pluridimensionnel*, Editions Albin Michel, Paris.

—— 1990. *The general theory of justice*, CERAS, Paris.

—— 1991a. 'The ethical economics of envy', CERAS, no. 90, German Bernacer Lecture, University of Alicante.

—— 1991b. 'Free and equal in rights', *Journal of Regional Policy*, 1: 5–62.

—— 1991c. 'Super-equity', CERAS, no. 98, German Bernacer Lecture, University of Alicante.

—— 1991d. 'Full process liberalism', IMF working paper (Division of Fiscal Affairs) and CGPC.

—— 1993a. 'Free and equal in rights: the philosophies of the 1789 Declaration of the Rights of Man and of the Citizen', *Journal of Political Philosophy*, 1(2): 158–183.

—— 1993b. 'Distributive justice'. In Goodin, R. and P. Pettit (eds), *A companion to political philosophy*, Blackwell, Oxford, 438–461.

—— 1993c. 'The impossibility of utilitarianism'. In Koslowski, P. and Y. Shionoya (eds), *The good and the economical*, Springer-Verlag, Berlin, Heidelberg, New York, 30–66.

—— 1993d. 'Equal liberty', CGPC.

—— 1994a. 'Rational normative economics against social choice and social welfare', *European Economic Review*, 38: 721–730.

—— 1994b. 'The meaning of fundamental preferences', *Social Choice and Welfare*, 11: 194–204.

—— 1994c. 'L'égalité de la liberté', *Recherches Economiques de Louvain*, 1: 81–86.
—— 1995a. 'The economics of social sentiments: the case of envy', *The Japanese Economic Review*, 46(1): 63–87.
—— 1995b. 'Economic justice: the central question', *European Economic Review*, 661–673.
—— 1995c. 'The modern theory of justice', *L'Année sociologique*, 5: 297–315.
—— 1996a. 'Moral public choice', *Public Choice*, 87: 117–148.
—— 1996b. 'The theory of justice', *Social Choice and Welfare*, 13: 151–182.
—— 1996c. 'Playing fair with fairness', *Journal of Economic Surveys*, 10(2).
—— 1996d. 'Rational just social choice'. In Arrow, K., A. Sen and K. Suzumura (eds), *Social choice revisited*, Macmillan, London, volume 2, 167–195.
—— 1996e. *Modern theories of justice*, The MIT Press, Cambridge, Massachusetts.
—— 1997a. *Justice and Equity*, English translation by H. See, with new foreword, MIT Press, Cambridge, Massachusetts.
—— 1997b. 'Macrojustice', paper presented at the conference on equality and responsibility, University of Cergy-Pontoise.
Melden, A.I. (ed.) 1970. *Human rights*, Belmont.
Mill, J.S. 1859. *On liberty*, McCallum, R.B. (ed.), Blackwell, Oxford.
Nino, C.S. 1980. *Introduccion al analisis del derecho*, Depalma, Buenos Aires.
Nozick, R. 1974. *Anarchy, state and utopia*, Basic Books, New York.
Paul, E.F., F.D. Miller, and J. Paul (eds) 1985. *Liberty and equality*, Basil Blackwell, Oxford.
Raphael, D.D. 1980. *Justice and liberty*, The Athlone Press, London.
Rawls, J. 1971. *A theory of justice*, Harvard University Press, Cambridge, Massachusetts.
Raz, J. 1986. *The morality of freedom*, Oxford University Press, Oxford.
Rials, S. (ed.) 1989. *La déclaration de 1789*, Presses Universitaires de France, Paris.
Roemer, J. 1986. 'Equality of resources implies equality of welfare', *Quarterly Journal of Economics*, 101: 751–784.
Ross, D. 1930. *The right and the good*, Clarendon Press, Oxford.
Rothbart, M. 1973. *For a new liberty*, Macmillan, New York.
Rousseau, J.J. 1973. *The social contract and discourses*, Dent and Sons, London.
Sartre, J.P. 1943, 1962. *Being and nothingness*, Harper and Row, New York.
Seidl, C. 1975. 'On liberal values', *Zeitschrift für Nationalökonomie*, 35.
Seidler, V.J. 1986. *Kant, respect and injustice: the limits of liberal moral theory*, Routledge, London.
Sher, G. 1987. *Desert*, Princeton University Press, Princeton.
Sterba, J. 1994. 'From liberty to welfare', *Ethics*, 105: 64–98.
Stolgar, S.J. 1984. *An analysis of rights*, The Macmillan Press, London and Basingstoke.
Summer, L.W. 1987. *The moral foundation of rights*, Oxford University Press, Oxford.
Tebaldeschi, I. 1979. *La vocazione filosofica del diritto*, Giuffré, Milan.
Tobin, J. 1970. 'On limiting the domain of inequality', *Journal of Law and Economics*, 13: 363–378.
Tocqueville, A. de 1856. *L'ancien régime et la révolution*, Laffont, Paris.
Vickrey, W. 1945. 'Measuring marginal utility by reactions to risk', *Econometrica*, 13: 319–333.
Waldron, J. (ed.) 1984. *Theories of rights*, Oxford University Press, Oxford.
Walzer, M. 1983. *Spheres of justice*, Blackwell, Oxford.
Weber, M. 1962. *Basic concepts in sociology*, Citadel Press, New York.

2

LIBERTY AND ITS VALUE

Daniel M. Hausman

In 'The Values of Freedom' Serge Kolm offers an extremely compressed and wide-ranging discussion of freedom, its meanings, its values, and its centrality to justice. He argues that justice is essentially concerned with the distribution of freedom. Indeed justice obtains if and only if individuals have equal (and maximal) liberty. This thesis is more a framework into which to cast controversies concerning justice than a substantive theory of justice, because all competing theories of justice can claim to defend equal liberty. Freedom itself is a certain kind of structure of causality–determination of action by features intrinsic to a person, such as will or reason. Freedoms can be distinguished along a number of different dimensions – 'cause, agent, nature, extent, constraint, value, action, use and conditions' (p. 24). The main kinds of freedom are 'act freedom' (or, closely related, 'process freedom') and 'means freedom.' Though Kolm never defines what an 'act' (in contrast to an 'action') is, act freedoms resemble what are often called 'negative liberties' – the absence of legal and social obstacles to doing certain kinds of things. 'Means freedoms' in contrast would not be called freedoms by many philosophers and economists. Means freedoms appear to be simply means (p. 31) – individual capacities, tools, resources, sources of social power, and so forth. Means make possible not only particular actions, but existence and agency itself, and hence they are clearly relevant to freedom. Finally, freedoms are of value for a variety of reasons that cluster around two issues: first, they are means to achieve ends and to exercise capacities. Second, freedoms are essential prerequisites for agency, dignity, and social recognition.

This is an immensely rich, intricate, and suggestive framework within which to address questions concerning the nature, importance, and extent of freedom and concerning the relations between freedom and other values. Indeed the framework is so intricate that Kolm himself can give only a fragmentary sketch, replete with references to the books and articles that constitute not only his life's work, but one of the most important

45

contemporary perspectives in normative social and political philosophy. In a brief note I cannot expound and criticize a whole social philosophy. What I shall do instead is to point to an awkward or elliptical feature of Kolm's framework and to propose an alternative that simplifies questions concerning freedom.[1] I do not mean to suggest that the difficulties in applying Kolm's framework cannot be surmounted. Indeed, I shall sketch how Kolm's set-up might account for the simple problem case I shall discuss and how it might subsume my alternative. But I do have doubts about its usefulness to theorists concerned to incorporate issues involving freedom into normative economics. Just as general relativity theory is too elaborate for the purposes of naval navigation, so, I suspect, Kolm's framework is overly complicated for the purposes of normative economics.

Kolm writes that 'liberty is a type of structure of causality' (p. 17) or simply 'a structure of causality' (p. 21). '"Free" is an instance of "caused by", and "freer" is an instance of "more caused by"' (p. 22). Kolm then goes on to say more about the relevant effects (mainly actions) and causes (states of individuals, in particular will and reason). But this notion of freedom fits some of the paradigm uses of the term awkwardly. Contrast the situations of two individuals, C (for 'Chinese') and I (for 'Indian.') I possesses political liberties that C lacks. In particular I is free to criticize the Indian government, while C is not free to criticize the Chinese government. Suppose that both print up leaflets criticizing their respective governments and spend a Tuesday morning distributing them. At noon on Tuesday I returns to work and to the criticisms or support of her fellow workers and to the anger of her boss, who, let us suppose, fires I for missing work. At noon on Tuesday C is simply arrested and begins a rather unpleasant period of re-education. The structure of causality concerning the distribution of the leaflets appears to be just the same, but most people would say that I possesses a liberty that C lacks. The notion of 'a structure of causality' badly needs fleshing out.

This is not intended as a refutation of the view that freedom is a structure of causality. The distinctions we draw between I's and C's liberties could be set out in terms of whether I and C can bring it about that the leaflets are distributed without their facing a risk of arrest. But there is, I would suggest, a more useful framework for raising questions about freedom. That framework was first presented by Gerald MacCallum (1967) and one might regard it as articulating the insight that freedom is a structure of causality, rather than as opposed to Kolm's perspective. MacCallum proposes that claims about freedom should be interpreted as claims about (a) what range of things can be done by (b) what entities, with or without (c) what sort of obstacles. To say that I possesses a (political) liberty of expression is to say that I is free to make speeches, distribute leaflets, and so forth without risk of legal sanctions. The assertion

46

specifies an agent, a domain or range of activities or states, and a set of obstacles.

> Such freedom is thus always *of* something (an agent or agents), *from* something, *to* do, not do, become, or not become something; it is a triadic relation. Taking the format '*x* is (is not) free from *y* to do (not do, become, not become) *z*, . . .'
>
> (1967, p. 314)

In this format, one can say that *C* is not free from government sanctions to distribute leaflets, while *I* is.

This framework makes freedom *univocal*. Political liberties, social freedoms, physical possibilities, 'act freedoms', and 'means freedoms' are not different species of freedoms. There is only a single kind of freedom of an agent from constraints to do or become something. Talk of kinds (and amounts) of 'freedom' is misleading and elliptical. One might say that *I* is politically free to pass out leaflets on Tuesday morning, but not economically free to do so. But why introduce different notions of freedom? The difference lies in the sort of obstacle from which *I* is or is not free, not in the nature of 'freedom'. Kolm's act freedom is freedom for an individual person to do some restricted set of things (see p. 31 for a rough specification of this set) without legal hindrance. Kolm's means freedom is also freedom for an individual person. It is freedom not only from legal and social hindrances, but also from various material and biological obstacles. The notion of means freedom (as Kolm implicitly notes) is, however, not well formulated until one specifies some range of states or activities. Someone who is starving is not free from biological obstacles to life. Someone who is uneducated is not free from material and social obstacles to develop certain abilities and to achieve a certain social status. Nothing is lost, and clarity is gained by insisting that there is but one kind of freedom, that there is no such thing as being free or freer (full stop), and that claims concerning freedoms are always claims concerning the freedoms of agents from obstacles to their doing (not doing) or becoming (not becoming) something.

Such a framework implies a radical deflation of the notion of freedom. Although this claim appears to put my remarks in radical opposition to Kolm's view, I'm not sure that the opposition is in fact great. Even when Kolm speaks of the 'existential-ontological' value of freedom, it is always of freedom as a means or a condition for something else. To say that freedom ceases to be a central concept in moral philosophy does not imply any diminution of the importance of people being free to do many things without particular obstacles. Adopting this perspective, one will not say, 'Freedom is the being of man' (as Sartre does in the passage quoted by Kolm). Such a claim might be the improbable assertion that certain sorts of purely physical or biological constraints do not apply to human decision-making. More plausibly it might assert that a certain sort of agency and indeed courage is the 'being of man'. Freedom is of the greatest practical importance, because if there are obstacles that prevent individuals from manifesting their agency, then human beings become at best glamorous potentialities. As bread is the staff of physical life, so freedom is the staff of moral life, but this fact does not imply that bread or freedom are central notions in moral philosophy, let alone ends in themselves.

All of this has, I believe, a moral for economists attempting to incorporate concerns about freedom into normative economics. Indeed I think that the above remarks about freedom find echoes in some of the formal results. Suppose one takes the agents whose freedom is of interest to be individual human beings, and suppose one takes the range of things the agent can be and do to be fully determined by the individual's complete and transitive preference ranking. Then all questions about the individual's freedom become questions about the obstacles that prevent the individual from progressing further up his or her preference ranking. Formalizations of the notion of the quantity or extent of freedom that accept such a starting point have appeared to many theorists to be impoverished, and in such work the extent of freedom readily collapses into merely the size of the feasible set or into utility itself. The view of freedom as a triadic relation presented here suggests that some progress might be made by distinguishing among *kinds* of obstacles. But more fundamentally it suggests that the problem lies not with the way freedom is understood, but with the notion of agency that is implicit in identifying what individuals would do or be with the objects of given preference rankings. If choice is simply taking the most preferred feasible option, then there is nothing to freedom but the range of feasible options. But there is more to freedom, and choice is much more than taking the most preferred feasible option.

NOTE

1 For more on freedom and rights and their relevance to normative economics, see Hausman and McPherson (1996, esp. ch. 9).

REFERENCES

Hausman, Daniel and Michael McPherson. 1996. *Economic Analysis and Moral Philosophy*. Cambridge: Cambridge University Press.
Kolm, Serge-Christophe. 1997. 'The Values of Freedom'. This volume, chapter 2.
MacCallum, Gerald C., Jr. 1967. 'Negative and Positive Freedom'. *Philosophical Review* 76: 312–334.

3

INDIVIDUAL FREEDOM AND SOCIAL CHOICE

Clemens Puppe[1]

INTRODUCTION

In the recent debate about the modelling of 'freedom of choice' in individual decision-making[2] several authors have proposed an approach incorporating a *set* of different preference orderings which an individual may take into account when evaluating his opportunities (see, for instance, Arrow [2], Jones and Sugden [8] and Pattanaik and Xu [15]). In such a model, which I shall refer to as the *multiple preference model* of freedom, the intrinsic value of opportunities is conceptualized through the libertarian notion of an autonomous agent who is 'free' to choose the preference that is right for him. Indeed, this seems to be the central idea behind the analysis of [8] and [15].

The purpose of this paper is to further advocate the multiple preference model of freedom and to establish its link to traditional social choice theory. In contrast to the approach of Pattanaik and Xu [15] who propose such a model in terms of a given 'reference' set of *reasonable* preferences, the interpretation of the model intended here is quite different. Following the approach of Nehring and Puppe [13], the present paper utilizes a fundamental representation theorem due to Kreps [10] and views the different relevant preference orderings not as *a priori* given but as induced ('revealed') by the individual's evaluations of opportunity sets. By Kreps' theorem, a transitive ranking of opportunity sets is representable by a set of weak orders defined on the set of alternatives if and only if it is monotonic with respect to set inclusion and satisfies a simple property, called 'contraction consistency'. In [13] it is argued that this property is indeed a very plausible general condition for evaluating opportunities. Consequently, under very mild assumptions a ranking of opportunity sets can be viewed as being generated by a set of weak orders corresponding to different, in general conflicting, evaluations of the alternatives. On the intended interpretation of the model these orderings may be thought of as corresponding to a decision-maker's different *multiple selves*. Of course, it might be the case that for *any* reasonable preference there exists

49

a corresponding 'self', as assumed in Pattanaik and Xu [15]. However, under the intended interpretation, this would only be accidental. Indeed, it is emphasized that in the present analysis the 'reference set' of orderings is endogenously determined by the individual's evaluations of opportunity sets.

In the context of freedom, the relevance of the analysis of Kreps [10] has sometimes been denied, arguing that it only accounts for the instrumental role of freedom, but not for its *intrinsic* value. While this might be true for the specific interpretation that Kreps lends to his model, it may not be true for the model itself. Indeed, as argued in Nehring and Puppe [13], Kreps' representation theorem may be given a much more general interpretation. For instance, one need not interpret the induced orderings ('multiple selves') as probable future preferences, as done by Kreps, but may allow – in terms of interpretation – for any relevant counter-factual preference as well. In particular, these orderings may include preferences which the decision-maker does *not* expect to have.

Given the intended interpretation of the multiple preference model, the problem of comparing opportunity sets in terms of freedom thus transforms into an *intrapersonal* social choice problem among the decision-maker's multiple selves. The contribution of this paper is to give a rigorous account of this idea and to demonstrate by means of two simple examples the applicability of such an approach. It is shown that any transitive ranking of opportunity sets satisfying contraction consistency corresponds to a certain social choice mechanism applied to the 'society' of the decision-maker's different selves. More specifically, the paper establishes a one-to-one correspondence between classes of rankings of opportunity sets and collective choice rules satisfying a certain invariance condition. Based on this result, one obtains characterizations of the classes that correspond to the unanimity rule and a modified 'majority rule', respectively.

This paper is organized as follows. First I present the general multiple preference model, as proposed in Pattanaik and Xu [15], and Nehring and Puppe [13], respectively. I also briefly review some of the related results obtained in Puppe [17]. The main results of the present analysis are then set out. The concept of an invariant collective choice rule is introduced and a one-to-one correspondence between such choice rules and rankings of opportunity sets is established. This result is then applied in order to characterize the class of rankings of opportunity sets which corresponds to the unanimity rule. It turns out that this class is precisely the class of all domination relations as introduced in [17]. Based on the analysis of Puppe and Xu [18], a modified 'majority rule' is defined, with a characterization of the class of rankings of opportunity sets generated by this rule. Unlike the unanimity rule, the modified 'majority rule' requires a restricted domain in order to generate a transitive ranking. I conclude with some final remarks.

INDIVIDUAL FREEDOM AND SOCIAL CHOICE

THE MULTIPLE PREFERENCE MODEL

Basic conditions

Let X be a finite set of alternatives and let $P^0(X)$ denote the set of all possible opportunity sets in X, i.e. $P^0(X) := \{A \subseteq X : A \neq \emptyset\}$. Furthermore, denote by $\succeq$ a preorder on $P^0(X)$, i.e. a reflexive and transitive binary relation on $P^0(X)$, with the interpretation that $A \succeq C$ if and only if A offers at least as much freedom as C. The symmetric part and the asymmetric part of $\succeq$ are defined as usual, i.e. $A \sim B :\Leftrightarrow [A \succeq B$ and $B \succeq A]$ and $A \succ B :\Leftrightarrow [A \succeq B$ and not $B \succeq A]$. Consider a set $\mathcal{R} = \{R_1, \ldots, R_n\}$ of weak orders, i.e. complete preorders, on X. The intended interpretation is that $\mathcal{R}$ represents the set of orderings which an individual takes into account when evaluating the degree of freedom offered by different opportunity sets. In the specific interpretation favoured by Pattanaik and Xu [15], $\mathcal{R}$ represents the set of preferences that a *reasonable person* may conceivably have. However, as shall be argued below, other interpretations are also possible. The basic question is the following. Given such a *reference set* $\mathcal{R}$ of orderings, when does an opportunity set A entail at least as much freedom as another opportunity set C, i.e. when does $A \succeq C$ hold? Before trying to answer this question in general, it may be advantageous to consider a simpler problem. First, suppose that C is a subset of A. In this case, it seems safe to assume that A offers at least as much freedom as C. Hence, $\succeq$ will be required to satisfy the following property.

M (Monotonicity with respect to set inclusion) For all $A, C \in P^0(X)$,

$$C \subseteq A \Rightarrow A \succeq C.$$

In the literature, this property is indeed one of the most uncontroversial conditions in the exercise of modelling 'freedom of choice'. Note that condition M is, however, not specific to the problem of freedom of choice. Rather, it may be viewed as defining the general 'context' of the analysis. Indeed, a property such as condition M will hold in any two-stage decision model where second-stage choices of the final alternative, given the opportunity set determined in a first stage, are not constrained by 'decision costs' or other restrictions on the decision-maker's ability to choose from his opportunities.

Next, consider the case where A is a subset of C, say $C = A \cup B$ for some $B \subseteq X$. In this case, the issue is to determine whether or not a certain expansion of the individual's opportunities enhances the freedom he enjoys. Given the notion of a reference set of orderings this seems to have a rather straightforward answer. Suppose first that for any 'relevant' preference $R_i \in \mathcal{R} = \{R_1, \ldots, R_n\}$ and any alternative $y \in B$ there exists an alternative $x \in A$ such that xR_iy. In this case, it seems that a restriction

51

to the alternatives in A entails no loss of freedom. Indeed, an agent fac with the opportunity set A is still 'free' to choose any reasonable pref ence ordering without sacrificing fulfilment in terms of his preferenc whatever reasonable preference he may choose to have, there exists : alternative in A which will leave him as happy as any alternative $A \cup B$. In contrast, suppose that there exists an alternative $y \in B$, i $y \in C \setminus A$, such that from the viewpoint of *some* relevant preference one has yP_ix for all $x \in A$, i.e. a strict preference for y over any alternati x in A. In this case, it seems clear that $C = A \cup B$ entails strictly more fre dom than the subset A. Indeed, given the opportunities in A, the agent no longer 'free' to choose being an 'i-type individual' without sacrificin fulfilment in terms of his preferences. Hence, one is led to postulate th: for all $A, B \in P^0(X)$,

$$A \sim A \cup B \Leftrightarrow$$

$$(3.1$$

for all i, and all $y \in B$, there exists $x \in A$ such that xR_iy.

Suppose that a ranking $\succeq$ satisfies (3.1) and condition M. Then $\succeq$ satisfie the following property which has been introduced in Nehring and Pupp [13].

CC (Contraction consistency) For all $A, B \in P^0(X)$ and all $x \in X$,

$$B \subseteq A \text{ and } A \cup \{x\} \succ A \Rightarrow B \cup \{x\} \succ B.$$

Contraction consistency states that if the addition of alternative x to the opportunity set A strictly increases the entailed freedom, then its addition to any subset B of A must have the same effect.

Suppose that for $A, B \in P^0(X)$ one has $A \sim A \cup B$, i.e. suppose that (3.1) holds. Then, by virtue of condition M and transitivity, one also has $A \succeq B$. Indeed, in this case A *dominates* B in the sense that joining B to A is of no value. Accordingly, define the induced domination relation $\succeq^*$ as follows (cf. [10], [17]). For all $A, B \in P^0(X)$,

$$A \succeq^* B :\Leftrightarrow A \sim A \cup B. \qquad (3.2)$$

The following results describes the impact of condition CC in terms of the induced domination relation (for a proof, see [17, Lemma 1]).

Fact 1 *Let $\succeq$ be a preorder on $P^0(X)$ satisfying condition M. Then $\succeq$ satisfies condition CC if and only if the induced domination relation $\succeq^*$ is transitive.*

Fact 1 suggests that property CC is indeed a very natural condition in the context of ranking opportunities (for a thorough discussion of the general-

52

ity of condition CC, see [13]). Moreover, in combination with condition M it characterizes the multiple preference model. This is the content of the following theorem which is due to Kreps [10] (for a proof of the version stated here, see [13]).

Theorem 1 (Kreps) *Let $\succeq$ be a preorder on $P^0(X)$ satisfying condition M. There exists a set $\{R_1, \ldots, R_n\}$ of weak orders on X such that (3.1) holds if and only if $\succeq$ satisfies condition CC.*

Note that by Fact 1 the existence of a set $\{R_1, \ldots, R_n\}$ as required in Theorem 1 is also equivalent to transitivity of the induced domination relation (cf. [17]).

It is important to distinguish two different interpretations of Theorem 1 which correspond to two different interpretations of the multiple preference model in general. First, one may take a 'reference set' $\mathcal{R}$ of weak orders as the primitive notion of the model and try to base the comparison of different opportunity sets on this given reference set, as in the approach suggested by Pattanaik and Xu [15]. On such an interpretation, Theorem 1 just asserts the validity of condition CC, or alternatively, the fact that the induced domination relation $\succeq^*$ is transitive. The second interpretation, in contrast, does not *assume* a given reference set $\mathcal{R}$ but argues for the plausibility of condition CC as a general condition for evaluating opportunities. From such a point of view, Theorem 1 becomes highly relevant since it allows one to *deduce* the existence of a set of weak orders on which the evaluation of opportunities is based according to (3.1). Hence, on this interpretation the set $\{R_1, \ldots, R_n\}$ of weak orders is a concept deduced from, or 'revealed' by, the decision-maker's evaluations of opportunities. As suggested in Nehring and Puppe [13], one may think of the orderings R_i as corresponding to a decision-maker's different 'selves'. Henceforth, a set $\{R_1, \ldots, R_n\}$ satisfying for all $A, B \in P^0(X)$ condition (3.1) will be referred to as a *representing family* for the preorder $\succeq$. Observe, however, that a *representing family* in this sense in fact only determines the domination relation $\succeq^*$ induced by $\succeq$.

Either of the two interpretations faces a problem. Indeed, the first interpretation of the multiple preference model raises the question of which preferences should enter the reference set $\mathcal{R}$. Although Pattanaik and Xu [15] offer an explicit suggestion, namely those preferences that a reasonable person may possibly have, this does not really solve the issue. First, such an interpretation raises the further question of which preferences should be regarded as reasonable. Secondly, even if one could single out the set of all preferences that a 'reasonable' person could have, it is not clear why *all* of those preferences should really matter uniformly across different agents. Indeed, the sets of preferences taken into account when evaluating opportunities might significantly differ across different individuals, even if those individuals find themselves in similar circumstances.

On the second interpretation there is no need to exogeneously specify a reference set of weak orders. Indeed, in this case an agent's evaluation of opportunity sets is taken as the primitive notion. Given that these evaluations satisfy condition CC, the set of weak orders which the agent may take into account can be inferred using Theorem 1. However, the problem here is that conditions M and CC do not *uniquely* determine a representing family, i.e. the 'revealed' set of weak orders, through condition (3.1). To see this, consider the following example.

Example 1 Let $X = \{x, y, z\}$ and suppose that $A \succeq B \Leftrightarrow B \subseteq A$. Clearly, this ranking satisfies conditions M and CC. Denote by $R_1 - R_6$ the following six weak orderings on X.

$$R_1 : xP_1yP_1z,$$
$$R_2 : xP_2zP_2y,$$
$$R_3 : yP_3xP_3z,$$
$$R_4 : yP_4zP_4x,$$
$$R_5 : zP_5xP_5y,$$
$$R_6 : zP_6yP_6x.$$

It is easily verified that a reference set $\mathcal{R} \subseteq \{R_1, \ldots, R_6\}$ is a representing family for the ranking corresponding to set inclusion if and only if the sets $\mathcal{R} \cap \{R_1, R_2\}$, $\mathcal{R} \cap \{R_3, R_4\}$ and $\mathcal{R} \cap \{R_5, R_6\}$ are all non-empty. Obviously, this condition does not uniquely determine $\mathcal{R}$. Also observe that allowing for indifference in the orderings of a representing family would yield an even greater multiplicity of 'admissible' reference sets.

Non-uniqueness of the representing family is obviously a serious problem for the intended interpretation of the model. On the other hand, as Kreps' theorem very clearly demonstrates, non-uniqueness is unavoidable if all information that is used derives from *ordinal* comparisons of opportunity sets. A possible way to treat this problem in the present purely ordinal framework will be suggested below.

A notion of essentiality

This section briefly discusses the notion of essential alternatives introduced in Puppe [17]. For all $A \in P^0(X)$, say that $x \in A$ is essential in A if either $A = \{x\}$, or [$\#A \geq 2$ and $A \succ A \setminus \{x\}$]. Thus, x is *essential* in A if by deleting it the reduced opportunity set would entail strictly less freedom. For each $A \in P^0(X)$, denote by $E(A)$ the subset of essential alternatives, i.e.

$$E(A) := \{x \in A : A \succ A \setminus \{x\}\}. \tag{3.3}$$

For notational convenience, we have set $A \succ \emptyset$ for all $A \in P^0(X)$ in (3.3) in order to cover also the case where A contains one single alternative. In the general multiple preference model as introduced above, $E(A)$ may be empty. To see this, consider the following example.

Example 2 Let $X = \{x, y, z, v\}$. Furthermore, let $\mathcal{R} = \{R_1, R_2\}$ with $x I_1 y P_1 z P_1 v$ and $z I_2 v P_2 x P_2 y$, where I_1 and I_2 denote the symmetric part of R_1 and R_2, respectively. If a ranking $\succeq$ satisfies (3.1) with respect to this reference set of weak orders, one obtains

$$\{x, y, z, v\} \sim \{x, y, z\} \sim \{x, y, v\} \sim \{x, z, v\} \sim \{y, z, v\},$$

hence $E(\{x, y, z, v\}) = \emptyset$.

As a response to this example, one might try to argue that the notion of essentiality induced by (3.1) via (3.3) does in fact not appropriately capture the intuitive meaning of essentiality in the multiple preference model. Rather, one might suggest defining an alternative $x \in A$ as essential in A whenever it is a *best* alternative with respect to some ordering $R_i \in \mathcal{R}$. Such a definition amounts to assuming that the addition of an alternative x to an opportunity set A strictly increases the freedom whenever x is a best alternative in $A \cup \{x\}$ with respect to some ordering R_i, regardless of whether or not there exists an $x' \in A$ such that $x' I_i x$. Formally, one may define for all $A \in P^0(X)$,

$$E'(A) := \bigcup_{i=1}^{n} \max_{R_i} A, \tag{3.3'}$$

where $\max_{R_i} A$ denotes the set of best elements in A with respect to R_i. Indeed, the set $E'(A)$ exactly corresponds to the set $\max(A)$ which plays a key role in the analysis of Pattanaik and Xu [15]. Clearly, $E'(A)$ is never empty. The claim that $A \succ A \setminus \{x\}$ whenever $x \in E'(A)$ amounts to suggesting the following modification of condition (3.1).

$$A \sim A \cup B \Leftrightarrow$$
$$\text{for all } i, \text{ and all } y \in B \setminus A, \text{ there exists } x \in A \text{ such that } x P_i y. \tag{3.1'}$$

Note that the difference to (3.1) is that $y \notin A$, and that the preference for x over y is now required to be strict. On the first interpretation of the multiple preference model which takes a specific reference set as given the two definitions of essentiality corresponding to (3.1) and (3.1'), respectively, indeed make a difference, and one might try to argue for one or the other. However, on the second interpretation which views the set of orderings on X as a deduced concept, the first definition described by (3.1 and (3.3) turns out to be completely general.

Fact 2 *Let $\succeq$ be a preorder on $P^0(X)$ satisfying condition M and suppose that there exists a set of weak orders $\mathcal{R}' = \{R'_1, \ldots, R'_m\}$ such that (3.1'), holds with respect to $\mathcal{R}'$. Then, there exists a set $\mathcal{R} = \{R_1, \ldots, R_n\}$ such that $\succeq$ satisfies (3.1) with respect to $\mathcal{R}$.*

The proof of Fact 2 consists in showing that a preorder satisfying conditions M and (3.1') with respect to some set $\mathcal{R}'$ also satisfies condition CC. Given this, Fact 2 follows at once from Theorem 1. Clearly, the set $\mathcal{R}$ in Fact 2 is necessarily different from $\mathcal{R}'$. Hence, on the second interpretation of the model we may confine ourselves to the notion of essentiality corresponding to condition (3.1).

The model with linear preferences

By Theorem 1, the internal structure of the general multiple preference model is exhaustively described by conditions M and CC. In view of the generality of these two conditions one may wish to endow the model with more structure. One way to do this is to assume all orderings in the reference set $\mathcal{R}$ to be *linear* orderings (cf. [13]).[3] This assumption greatly simplifies the analysis and seems to be attractive in many ways. Indeed, suppose that $\succeq$ satisfies conditions M and (3.1) with respect to a set $\mathcal{R}$ of linear orderings. Then, for all $A \in P^0(X)$ the set $E(A)$ as defined in (3.3) is non-empty. Hence, one has the following property (cf. [17]).

F (Non-emptiness of E)   For all $A \in P^0(X)$ there exists $x \in A$ such that,

$$A \succ A \setminus \{x\}.$$

As before, we have set here $A \succ \emptyset$ for all $A \in P^0(X)$ in order to economize notation. Another consequence of the linearity assumption is that for all $A \in P^0(X)$, the set $E(A)$ coincides with the set $E'(A)$ as defined in (3.3'). Moreover, linearity of the preferences in a 'reference set' implies the following property which has been introduced in [17].

I (Independence of non-essential alternatives)   For all $A \in P^0(X)$,

$$A \sim E(A).$$

Condition I states that all what matters in comparing opportunity sets are the induced sets of essential alternatives. In particular, condition I implies by transitivity that for all $A, B \in P^0(X)$, $A \succeq B \Leftrightarrow E(A) \succeq B \Leftrightarrow A \succeq E(B)$.

In this sense, the ranking $\succeq$ is thus independent of non-essential alternatives. It seems that condition I is indeed a very appealing regularity condition, a view which is strongly supported by the analysis in [13].

In our present context, the main interest in conditions F and I lies in the fact that in combination with conditions M and CC they jointly characterize the multiple preference model in the linear case.

Theorem 2 *Let $\succeq$ be a preorder on $P^0(X)$ satisfying conditions M and CC. There exists a representing family of linear orderings for $\succeq$ if and only if $\succeq$ satisfies conditions F and I.*

A proof of Theorem 2 may be obtained using the result of Aizerman and Malishevski [1] on the rationalizability of choice functions by means of a set of linear orderings (see also Moulin [11]). Indeed, one can show that under the conditions of Theorem 2, the 'choice function' $E : P^0(X) \rightarrow P^0(X)$ which associates to each opportunity set A its subset of essential alternatives $E(A)$ satisfies the following so-called 'Aizerman condition'. For all $A, B \in P^0(X)$,

$$B \subseteq A \text{ and } E(A) \subseteq B \Rightarrow E(B) \subseteq E(A).$$

Furthermore, condition CC implies that the correspondence E satisfies property (α). By the Aizerman/Malishevski theorem these conditions are equivalent to the existence of a set of linear orderings $\{R_1, \ldots, R_n\}$ such that for all $A \in P^0(X)$, $E(A) = \cup_i \max_{R_i} A$. It is then easily verified that the set $\{R_1, \ldots, R_n\}$ is indeed a representing family (for a detailed analysis of the connection between the representation results of Aizerman/Malishevski and Kreps, and for a slightly more general result than Theorem 2, see Nehring and Puppe [13]).

RANKINGS OF FREEDOMS AND SOCIAL CHOICE MECHANISMS

Given the intended interpretation of the multiple preference model, the problem of ranking different opportunity sets may be viewed as a *social choice* problem between a decision-maker's different 'multiple selves'. The aim of this section is to give a rigorous account of this idea. In particular, it is shown by means of simple examples that such an approach is feasible even in the somewhat restrictive ordinal framework of the present paper. The first part of this section offers a formal analysis in terms of the concepts of social choice theory and provides the links to the problem of ranking opportunities. Subsequently, the two main examples are given. The first is the unanimity ordering which turns out to correspond to the domination relation defined in (3.2). The second example is a modified 'majority rule' which corresponds to the ranking suggested in Puppe and Xu [18].

Basic concepts and definitions

Let $\succeq$ be a preorder on $P^0(X)$ satisfying conditions M and CC. According to Theorem 1 there exists a representing family for $\succeq$, i.e. a set $\mathcal{R} = \{R_1, \ldots, R_n\}$ of weak orders on X such that condition (3.1) holds. Consequently, the ranking $\succeq$ may be viewed as resulting from a certain social choice mechanism applied to the 'society' $\{R_1, \ldots, R_n\}$ of the decision-maker's different multiple selves. In order to formulate this idea more precisely, observe first that in such a framework the 'social states' are the different opportunity sets, so that society's preferences have to be defined on the state space $P^0(X)$. Consequently, one has to look for a suitable social choice mechanism defined on the set of n-tuples of indirect utility preferences induced by the orderings R_i. For each $i \in \{1, \ldots, n\}$, denote by $\succeq_i$ the *indirect utility* preference induced by R_i, i.e. for all $A, B \in P^0(X)$,

$$A \succeq_i B :\Leftrightarrow \text{ for all } y \in B \text{ there exists } x \in A \text{ such that } xR_i y.$$

Note that with this notation condition (3.1) simplifies to the following condition. For all $A, B \in P^0(X)$,

$$A \sim A \cup B \Leftrightarrow \text{ for all } i, A \succeq_i B. \tag{3.4}$$

Henceforth, we will also refer to a set $\{\succeq_1, \ldots, \succeq_n\}$ of indirect utility preferences satisfying (3.4) as a representing family for $\succeq$. Clearly, $\{\succeq_1, \ldots, \succeq_n\}$ is a representing family in this sense if and only if the set of the corresponding weak orders on X is a representing family in the sense defined previously.

Recall the following definitions from social choice theory (see e.g. Sen [19]). A collective choice rule (CCR) f is a functional relation which associates to each n-tuple $(\succeq_1, \ldots, \succeq_n)$ of indirect utility preferences on $P^0(X)$ one and only one 'social' preference relation $\succeq_f := f(\succeq_1, \ldots, \succeq_n)$ on $P^0(X)$. The function f will be called a *transitive* collective choice rule (TCCR) if and only if its range is restricted to the set of all preorderings on $P^0(X)$.[4] A CCR f is called *Pareto-inclusive* if and only if for all 'social states' $A, B \in P^0(X)$,

$$\text{for all } i \in \{1, \ldots, n\}, A \succeq_i B \Rightarrow A \succeq_f B,$$

with strict social preference if at least one of the preferences $A \succeq_i B$ is strict. For future reference, we denote by $\succeq^P_{(\succeq_1, \ldots, \succeq_n)}$ the Pareto-relation

58

(unanimity ordering) corresponding to the n-tuple $(\succeq_1, \ldots, \succeq_n)$, i.e. for all $A, B \in P^0(X)$,

$$A \succeq^P_{(\succeq_1,\ldots,\succeq_n)} B :\Leftrightarrow \text{ for all } i \in \{1, \ldots, n\}, A \succeq_i B.$$

When no confusion is likely to arise we will omit the subscript and simply write $\succeq^P$ for the Pareto-relation. Clearly, a CCR f is Pareto-inclusive if and only if for all n-tuples of preferences the corresponding Pareto-relation is a subrelation of the social preference, i.e. if and only if for all $(\succeq_1, \ldots, \succeq_n)$,

$$\succeq^P_{(\succeq_1,\ldots,\succeq_n)} \subseteq \succeq_f, \text{ and}$$

$$\succ^P_{(\succeq_1,\ldots,\succeq_n)} \subseteq \succ_f.$$

It has been observed above that a ranking $\succeq$ on $P^0(X)$ satisfying conditions M and CC does not uniquely determine a representing family of weak orders on X, or equivalently, a representing family of the corresponding indirect utility preferences on $P^0(X)$. Hence, in order to identify a common social choice mechanism underlying a ranking $\succeq$ of opportunity sets one has to require *invariance* with respect to the choice of the representing family. In order to rigorously formulate this idea we need the following definition.

Definition Say that the tuples $(\succeq_1, \ldots, \succeq_n)$ and $(\succeq'_1, \ldots, \succeq'_m)$ are *equivalent*, denoted by

$$(\succeq_1, \ldots, \succeq_n) \approx (\succeq'_1, \ldots, \succeq'_m),$$

if and only if for all $A, B \in P^0(X)$ they induce the same ranking between A and $A \cup B$ via condition (3.4), i.e. if and only if for all $A, B \in P^0(X)$,

for all $i \in \{1, \ldots, n\}, A \succeq_i B \Leftrightarrow$ for all $j \in \{1, \ldots, m\}, A \succeq_j B$.

Clearly, $(\succeq_1, \ldots, \succeq_n) \approx (\succeq'_1, \ldots, \succeq'_m)$ if and only if the sets $\{\succeq_1, \ldots, \succeq_n\}$ and $\{\succeq'_1, \ldots, \succeq'_m\}$ represent the same preorder $\succeq$ (or rather its induced domination relation $\succeq^*$) in the sense of condition (3.4). It is also easily verified that the relation $\approx$ just defined is indeed an equivalence relation on the set of all tuples of indirect utility preferences on $P^0(X)$. Given this notion of equivalence one may now define a concept of invariance for CCRs.

Definition A CCR f is called $\approx$-*invariant* if and only if f is defined on the quotient space of all tuples of indirect utility preferences, i.e. if and only if

$$f(\succeq_1, \ldots, \succeq_n) = f(\succeq'_1, \ldots, \succeq'_m)$$

whenever $(\succeq_1, \ldots, \succeq_n) \approx (\succeq'_1, \ldots, \succeq'_m)$.

It is noted that this concept of $\approx$-invariance implies strong restrictions on the shape of a CCR f. For instance, $\approx$-invariance implies anonymity. Indeed, any permutation of an n-tuple $(\succeq_1, \ldots, \succeq_n)$ is in our sense equivalent to $(\succeq_1, \ldots, \succeq_n)$. Hence, a permutation of society's preferences cannot affect the social preference. More generally, $\approx$-invariance implies that social preference depends only on the *set* of society's preferences. In particular, this entails a property of replication neutrality in the sense that a replication of a certain preference in a society cannot affect the resulting social preference. Of course, the reason is that such a replication does not alter the set of society's preferences. This property turns out to be very useful in what follows. Let N denote the number of all different weak orders on X, or equivalently, the number of all different indirect utility preferences on $P^0(X)$, and let f be an $\approx$-invariant CCR. Given the property of replication neutrality, we need not consider tuples of different length as done so far, but may assume without loss of generality that f is defined on the set of all N-tuples of indirect utility preferences. Indeed, for any tuple $(\succeq_1, \ldots, \succeq_n)$ one can construct an equivalent N-tuple either by successive replication or successive deletion of preferences. To give a simple example of an $\approx$-invariant CCR consider the *unanimity rule* which associates to each N-tuple of preferences the Pareto-relation. Obviously, for all $A, B \in P^0(X)$,

$$A \succeq^P_{(\succeq_1, \ldots, \succeq_N)} B \Leftrightarrow A \succeq^P_{(\succeq'_1, \ldots, \succeq'_N)} B,$$

whenever $(\succeq_1 \ldots, \succeq_N) \approx (\succeq'_1, \ldots, \succeq'_N)$. Hence, the unanimity rule is indeed an $\approx$-invariant TCCR.

The following result demonstrates that the notion of an $\approx$-invariant social choice mechanism is indeed the appropriate concept in our context.

Theorem 3 *Let $\succeq$ be a binary relation on $P^0(X)$. Then, $\succeq$ is a preorder satisfying conditions M and CC if and only if there exists a Pareto-inclusive, $\approx$-invariant TCCR f such that $\succeq$ is an element of the range of f, i.e. such that for some N-tuple $(\succeq_1, \ldots, \succeq_N)$ one has*

$$\succeq = f(\succeq_1, \ldots, \succeq_N).$$

Proof In order to verify sufficiency of conditions M and CC for the existence of a TCCR f with the desired properties, let $\{R_1, \ldots, R_n\}$ be a representing family for $\succeq$ according to Theorem 1. Furthermore, let $(\succeq_1 \ldots, \succeq_n)$ be the representing family of the corresponding indirect utility preferences. Without loss of generality we may replicate or delete preferences and assume $n = N$. Define a CCR f as follows. For all $(\succeq'_1 \ldots, \succeq'_N)$,

$$f(\succeq'_1, \ldots, \succeq'_N) := \begin{cases} \succeq & \text{if } (\succeq'_1, \ldots, \succeq'_N) \approx (\succeq_1, \ldots, \succeq_N) \\ \succeq^P_{(\succeq'_1, \ldots, \succeq'_N)} & \text{if } (\succeq'_1, \ldots, \succeq'_N) \not\approx (\succeq_1, \ldots, \succeq_N) \end{cases}$$

Hence, the CCR f associates to an N-tuple $(\succeq'_1, \ldots, \succeq'_N)$ the given preorder $\succeq$ if the N-tuple is equivalent to the representing family for $\succeq$, and the corresponding Pareto-relation otherwise. Obviously, the CCR f always yields a transitive social preference, hence is a TCCR. It is also easily established that the function f as defined is $\approx$-invariant. Indeed, this follows immediately from the fact that the unanimity rule is $\approx$-invariant. Hence, it remains to show that f is Pareto-inclusive. This is true by definition for any N-tuple which is not equivalent to the N-tuple induced by $\succeq$. Thus, consider the representing family $(\succeq_1, \ldots, \succeq_N)$ and suppose that $A, B \in P^0(X)$ are such that for all $i \in \{1, \ldots, N\}$, $A \succeq_i B$. By (3.4) this implies $A \sim A \cup B$, hence by transitivity and condition M, $A \succeq B$. If one of the preferences $A \succeq_i B$ is strict, one obtains by (3.4) and condition M, $A \cup B \succ B$, hence by transitivity, $A \succ B$. Consequently, the Pareto-relation corresponding to $(\succeq_1, \ldots, \succeq_N)$ is a subrelation of $f(\succeq_1, \ldots, \succeq_N) = \succeq$.

Conversely, let there be given a Pareto-inclusive, $\approx$-invariant TCCR f. We have to show that each element of the range of f satisfies conditions M and CC. Thus, let $\succeq = f(\succeq_1, \ldots, \succeq_N)$ for some N-tuple of preferences. First, suppose that $B \subseteq A$ for some $A, B \in P^0(X)$. Since all preferences $\succeq_i$ are indirect utility preferences, one clearly obtains $A \succeq_i B$ for all $i \in \{1, \ldots, N\}$. Since f is Pareto-inclusive this implies $A \succeq B$, hence $\succeq$ satisfies condition M. Next, suppose that $B \subseteq A$ and $A \cup \{x\} \succ A$ for some $A, B \in P^0(X)$ and some $x \in X$. As before, one must have $A \cup \{x\} \succeq_i A$ for all $i \in \{1, \ldots, N\}$ since these are all indirect utility preferences. However, the preference for $A \cup \{x\}$ over A must be strict for some $i_0 \in \{1, \ldots, N\}$. Indeed, assume to the contrary that $A \sim_i A \cup \{x\}$ for all $i \in \{1, \ldots, N\}$. Then, by Pareto-inclusiveness of f, one would obtain $A \sim A \cup \{x\}$ which is false by assumption. Hence, one has $x P_{i_0} y$ for all $y \in A$ where R_{i_0} is the ordering on X corresponding to $\succeq_{i_0}$. Since $B \subseteq A$ this implies $B \cup \{x\} \succ_{i_0} B$. Hence, again by the fact that f is Pareto-inclusive, $B \cup \{x\} \succ B$, i.e. $\succeq$ satisfies condition CC, and the proof is complete.

By Theorem 3, a given preorder $\succeq$ satisfying conditions M and CC thus corresponds to a certain $\approx$-invariant TCCR f evaluated at a representing family $(\succeq_1, \ldots, \succeq_N)$ of indirect utility preferences. Consequently, an $\approx$-invariant TCCR f as a whole corresponds to a *class* of rankings of opportunity sets satisfying conditions M and CC. Such a class of rankings may be referred to as a rule of comparing opportunity sets.

Definition Let Δ be a set of preorderings on $P^0(X)$ each of which satisfies conditions M and CC. Then Δ is called a *rule* for comparing opportunity sets if and only if there exists a Pareto-inclusive, $\approx$-invariant TCCR f with range Δ.

In the following we examine two examples of such rules for comparing opportunity sets. The first corresponds to the unanimity rule, the second to a modified 'majority rule'.

The unanimity rule

It has already been observed that a simple example of an $\approx$-invariant TCCR is the unanimity rule. Surely, it is Pareto-inclusive. Consequently, by Theorem 3 above it defines a certain rule for comparing opportunity sets, i.e. a certain class of preorderings on $P^0(X)$ satisfying conditions M and CC. It turns out that this class is precisely the class of all domination relations $\succeq^*$ defined in (3.2). A preorder $\succeq$ on $P^0(X)$ coincides with its induced domination relation $\succeq^*$ if and only if it satisfies the following condition (see [17], also cf. [10]).

D (Domination principle) For all $A, B \in P^0(X)$,

$$A \succeq B \Leftrightarrow A \sim A \cup B.$$

Note that condition D in particular implies condition M. Indeed, for $B \subseteq A$ one obtains $A \cup B = A$, hence by reflexivity $A \sim A \cup B$ which by condition D implies $A \succeq B$. Furthermore, since $\succeq$ is transitive condition D implies condition CC by Fact 1. The following result shows that the unanimity rule corresponds to the class of all preorderings on $P^0(X)$ that satisfy the domination principle.

Theorem 4 *Let $\succeq$ be a preorder on $P^0(X)$. Then, $\succeq$ is an element of the range of the unanimity rule if and only if it satisfies condition D.*

Proof In order to show sufficiency of condition D, let $(\succeq_1, \ldots, \succeq_N)$ be a representing family for $\succeq$. It will be shown that $\succeq$ coincides with the Pareto-relation $\succeq^P$ corresponding to the representing family. Hence, assume that $A \succeq B$. By condition D, this is equivalent to $A \sim A \cup B$, which by condition (3.4) is in turn equivalent to $A \succeq_i B$ for all $i \in \{1, \ldots, N\}$, i.e. to $A \succeq^P B$.

Conversely, in order to verify necessity let $\succeq$ be an element of the range of the unanimity rule, i.e. $\succeq = \succeq^P_{(\succeq_1, \ldots, \succeq_N)}$ for some N-tuple $(\succeq_1, \ldots, \succeq_N)$ of indirect utility preferences. In order to verify condition D, suppose that $A \succeq^P B$, i.e. $A \succeq_i B$ for all $i \in \{1, \ldots, N\}$. This implies by virtue of each $\succeq_i$ being an indirect utility preference, that $A \sim_i A \cup B$ for all $i \in \{1, \ldots, N\}$, hence $A \sim^P A \cup B$. Conversely, since $\succeq^P$ is transitive and satisfies condition M, it is clear that $A \sim^P A \cup B$ implies $A \succeq^P B$ and the proof is complete.

By Theorem 4, the range of the unanimity rule is precisely the set of all preorderings on $P^0(X)$ satisfying condition D. In case one restricts the analysis to TCCRs defined on the set of all indirect utility preferences which are generated by *linear* orderings on X, it is possible to give a very simple representation of the unanimity rule in terms of essential alternatives. Denote by $\mathcal{L}$ the set of all indirect utility preferences that are generated by linear orderings on X. First, note that Pareto-inclusive, $\approx$-invariant TCCRs defined on $\mathcal{L}^N$ correspond to (classes of) preorderings on $P^0(X)$ which satisfy conditions F and I in addition to M and CC. Indeed, the following fact easily follows from Theorems 2 and 3.

Fact 3 *Let $\succeq$ be a binary relation on $P^0(X)$. Then, $\succeq$ is a preorder satisfying conditions M, CC, F and I if and only if there exists a Pareto-inclusive, $\approx$-invariant TCCR f defined on $\mathcal{L}^N$ such that $\succeq$ is in the range of f.*

The following theorem is based on [17, Prop. 1] and can be verified using Fact 3.

Theorem 5 *Let $\succeq$ be preorder on $P^0(X)$. Then, $\succeq$ is an element of the range of the unanimity rule defined on $\mathcal{L}^N$ if and only if the correspondence E induced by $\succeq$ via (3.3) is non-empty, satisfies Sen's property (α), and for all $A, B, \in P^0(X)$,*

$$A \succeq B \Leftrightarrow E(A \cup B) \subseteq A.$$

Hence, by Theorem 5 the unanimity rule restricted to $\mathcal{L}^N$ generates the following rule for comparing opportunity sets: A offers at least as much freedom as B if and only if every essential alternative of $A \cup B$ is available in A.

A modified 'majority' rule

An obvious problem with the analysis presented so far is the fact that a representing family for a preorder $\succeq$ only determines its induced domination relation $\succeq^*$ which, in general, may be rather incomplete. Indeed, as has been shown, $\succeq^*$ is precisely as incomplete as the unanimity rule to which it corresponds. An important question is therefore how one could reasonably extend a given domination relation. The purpose of this paragraph is to apply the established link between rankings of opportunities and social choice mechanisms to that problem. Using this analogy, the problem of extending the domination relation corresponds to the problem of finding a suitable CCR extending the unanimity rule. Of course, the latter problem has a long tradition in social choice theory. In the following, I will concentrate on one obvious candidate for such a CCR, the *majority rule.* An immediate problem with the standard majority rule in our context is that it is *not* an $\approx$-invariant CCR. For instance, it does not satisfy replication neutrality. Therefore, we will have to consider a certain modification of the majority rule that accounts for the problem of non-uniqueness of a representing family. Intuitively, this modified majority rule corresponds to a rule of majority of 'types' rather than individuals, where the 'types' are defined relative to a given opportunity set. Specifically, consider an N-tuple $(\succeq_1, \ldots, \succeq_N)$ of indirect utility preferences, and assume that these are generated by linear orderings on X. Given an opportunity set A, let $E(A)$ denote the set of essential alternatives as defined in (3.3), or equivalently (3.3'). For any $x \in E(A)$, think of all orderings for which x is uniquely best in A as one 'type' of preference (given A). Suppose that for all $A, B \in P^0(X)$, $A \succeq B$ if and only if

$$A \succeq_{\#E} B :\Leftrightarrow \#[E(A \cup B) \cap A] \geq \#[E(A \cup B) \cap B]. \qquad (3.5)$$

Hence, the assumption is that A entails at least as much freedom as B if and only if a *majority of types* (given $A \cup B$, i.e. given all alternatives under consideration) would prefer A to B. This rule for comparing opportunity sets in terms of freedom has been introduced and axiomatically characterized in Puppe and Xu [18]. Note that it indeed induces a complete ranking of opportunity sets. According to (3.5), define a CCR f_{MR}, the *modified* majority rule, as follows. For all $(\succeq_1, \ldots, \succeq_N) \in \mathcal{L}^N$,

$$f_{MR}(\succeq_1, \ldots, \succeq_N) := \succeq_{\#E},$$

where $E : P^0(X) \to P^0(X)$ is the correspondence induced by the N-tuple $(\succeq_1, \ldots, \succeq_N)$ via (3.3').

Fact 4 *f_{MR} is a Pareto-inclusive and $\approx$-invariant CCR on the domain $\mathcal{L}^N$.*

In order to verify this, suppose that for all $i \in \{1, \ldots, N\}$, $A \succeq_i B$. By virtue of each ordering being an indirect utility preference this implies $A \sim_i A \cup B$ for all i. However, this immediately implies $E(A \cup B) \subseteq A$, hence $A \succeq_{\#E} B$. If one of the preferences $A \succeq_i B$ is strict one obtains $E(A \cup B) \not\subseteq B$, hence $A \succ_{\#E} B$. This shows that f_{MR} is Pareto-inclusive. In order to verify $\approx$-invariance, note that any two equivalent N-tuples of indirect utility preferences in $\mathcal{L}^N$ induce the same correspondence $E : P^0(X) \to P^0(X)$. Consequently, f_{MR} cannot differ on equivalent N-tuples. In fact, it is easily verified that on the domain $\mathcal{L}^N$ a CCR f is $\approx$-invariant if *and only if* it depends only on the induced correspondence $E : P^0(X) \to P^0(X)$.

In Puppe and Xu [18] it has been observed that the ranking $\succeq_{\#E}$ as defined in (3.5) is not necessarily transitive, indeed in general it is not even acyclic. Given the present analysis, this of course comes as no surprise since majority decisions are well known to induce cyclic choices in many cases. Consequently, if f_{MR} is supposed to induce transitive rankings of opportunities one has to impose *domain restrictions*. In [18] it has been shown that the ranking $\succeq_{\#E}$ is transitive if and only if the induced correspondence $E : P^0(X) \to P^0(X)$ satisfies Sen's properties (α) and (β) (cf. Sen [19]). For all $A, B \in P^0(X)$ and all $x, y \in X$,

(α) $[B \subseteq A$ and $x \in B \cap E(A)] \Rightarrow x \in E(B)$,

(β) $[B \subseteq A$ and $\{x, y\} \subseteq E(B)] \Rightarrow [x \in E(A) \Leftrightarrow y \in E(A)]$.

The key to the following analysis is the observation that in our context these rationalizability conditions on the correspondence E may in fact be interpreted as domain restrictions on the CCR f_{MR}. In order to formalize this idea, let for any $S \in P^0(X)$ and $x \in S$, $\mathcal{B}(x, S)$ stand for 'for some individual preference $\succeq_i$, $\{x\} \sim_i S$' (i.e. with respect to the underlying linear ordering R_i, 'x is uniquely best in S'). Note that on the set $\mathcal{L}^N$, the statement $\mathcal{B}(x, S)$ is equivalent to $x \in E(S)$. With this notation, properties (α) and (β) may be rewritten as follows. For all $S, T \in P^0(X)$ and all $x, y \in X$

(α^*) $[x \in T \subseteq S$ and $\mathcal{B}(x, S)] \Rightarrow \mathcal{B}(x, T)$,

(β^*) $[T \subseteq S, \mathcal{B}(x, T), \mathcal{B}(y, T)$ and $\mathcal{B}(x, S)] \Rightarrow \mathcal{B}(y, S)$.

Note that any N-tuple in $\mathcal{L}^N$ automatically satisfies condition (α^*). Indeed, this follows at once from the fact that these preferences are all indirect utility preferences. However, the same does not apply to condition (β^*). Hence, the latter condition represents a proper domain restriction. Denote by $\mathcal{L}^N(\beta^*)$ the set of all N-tuples in $\mathcal{L}^N$ satisfying property (β^*). By the analysis of [18] one has the following result.

Fact 5 $\mathcal{L}^N(\beta^*)$ *is the largest domain on which* f_{MR} *yields a transitive ranking of opportunity sets.*

Suppose that an N-tuple in $\mathcal{L}^N$ contains *every* possible linear ordering on X (or, more precisely, the corresponding indirect utility preference). It is easily verified that such an N-tuple is indeed an element of the domain $\mathcal{L}^N(\beta^*)$. The CCR f_{MR} evaluated at such an N-tuple yields the following ranking of opportunity sets. For all $A, B \in P^0(X)$,

$$A \succeq B \Leftrightarrow \#A \geq \#B.$$

This is the ranking originally suggested and characterized in Pattanaik and Xu [14]. In the present analysis it thus appears as a specific element of the range of a modified 'majority rule'.

By a result of Puppe and Xu [18], a preorder on $P^0(X)$ is in the range of f_{MR} restricted to $\mathcal{L}^N(\beta^*)$ if and only if it satisfies conditions M, F, CC, Sen's property (γ) (applied to the induced correspondence $E : P^0(X) \rightarrow P^0(X)$) and a symmetry axiom which explicitly restricts the informational basis for the comparison of opportunities to the induced notion of essentiality (for the details, see [18]).

CONCLUDING REMARKS

In this paper, a link between the problem of ranking opportunity sets in terms of freedom of choice and the problem of preference aggregation has been established. The central concept providing that link is the notion of an $\approx$-invariant collective choice rule applied to the 'society' of a decision-maker's 'multiple selves'. A simple example of such a collective choice rule is the unanimity rule which has been shown to correspond to a certain notion of domination of opportunity sets. It turned out that the problem of comparing undominated opportunity sets amounts to finding an appropriate collective choice rule extending the unanimity rule. As an example, a modified 'majority rule' has been examined, retaining as closely as possible the spirit of standard majority decisions. An investigation of other extensions of the unanimity rule seems to be a worthwhile topic for future research.

It is emphasized that the link between individual freedom and social choice may be applied in both directions. In this paper, some well-known preference aggregation procedures have been applied in order to sharpen our intuitions about individual freedom. Conversely, one might also try to assess the merits of different aggregation procedures in promoting *social* freedom on the basis of our intuitions about rankings of individual opportunities.

NOTES

1 I would like to thank participants of the conference on 'Ethics and Economics of Liberty' at the University of Cergy-Pontoise, and seminar participants at the University of Graz and the University of California at Riverside for valuable comments on earlier drafts of this paper.

2 See, among others, Arrow [2], Gravel [5, 6], Gravel, Laslier and Trannoy [7], Jones and Sugden [8], Klemisch-Ahlert [9], Nehring and Puppe [13], Pattanaik and Xu [14, 15], Puppe [16, 17], Puppe and Xu [18], Sen [20–22] and Suppes [23]. See also Bossert [3], Bossert, Pattanaik and Xu [4] and Nehring and Puppe [12] on closely related topics.

3 By definition, a linear ordering is an antisymmetric weak order.

4 Note that this concept of a TCCR is strictly weaker than the concept of a social welfare function, since it does not assume completeness of the social preference. On the other hand, completeness could formally be obtained by subsuming incomparability under indifference. In this case, a TCCR would correspond to a quasi-transitive social decision function. I am grateful to Maurice Salles for his clarifying comment on terminology.

REFERENCES

[1] Aizerman, M.A. and A.V. Malishevski (1981), 'General Theory of Best Variants Choice: Some Aspects', *IEEE Transactions on Automatic Control* 26, 1030–1040.

[2] Arrow, K. (1995), 'A Note on Freedom and Flexibility', in K. Basu, P.K. Pattanaik and K. Suzumura (eds), *Choice, Welfare and Development, A Festschrift in Honour of Amartya K. Sen*, Oxford: Oxford University Press.

[3] Bossert, W. (1997), 'Opportunity Sets and Well-Being', *Social Choice and Welfare* 14, 97–112.

[4] Bossert, W., P.K. Pattanaik and Y. Xu (1994), 'Ranking Opportunity Sets: An Axiomatic Approach', *Journal of Economic Theory* 63, 326–345.

[5] Gravel, N. (1994), 'Can a Ranking of Opportunity Sets Attach an Intrinsic Importance to Freedom of Choice?' *American Economic Review Papers and Proceedings* 84, 454–458.

[6] Gravel, N. (1996), 'Ranking Opportunity Sets on the Basis of their Freedom of Choice and their Ability to Satisfy Preferences: A Difficulty', *Social Choice and Welfare*.

[7] Gravel, N., J.F. Laslier and A. Trannoy (1997), 'Individual Freedom of Choice in a Social Setting', this volume, chapter 5.

[8] Jones, P. and R. Sugden (1982), 'Evaluating Choice', *International Review of Law and Economics* 2, 47–65.

[9] Klemisch-Ahlert, M. (1993), 'Freedom of Choice: A Comparison of Different Rankings of Opportunity Sets', *Social Choice and Welfare* 10, 189–207.

[10] Kreps, D.M. (1979), 'A Representation Theorem for "Preference for Flexibility"', *Econometrica* 47, 565–577.

[11] Moulin, H. (1985), 'Choice Functions over a Finite Set: A Summary', *Social Choice and Welfare* 2, 147–160.

[12] Nehring, K. and C. Puppe (1996a), 'Continuous Extensions of an Order on a Set to the Power Set', *Journal of Economic Theory* 68, 456–479.

[13] Nehring, K. and C. Puppe (1996b), 'On the Multi-Preference Approach to Evaluating Opportunities', mimeograph.

[14] Pattanaik, P.K. and Y. Xu (1990), 'On Ranking Opportunity Sets in Terms of Freedom of Choice', *Récherches Economiques de Louvain* 56(3–4), 383–390.

[15] Pattanaik, P.K. and Y. Xu (1995), 'On Preference and Freedom', mimeograph.

[16] Puppe, C. (1995), 'Freedom of Choice and Rational Decisions', *Social Choice and Welfare* 12, 137–153.

[17] Puppe, C. (1996), 'An Axiomatic Approach to "Preference for Freedom of Choice"', *Journal of Economic Theory* 68, 174–199.

[18] Puppe, C. and Y. Xu (1995), 'Assessing Freedom of Choice in Terms of Essential Alternatives', mimeograph.

[19] Sen, A.K. (1970), *Collective Choice and Social Welfare*, San Francisco: Holden-Day.

[20] Sen, A.K. (1988), 'Freedom of Choice: Concept and Content', *European Economic Review* 32, 269–294.

[21] Sen, A.K. (1991), 'Welfare, Preference and Freedom', *Journal of Econometrics* 50, 15–29.

[22] Sen, A.K. (1993), 'Markets and Freedoms: Achievements and Limitations of the Market Mechanism in Promoting Individual Freedoms', *Oxford Economic Papers* 45, 519–541.

[23] Suppes, P. (1987), 'Maximizing Freedom of Decision: An Axiomatic Analysis', in G. Feiwel (ed.), *Arrow and the Foundations of the Economic Policy*, New York: New York University Press.

4

FREEDOM OF CHOICE AND INDIVIDUAL PREFERENCES

A comment on Clemens Puppe's 'Individual freedom and social choice'

Nicolas Gravel, Jean-François Laslier and Alain Trannoy

In 'Individual freedom and social choice', Clemens Puppe relates the problem of ranking individuals' opportunity sets on the basis of their freedom of choice to the issue of preferences aggregation. Although the connection may seem surprising, it derives quite naturally from a whole body of literature (see, e.g. Arrow [2], Foster [3], Kreps [8] and Pattanaik and Xu [11]) that locates the main reason for attaching importance to freedom of choice in the individual's ignorance of the preferences used when choosing from an opportunity set. This ignorance is naturally modelled by a set of possible preference orderings that the individual could have when choosing from any particular opportunity set. Every preference from this set generates a unique 'indirect utility ranking' of opportunity sets in the usual fashion: set A is better than set B if A's most preferred option is preferred to B's most preferred option. In this sense, the exercise of generating a unique ranking of opportunity sets from the multiplicity of 'indirect utility rankings' bears a strong formal similarity with that of generating a unique (social) ranking from a profile of (individual) rankings of alternatives extensively examined in social choice theory.

Exploiting this similarity, Clemens Puppe offers axiomatic characterizations of two rules that rank opportunity sets on the basis of the set of possible preferences that the individual can have: a unanimity rule, and what the author calls a 'modified majority rule'. The unanimity rule has been first introduced and discussed extensively in [3]. It ranks set A above set B when and only when, given any preference ordering that the individual could possibly have, the individual prefers choosing from A than choosing from B. The 'modified majority rule' says, roughly, that set A is better than set B if, for a majority of preferences that the individual could have, the individual would prefer choosing from A than from B.

It is worth noticing that in this approach, freedom matters normatively only because it enables individuals to make better choice according to their possible preferences. As Sen ([16], [17], [18]) has argued, it is also possible to value freedom of choice for its own sake, as an intrinsic source of well-being that is independent from (although not incompatible with) its effect on the individual's ability to make better choices according to some of her possible preferences. The purpose of this note is not to re-emphasize this distinction. Instead, our aim is to question the particular justification given by Puppe to the particular notion of freedom of choice in terms of multiple preferences.

The cornerstone of this justification is a remarkable representation theorem due to Kreps [8] and generalised by Puppe. In order to accept Kreps's theorem as a justification for defining freedom in terms of multiple preferences, it is necessary to accept that the binary relation generated by the statement 'offers at least as much freedom as' applied to alternative opportunity sets satisfies two properties. The first property is the standard (and hardly controversial) weak monotonicity with respect to set inclusion (WMSI) which states that adding new options to an opportunity set does not reduce freedom. The second property is the following axiom of contraction consistency (CC).

CC (contraction consistency) Given any two opportunity sets A, B such that $A \supseteq B$, and for every option x, if adding x to the opportunity set A strictly enlarges its freedom, then adding x to B should also strictly enlarge the freedom offered by B.

Before discussing more fully Kreps's theorem and its implication for the multiple preferences approach to freedom, it is legitimate to question the general plausibility of CC as an axiom designed to capture our intuition about freedom. To say the least, the link between CC and the statement 'offers at least as much as' is not immediately transparent. An argument that can be given in its favour is that some of the freedom-based rankings of opportunity sets considered in the literature (for instance set inclusion, the cardinality ranking characterized in [19] and [10] and the 'weighted cardinality' ranking characterized in our own contribution to the volume) satisfy CC. But this is no evidence that CC is a necessary condition to impose on any ranking of opportunity sets based on freedom of choice. As a matter of fact, it is not difficult to think of circumstances in which our intuition with respect to freedom goes against a ranking prescribed by CC. Consider for example a country – say, pre-Gorbachev Soviet Union – in which only candidates from the communist party are allowed to run for elections. The typical opportunity set of a person entitled to vote in this country at a standard election is {vote for the communist candidate, stay home}. By contrast the opportunity set of a person not entitled to vote is the singleton {stay home}. Given such an electoral system, it is not unreasonable to claim that the fact of being given the right to vote does not enlarge significantly one's freedom to affect the outcome of the election. That is, it is not unreasonable to claim that the set {vote for the communist candidate, stay home} does not offer more freedom of choice than the set {stay home}. Suppose now that we consider the same country in, say, the Yeltsin era where more than one candidate is allowed to run for elections. Suppose that, for some (perhaps understandable) reason, candidates from the communist party are not allowed to run for elections and that there are two parties that present candidates at the election: party A and party B. The typical voter's opportunity set is {stay home, vote for party A, vote for party B}. Now, given political plurality, it could be claimed – once again plausibly – that allowing the communist party to present candidates would enlarge the freedom of choice of the voters. That is, it could be claimed that the set {stay home, vote for party A, vote for party B, vote for the communist party} offers strictly more freedom of choice than the set {stay home, vote for party A, vote for party B}. Yet the two pairs of judgements violate CC. What this example illustrates is that, in many circumstances, normal judgements concerning the freedom offered by an opportunity set depend upon the whole opportunity set and not only upon the availability of an option in the set. That is, many standard judgements about freedom are 'menu dependent'. In the example, adding the option 'voting for the communist party' in a situation where the only other choice is staying home does not have the same effect of freedom that adding this same option in a situation of political plurality has. By having a flavour of menu independence, at least on opportunity sets related by set inclusion, CC can therefore contradict some plausible judgements about freedom.

Hence, it is legitimate to question the relevance of Kreps's representation theorem for justifying the notion of freedom of choice in terms of multiple preferences from the very beginning: By questioning the plausibility of CC as a general condition to impose on a ranking of opportunity sets. But it is also possible to question Clemens Puppe's main justification for the multiple preferences approach to freedom even if one accepts CC as a plausible property for a ranking of opportunity sets. Indeed, Kreps's representation theorem states that a complete and transitive ranking of all non-empty subsets (opportunity sets) of a finite set of objects of choice satisfies WMSI and CC if and only if it can be represented by a function Ψ from the set of opportunity sets to the non-negative real line which, for every opportunity set A, can be written as: $\Psi(A) = F(\max_{a \in A} u_1(a), \ldots, \max_{a \in A} u_n(a))$ for some (finite) list of functions $u_1(.), \ldots, u_n(.)$ from the set of options to the non-negative real line and for some strictly increasing function $F: \mathfrak{R}_+^n \to \mathfrak{R} +$.[1]

Kreps and Puppe interpret the functions $u_i(.)$ as being different 'utility functions' that the individual can possibly have over the various objects of choice. With this interpretation, the theorem tells us that a freedom-based ranking of opportunity sets performed by a complete and transitive ranking satisfying CC and WMSI can be though of as a resulting from a procedure in two steps:

1 A comparison of the maximal utility achieved in each set for each 'utility function'

2 an aggregation of the rankings obtained in step 1 into a unique ranking of opportunity sets by a 'Pareto-inclusive' function F.

In this sense, this theorem seems to provide foundation for the multi-preference approach to freedom. Yet it is important to understand that the theorem does not tell us that we *ought to* think of a complete and transitive ranking of opportunity set satisfying WMSI and CC that way. The functions $u_i(.)$ of the theorem as well as the aggregation function F are just mathematical entities, with no necessary relationship with the individual 'real' utilities or preferences (provided that such things are part of the model). In the context of Kreps's theorem, these functions are representational constructions and that is all! Of course one is free to interpret them as one wishes. And there are good arguments for relating freedom of choice with multiplicity of preferences. But these arguments cannot be derived from Kreps's theorem alone. Their validity must be assessed on other grounds. In short, we can serve to Clemens Puppe the same criticism that was addressed by Sen ([13], [14], [15]) to Harsanyi's ([4], [5]) (see also [6], [7] for a response of Harsanyi to Sen's critique and [20] for a thorough discussion of the Harsanyi–Sen debate): Nothing else than representational constructions can be obtained from a representation theorem.

Furthermore, as compared to Harsanyi's case, Kreps's representation theorem introduces additional difficulties of interpretation. Indeed, as Clemens Puppe acknowledges, there can be many systems of functions $u_i(.)$ and $F(.)$ that represent a given ranking of opportunity sets satisfying CC and WMSI. But contrary to Harsanyi's aggregation theorem, these multiple systems of functions $u_i(.)$ – 'representing families' in Puppe's terminology – may correspond to as many different collections of *orderings* of the options (and not just to different representations of a same collection of orderings). In short, in Puppe's framework, an individual is modelled as having different possible sets of different possible preferences. Moreover, these 'representing families' of preferences are related each to another in a complicated way as can be seen in Puppe's illuminating example. It is not entirely clear how these multiple 'representing families' should be interpreted. It is very intuitive to admit that an individual can have a set of many possible preferences. But what does it mean for an individual to have many sets of different preferences?

72

COMMENT

An interesting – as well as surprising – corollary of Kreps's theorem, also proved in Kreps [8], is that, for a complete and transitive ranking of opportunity sets satisfying CC and WMSI, there exists a list of function $v_1, \ldots, v_I$ from the set of options to the non-negative real line such that the function Φ from the set of all opportunity sets to the real line defined, for every opportunity set A, by

$$\Phi(A) = \sum_{i=1}^{I} \max_{a \in A} v_i(a)$$

represents this ranking exactly. That is, insofar as an individual has a complete and transitive ranking of opportunity sets satisfying CC and WMSI, the individual's multiple preferences revealed by Kreps's theorem can be aggregated in a utilitarian-like fashion. This result, to which the menu independence flavour of axiom CC contributes for no small part, re-emphasizes the stringency of CC. Now, given this result, the reader may ask: what is the interest of characterizing aggregation rules like unanimity or majority voting when one can rank opportunity sets by comparing the sum of their best elements as evaluated by a set of admissible utility function?

The answer to this question lies in the fact that Clemens Puppe has provided us with a version of Kreps's theorem that drops the condition of completeness imposed on the ranking of opportunity sets. Since completeness is not imposed, no numerical representation of the ranking can be obtained and, for this reason, no utilitarian rule is available. Although Puppe's abandonment of completeness does not yield a numerical representation of the ranking, it does yield a 'representing family' of orderings – or utility functions – of the options contained in opportunity sets. These functions relate to the original ranking of opportunity sets in roughly the same way as they do in Kreps's theorem.[2] For this reason, everything said thus far about the meaning of these 'representing families' for Kreps's theorem remain valid. Restating Kreps's theorem without imposing completeness is a very natural thing to do if one is interested in using the theorem to justify a particular approach to freedom of choice. For there is little reason to expect comparisons on the basis of freedom to yield definite conclusion in every circumstance.

Yet, if the possible incompleteness of the ranking of opportunity sets leaves open the problem of aggregating the multiple rankings of opportunity sets induced by the 'representing family' of utility functions, it is not clear that the majority rule characterized by Puppe is a natural solution of this problem. Indeed, the aggregation problem faced by Puppe looks more like a multi-criteria decision problem (see for instance [12],[9] and [1]) than an Arrovian social choice exercise. In a social choice context, the appeal of the majority rule is derived from its equal treatment of all individuals ('one man one vote'). Such a justification does not translate easily in the multiple preferences setting considered by Puppe. Why would an individual who evaluates opportunity sets by means of a list of preferences that she could have over the options attach an equal importance to every preference in the list? Why not instead weight some preference (say because they are more widespread) more heavily than others? Without a plausible answer to these question, the appeal of the majority rule for aggregating the multiple possible preferences of an individuals is unclear.

NOTES

1 In Kreps's [8] original paper, CC does not appear as such and is replaced by property (1.5) (see [8]; p. 567). Yet, when applied to a transitive ranking of all non-empty subsets of a finite set of options satisfying weak monotonicity with respect to set inclusion, CC and Kreps's property (1.5) are equivalent.
2 The absence of a numerical representation of the ranking of opportunity sets in Puppe makes the relationship between the 'representing family' of utility functions more cumbersome to state formally. It is for this reason that we have based most of our comments on Kreps's version of the theorem.

REFERENCES

[1] K. Arrow and H. Reynaud (1986) *Social Choice and Multicriterion Decision Making*. MIT Press, Cambridge, Massachusetts.
[2] K. J. Arrow (1995) 'A note on freedom and flexibility'. In P. P. K. Basu and K. Suzumura (eds), *Choice, Welfare and Development: A Festschrift in Honour of Amartya K. Sen*, chapter 1, pages 7–15. Oxford University Press, Oxford.
[3] J. Foster (1993) 'Notes on effective freedom'. Mimeo, Vanderbilt University.
[4] J. C. Harsanyi (1953) 'Cardinal utility in welfare economics and in the theory of risk-taking'. *Journal of Political Economy*, 63: 434–435.
[5] J. C. Harsanyi (1955) 'Cardinal utility, welfarist ethics, and interpersonnal comparisons of utility'. *Journal of Political Economy*, 63: 309–321.
[6] J. C. Harsanyi (1975) 'Nonlinear social welfare functions: Do welfare economists have a special exemption from bayesian rationality?' *Theory and Decision*, 6: 311–332.
[7] J. C. Harsanyi (1977) 'Nonlinear social welfare functions: A rejoinder to Professor Sen'. In R. Butts and J. Hintikka (eds), *Foundational Problems in the Special Sciences*, pages 293–296. D. Reidel, Dordrecht.
[8] D. M. Kreps (1979) 'A representation theorem for "preference for flexibility"'. *Econometrica*, 47: 565–577.
[9] V. Mousseau and B. Roy (1996) 'A theoretical framework for analysing the notion of relative importance of criteria'. *Journal of Multi-Criteria Decision Analysis*, 5: 145–159.
[10] P. K. Pattanaik and Y. Xu (1990) 'On ranking opportunity sets in terms of freedom of choice'. *Récherches Economiques de Louvain*, 56: 383–390.
[11] P. K. Pattanaik and Y. Xu (1995) 'On freedom and preferences'. Mimeo, University of California, Riverside.

[12] B. Roy (1985) *Aide Multicritère à la Decision*. Economica, Paris.

[13] A. K. Sen (1976) 'Welfare inequalities and Rawlsian axiomatics'. *Theory and Decision*, 7: 243–262.

[14] A. K. Sen (1977) 'Non-linear social welfare functions: A reply to Professor Harsanyi'. In R. Butts and J. Hintikka (eds), *Foundational Problems in the Special Sciences*, pages 297–302. D. Reidel, Dordrecht.

[15] A. K. Sen (1986) 'Social choice theory'. In K. Arrow and M. D. Intriligator (eds), *Handbook of Mathematical Economics: Volume III*, pages 1073–1181. North-Holland, Amsterdam.

[16] A. K. Sen (1988) 'Freedom of choice: Concept and content'. *European Economic Review*, 32: 269–294.

[17] A. K. Sen (1990) 'Welfare, freedom and social choice'. *Recherches Economiques de Louvain*, 56: 451–486.

[18] A. K. Sen (1991) 'Welfare, preferences and freedom'. *Journal of Econometrics*, 50: 15–29.

[19] P. Suppes (1987) 'Maximizing freedom of decision: An axiomatic approach'. In G. Feiwel (ed.), *Arrow and the Foundations of the Theory of Economic Policy*, pages 243–254. New York University Press.

[20] J. A. Weymark (1991) 'A reconsideration of the Harsanyi-Sen debate on utilitarianism'. In J. Elster and J. Roemer (eds), *Interpersonal Comparisons of Well-Being*, pages 255–320. Cambridge University Press, Cambridge.

5

INDIVIDUAL FREEDOM OF CHOICE IN A SOCIAL SETTING

Nicolas Gravel, Jean-François Laslier and Alain Trannoy

ABSTRACT

In this paper, we examine the problem of ranking individual opportunity sets on the basis of their freedom of choice in a social setting. By a social setting, we mean a framework in which the number of individuals whose freedom is evaluated is larger than one and where the access to the options contained in opportunity sets may be subjected to scarcity constraints. We propose two axioms that a freedom-based ranking could plausibly satisfy in such a context. The first axiom is the standard monotonicity with respect to set inclusion. The second axiom is a requirement which rules out the possibility that a mere redistribution of access to options among a given number of individuals leads to unanimous improvement in individual freedom. Using the formal similarity between this framework and the one considered in the problem of representing ordinal probability binary relations by a numerical measure (de Finetti (1937), Kraft, Pratt and Seidenberg (1959), Scott (1964) and Fishburn (1969)), we show that any ranking that satisfies the two axioms has a very simple numerical representation where the freedom associated to any set is the sum of some positive weights assigned to its elements.

INTRODUCTION

The issue of defining and measuring individual freedom of choice has received considerable attention recently (see, *inter alia*, Arrow (1995), Bossert, Pattanaik and Xu (1994), Gravel (1994; 1996), Jones and Sugden (1982), Klemisch-Ahlert (1993), Pattanaik and Xu (1990; 1995), Puppe (1995; 1996a; b), Puppe and Xu (1995), Sen (1988; 1990; 1991; 1993a), Sugden (1985) and Suppes (1987)). Typically, this question is handled by studying the consequences of imposing 'plausible' properties, or axioms, on the binary relation induced by the statement 'offers at least as much freedom as' applied to alternative individual opportunity sets. In this approach, an opportunity set is interpreted as the set of all options (commodity bundles, political candidates, lawful activities, etc.) to which an individual has access and from which she will, in some latter stage, make a choice.

The axioms usually proposed to capture the intuitive notion of freedom are all concerned with the way by which the addition of an option to an opportunity set contributes to its freedom of choice. More precisely, the axioms try to capture the idea that the mere *availability* of an option, independently of its immediate subjective merit for the chooser, increases the freedom of choice of the set containing it. This principle for ranking opportunity sets contrasts with that used in conventional welfare economics where the opportunity sets are compared on the basis of the immediate subjective welfare – or utility – that the chosen option is assumed to give to the chooser. This latter approach could be referred to as 'subjectivist' since the criterion underlying the ranking of opportunity sets is the immediate subjective evaluation of the options by the chooser. On the other hand, the notion of freedom of choice considered in the literature could be viewed as 'objectivist' in the sense that it induces a ranking of opportunity sets based upon the physical attributes of the set itself and not upon the immediate subjective preferences of the chooser.

Of course, this distinction between 'subjectivist' immediate utility-based and 'objectivist' freedom-based principles for ranking opportunity sets leaves open the question of how the two principles could be articulated in an overall 'well-being' ranking of individual opportunity sets which, presumably, would depend upon both freedom and preference considerations. Aspects of this question have been explored in Bossert (1997), Bossert, Pattanaik and Xu (1994), Gravel (1994; 1996) and Puppe (1995; 1996b) among others. The distinction raises also the more fundamental question as to why an objectivist notion of freedom of choice should play any role in a ranking of individual opportunity sets beyond that of enabling the individual to make better choices according to her immediate subjective preferences. With respect to this latter question, one can find three different answers in the literature.

The first is given by Sen (1991) and consists in rejecting altogether the 'objectivist' conception of freedom set forth in the literature and the dissociation of freedom from preference on which such a conception is based. As he writes, 'any plausible axiomatic structures in the comparison of the extent of freedom . . . have to take some account of the person's preferences' (p. 22). Sen's argument is, however, difficult to follow since he does not state explicitly what he means by 'preferences'. As he recognizes himself, 'the term preference is ambiguous' (p. 19). Yet, one of its commonly attributed meanings, to which we ourselves refer when we use that term in the present paper, is as an index of the individual eudemonistic welfare, or utility. Diana prefers a pint of beer to a glass of wine if and only if

77

drinking a pint of beer make her eudemonistically better off than drinking a glass of wine. Since Sen's opposition to the use of welfarist information in establishing normative criteria is notorious, this interpretation is not what he has in mind. Another commonly accepted meaning of the word 'preferences' is that of being the binary relation which rationalizes the individual's choice behaviour. Obviously, such a meaning is valid only if the choice behaviour under consideration satisfies the 'internal consistency' requirements, such as Sen's (1970) properties α and β, which renders it rationalizable by a binary relation. But, as Sen (1993b) again recognizes, 'there is no internal way . . . of determining whether a particular behaviour pattern is or is not consistent' (p. 498). 'Indeed, being consistent or not consistent is not the kind of thing that can happen to choice functions *without* interpretation – without a presumption about the context that takes us beyond the choices themselves' (p. 499; Sen's italic). It is precisely because it does not provide us with such 'a presumption about the context' which would clarify the meaning of the word 'preferences' that Sen's (1991) argument is difficult to accept.

Another answer to that question, provided by Arrow (1995), Foster (1993), Kreps (1979), Pattanaik and Xu (1995) and Puppe (1996a), among others, asserts that the importance of freedom of choice for an individual is the result of the individual's ignorance with respect to her future preferences. Since the individual does not know exactly the preferences she will have when asked to choose from an opportunity set, it makes sense for her to value positively the objective availability of an option, even if the option is not considered valuable from the subjective view point of her immediate preferences. Although this type of answer introduces a 'remote subjectivist' explanation for the normative importance of freedom, it does not reject the objectivist conception of freedom of choice. In this approach indeed, freedom remains an attribute of the opportunity set which does not depend upon the immediate subjective preferences of the chooser (although it may well depend upon the set of all possible preferences that such a person may conceivably have).

Finally, a third answer to that question is found in the point of view, forcefully developed by Jones and Sugden (1982), that the importance of freedom of choice is *intrinsic* or, more simply, that freedom of choice is important for its own sake, irrespective of any consequences it may entail for the chooser. This point of view is, perhaps, best expressed by the following statement by Tocqueville (1856):

> Ce qui, dans tous les temps a attaché à la liberté le coeur de certains hommes, ce sont ses attraits mêmes, son charme propre indépendant de ses bienfaits. . . . Qui cherche dans la liberté autre chose qu'elle même est fait pour servir.

(p.217)[1]

Aside from this objectivist conception, another salient feature of the approach to individual freedom considered thus far in the literature is its complete abstraction from the social and economic context in which the evaluation of individual freedom is performed. In effect, the axioms proposed to capture the intuitive meaning of individual freedom are typically applied to an environment which makes no reference whatsoever to the fact that the individual whose freedom is evaluated is not Robinson Crusoe but, rather, a member of a larger community in which access to the various options may be subject to scarcity constraints. *A priori*, such an abstraction from the social context and the scarcity constraints seems surprising, given the typical interpretation of freedom of choice in terms of accessibility to options set forth in the literature. For in a social environment submitted to scarcity constraints, giving someone access to some option implies, very often, depriving someone else of that option. For example, in a society in which the number of hospital beds is smaller than the number of individuals, adding to Diana's opportunity set an option which, among other things, gives her the certainty of spending a night in an hospital at any time she wishes means depriving some other individual from this benefit. Moreover, such a neglect of the social setting in which individual freedom is evaluated contrasts sharply with the way by which this notion is traditionally examined by philosophers (for instance Hayek (1960) and Rawls (1971)).

In this paper, we remain in tune with the objectivist conception of individual freedom sketched above. However we enrich the standard framework by introducing in the analysis the social context in which an individual evolves. By a social context, we simply mean a list of individual opportunity sets, one such opportunity set for every individual member of the society. Intuitively, a list of individual opportunity sets reveals information about the aggregate scarcity constraints under which the society operates, as well as the distributional rule used to allocate this scarcity among the society members. This information is useful to modelling individual freedom of choice because, together with the objectivist conception of this notion, it points to new directions along which the properties of the freedom-based ranking of individual opportunity sets can be examined. One of these directions, explored in this paper, links together the different freedom-based comparisons of the society members' opportunity sets between alternative social contexts. This direction stands on the presumption that, in a social setting, freedom comparisons of all individuals' opportunity sets are performed by the same ranking. In our view, this postulate suits the objectivist conception of freedom quite well. If the freedom of choice offered by a set depends upon its physical attribute and not upon the subjective evaluation of the person facing the set, it is difficult to see how a comparison of two opportunity sets based on freedom alone could vary from one individual to another. At given prices, $10,000 to spend on

79

commodity bundles gives Charles just the same amount of freedom of choice as it gives Diana.

Given this postulate, we examine an axiom that the freedom-based ranking of individual opportunity sets could plausibly satisfy when applied in a social context. We call this axiom 'impossibility of unanimous gains from redistribution' (IUGR). Very roughly, as its name indicates, this axiom rules out the possibility for a mere redistribution in the accesses to each alternative among a given number of individuals to strictly improve the freedom of someone without strictly reducing that of at least someone else.

It turns out that, when combined with a property of monotonicity with respect to set inclusion commonly used in the literature, the axiom of IUGR has important consequences for the way by which individual freedom is defined (under the proviso that it is defined in the same way for all individuals). Monotonicity with respect to set inclusion simply requires any set to offer strictly more freedom (or at least no less freedom) than any of its proper subsets. The main result of this paper is that, provided that the universal set of options is finite, a ranking of opportunity sets satisfies IUGR and monotonicity with respect to set inclusion if, and only if, the freedom offered by each set can be expressed as a sum of nonnegative weights assigned to each of its elements. This class of rankings of opportunity sets is considered, but not characterized axiomatically, by Klemisch-Ahlert (1993). It contains, as a particular case, the famous cardinality rankings of opportunity sets studied formally by Suppes (1987) and Pattanaik and Xu (1990) and informally by Hayek (1960; p. 35) in which the same weight is applied to every option. As it turns out, this characterization is obtained immediately after it is realized that, when applied to our framework, the axiom of Impossibility of Unanimous Gains from Redistribution is formally equivalent to an axiom known as 'strong additivity' in the classical literature on the problem of representing ordinal probability relations by numerical measures (see de Finetti (1931), Kraft, Pratt and Seidenberg (1959), Scott (1964) and Fishburn (1969; 1970) among others). To this respect, a conclusion of this paper is that the binary relation generated by the statement 'offers at least as much freedom as' applied to alternative individual opportunity sets is formally indistinguishable from the binary relation induced by the statement 'is at least as probable as' applied to alternative events. More importantly perhaps, the contribution of this paper is to identify an axiom which, in a plausible social setting, characterizes all rankings of opportunity sets which, like the well-known cardinality ones, have an additive numerical representation.

The plan of this paper is as follows. First we present and interpret the formal framework and the axioms. We then proceed to state, prove and interpret our main result. In the conclusion we summarize the discussion.

THE FORMAL FRAMEWORK

Notation

The notation and definitions used in this paper are standard. The logical operators are $\forall$ ('for all'), $\exists$ ('there exists'), $\neg$ ('not'), $\wedge$ ('and'), $\vee$ ('or'), $\Longrightarrow$ ('if . . . then'), $\Longleftrightarrow$ ('if and only if'). By a (strict) binary relation $\succ$ on a set Ω, we mean a subset of $\Omega \times \Omega$. Following the convention used in economics, we write $x \succ y$ instead of $(x, y) \in \succ$. Corresponding to a strict binary relation $\succ$, we define its weak companion $\succeq$ by $x \succeq y \Longleftrightarrow \neg(y \succ x)$ and we define the symmetric factor $\sim$ of $\succeq$ by $x \sim y \Longleftrightarrow (x \succeq y) \wedge (y \succeq x)$. Hence, in terms of the strict binary relation, $x \sim y \Longleftrightarrow \neg(x \succ y) \wedge \neg(y \succ x)$. A strict binary relation $\succ$ on Ω is asymmetric if $\neg(x \succ y \wedge y \succ x)$ holds for all (not necessarily distinct) $x, y \in \Omega$, is irreflexive if $\neg(x \succ x)$ holds for all $x \in \Omega$, and is negatively transitive if $x \succ z \vee z \succ y$ follows $x \succ y$ for all x, y and $z \in \Omega$. A weak binary relation $\succeq$ on Ω is complete if for any (possibly non-distinct) x, $y \in \Omega$, either (or both) of the statements $(x \succeq y)$ or $(y \succeq x)$ hold, is reflexive if the statement $x \succeq x$ holds for every x in Ω, and is transitive if $x \succeq z$ follows $x \succeq y$ and $y \succeq z$ for any x, y, $z \in \Omega$. Clearly, for every strict binary relation $\succ$ and its weak companion $\succeq$, $\succ$ is asymmetric if and only if $\succeq$ is complete, $\succ$ is negatively transitive if and only if $\succeq$ is transitive and $\succ$ is irreflexive if and only if $\succeq$ is reflexive. Given any set Ω, we denote its n-fold Cartesian product by Ω^n and its cardinality by $\#\Omega$. The sets of real numbers, non-negative real numbers and strictly positive real numbers are denoted respectively by $\Re$, $\Re_+$ and $\Re_{++}$ while the sets of integers, non-negative integers and strictly positive integers are denoted by N, N_+ and N_{++} respectively. The origin in $\Re^n$ is denoted by 0^n. Given any two vectors $\widehat{V}$ and $\widehat{W}$ in $\Re^n$, we denote by $\widehat{V}.\widehat{W}$ their dot product defined by $\widehat{V}.\widehat{W} = \sum_{i=1}^{n} \widehat{V}_i \widehat{W}_i$.

Statements and interpretation of the basic concepts

Let X (with generic element x, y, z, etc.) be a finite set of all conceivable objects of concern for any given individual and let $Z = 2^X \setminus \emptyset$ (with generic elements A, B, C etc.) denote the set of all non-empty subsets of X. An element of X shall be called an option and an element of Z, an opportunity set. As mentioned in introduction, we are interested in defining individual freedom of choice in a social context. Formally, a social context is a pair $(n, \widehat{A^n})$ where $n \in N_{++}$ is the number of society members and $\widehat{A^n} \in Z^n$ is an n-dimensional vector of individual opportunity sets. We refer to any such n-dimensional vector as an allocation of opportunities. Denoting by S the domain of all admissible social contexts, we assume the following:

Assumption 1 *(Unrestricted domain):* $S = \bigcup_{n \in N_{++}} \{n\} \times Z^n$

That is, we impose *a priori* no restrictions on the type of social contexts in which individual freedom is to be evaluated. Hence we are looking for a definition of freedom of choice which applies to any society with a finite number of individuals. As can be suspected, this assumption is not innocuous.

We compare alternative individual opportunity sets on the basis of their freedom of choice by mean of a strict binary relation $\succ$ ('offers strictly more freedom as') defined over Z. Corresponding to $\succ$, we denote its weak companion ('offers at least as much freedom as') by $\succeq$ and the symmetric factor of $\succeq$ ('offers just as much freedom as') by $\sim$.[2] We emphasize that $\succeq$ (or $\succ$) is interpreted as assessing the freedom of choice of any individual in any social context. The use of the same binary relation to evaluate the freedom of different individuals rests on the objectivist conception of freedom discussed above.

We now state the axioms imposed on $\succ$. The first axiom is one of the following two versions of the axiom of monotonicity with respect to set inclusion.

Assumption 2 *Strong monotonicity with respect to set inclusion (SMSI):*
$\forall A, B \in Z$ such that $B \subset A$, $A \succ B$.

Assumption 3 *Weak monotonicity with respect to set inclusion (WMSI):*
$\forall A, B \in Z$ such that $B \subseteq A$, $A \succeq B$ and $\exists \ x \in X$ such that $X \succ \{x\}$.

SMSI requires any opportunity set to offer strictly more freedom of choice than any of its proper subset. Hence, under SMSI, adding any option to an opportunity set leads to a strict improvement in freedom of choice. Some (e.g. Puppe (1996b)) have criticized this requirement, arguing that the addition of 'very bad' options such as 'being beheaded at dawn' to an opportunity set may not strictly increase the freedom of choice offered by the set. Although we are not entirely convinced that such an argument really applies to a freedom-based ranking of opportunity sets (as opposed to a *utility*-based one), the result presented herein does not depend upon the full strength of SMSI. With minor qualification (see remark 1 below), the result may be restated using WMSI instead.[3] WMSI requires any set to offer at least as much freedom as any of its subset and states that, for at least one option (like, say, 'being beheaded at dawn'), the universal set of all conceivable options offers strictly more freedom than the opportunity set which leaves no other choice than to 'be beheaded at dawn'.

To introduce the key axiom of impossibility of unanimous gains from redistribution, we need some further definitions.

Definition 1 *Given any number $n > 1$ of individuals and any two allocations of opportunities $\widehat{A^n}$, $\widehat{B^n}$ we say that $\widehat{A^n}$ is obtained from $\widehat{B^n}$ by a bilateral transfer of an option a from individual j to individual i (denoted $\widehat{A^n} \beta_{aij} \widehat{B^n}$) if and only if the following holds (i) $\forall h \neq i, j$ $\widehat{A^n_h} = \widehat{B^n_h}$, (ii) $a \in \widehat{B^n_j}$, $\widehat{A^n_j} = \widehat{B^n_j} \backslash \{a\}$ and (iii) $a \notin \widehat{B^n_j}$, $\widehat{A^n_j} = \widehat{B^n_j} \cup \{a\}$.*

Definition 2 *Given any number n of individuals and any two allocations of opportunities $\widehat{A^n}$, $\widehat{B^n}$ we say that $\widehat{A^n}$ is obtained from $\widehat{B^n}$ by a sequence of bilateral transfers (denoted $\widehat{A^n} \beta \widehat{B^n}$) if and only if there exists a (finite) sequence of options $\{a(t)\}_{t=1}^{T}$ with $T \in N++$, a sequence of pairs of individuals $\{i(t), j(t)\}_{t=1}^{T}$ and a sequence of allocations of opportunities $\{\widehat{C^n}(t)\}_{t=1}^{T+1}$ such that $\widehat{C^n}(T) = \widehat{B^n}$, $\widehat{C^n}(1) = \widehat{A^n}$ and $\widehat{C^n}(t) \beta_{a(t)i(t)j(t)} C^n(t+1)$ $\forall t = 1, \ldots, T$.*

In words, a bilateral transfer of option a from individual j to individual i is simply a move by which access to option a is transferred from individual j to individual i. An allocation of opportunities is obtained from another by a sequence of bilateral transfers if one can find a sequence of bilateral transfers that leads from the latter to the former.

We are now equipped to introduce our fourth assumption.

Assumption 4 *Impossibility of unanimous gains from redistribution (IUGR): Given any number $n > 1$ of individuals and any two allocations of opportunities $\widehat{A^n}$ and $\widehat{B^n}$ such that $\widehat{A^n} \beta \widehat{B^n}$ if $\widehat{A^n_i} \succ \widehat{B^n_i}$ for some individual i, then there is at least one individual j for which $\widehat{B^n_j} \succ \widehat{A^n_j}$.*

As said in the introduction, this axiom rules out the possibility for a simple reallocation of the accessible options among a given number of opportunity sets to improve strictly the freedom of someone without reducing that of someone else. A priori, this requirement seems a reasonable one to impose on a rule for evaluating individual freedom. To see why, suppose it was not satisfied. Then, this would imply the possibility of improving the freedom of someone without reducing that of someone else by simply redistributing the access to some (or to all) of the options. But if we simply redistribute the access to every option (by a sequence of bilateral transfers), it means that, for every individual who *gains* access to a new option, there is another individual who *loses* access to that same option. Provided that individual freedom of choice is conceived in terms of accessibility to the various options, it seems counter-intuitive that someone's freedom can be enlarged from such a change without having at least someone else's being reduced. In order to get a somewhat less abstract picture of the concepts presented so far, it may be helpful to consider the following two examples.

Example 1 Assume a country where the right to vote at national elections is given only to male adults and in which there are as many male as female adults. Without being specific about the way options are defined, one can say that in such a society, every male adult has the option of going to the polling station at national election and voting for whichever candidate suits his taste best. However, no female adult has this option. Imagine now that, for some reason, it is decided that only the female adults will be given the right to vote. Provided that this decision has no effects other than transferring the option of voting from male to female adults, it is clear that the new allocation of opportunities brought about by the decision has been obtained from the previous one by a sequence of bilateral transfers. It seems also fairly safe to say that this decision does not lead to a unanimous strict improvement in individual freedom.

Example 2 Assume a two-individuals society, involving, say Charles and Diana, in which only a given quantity of some good, say one cake, is physically available. To make this problem fit within our finite framework, we assume that the cake can only be cut in a finite number (say ten) of slices. Assume that the universal set of options is $X = \{0, \ldots, k\}$ with k being any finite number of slices (1/10th of one cake). Hence, in this problem an option is simply a number of slices of cake. For convenience, we assume free disposal so that if an individual is given, say, half a cake, he or she is given access *de facto* to the opportunity set $\{0, 1, 2, 3, 4, 5\}$. In this example, it is not difficult to see that all allocations of the ten slices between Charles and Diana are related each with another by a sequence of bilateral transfers. Hence, according to IUGR, it would be impossible to increase the freedom of one of these two individuals without reducing that of the other by reallocating differently the ten slices. Here again, this impossibility fits intuition quite well.

After such a defence of IUGR, let us turn to a criticism. Quite clearly, the plausibility of the axiom stands upon the acceptability of the objectivist notion of freedom defined only in terms of access to options. As a matter of fact, the axiom IUGR implies a strong idea of independence of the contribution of an option to the freedom of choice of an opportunity set from both the other options to which it is added or deleted and the specific characteristics of the decision-maker. In this respect, it may be noted that IUGR implies a more standard independence condition (used in particular by Pattanaik and Xu (1990), Bossert, Pattanaik and Xu (1994), Bossert (1996) and Suppes (1987)) as shown by the following proposition.

Proposition 1 *Under assumption 1, an irreflexive strict binary relation $\succ$ on Z which satisfies IUGR satisfies also the condition that for any $A, B, C \in Z$ such that $A \cap C = B \cap C = \emptyset$, $A \succeq B \Leftrightarrow (A \cup C \succeq B \cup C)$.*

Before proving this proposition, we need the following lemma.

Lemma 1 $\forall n \in N + +$, $\forall \widehat{A^n}, \widehat{B^n} \in Z^n$, $\widehat{A^n} \ \beta \ \widehat{B^n} \Longleftrightarrow \forall x \in X, \#\{i \in \{1, \dots, n\} \mid x \in \widehat{A_i^n}\} = \#\{i \in \{1, \dots, n\} \mid x \in \widehat{B_i^n}\}$.

Proof The necessity part is obvious. For sufficiency, let $\widehat{A^n}, \widehat{B^n} \in Z^n$ be such that $\forall x \in X, \#\{i \in \{1, \dots, n\} \mid x \in \widehat{A_i^n}\} = \#\{i \in \{1, \dots, n\} \mid x \in \widehat{B_i^n}\}$ and let $A(x) = \{i \in \{1, \dots, n\} \mid x \in \widehat{A_i^n}\}$ and $B(x) = \{i \in \{1, \dots, n\} \mid x \in \widehat{B_i^n}\}$. If $A(x) = B(x)$, the implication is trivial. If $A(x) \neq B(x)$, then $\#(A(x)\backslash B(x)) = \#(B(x)\backslash A(x))$ and, since $(A(x)\backslash B(x)) \cap (B(x)\backslash A(x)) = \emptyset$, there exists a one-to-one mapping $m : B(x)\backslash A(x) \to A(x)\backslash B(x)$ that associates to every individual $j \in B(x)\backslash A(x)$ a *distinct* individual $i \in A(x)\backslash B(x)$. Given such a mapping $m(.)$, define the sequence of allocations of opportunities $\{\widehat{B^n}(j, m(j), x)\}_{j=0}^{\#B(x)\backslash A(x)}$ by $\widehat{B_h^n}(j, m(j), x) = \widehat{B_h^n}(j - 1, m(j - 1), x)$ $\forall h \neq j, m(j - 1)$ and by $\widehat{B_j^n}(j, m(j), x) = \widehat{B_j^n}(j - 1, m(j - 1), x)\backslash\{x\}$ and $\widehat{B_{m(j)}^n}(j, m(j), x) = \widehat{B_{m(j)}^n}(j - 1, m(j - 1), x) \cup \{x\}$ with $\widehat{B^n}(0, m(0), x) = \widehat{B^n}$. By construction, $\widehat{B^n}(j, m(j), x) \ \beta_{xj-1m(j-1)} \ \widehat{B^n}(j - 1, m(j - 1), x)$ and $\widehat{B^n}(\#B(x)\backslash A(x), m(\#B(x)\backslash A(x)), x)$ so that $\widehat{A^n} \ \beta \ \widehat{B^n}$ holds. QED.

We turn now to the proof of the proposition. Assume that A, B and C are three sets such that $A \cap C = B \cap C = \emptyset$ and consider a three persons society with the two allocations of opportunities $(A, C, B \cup C)$ and $(B, C, A \cup C)$. It is easy to show that, for any option x, there are as many individuals who have x in their opportunity set in the allocation $(A, C, B \cup C)$ as there are in $(B, C, A \cup C)$. By the lemma we thus have $(A, C, B \cup C) \ \beta \ (B, C, A \cup C)$. By irreflexivity $\neg \ C \succ C$ so that if $A \succeq B$, then $A \cup C \succeq B \cup C$ follows at once from IUGR and, similarly, if $A \cup C \succeq B \cup C$, $A \succeq B$ follows from IUGR. QED.

The independence condition implied by proposition 1 is open to criticism. As discussed in Pattanaik and Xu (1990), a ranking of opportunity sets which satisfies the independence condition of proposition 1 pays no attention whatsoever to the diversity of the options. For example, a ranking satisfying the independence condition implied by IUGR can no consider a restaurant offering only roasted chicken as freedom-wise equivalent to another where raviolis only are available and at the same time rank a restaurant in which roasted chicken and tortellini are available above a restaurant where ravioli and tortellini appear on the menu.

But IUGR conveys more than an idea of independence. Among its other implications (the more striking of which being perhaps the content of the theorem below), it is worth noticing that it entails transitivity or quasi-transitivity as shown by the following proposition.

Proposition 2 *Under assumption 1, A binary relation $\succ$ on Z which satisfies IUGR is negatively transitive.*

Proof Consider a three member society with two allocations of opportunities (A, B, C) and (B, C, A) where A, B and C are any three opportunity sets. It is obvious that $(A, B, C)\ \beta\ (B, C, A)$. Now, if $A \succ B$, IUGR requires either that $C \succ B$ or $A \succ C$. QED.

As a final interpretative remark, it is important to note that the full strength of IUGR, in particular the fact that it implies transitivity and the independence condition of proposition 1 as well as the stronger result contained in the theorem below is attributable for a large part to the wide domain of application of the axiom rather than to its substantive content. For the power of IUGR arises to a large extent from the fact that it applies to a ranking which compares indistinctly all individual opportunity sets in every conceivable social context involving any finite number of individuals. That is to say, it is the ambition of defining individual freedom on a domain of social context as large as S which, for a significant part, is responsible for the strength of the axiom. In effect, the application of IUGR to such a large domain of social contexts as S renders IUGR formally analogous to an axiom known in ordinal probability theory as strong additivity (see Fishburn (1970) for a discussion and a proof of formally analogous results based on this axiom). Once this is recognized, the theorem stated in the next section is just a restatement of the theorem, proved for the first time by Kraft, Pratt and Seidenberg (1959), that strong additivity is a necessary and sufficient condition for a binary relation defined on a σ-algebra of sets to have an additive representation (see also Scott (1964; theorem 4.1), Fishburn (1970; theorem 4.1 and chap. 14, exercise 1)). The substantive content of the axiom, that is, intuitively, the fact of ruling out unanimous improvements in terms of freedom in the case of a simple reallocation of options among the same number of people could have more modest implication (if any) if it was applied to a more restricted domain of social contexts.

THE RESULT

We have the following theorem. In the appendix, we give a proof for the sake of completeness, although it can be found in the aforementioned references on ordinal probability.

Theorem 1 *A complete binary relation $\succeq$ on Z satisfies SMSI and IUGR if and only if there exists a function $v : X \longrightarrow \Re_{++}$ such that, for all $A, B \in Z$, $A \succeq B \Longleftrightarrow \sum_{x \in A} v(x) \geq \sum_{y \in B} v(y)$.*

Remark IUGR alone entails the existence of an additive representation for $\succeq$. The role played by SMSI is to force the weights to be strictly positive. Using WMSI instead would only weaken the requirement for the weights to be non-negative with at least one weight being positive.

In words, the theorem says that a freedom-based rule for comparing opportunity sets that satisfy SMSI and IUGR is formally indistinguishable from a rule obtained by first assigning strictly positive weights to every conceivable option and second, by defining the freedom offered by any opportunity set as the sum of the weights of its elements. This class of rankings is a generalization of the well-known cardinality rankings of opportunity sets (examined by Pattanaik and Xu (1990; 1995), Suppes (1987), Bossert, Pattanaik and Xu (1993)) by allowing the weights to differ across the options.

CONCLUSION

In this paper we examine an axiom – impossibility of unanimous gains from redistribution – that a ranking of individuals' opportunity sets can plausibly satisfy when applied to a general class of social environments. Under the postulate, consistent with an objectivist conception of freedom, that the extent of freedom of all individuals is evaluated by the same ranking, we characterize with this axiom the class of all rankings that compare any two sets by summing some predefined weights assigned to their elements. This of course raises the question of the intuitive meaning attached to the weights. Given the objectivist conception of freedom which motivates the present framework, it would be misleading to interpret the weights as indices of individual welfare such as utility. A more natural (but clearly less informative) interpretation is that the weight of an option reflects the option's contribution to the overall individual's freedom. Yet it remains to be seen what this objective contribution to individual freedom is supposed to mean. An immediate answer to this question is to define the contribution of an option to the freedom of an opportunity set only in terms of accessibility. An option contributes to freedom if and only if it is available. In this respect, the availability of option x in an opportunity set is worth exactly that of option y. While this interpretation is consistent with the particular case of the cardinality rankings of opportunity sets considered in Pattanaik and Xu (1990) and Suppes (1987) where the same weight is assigned to every option (the function $v(.)$ of the theorem is constant), it does not apply very well in all other cases where the weights may vary from an option to the other. Why, in an objectivist conception of freedom where the freedom of all individuals is evaluated by the same ranking, would the contribution of an option to the freedom offered by an opportunity set be different from that of another option? Our paper provides no answer to that question which, undoubtedly, deserves further investigation.

APPENDIX

Proof of the theorem

Necessity Assume that $\succeq$ is such that there exists some function $v : X \longrightarrow \Re + +$ for which $A \succeq B \Longleftrightarrow \sum_{x \in A} v(x) \geq \sum_{y \in B} v(y)$ for all A, $B \in Z$. Since $v(x) > 0$ for every $x \in X$, it is immediately seen that $\succeq$ satisfies SMSI (as well as WMSI). To see that it satisfies IUGR as well, and given the lemma, let, for some n, $(A_1, \ldots, A_n)$ and $(B_1, \ldots, B_n)$ be two allocations of opportunities such that $\forall x \in X, \#\{i \in \{1, \ldots, n\} \mid x \in A_i^n\} = \#\{i \in \{1, \ldots, n\} \mid x \in B_i^n\}$ and assume that, for some individual i, $A_i \succ B_i$. Then

$$\sum_{x \in A_i} v(x) > \sum_{y \in B_i} v(y). \tag{5.1}$$

On the other hand, since, for every $x \in X$, $\#\{i \in \{1, \ldots, n\} \mid x \in A_i\} = \#\{i \in \{1, \ldots, n\} \mid x \in B_i\}$ we have

$$\sum_{i=1}^{n} \sum_{x \in A_i} v(x) = \sum_{i=1}^{n} \sum_{y \in B_i} v(y). \tag{5.2}$$

Clearly, since $v(x) > 0$ for every $x \in X$, the consistency of (5.1) and (5.2) requires that there be some j for which

$$\sum_{y \in B_j} v(y) > \sum_{x \in A_j} v(x)$$

which gives the desired conclusion.

Sufficiency Assume that $\succeq$ satisfies IUGR and let $I = \{1, \ldots, \#X\}$ be any index set of X. The strategy of the proof is to map the problem of comparing finite opportunity sets into one of comparing I-dimensional real valued vectors and to apply to this new problem the so-called 'theorem of the alternative' (see Fishburn (1970; theorem 4.2 for a proof). For this task, let $C : Z \longrightarrow \{0, 1\}^{\#X} \backslash \{0^{\#X}\}$ be the characteristic function of Z defined by

$$\forall A \in Z, \forall i = 1, \ldots, \#X, \, C_i(A) = 1 \text{ if } x_i \in A$$

$$= 0 \text{ otherwise}$$

It is easy to see that C is one-to-one so that without loss of generality, the binary relation $\succeq$ can be defined on $\{0, 1\}^{\#X} \backslash \{0^{\#X}\}$. Let $K = \# \succ$ (the number of pairs of opportunity sets (A, B) such that $A \succ B$ holds) and let M be such that $M - K = (\# \sim)/2$ (half the number of pairs (A, B) for which $A \sim B$ holds). To every ordered pair of opportunity sets A_i and B_i such that $A_i \succ B_i$ for $i = 1, \ldots, K$, one can associate the vector difference $C(A_i) - C(B_i)$. For ordered pairs $(C, D) \in \sim$ we know from the definition of a symmetric factor that $(C, D) \in \sim \Longleftrightarrow (D, C) \in \sim$ for any $C, D \in Z$. Select arbitrarily one ordered pair out of any two symmetric pairs belonging to $\sim$ and index the selected pair by a number $i = K + 1, \ldots, M$. Associate to each of the selected pairs (A_i, B_i) for $i = K + 1, \ldots, M$ the vector difference $C(A_i) - C(B_i)$. We can now apply the theorem of the alternative to the K vectors differences generated by $\succ$ and to the $M - K$ vectors differences induced by $\sim$ in the way just described. Applied to this setting, the theorem of the alternative states that either:

1 there exists a vector $V \in \mathfrak{R}^{\#X}$ such that $V.(A_i - B_i) > 0$ for $i = 1, \ldots, K$ and $V.(A_i - B_i) = 0$ for $i = K + 1, \ldots, M$; or
2 there exist non-negative real numbers $r_1, \ldots, r_K$, not all of which are equal to 0, and real numbers $r_{K+1}, \ldots, r_M$ such that, for all $i = 1, \ldots, \#X$,

$$\sum_{k=1}^{M} r_k(C_i(A_k) - C_i(B_k)) = 0.$$

Note that if the alternative (1) is true, the proof is complete (after noticing that SMSI forces the vector V to be strictly positive). Hence the rest of the proof consists in showing that alternative (2) is inconsistent with IUGR. Indeed, assume that alternative (2) holds. Given the definition of the characteristic function C, one can note that all vectors $(C(A_i) - C(B_i))$ for $i = 1, \ldots, M$ have coordinates in the set $\{-1, 0, 1\}$ (a subset of N). For this reason, it is easy to show that the numbers $r_1, \ldots, r_M$ can all be chosen to be integers. Moreover, any negative $r_k \in \{r_{K+1}, \ldots, r_M\}$ can be replaced by $-r_k$ after replacing the corresponding vector $C(A_k) - C(B_k)$ by $C(B_k) - C(A_k)$ and replacing the pair of opportunity set (A_k, B_k) in $\sim$ by its symmetric companion (B_k, A_k). It is obvious that such a change does not alter significantly the representation of $\succeq$ provided by the system of vectors $\{C(A_i) - C(B_i)\}_{i=1}^{M}$. Hence alternative (2) implies the existence of non-negative integers $r_1, \ldots, r_M$ (one of the first K ones being strictly positive) such that for all $i = 1, \ldots, \#X$, $\sum_{k=1}^{M} r_k(C_i(A_k) - C_i(B_k)) = 0$. Moreover, since $\geq$ is reflexive, there is no loss of generality in supposing $r_k > 0$ for all $k > K$ for which the associated pairs of opportunity sets consists of identical sets. Consider then the two allocations of opportunities:

$$A^{\sum_{k=1}^{M} r_k} = (\underbrace{A_1, A_1, \ldots, A_1}_{r_1}, \underbrace{A_2, \ldots, A_2}_{r_2}, \ldots, \underbrace{A_M, \ldots, A_M}_{r_M})$$

and

$$B^{\sum_{k=1}^{M} r_k} = (\underbrace{B_1, B_1, \ldots, B_1}_{r_1}, \underbrace{B_2, \ldots, B_2}_{r_2}, \ldots, \underbrace{B_M, \ldots, B_M}_{r_M})$$

in a society containing $\sum_{k=1}^{M} r_k$ members. Since $\sum_{k=1}^{M} r_k > 1$, the condition $\sum_{k=1}^{M} r_k(C_i(A_k) - C_i(B_k)) = 0$ for all $i = 1, \ldots, \#X$ implies that $\#\{i \in \{1, \ldots, n\} \mid x \in A_i^{\sum_{k=1}^{M} r_k}\} = \#\{i \in \{1, \ldots, n\} \mid x \in B_i^{\sum_{k=1}^{M} r_k}\}$ for all $x \in X\}$.

By the lemma, $A^{\sum_{k=1}^{M} r_k} \beta \, B^{\sum_{k=1}^{M} r_k}$. Since, by construction, $A_i \succ B_i$ holds for the first $\sum_{k=1}^{K} r_k$ pairs of opportunity sets of these two allocations and $A_i \sim B_i$ for the $\sum_{k=K+1}^{M} r_k$ remaining ones, this gives the required violation of IUGR.

QED.

NOTES

1 'What, in all times, has attached to liberty the heart of some men, are its own attraction, its own charm, independent from its benefits. He who seeks in liberty something else than itself is borne to serve'. (Free translation.)
2 Hence we somewhat depart from the standard notational (and conceptual) custom in economics by treating the strict binary relation $\succ$ as 'basic'.
3 Strictly speaking, WMSI is weaker than SMSI (in the sense of being implied by the latter but not vice versa) only in the case where $\geq$ is reflexive. If $\geq$ is not reflexive, the two axioms are independent.

90

REFERENCES

[1] Arrow, K. (1995) 'A Note on Freedom and Flexibility' in K. Basu, P. Pattanaik and K. Suzumura (eds), *Choice, Welfare and Development. A Festschrift in Honour of Amartya K. Sen*, Oxford, Oxford University Press.

[2] Bossert, W., P. K. Pattanaik and Y. Xu (1994) 'Ranking Opportunity Sets: An Axiomatic Approach' *Journal of Economic Theory*, **63**, 326–345.

[3] Bossert, W. (1997) 'Opportunity Sets and Individual Well-Being', *Social Choice and Welfare*, **14**, 97–112.

[4] de Finetti, B. (1937) 'La Prévision: Ses Lois Logiques, ses Sources Subjectives', *Annales Inst. Henri Poincaré*, **7**, 1–68.

[5] de Tocqueville, A. (1856) 'L'Ancien Régime et la Révolution, tome 2, Paris, Gallimard, 1952.

[6] Fishburn, P. (1969) 'Weak Qualitative Probability on Finite Sets' *Annals of Mathematical Statistics*, **40**, 2118–2126.

[7] Fishburn, P. (1970) *Utility Theory for Decision Making*, New York, John Wiley & Son.

[8] Foster, J. (1993) Notes on Effective Freedom, Mimeo, Vanderbilt University.

[9] Gravel, N. (1994) 'Can a Ranking of Opportunity Sets Attach an Intrinsic Importance to Freedom of Choice?', *American Economic Review, Papers and Proceedings*, **84**, 454–458.

[10] Gravel, N. (1996) 'Ranking Opportunity Sets on the Basis of their Freedom of Choice and their Ability to Satisfy Preferences: A Difficulty', *Social Choice and Welfare*.

[11] Hayek, F. V. (1960) *The Constitution of Liberty*, Chicago, Chicago University Press.

[12] Jones, P. and R. Sugden (1982) 'Evaluating Choices', *International Journal of Law and Economics*, **2**, 47–65.

[13] Klemisch-Ahlert (1993) 'Freedom of Choice: A Comparison of Different Rankings of Opportunity Sets', *Social Choice and Welfare*, **10**, 189–207.

[14] Kraft, C. H., J. W. Pratt and A. Seidenberg (1959) 'Intuitive Probability on Finite Sets', *Annals of Mathematical Statistics*, **30**, 408–419.

[15] Kreps, D. M. (1979) 'A Representation Theorem for "Preference for Flexibility"', *Econometrica*, **47**, 454–458.

[16] Pattanaik, P. K. and Y. Xu (1990) 'On Ranking Opportunity Sets in Terms of Freedom of Choice', *Recherches Economiques de Louvain*, **56**, 383–390.

[17] Pattanaik, P. K. and Y. Xu (1995) 'On Preference and Freedom', Mimeo, University of California, Riverside.

[18] Puppe, C. (1995) 'Freedom of Choice and Rational Decisions', *Social Choice and Welfare*, **12**, 137–153.

[19] Puppe, C. (1996a) 'Individual Freedom and Social Choice', this volume, chapter 3.

[20] Puppe, C. (1996b) 'An Axiomatic Approach to "Preference for Freedom of Choice"', *Journal of Economic Theory*, **68**, 174–199.

[21] Puppe, C. and Y. Xu(1995) 'Assessing Freedom of Choice in Terms of Essential Alternatives', Mimeo.

[22] Scott, D. (1964) 'Measurement Structure and Linear Inequalities', *Journal of Mathematical Psychology*, **1**, 233–247.

[23] Sen, A. K. (1970) *Collective Choice and Social Welfare*, San Francisco, Holden-Day.

[24] Sen, A. K. (1988) 'Freedom of Choice: Concept and Content', *European Economic Review*, **32**, 269–294.

[25] Sen, A. K. (1990)'Welfare, Freedom and Social Choice: A Reply', *Recherches Economiques de Louvain*, **56**, 451–486.

[26] Sen, A. K. (1991) 'Welfare, Preference and Freedom', *Journal of Econometrics*, **50**, 15–29.

[27] Sen, A. K. (1993a) 'Markets and Freedoms: Achievements and Limitations of the Market Mechanism in Promoting Individual Freedoms', *Oxford Economic Papers*, **45**, 519–541.

[28] Sen, A. K. (1993b) 'Internal Consistency of Choice', *Econometrica*, **61**, 495–522.

[29] Sugden, R. (1985) 'Liberty, Preferences and Choice', *Economics and Philosophy*, **1**, 213–229.

[30] Suppes, P. (1987) 'Maximizing Freedom of Decision: An Axiomatic Analysis' in G. Feiwell (ed.) *Arrow and the Foundations of the Economic Policy*, New York, New York University Press.

6

IMPERSONAL VERSUS OBJECTIVIST CONCEPTIONS OF FREEDOM

A comment on 'Individual freedom of choice in a social setting'

Clemens Puppe[1]

The aim of the contribution by N. Gravel, J. F. Laslier and A. Trannoy is to specify properties that a ranking of opportunity sets in terms of individual freedom of choice would plausibly satisfy. The most obvious feature that distinguishes the authors' approach from almost all of the existing literature on the modelling of freedom of choice is the use of what is called a 'social setting'. By this the authors mean a framework in which there is more than one individual involved and in which the 'states' to be evaluated are not single opportunity sets but rather *profiles* of opportunity sets, one set for each individual in the society. The main justification that the authors give for expanding the standard framework in this way is that only such a framework is capable of representing the scarcity constraints under which a society operates. Of course, this raises the question of what role these scarcity constraints play in assessing individual freedom. It is intuitively clear that these constraints do play an important role in determining the total opportunities of a society and the possibilities to distribute them among individuals. However, *a priori* it is not obvious how scarcity constraints influence the evaluation of *individual* freedom as such. The key twist of the paper is the particular way in which properties of different opportunity profiles are related to properties of the ranking $\succeq$ of individual freedom. The crucial condition here is an assumption called 'impossibility of unanimous gain from redistribution' (IUGR). In order to understand its meaning and impact in the present context, an important issue that has to be addressed first is what the precise interpretation of the ranking $\succeq$ of individual freedoms should be. Given the 'social context' proposed by the authors, one may think of two fundamentally different interpretations. On the first, the ranking $\succeq$ may be viewed as an *impersonal* (or 'social') ranking of individual freedom abstracting from any specific characteristic of the person whose freedom is to be evaluated.

Alternatively, the ranking $\succeq$ could be viewed as a description of the individuals' *own* evaluation of the freedom they enjoy in different situations. Of course, the latter interpretation only fits the particular conception of freedom put forward by the authors if one imposes additional restrictions guaranteeing that the rankings of freedom are the same for *all* individuals. In the following I will refer to the first interpretation as the impersonal interpretation, and to the latter as the *individualistic* interpretation. It is important to realize that unlike the impersonal interpretation, which implies an 'objectivist' view of freedom, the 'individualistic' conception of freedom arguably entails no precommitment with respect to the 'objectivist/subjectivist' distinction. The main purpose of this note is to argue that a coherent account of the authors' approach is only possible under the impersonal interpretation of freedom. This seems to be an important observation since, as I shall also argue, the impersonal interpretation of freedom is even more restrictive than an 'objectivist' conception of freedom necessarily has to be.[2] Indeed, unlike a general objectivist conception of freedom, the impersonal interpretation not only neglects the subjective value of opportunities for the chooser but also the (objective) *abilities* of the chooser to use her opportunities in a certain way. The central claim of this note is thus in brief as follows. Even under an objectivist conception of freedom, given their different abilities, $10,000 to spend on commodity bundles may *not* give Charles the same amount of freedom as it gives Diana.

In the following I shall try to work out the restrictions that an impersonal interpretation of the ranking $\succeq$ of individual freedom entails. In order to do so, it will be useful to reformulate the authors' primitive concepts within a general individualistic framework, viewing the impersonal interpretation as the limiting case of the individualistic framework in which all individuals are treated symmetrically. Thus, consider the most general form of individualistic evaluations of individual freedom in the authors' social context. Let $\succeq_i'$ denote individual i's evaluation of the freedom she enjoys, where this relation is defined on the set $\bigcup_{n \in N_{++}} Z^n$ of all tuples of opportunity sets. The intended interpretation of $\succeq_i'$ is thus that $(A_1, \ldots, A_n) \succeq_i' (B_1, \ldots, B_n)$ if and only if the freedom that individual i enjoys in the profile $(A_1, \ldots, A_n)$ is at least as large as the freedom that she enjoys in the profile $(B_1, \ldots, B_n)$. The first restriction implicit in the authors' approach is that each individual ranking only depends on the individual's own 'consumption' of opportunities. The effect of this assumption is that the individual rankings are not defined over opportunity *profiles* but in fact over the (individual) opportunity sets themselves. Formally, this amounts to the following strong *separability* condition on the freedom rankings $\succeq_i'$. For all $n \in N_{++}$, all $i \in \{1, \ldots, n\}$ and all A, B, C_1, $\tilde{C}_1, \ldots, C_n, \tilde{C}_n, D_1, \tilde{D}_1, \ldots, D_n, \tilde{D}_n \in Z$,

$$(C_1, \ldots, C_{i-1}, A, C_{i+1}, \ldots, C_n) \succeq_i' (\tilde{C}_1, \ldots, \tilde{C}_{i-1}, B, \tilde{C}_{i+1}, \ldots, \tilde{C}_n)$$

$$\Leftrightarrow (D_1, \ldots, D_{i-1}, A, D_{i+1}, \ldots, D_n) \succeq_i' (\tilde{D}_1, \ldots, \tilde{D}_{i-1}, B, \tilde{D}_{i+1}, \ldots, \tilde{D}_n) \quad (6.1)$$

Obviously, if one starts with a framework where the individuals' rankings of freedom are defined on $\bigcup_{n \in N_{++}} Z^n$ then the separability condition (6.1) allows to represent each of these rankings by a ranking $\succeq_i$ defined on Z in the following way. For all $A, B \in Z, A \succeq_i B$ if and only if there exists a number $n \in N_{++}$ and a collection $C_1, \tilde{C}_1, \ldots, C_n, \tilde{C}_n$ of sets such that $(C_1, \ldots, C_{i-1}, A, C_{i+1}, \ldots, C_n) \succeq_i' (\tilde{C}_1, \ldots, \tilde{C}_{i-1}, B, \tilde{C}_{i+1}, \ldots, \tilde{C}_n)$. Consequently, the authors' approach appears as a special case of a more general framework in which the individual freedom rankings are not necessarily separable in the sense of condition (6.1). To avoid misunderstandings, I should emphasize that I consider the separability assumption (6.1) implicit in the authors' analysis as a perfectly legitimate starting point. However, given the social context and the authors' argument on the relevance of the scarcity constraints it might be interesting to explore the more general scenario, too. Indeed, one might argue that the overall scarcity constraints have a certain indirect influence on the assessment of individual freedom in the sense that an individual's freedom has to be evaluated *relative to* society's overall opportunities. Take the following simple example. Suppose that the universal set of alternatives is $\{x, y, z\}$, and consider the following two scenarios. In the first, all individuals have only access to the options x and y. Formally, this scenario may thus be described by the profile $(\{x, y\}, \ldots, \{x, y\})$. In the second, assume that all individuals have access to all three of the different opportunities except for one individual, say i, who has access to x and y only. Hence, the second scenario is represented by the profile $(\{x, y, z\}, \ldots, \{x, y\}, \ldots, \{x, y, z\})$, where the set $\{x, y\}$ appears as the ith component. One might argue that in such a situation individual i's evaluation of freedom could well be

$$(\{x, y\}, \ldots, \{x, y\}, \ldots, \{x, y\}) \succ_i' (\{x, y, z\}, \ldots, \{x, y\}, \ldots, \{x, y, z\}),$$

in violation of assumption (6.1). Note that the argument is *not* that individuals may be envious, nor that they would prefer an 'egalitarian' distribution of opportunities. The reason for the above ranking of individual i's freedom may simply be that although in both cases her opportunities are $\{x, y\}$, in one case she has access to *all* opportunities available to society. Hence, the argument rests upon the presumption that societal opportunities are the yardstick by which individual freedom has to be measured. Indeed, the freedom that we experience crucially depends on the other person's opportunities that we observe. Admittedly, the incorporation of such an idea could considerably complicate the analysis. Hence, it is certainly justified to start with the simplest possible framework in which individual rankings satisfy the separability assumption (6.1). On the other hand, in that case there seems to be no inherent link between the structure of individual freedom rankings and the overall scarcity constraints.

Let me now turn to the crucial assumption that all individuals' freedom has to be evaluated by the *same* ranking. Formally, for all individuals, i, j,

$$\succeq_i = \succeq_j . \qquad (6.2)$$

Of course, the effect of postulate (6.2) is that there is only a single freedom ranking under consideration, denoted by $\succeq$. Unlike the first restriction mentioned above, this second assumption is made explicit in the paper and discussed in some detail. The main argument for assumption (6.2) rests on the authors' distinction between what they call the 'objectivist' and the 'subjectivist' conception of freedom. According to the 'objectivist' conception of freedom to which the authors subscribe, only the physical attributes of a set should matter for assessing the entailed freedom. For instance, what may matter for freedom is the implied accessibility of certain options, not their subjective value to the chooser. Consequently, since the physical attributes of a set are independent of the person who faces this particular set, the relevant rankings of freedom should be independent of individuals, too. It is emphasized that also the plausibility of the central assumption IUGR proposed by the authors hinges crucially on that presumption. Assumption IUGR states that a mere redistribution of the opportunities available to a society cannot unanimously improve the freedom of all individuals.[3] To see why this can plausibly be true only under the assumption that all individuals' opportunities are evaluated by the same ranking, consider the following simple example. Suppose there are two individuals, the first of whom ranks set A freedom-wise strictly above set B, whereas the second individual has the opposite freedom ranking between A and B. Clearly, the transition from (B, A) to (A, B) involves only a redistribution and represents an unanimous strict improvement in terms of freedom.

As I already mentioned, my main concern with the authors' approach is that the impersonal interpretation of the ranking $\succeq$ entailed by assumption (6.2) goes well beyond what an 'objectivist' conception of freedom by itself would normally imply. The reason is that even an objectivist view of freedom does not imply that only the physical attributes of the *sets* under consideration should matter. The individuals' physical attributes might be equally relevant. People not only differ in tastes but also in their *abilities*, a point which has been repeatedly emphasized by Amartya Sen. Clearly, at least some of the relevant abilities materialize in physical attributes. Consequently, there seems to be no reason why under an objectivist conception of freedom these attributes should not be taken into account.

96

COMMENT

In order to make the point as clear as possible, consider the following slightly extreme example. There are two individuals, one of whom is deaf, the other blind. Suppose both individuals are endowed with the same set A of opportunities. In addition, there are two more alternatives available, x and y, where x stands for 'going to a concert of classical music' and y denotes 'visiting an art gallery'. Each additional alternative can be given to either of the two individuals, but neither can be given to both individuals. In this situation it seems highly plausible that the deaf person would see her freedom being strictly greater in the set $A \cup \{y\}$ than in $A \cup \{x\}$, whereas the converse would hold for the blind person. Consequently, the two individuals would not share the same freedom ranking over opportunity sets. Moreover, starting with an initial state where the deaf person holds x and the blind person holds y, it is obvious that a redistribution of alternatives could make both individuals freedom-wise strictly better off. Note that the example does not refer to the subjective tastes of the involved persons but rather to their objective abilities which determine what the individuals can achieve from their opportunities. As a response to this example, one might try to defend assumption (6.2) by redefining the universal set of alternatives in the following way. Instead of considering the alternative '*going to* a concert of classical music', one might suggest the alternative '*enjoying* a concert of classical music'. However, it is not clear whether such a move could successfully overcome the difficulty. For instance, one problem is how to distinguish the redefined alternatives by their physical (objective) characteristics.

Summarizing, I think that the authors' contribution provides an interesting new angle to the modelling of freedom of choice. I am particularly sympathetic with the view that an individual's freedom should not be considered in isolation but has to be evaluated in the light of a 'social context' specifying what the other individuals' opportunities are. Furthermore, given an impersonal (rather than merely 'objectivist') conception of freedom, the authors' main result may provide an appealing characterization of freedom rankings. However, as I also have tried to argue, such an impersonal conception of freedom neglects important aspects that should be included in considerations about freedom.

NOTES

1 This note has been prepared while I was visiting the Department of Economics at the University of California, Davis. I would like to express my gratitude for the hospitality I received there. I thank Klaus Nehring and Prasanta Pattanaik for inspiring discussions that helped me to clarify some of the issues discussed in this note. Clearly, I alone bear responsibility for all possible shortcomings that remain.

2 At this point it seems only fair to say that my own intuitions concerning the 'objectivist/subjectivist' dichotomy tend to favour the subjectivist side (or rather, the 'remote subjectivist' position, in the authors' terminology). However, nothing of what I shall say here should depend on that.

3 As the authors themselves note, assumption IUGR, as well as the implied standard independence condition, completely neglects the effect that 'diversity' (of opportunities) may have on freedom. It is not clear, however, whether in a freedom context one can legitimately abstract from the impact of diversity. A further issue is whether there can be an 'objectivist' conception of diversity at all, or whether the concept of diversity is rather inherently subjectivist. For a thorough critique of the standard independence condition implied by IUGR, see Nehring and Puppe, 'Continuous extensions of an order on a set to the power set', *Journal of Economic Theory* 68 (1996), 456–479.

Part II
RIGHTS

7

INTERPRETATIVE, SEMANTIC AND FORMAL DIFFICULTIES OF THE SOCIAL CHOICE RULE APPROACH TO RIGHTS

Anne Brunel and Maurice Salles

ABSTRACT

We comment on Sen's original treatment of rights in social choice theory. We underline three difficulties: interpretative difficulties, difficulties regarding the meaning of liberalism, and mathematical difficulties. We finally present a research programme.

The traditional approach (social choice rule approach) to rights and liberty is rather under-represented in this book. However, if Sen's five-page paper of 1970 (Sen (1970)) had not been published, it is very likely that this book would have not existed. The purpose of this chapter is partly to repair this under-representation by providing comments on Sen's original approach and to indicate some possible routes for new developments (new developments different from the literature on liberty based on opportunity sets and the literature based on game forms).

We shall proceed as follows. First, we recall the social choice basic formalism and Sen's theorems. Second, we focus on three difficulties of this formalism. A first difficulty concerns the interpretation, made by some authors (Hammond (1982), (1995), Bernhoz (1974), Gibbard (1974), and Sen himself in a footnote (1970)), of Sen's paradox in terms of a conflict between a right of making externalities and Pareto efficiency. The second type of difficulty is more semantic in nature and is related to the definition of rights in terms of power. The last type of difficulty is formal (Saari (1998)). According to Saari, the liberalism conditions entail that the procedure cannot distinguish the rational preferences of individuals from the preferences of non-existent cyclic individuals. Consequently, cyclic outcomes occur when the societal rankings reflect the wishes of non-existent cyclic individuals rather than the actual, but indistinguishable, rational individuals. Finally, we conclude by commenting on the meaning of social states, rights and liberty, and by mentioning some work in progress based on the use of modal (deontic) logic.

THE SOCIAL CHOICE RULE APPROACH

We consider a set of social states (alternatives, options), X, and a set of individuals, N. These sets have no specific structures. Even N need not be finite. Each individual $i \in N$ has a preference over X given by a complete preorder $\succeq_i$ over X. (A complete preorder $\succeq$ over X is a binary relation satisfying (i) for all $x, y \in X$, $x \succeq y$ or $y \succeq x$ and (ii) for all $x, y, z \in X$, $x \succeq y$ and $y \succeq z \Rightarrow x \succeq z$.) We denote the set of complete preorders over X by $Ord(X)$. A profile π is a function from N to $Ord(X)$ (for N being finite of size n, it is an n-list $(\succeq_1, \ldots, \succeq_n)$). Π denotes the set of profiles. The social preference over X is given by a binary relation $\succeq_S$, the asymmetric component of which, $\succ_S$, is acyclic. $\succ$, the asymmetric part of $\succeq$, is defined by $x \succ y \Leftrightarrow x \succeq y$ and $\neg y \succeq x$. $\succ$ over X is acyclic if there is no finite set $\{x_1, \ldots, x_k\} \subseteq X$ such that $x_1 \succ x_2$ and $x_2 \succ x_3$ and ... and $x_{k-1} \succ x_k$ and $x_k \succ x_1$. Let $AC(X)$ be the set of binary relations with acyclic asymmetric components. A social decision function is a function from Π to $AC(X)$.

Given a social decision function f, we say that individual i is decisive for $a \in X$ against $b \in X$ if $a \succ_S b$ whenever $a \succ_i b$, i.e., for all profiles π in which $a \succ_i b$, $f(\pi)$ gives a social preference $\succeq_S$ for which $a \succ_S b$. An individual who is decisive for a against b and for b against a will be said to be decisive over $\{a, b\}$.

Sen has introduced two definitions of liberalism.

Condition L (Liberalism) For each $i \in N$, there exist two social states, a_i and b_i such that individual i is decisive over $\{a_i, b_i\}$.

A version of Sen's result can also be obtained with the following weaker condition.

Condition L* (Minimal liberalism) There are at least two individuals i and j, and for each of them two social states, a_i, b_i, and a_j, b_j, such that i is decisive over $\{a_i, b_i\}$, and j is decisive over $\{a_j, b_j\}$.

The classical Paretian requirement is similar to the Pareto principle in Arrow's book (Arrow (1963)):

Condition P Let $\pi \in \Pi$ and $a, b \in X$. If $a \succ_i b$ for all $i \in N$, then $a \succ_S b$ where $\succ_S$ is the asymmetric component of $\succeq_S = f(\pi)$.

We can now state Sen's theorem.

102

Theorem 1 *There does not exist a social decision function satisfying Conditions L* and P.*

Of course, as a corollary, we obtain the inconsistency of conditions L, P, and the existence of a social decision function.

Theorem 2 *There does not exist a social decision function satisfying Conditions L and P.*

Note that in our presentation Sen's Condition U (unrestricted domain) which asserts that the social decision function is defined on the set of profiles is built in our definition of the social decision function.

THREE DIFFICULTIES

The illustrations and the conflict externality/optimality

A famous example given by Sen in his original paper and in the relevant chapter of his book (Sen (1970a)) involves two individuals, a prude (*PR*) and a lascivious person (*LA*), and a (social) choice between three alternatives *a*, *b* , and *c* standing respectively for *PR* reading a copy of *Lady Chatterley's Lover*, *LA* reading it, or neither reading it. For some reason *PR*'s preference is $c \succ_{PR} a \succ_{PR} b$ and *LA*'s preference is $a \succ_{LA} b \succ_{LA} c$. According to the example *PR* is decisive over $\{a, c\}$ and *LA* is decisive over $\{b, c\}$. Since both individuals prefer *a* to *b*, we obtain $a \succ_S b \succ_S c \succ_S a$.

This example is rather ambiguous since it does not consider the possibility that both individuals read the book. To make sense of this example, we must assume that there is only one copy of the book and an equivalence between having the book and reading it. Let us construct ordered pairs of *Y* (for yes) and *N* (for no) where (Y, N) means *PR* (first component) reads the book and *LA* (second component) does not read the book. Our three options become (Y, N), (N, Y), and (N, N), and the preferences $(N, N) \succ_{PR} (Y, N) \succ_{PR} (N, Y)$ and $(Y, N) \succ_{LA} (N, Y) \succ_{LA} (N, N)$. In this case, we can see easily that *PR* being decisive over $\{(N, N), (Y, N)\}$ has basically no effect on *LA* since for both options he does not read the book. The same is true of *LA* over $\{(N, Y), (N, N)\}$. Suppose now there are two copies of the book (or that both individuals reading the book is an available option) and that the preferences are $(N, N) \succ_{PR} (Y, N) \succ_{PR} (N, Y) \succ_{PR} (Y, Y)$ and $(Y, Y) \succ_{LA} (Y, N) \succ_{LA} (N, Y) \succ_{LA} (N, N)$. These preferences are unconditional in the sense of Hammond (1982) (applied to *PR*, this means that $(N, .) \succ_{PR} (Y, .)$ whatever is the second component; in other contexts, this property is sometimes called *separability* (Blackorby, Primont and Russell (1979), Varian (1992)). It is easily checked that we do not obtain one but two cycles if we consider that PR is decisive over $\{(N, N), (Y, N)\}$ and over $\{(N, Y), (Y, Y)\}$, and LA is decisive over $\{(Y, Y), (Y, N)\}$ and $\{(N, Y), (N, N)\}$. This four-alternative version of the example is proposed for instance in Salles (1997) and in Hausman and McPherson (1996), though Hausman and McPherson do not formally construct ordered pairs and do not mention that it gives rise to two cycles.

We believe that the introduction of a Cartesian product structure in the illustrations is essential for a correct understanding of an important interpretation of Sen's theorem as saying that granting a right to individuals to create an externality is bound to conflict with Pareto optimality. It should be noted, however, that this interpretation takes us rather far from Condition L*, which is a condition about individual power. In some sense, we need to restrict the space of options by introducing a Cartesian product structure before we can make such an interpretation. Given this structure, it is natural to restrict individuals' preferences as well, as does Hammond with his privately oriented preferences, asserting that if an individual i is decisive over $\{a_i, b_i\}$, then all the other individuals must be indifferent between these options (see Hammond (1982), (1995)). Then the inconsistency vanishes and further results can even be obtained (see Coughlin (1986), Hammond (1995), (1997)).

In our former example, PR and LA's personal spheres are identical and limited to $\{Y, N\}$. Then, a question arises. Is the individual preference defined over the individual's personal sphere or over the Cartesian product? If it is defined over the personal sphere, how must we define the liberalism condition and the Pareto condition? It is clear that the usual decisiveness condition as well as the Pareto principle imply that the individual and the social preferences are both defined over the Cartesian product. Of course, an easy answer can be given, but depending on this answer we get different basic structures for the model and the differences should be carefully studied. Consequently, the Cartesian product structure should force us to consider problems that also occur in social choice in economic environments (see for recent surveys Le Breton (1997), Le Breton and Weymark (1996) and Redekop (1995)). It seems difficult to deal with externalities in a social choice context. An illuminating illustration of this was recently given in a paper by Chichilnisky (1996) responding to Allen (1996). The central question was about the condition of monotonicity of individual preferences. Consider an exchange economy with a finite set of agents $N = \{1, \ldots, n\}$ and a commodity space $\mathfrak{R}^\ell_+ = \{x \in \mathfrak{R}^\ell : x = (x_1, \ldots, x_\ell), x_k \geq 0$ for all $k = 1, \ldots, \ell\}$. Each individual has a preference over $\mathfrak{R}^\ell_+$ given by a complete preorder $\succeq_i$. A commodity bundle of the individual i is denoted by x^i and x^i_k is the quantity of good k available to individual i. Each agent has an initial endowment $e^i \in \mathfrak{R}^\ell_+$. An allocation is a vector $x = (x^1, \ldots, x^n) \in \mathfrak{R}^{n\ell}_+$ and x is a feasible allocation if $\sum_i x^i = \sum_i e^i$. The set of feasible allocations in an exchange economy is the so-called Edgeworth hyperbox. The Edgeworth hyperbox is denoted by EB. By the first welfare economics theorem, every competitive allocation is Pareto optimal. Since under standard conditions we know that there exist competitive equilibria, but generally not a unique equilibrium, social choice over the set of competitive allocations could be the last part (always missing, because many economists since Robbins consider that the only normative judgements they can make must be based on Pareto optimality) of general equilibrium theory. But social choice over feasible allocations involves many difficulties. Consider first the assumption of monotonicity of consumers' preferences. A form of this assumption says that if $x^i > x^{\prime i}$ (which means $x_k^i \geq x_k^{\prime i}$ for all $k \in \{1, \ldots, \ell\}$ and $x_k^i > x_k^{\prime i}$ for some k) then $x^i \succ x^{\prime i}$. Now this condition holds for individual preferences over $\mathfrak{R}_+^\ell$. However, the social choice is over a subset of the Edgeworth hyperbox. This subset is itself a subset of the Pareto-optimal feasible allocations. Let us define Pareto optimality. A feasible allocation x is Pareto-superior to a feasible allocation $x^\prime$ (denoted $x \succ_{PAR} x^\prime$) if $x^i \succeq_i x^{\prime i}$ for all $i \in \{1, \ldots, n\}$ and $x^i \succ_i x^{\prime i}$ for some i. x is Pareto optimal if it is a maximal element of $\succ_{PAR}$. In passing, we note that $\succ_{PAR}$ is defined over EB but $\succ_{PAR}$ is derived from individual preferences over $\mathfrak{R}_+^\ell$. Since social choice is a choice between elements in EB, we must consider individual preferences over EB. We can, of course, say that an individual preference $\succeq_i^{EB}$ over EB coincides with the individual i's component of the EB allocation, i.e., $x \succeq_i^{EB} x^\prime \Leftrightarrow x^i \succeq_i x^{\prime i}$. This is the point of view adopted by Chichilnisky. But this appears to us as a denial of social choice where decisions should be based on ethical judgements about social justice, inequality, redistribution and so forth. Some individuals may be selfish. To impose that all individuals be selfish is an extreme assumption in this context. So a kind of monotonicity assumption in EB would assert that if $x > x^\prime$ for $x, x^\prime \in EB$ then $x \succ_S^{EB} x^\prime$. But obviously, it is impossible to have two points $x, x^\prime \in EB$ with $x > x^\prime$ and, therefore, the monotonicity assumption is trivially satisfied.

The same kind of difficulty arises with the Pareto principle. If we impose a Pareto-type condition on the set of Pareto-optimal-competitive allocations this must say something like $x \succ_S^{EB} x^\prime$ whenever $x \succ_i^{EB} x^\prime$ for all i.

There is now a large literature on social choice in economic environments. However, to the best of our knowledge, this literature does not take account of the difficulties mentioned above (in particular, as far as the different forms of the Pareto principle are concerned).

In the individual and group rights literature, papers by Bernholz (1974), Gibbard (1974), Hammond (1982, 1995) introduce the Cartesian structure over social states. This structure seems to us to be a good step in the right direction and is a good way to analyse the social choice rule approach to rights as granting to individuals (or groups of individuals) rights to create externalities, and consequently to suggest remedies to this.

105

But this somewhat dissimulates the original formal structure of the approach, which is about power.

The basic formalism: A conflict of power and a semantic confusion

The social choice research programme in modern times (essentially since Arrow's work) has generated a great number of definitions of asymmetrical power distribution: decisiveness, quasi-decisiveness, almost-decisiveness, dictatorship, vetoers etc. In fact the weak form of the Pareto principle that is generally used is such a condition. Let us call coalition any non-empty subset of N (including singletons, to misuse the term). A coalition $C \subseteq N$ is said to be decisive for a against b ($a, b \in X$) if $a \succ_S b$ whenever for all $i \in C$, $a \succ_i b$, i.e., if for all profiles $\pi \in \Pi$ for which for all $i \in C$, $a \succ_i b$, $a \succ_S b$ obtains, where $\succ_S$ is the asymmetric component of $\succeq_S = f(\pi)$. In the same way as for individuals, we will say that a coalition C is decisive over $\{a, b\}$ if it is decisive for a against b and for b against a. Then, Condition P can be restated.

Condition P The set of individuals N is decisive over $\{x, y\}$ for any $x, y \in X$.

Sen's Theorem 1 then appears as an inconsistency between collective rationality (given by the acyclicity of $\succ_S$), the universal power of N and the limited power of at least two individuals. That is, for acyclic social preferences, it is impossible for N to be decisive over every two-element subset of X and, at the same time, for each of two individuals to be decisive over a two-element subset of X.

A restated definition of an Arrovian dictator is the following. An individual i is a dictator for a social decision function f if i is decisive over every two-element subset of X. Note that if the social decision function is restricted to be a social welfare function, i.e., if $\succeq_S$ is a complete preorder, given the independence condition and n finite, Arrow's Theorem states that N is decisive over all $\{x, y\} \subseteq X$ only if a single individual is himself decisive over all $\{x, y\} \subseteq X$. In Sen's book (1970a), a Condition D* is introduced, which asserts that there is no individual for which there exist two options a and b in X such that for all $\pi \in \Pi$ either $a \succ_i b \Rightarrow a \succ_S b$ or $a \succeq_i b \Rightarrow a \succeq_S b$. In his comments, Sen writes: 'D* rules out even a local dictator.'

This comment obviously refers to the first part of the definition, i.e., to the fact that i is decisive for a against b, with a and b being two specific options. The individual that Sen calls a *local* dictator here has *less* power than the two individuals of Condition L*, since each of these two individuals is decisive over a two-element subset of X, say $\{a, b\}$, which means decisive for a against b and for b against a. It is at this point that we find that there is a semantic ambiguity: how a condition in which

106

some power is conferred to two individuals can be called a *liberalism* condition, and, at the same time, another statement about an individual having less power than that be in reference to a local dictator? The terminological contrast between the two terms – liberalism and (local) dictator – is surprising.

A formal difficulty: Saari's analysis

Suppose we have a function $y = a/(x - b)$. We all interpret it, for $a \neq 0$, as a continuous, differentiable real function whose curve is an hyperbola with asymptotes $x = b$ and $y = 0$. Now consider the following presentation. Let $\mathcal{L}(\mathfrak{R}, \mathfrak{R})$ be the set of real functions of a real single variable. Let f be a function in this set satisfying (i) continuity, (ii) differentiability, (iii) $f(x)(x - b) = a$ for $a \neq 0$ and $b \in \mathfrak{R}$. It is obvious that we have the following impossibility theorem: there does not exist a function $f \in \mathcal{L}(\mathfrak{R}, \mathfrak{R})$, satisfying conditions (i), (ii), and (iii). Condition (iii) entails that f be defined over $\mathfrak{R} - \{b\}$ and is, accordingly, not defined over $\mathfrak{R}$. This example is adapted from an example in Saari (1998). We consider Saari's way to deal with Sen's Theorem as revolutionary though we are convinced that many specialists will not share our enthusiasm. Let us restrict our analysis to the three-alternative case: $X = \{a, b, c\}$ with individual 1 and individual 2 being decisive respectively over $\{a, b\}$ and over $\{a, c\}$. The social preference over $\{a, b\}$ does not depend on the preferences of individuals other than 1 over $\{a, b\}$, and the social preference over $\{a, c\}$ does not depend on the preferences of individuals other than 2 over $\{a, c\}$. The domain of the aggregation procedure, implicitly considered when Condition L* is imposed, only requires each individual to have a preference over two-alternative subsets, preference which, to quote Saari

> needs not satisfy any sequencing requirement such as transitivity. Thus, it is appropriate to treat the L* admissible procedures as being intended for unsophisticated societies with primitive individuals who can only rank pairs.

Of course, when we defined the social decision function, we used as its domain Π, the set of profiles of individual *complete preorders*. What Saari outlines is the following. If we impose a liberalism condition on an aggregation function, this entails that the function is not defined over the set of profiles of complete preorders. Consequently, if we want to have an aggregation function whose domain is the set of profiles of complete preorders, we must abandon the liberalism condition. We will not develop this any further. Doing it would oblige us to paraphrase Saari's paper; we consider it better for our readers to study the original. Note, furthermore, that Saari makes for the independence condition and Arrow's Theorem the same sort of analysis as the one made for the L* condition and Sen's Theorem.

A RESEARCH PROGRAMME

A natural question arises at this point. What should we do to overcome (some of) these difficulties? First, though our objective, partially defined by the editors of this volume, was to discuss Sen's original contribution. We must underline that the enormous development of the literature since 1970 has given us two major routes of research: the game-form approach (already mentioned above) and the freedom of choice approach (see Pattanaik (1994), (1997), and some chapters of this book).

From the beginning of the modern rebirth of social choice, we have worked on sets of alternatives, these alternatives being often interpreted as social states. It seems to us that a social state is a very vague notion, and at the same time a very large concept, so large that we can easily imagine that it can accommodate individual rights. The *Déclaration des Droits de l'Homme et du Citoyen* which serves as a preamble to several constitutions is an example of this. The social choice, here, is between alternatives within which rights are included, or at least some kind of rights (see Kolm (1993)). There is no need, then, to define them through an aggregation procedure. Nozick (1974) develops a similar argument. For Nozick, individual rights define constraints on the set of social states. In some sense, they define a subset of social states on which the social choice has to be made (if this subset is non-empty!). Sen (1976) provides illuminating comments on Nozick's views. We believe that this concept of social state and its use in social choice must be clarified. One step toward this end, at least from a formal point of view, is the structural analysis considered earlier.

This forces us to get a clear view of what rights are. Rather than carrying on a research programme characterized by the complexification of the basic formalism, we could possibly return to the concept of rights itself. Though the links between economics and philosophy have been recently revived as exemplified, for instance, by the books of Sen (1987), Binmore (1994), Broome (1991) and Hausman and McPherson (1996), and the publication of the journal *Economics and Philosophy*, the upsurge of books by moral philosophers on rights, liberty, and freedom has been largely unnoticed by economists working on this topic within the social choice area. Without trying to be exhaustive, we think of Raz (1986), Sumner (1989), Thompson (1990), Wolf (1990), Jacobs (1993), Martin (1993), Steiner (1994), Weinreb (1994), Wellman (1995), Gewirth (1996), Kristjansson (1996), and Zimmerman (1996). In her chapter on rights in *A Companion to Ethics*, Almond (1991) focused on the fact that the word *rights* can be differently interpreted depending on the meaning given to it (claim, power, liberty, immunity . . . .). What is the common feature of the right o drive at 130 kilometres per hour on a French motorway and any of the so-called human rights? All the aforementioned authors gave replies to questions of this sort. Though they do not agree, a knowledge of their work should be considered as essential for a future research. Some of the most famous contemporary moral philosophers provide detailed analysis of the moral problems met by human beings in modern times. This is the case, for instance, of Bernard Williams (1985). In his book, Williams favours a return to moral philosophers of the antiquity and to Kant, and he explains why. In particular, he shows that his point of view has moral consequences for the definition of rights.

The third and last point in this research programme is more technical. In the social choice rule approach, we showed that there is a semantic ambiguity in the asymmetric distribution of power. Indeed Sen interprets as liberalism the situation where two individuals are decisive each over a two-element subset of the set of alternatives, while he calls local dictatorship the situation where there is only one such individual. There is another ambiguity concerning the meaning of the definition of the exercise of a right. This ambiguity is clearly described in Pattanaik (1997). It refers to the impossibility for Sen's definition of rights to distinguish between the *ability* for an individual i to obtain $a \succ_S b$ whenever $a \succ_i b$ and the *obligation* to have $a \succ_S b$ whenever $a \succ_i b$. The two interpretations are possible, though many people would consider that only the second one is correct. In most cases, however, it seems to us that the idea of a right refers to the ability (it is possible that . . .), rather than to the obligation (it is necessary that . . .). We believe that we cannot be satisfied by a simple comment on this. We should take account of this particularity and accordingly we should study a logic of rights and see how this logic can be used in the social choice framework. Modal logic (see, for instance, Hughes and Cresswell (1996)) is the logic of necessity and possibility. Within modal logic, deontic logic is devoted to questions of obligation, prohibition, permission, commitment etc. (see von Wright (1951), Åqvist (1984), Horty and Belnap (1995)). Preliminary steps toward the use of deontic logic in the social choice framework have already been carried out by van Hees (1995).

To conclude, we believe that a lot of work remains to be done on the definition of rights and social states, and that we need to base our future technical work on the most recent findings of logicians.

ACKNOWLEDGEMENTS

We are very grateful to Don Saari for conversations and correspondence on this topic, and to Richard Barrett and Peter Hammond for their comments on an entirely different earlier draft. In particular, the present version owes much to Hammond's insightful remarks. The final version benefited from Nicolas Gravel's very detailed remarks and comments.

REFERENCES

Allen, B., 1996, 'A remark on a social choice problem', *Social Choice and Welfare*, Vol. 13, 11–16.

Almond, B., 1991, 'Rights', in Singer P. (ed.), *A Companion to Ethics*, Oxford, Basil Blackwell.

Åqvist, L., 'Deontic logic', in Gabbay D. and F. Guenthner (eds), *Handbook of Philosophical Logic*, Vol. 2, Dordrecht, Reidel, 605–714.

Arrow, K.J., 1963, *Social Choice and Individual Values*, 2nd edition, New York, Wiley.

Bernholz, P., 1974, 'Is a Paretian liberal really impossible?', *Public Choice*, Vol. 20, 99–107.

Binmore, K., 1994, *Game Theory and the Social Contract, Volume 1: Playing Fair*, Cambridge, Massachusetts, M.I.T. Press.

Blackorby, C., Primont, D., and R. R. Russell, 1979, *Duality, Separability, and Functional Structure: Theory and Economic Applications*, New York, North-Holland.

Broome, J., 1991, *Weighing Goods*, Oxford, Basil Blackwell.

Chichilnisky, G., 1996, 'A robust theory of resource allocation', *Social Choice and Welfare*, Vol. 13, 1–10.

Coughlin, P., 1986, 'Rights and the private Pareto principle', *Economica*, Vol. 53, 303–320.

Gewirth, A., 1996, *The Community of Rights*, Chicago, The University of Chicago Press.

Gibbard, A., 1974, 'A Pareto consistent claim', *Journal of Economic Theory*, Vol. 7, 388–410.

Hammond, P. J., 1982, 'Liberalism, independent rights and the Pareto principle', in Cohen L. J., Lós J., Pfeiffer H. and K.-P. Podewski (eds), *Logic, Methodology and Philosophy of Science*, Vol. 6, 217–243.

Hammond, P. J., 1995, 'Social choice of individual and group rights', in Barnett W. A., Moulin H., Salles M. and N. Schofield (eds), *Social Choice, Welfare and Ethics*, Cambridge, Cambridge University Press, 55–77.

Hammond, P. J., 1997, 'Game forms versus social choice rules as models of rights', in Arrow K. J., Sen A. K. and K. Suzumura (eds), *Social Choice Re-examined*, London, Macmillan.

Hausman, D. M., and M. S. McPherson, 1996, *Economic Analysis and Moral Philosophy*, Cambridge, Cambridge University Press.

Horty, J. F., and N. Belnap, 1995, 'The deliberative stit: A study of action, omission, ability, and obligation', *Journal of Philosophical Logic*, Vol. 24, 583–644.

Hugues, G. E., and M. J. Cresswell, 1996, *A New Introduction to Modal Logic*, London, Routledge.

Jacobs, L. A., 1993, *Rights and Deprivation*, Oxford, Clarendon Press.

Kolm, S.-C., 1993, 'Free and equal in rights: The philosophies of the declaration of 1789', *The Journal of Political Philosophy*, Vol. 1, 158–183.

Kristjánsson, K., *Social Freedom: The Responsibility View*, Cambridge, Cambridge University Press.

Le Breton, M., 1997, 'Arrovian social choice on economic domains', in Arrow K. J., Sen A. K. and K. Suzumura (eds), *Social Choice Re-examined*, London, Macmillan.

Le Breton, M., and J. Weymark, 1996, 'An introduction to Arrovian social welfare functions on economic and political domains', in N. Schofield (ed.), *Collective Decision Making: Social Choice and Political Economy*, Dordrecht, Kluwer.

DIFFICULTIES OF THE SOCIAL CHOICE RULE

Martin, R., 1993, *A System of Rights*, Oxford, Clarendon Press.

Nozick, R., 1974, *Anarchy, State, and Utopia*, Oxford, Basil Blackwell.

Pattanaik, P. K., 1994, 'Some non-welfaristic issues in welfare economics', in Dutta B. (ed.), *Welfare Economics*, Delhi, Oxford University Press.

Pattanaik, P. K., 1997, 'On modelling individual rights', in Arrow K. J., Sen A. K. and K. Suzumura (eds), *Social Choice Re-examined*, London, Macmillan.

Raz, J., 1986, *The Morality of Freedom*, Oxford, Clarendon Press.

Redekop, J., 1995, 'Arrow theorems in economic environments', in Barnett W. A., Moulin H., Salles M. and N. Schofield (eds), *Social Choice, Welfare, and Ethics*, Cambridge, Cambridge University Press.

Saari, D. G., 1998, 'Connecting and resolving Sen's and Arrow's theorems', *Social Choice and Welfare*, Vol. 15.

Salles, M., 1997, 'Rights, permission, obligation: Comments on Prasanta K. Pattanaik, On modelling individual rights', in Arrow K. J., Sen A. K. and K. Suzumura (eds), *Social Choice Re-examined*, London, Macmillan.

Sen, A. K., 1970, 'The impossibility of a Paretian liberal', *Journal of Political Economy*, Vol. 78, 152–157.

Sen, A. K., 1970a, *Collective Choice and Social Welfare*, San Francisco, Holden-Day.

Sen, A. K., 1976, 'Liberty, unanimity and rights', *Economica*, Vol. 43, 217–245.

Sen, A. K., 1987, *On Ethics and Economics*, Oxford, Basil Blackwell.

Steiner, I., 1994, *An Essay on Rights*, Oxford, Basil Blackwell.

Sumner, L. W., 1989, *The Moral Foundations of Rights*, Oxford, Clarendon Press.

Thomson, J. J., 1990, *The Realm of Rights*, Cambridge, Massachusetts, Harvard University Press.

Van Hees, M., 1995, *Rights and Decisions*, Dordrecht, Kluwer.

Varian, H. R., 1992, *Microeconomic Analysis*, 3rd edition, New York, W. W. Norton.

Von Wright, H., 1951, 'Deontic logic', *Mind*, Vol. 60, 1–15.

Weinreb, L. L., 1994, *Oedipus at Fenway Park: What Rights Are and Why There Are Any*, Cambridge, Massachusetts, Harvard University Press.

Wellman, C., 1995, *Real Rights*, New York, Oxford University Press.

Williams, B., 1985, *Ethics and the Limits of Philosophy*, London, Fontana Press/Collins.

Wolf, S., 1990, *Freedom within Reason*, New York, Oxford University Press.

Zimmerman, M. J., 1996, *The Concept of Moral Obligation*, Cambridge, Cambridge University Press.

8

DIFFICULTIES WITH THE SOCIAL CHOICE RULE APPROACH TO RIGHTS

Some comments on Brunel and Salles

Peter J. Hammond

The paper by Brunel and Salles does well to remind us how Sen's (1970) pioneering social choice rule (SCR) approach to rights is really the essential starting point for economists' interest in the theme of this book. The paper also succeeds in identifying some reasons for dissatisfaction with this SCR approach. Though it mentions the alternative game form approach, this is not discussed in any detail. Yet the game form approach does help to resolve at least one of the difficulties, as I shall argue below.

FIRST DIFFICULTY: SOCIAL CHOICE IN ECONOMIC ENVIRONMENTS

To quote: 'social choice over feasible allocations involves many difficulties'. This is true. Moreover, when the feasible set of economic allocations is an Edgeworth hyperbox (*EB*), the authors go on to claim: 'Since social choice is a choice between elements in *EB*, we must consider individual preferences over *EB*.' Also true. But it is not true that we must consider only individual preferences over *EB*, even if one imposes Arrow's independence of alternatives condition. In particular, consider the alleged difficulty over monotonic preferences. When only allocations within *EB* are included in the domain of social states, every consumer with the usual 'selfish' preferences for personal consumption has a point of satiation at one corner of *EB*. Monotonicity is then violated. However, really the relevant domain of social states consists of all possible consumption allocations in the Cartesian product space of different individuals' consumption sets. After all, social choice theory should be able to decide how to reallocate goods in any Edgeworth hyperbox, no matter what the total endowments of different goods may be. That is exactly what a social preference ordering is meant to do. But once this product space is allowed, preferences will be monotone whenever they are in the exchange economy, in the usual sense discussed in general equilibrium theory. Thus, the alleged difficulty with monotone preferences is entirely the result of artificially restricting the domain of social states to allocations within one single Edgeworth hyper-box.

Next, in order to apply the Pareto criterion of social choice theory to allocations within EB, it is noted that individuals' preferences must be extended to entire economic allocations. The obvious way of doing this is to follow every microeconomics textbook and assume that individuals are indifferent to all changes in the consumption vectors of other individuals. Thus, in comparing any two economic allocations, an individual is assumed to compare only his or her own two consumption bundles.

Now, the authors claim that 'this appears to us a denial of social choice where decisions should be based on ethical judgements about social justice, inequality, redistribution, and so forth'. But I would argue that normative social choice theory should be about how to heed individuals' legitimate interests – selfish or otherwise – when making social decisions in an ethically appropriate way. This being so, in my view the most important ethical judgements are those which are reflected in the social choice rule rather than in individual ethical values. Of course, it might be much easier to implement ethically satisfactory decision rules in a society of ethically sensitive individuals. But one should beware of basing social ethical judgements too heavily on individuals' ethical values, or lack of them. Otherwise there is a danger that, for instance, the selfish beneficiaries of altruistic sentiments will receive undue weight compared to those expressing such sentiments.

So there really are some difficulties. But it is easy to add to them unnecessarily by following Chichilnisky (1996) in restricting unduly the domain of social states one is willing to consider, or by confusing ethical values that should be captured in the social choice rule with those that are relevant to individuals' own preferences. And by confusing individuals' preferences with the appropriate concepts of ethical well-being or value, suitably modified, which are what one needs as a basis for making rational ethical decisions.

SECOND DIFFICULTY: RIGHTS IMPLY LOCAL DICTATORSHIP

In Sen (1970a, Chapter 4) Condition D* is defined, requiring that there should be no local dictator who is decisive for a over b, for some pair of social states a, b. Brunel and Salles point out that minimal liberalism actually requires the existence of at least two local dictators in this sense! Now, recall that Arrow's definition of a dictator is used to show how dictatorship cannot be avoided, given the other conditions of Arrow's impossibility theorem. With this in mind, it should be pointed out that Sen proves possibility results showing how the Pareto rule can be satisfied without there being local dictators. Indeed, the Pareto rule actually prevents the existence of local dictators. In some sense, the liberal paradox is a corollary of this result.

First thoughts make Brunel and Salles seem clearly right in describing this as a 'semantic confusion'. But second thoughts may be more reliable. After all, the social choice rule approach to rights really does require people to be 'local dictators' over personal matters where it is accepted that they should be free to exercise their rights. In the social choice rule approach, therefore, local dictatorship actually becomes a desideratum, provided that the 'localities' are appropriate. Our feelings of revulsion should be reserved for non-local dictatorships, or local dictatorships affecting issues that should not be treated as personal.

THIRD DIFFICULTY: MATHEMATICS

Papers not due to be published for two years are not always easily accessible. So I have not seen Saari (1998), and any remarks I make should not be interpreted in any way as a criticism of his article. Nevertheless, based on the discussion by Brunel and Salles, it seems to me that the difficulty which concerns Saari relates to the fact a binary social preference relation respecting individual preferences over appropriate personal issues may violate even acyclicity, as a famous example due to Gibbard (1974) makes clear. This is a real difficulty for the social choice rule approach to rights. But if individuals have rights to play strategies in game forms, rather than to dictate locally the social preference relation, the difficulty largely disappears.

The same distinction, by the way, bears on Pattanaik's (1997) claim that, where a personal matter is concerned, the theory of rights does not distinguish between the ability of an individual to determine a social preference, and the obligation of society's preference relation to respect an individual's preference. After all, to use an example based on a presentation by Sen of Gibbard's famous example, there is an obvious game form which grants each of two sisters the power to determine what colour dress she wears, but there is no game which simultaneously meets any obligation by society to respect the wish of one of them to wear a dress of the same colour as the other – especially when the other sister wants to wear a dress of a different colour. Pattanaik's claim is discussed as part of Brunel and Salles' 'research programme'. My comments here are intended merely to suggest a more suitable direction for research rather than argue that the issue has been entirely resolved.

THE RESEARCH PROGRAMME

The difficulties noted by Brunel and Salles may have been somewhat exaggerated. But difficulties certainly do remain. In their formal models, social choice theorists have so far only embodied a very limited conception of rights. Human rights and the rights of the citizen, as usually understood, and especially the degree to which those rights are respected, should be included within the description of a social state – as should other conceptions of rights which have been discussed by philosophers and jurists, though they have been largely ignored by economists and social choice theorists. Brunel and Salles do us a service to remind us of this other literature, and they draw our attention to some of the most recent relevant writings. But it should also be recalled that some of that literature addresses ideas that bear little on how to make good decisions, which is what social choice theory should be about. Also, just as many economists and social choice theorists have read too little of the relevant literature in philosophy, so too many philosophers know less about economics or decision and game theory than they really need to, if social choice theorists and economists are to find much of value in their work. So the literature that goes beyond social choice theory and economics needs to be read carefully and critically, without losing sight of the main decision theoretic issues that should concern us.

9

EFFECTIVITY FUNCTIONS, GAME FORMS, GAMES AND RIGHTS*

Bezalel Peleg

ABSTRACT

In this paper we offer an axiomatic approach for the investigation of rights by means of game forms. We give a new definition of constitution which consists of three components: the set of rights, the assignment of rights to groups of members of the society, and the distribution of power in the society (as a function of the distribution of rights). Using the foregoing definition we investigate game forms that faithfully represent the distribution of power in the society, and allow the members of the society to exercise their rights simultaneously. Several well-known examples are analysed in the light of our framework. Finally, we find a connection between Sen's minimal liberalism and Maskin's result on implementation by Nash equilibria.

INTRODUCTION

This paper consists of an attempt to use the axiomatic approach in investigating rights by means of game forms (for a recent paper which explores the relationship between rights and game forms see Hammond (1994)). The assignment of rights to the members of a society is, usually, part of the constitution of the society. Therefore, in order to investigate it we need a definition of constitution. Such a definition is given in Arrow (1967). However, if we adopt Arrow's definition of constitution (i.e., that a constitution is a 'well-behaved' social welfare function – see Arrow (1967)), then we have to accept the conclusion of Arrow's Impossibility Theorem that there is no satisfactory constitution. We quote from (Arrow, (1967, p. 228)):

> This conclusion is quite embarrassing, and it forces us to examine the conditions which have been stated as reasonable. It's hard to imagine anyone quarreling either with the Pareto Principle or the condition of Non-Dictatorship. The principle of Collective Rationality may indeed be questioned. One might be prepared to allow that the choice from a given environment be dependent on the history of previous choices made in earlier environments, but I think many would

116

find that situation unsatisfactory. There remains, therefore, only the Independence of Irrelevant Alternatives, which will be examined in greater detail in Section IV below.

In that Section we find (Arrow (1967, p. 231)):

Unfortunately, it is clear, as I have already suggested, that social decision processes which are independent of irrelevant alternatives have strong practical advantages, and it remains to be seen whether a satisfactory social decision procedure can really be based on other information.

The only way to resolve this impasse is to use a different, less known, definition of constitution. We follow this path in this paper. Our approach is based on Gardenfors (1981).

We now briefly review the contents of the paper. The first section introduces a definition of constitution which is a generalization of Gardenfors's definition of rights system. In our model rights are common knowledge and preferences, that may be private information, do not enter the definition of constitution. We also compute the constitutions for several examples. We then show how a constitution leads in a natural way to an effectivity function which describes the 'distribution of power' in a given society as a result of the assignment of rights (see Deb (1994) for somewhat similar ideas). We proceed to describe how game forms, that faithfully represent the foregoing effectivity function, are used by the members of the society to simultaneously exercise their rights. There then follows a study of games that are related to Gibbard's Paradox (Gibbard (1974)). Also, we show that it is possible to choose constitutions whose games forms have a non-empty set of equilibria for each profile of preferences of the members of the society. We then investigate the connection between Sen's Liberal Paradox and the implementability of social choice correspondences. A comparison of our paper with some closely related contributions to the theory of rights is then presented.

THE MODEL AND EXAMPLES

The legal rules of a democratic society are given in terms of rights of subgroups of members of the society (including, of course, individuals). We attempt to precisely define in such a situation the notion of constitution. Later we shall compare the current definition of this notion in terms of preferences (see, e.g., Arrow (1967) and Gibbard (1974)), with our definition.

A society S is a list $\langle N, A, \rho, \alpha, \gamma \rangle$ where:

1 $N = \{1, \ldots, n\}$ is the set of members of S.
2 A is the set of social states (which may be finite or infinite).

3 $\rho = \{\rho_1, \ldots, \rho_\ell\}$ is the (finite) set of rights.

4 $\alpha: 2^N \to 2^\rho$ is the (current) assignment of rights to groups of individuals.

5 γ, the access correspondence, determines the sets of attainable social states by groups of members of S as a function of their rights. Thus, γ: $2^N \times 2^\rho \to\to 2^A$. ($\to\to$ denotes a correspondence, i.e., a set-valued function.)

We always assume the following: (i) $\alpha (\emptyset) = \emptyset$, and (ii) $\gamma(\emptyset, \theta) = \gamma(S, \emptyset) = \{A\}$ for all $\theta \subset \rho$ and $S \subset N$. (i) is a convenient agreement. (ii) is true if A is the set of *all* possible social states.

The following remarks are in order. (We shall consistently use the foregoing notations.)

Remark 1 A social state is, intuitively, a complete description of all aspects relevant to the members of the society of a (possible) social situation. Formally, the set of ρ is an abstract set. However, intuitively, rights serve as vehicles for obtaining certain social states. Or, more concretely, they determine some major aspects of the 'distribution of power' in S.

Remark 2 The definition of the access correspondence deserves detailed explanation. If S is a coalition (of the members of the society), and $\theta \subset \rho$ is a set of rights, then $\gamma(S, \theta) = \{B_1, \ldots, B_m\}$ has the following interpretation. It is not (legally) excluded that the social outcome is in each of the sets $B_1, \ldots, B_m$ separately. For coherent models of rights a stronger interpretation is available.

Example 1 Let S be described in the following way. $N = \{1, 2\}$. Each member $i \in N$ has two shirts, white and blue, and he must wear one of the two. Denoting w for white and b for blue, the set A of social states is $A = \{(w, w), (w, b), (b, w), (b, b)\}$ (here, if $(x, y) \in A$ then x is the colour of 1's shirt and y is the colour of 2's shirt.) $\rho = \{\rho_1\}$ where ρ_1 is the right to freely choose one's own shirt. (Henceforth, we shall denote a singleton $\{a\}$ by a.) α is given by $\alpha(\emptyset) = \emptyset$, $\alpha(1) = \alpha(2) = \alpha(N) = \rho_1$. Finally, γ is given by $\gamma(S, \emptyset) = A$ for all $S \subset N$, $\gamma(\emptyset, \rho_1) = A$, $\gamma(1, \rho_1) = \{\{(w, w), (w, b)\}, \{(b, w), (b, b)\}\}$, $\gamma(2, \rho_1) = \{\{(w, w), (b, w)\}, \{(w, b), (b, b)\}\}$, and $\gamma(N, \rho_1) = 2^A \setminus \{\emptyset\}$.

Example 1 plays an important role in Gibbard (1974), and Gaertner, Pattanaik, and Suzumura (1992). Also, in choosing $\gamma(N, \rho_1)$ we have assumed that 1 and 2 may exercise ρ_1 *simultaneously*. Such a possibility may not always exist. The exact relationship between the foregoing example and Gibbard's (first) paradox (in Gibbard (1974)), will be clarified later.

Definition 1 Let $S = \langle N, A, \rho, \alpha, \gamma \rangle$ be a society. The triple $\langle \rho, \alpha, \gamma \rangle$ is called a *constitution*.

118

Thus, a constitution consists of a set of rights, an assignment of rights to groups of members of the society, and a function which specifies for each coalition (of members) its set of attainable (sets of) outcomes.

Remark 3 In our model, rights are personal because α and γ depend on the names of the members. In real-life situations this is usually not the case. To render our model more realistic we may assume that there is a set of parameters π such that each member i of the society is completely specified, for the sake of the analysis of rights and power, by a non-empty subset π_i of π. Under this assumption, two members $i, j \in N$ will be *symmetric* if $\pi_i = \pi_j$. Also, the constitution $\langle \rho, \alpha, \gamma \rangle$ satisfies equal treatment (ET), if for every pair of symmetric players $i, j \in N$ the transposition (i, j) is a symmetry of the pair $\langle \alpha, \gamma \rangle$ (more precisely, if $i, j \in N$, $\pi_i = \pi_j$, and $S \subset N \setminus \{i, j\}$, then $\alpha(S \cup \{i\}) = \alpha(S \cup \{j\})$ and $\gamma(S \cup \{i\}, \theta) = \gamma(S \cup \{j\}, \theta)$ for every $\theta \subset \rho$.)

In the sequel we shall use this approach of describing members of a society S by sets of parameters. Also, rights are very often associated with roles of certain members in S (e.g., mother, student, policeman, etc.). In the foregoing approach we may include the roles of a member i of S in his set of personal parameters π_i.

Remark 4 In our model, rights should be interpreted in a broad sense: all obligations to society (e.g., paying taxes) are rights. Thus, our notion of constitution is similar to the usual one. The observation that a constitution must contain both rights and obligations is not new (see, e.g., Kanger and Kanger (1972)). (I am indebted to the referee of this paper for this remark.)

The following example illustrates Remarks 3 and 4.

Example 2 A set $N = \{1, \ldots, n\}$ of workers share the same office. Let $\pi = \{\sigma, \upsilon\}$ be the set of the following two habits: $\sigma \equiv$ smoker, and $\upsilon \equiv$ non-smoker. The set of smokers N_1 is determined by a function $L : N \to \pi$, that is, $N_1 = \{i \in N | L(i) = \sigma\}$. Thus, $N_2 = \{i \in N | L(i) = \upsilon\} = N \setminus N_1$. The set A describes the possible states of the air at the office, that is, $A = \{\text{smoky}, \text{clear}\}$. Assume that ρ is a singleton which is the following obligation: 'Refrain from smoking, at the office, in the presence of at least one non-smoker,' Furthermore, assume that α, the assignment of rights, is given by $\alpha(\emptyset) = \emptyset$, and $\alpha(S) = \rho$ for all $S \subset N, S \neq \emptyset$. If we follow the usual meaning of the foregoing assumptions, then the access function γ is given by

$$\gamma(S, \rho) = \begin{cases} 2^A \setminus \{\emptyset\}, S \cap N_2 = \emptyset, S \neq \emptyset \\ \{\{\text{clear}\}, A\}, S \cap N_2 \neq \emptyset \end{cases}$$

and $\gamma(S, \emptyset) = \gamma(\emptyset, \rho) = A$ for all $S \subset N$.

Notice that in Example 2 every two (non-)smokers are symmetric (in the sense of Remark 3), and this is, indeed, reflected by α and γ. Also, formally we could define γ in an arbitrary manner. However, that might render our example senseless. Moreover, the values $\gamma(S, \theta)$ where $\theta \neq \alpha(S)$ do not enter the analysis of a society at a given date. However, if $\alpha(\bullet)$ changes over time, then all the values of γ matter. Finally, the description of Example 2 may be shortened. We chose the foregoing way in order to illustrate the use of parameters in describing the members of the society.

Remark 5 A constitution $\langle \rho, \alpha, \gamma \rangle$ is, at a given point of time, the result of the past continuous political process. In a democracy, at a given time, $\langle \rho, \alpha, \gamma \rangle$ represents the *status quo* of the rules of the state. Thus, it may be changed by the legislative institutions by voting or by other procedures (e.g., a referendum). Therefore, in our model rights are politically determined (see Sen (1994)). At each point in time t of change the members of S have a profile of preferences (on A), $R^N(t)$, that determines the direction of change. So, in our framework the problem of choosing the constitution does not arise because the constitution at a given period determines all possible (legal) constitutions at the next period. Illegal changes (e.g., *coups d'état*) are not covered by our model. However, we do not investigate in this work the dynamics of constitutions.

Remark 6 Let $S \subset N, S \neq \emptyset$, be a coalition, and let $\theta \subset \rho, \theta \neq \emptyset$. Then $\gamma(S, \theta)$ is a collection of subsets of A (i.e., a subset of 2^A). The reader may ask why we need such a 'complex' definition. In order to convince him that we have the right concept, let us consider the following example. Let N be the population of Israelis who have finished high school, are not older than 22, and look for a job in Israel. Let A be the set of all possible states of the job market in Israel and ρ be 'the right to work'. All the members of N have the right ρ, which guarantees a certain (low) payment in case of unemployment. A member $i \in N$ exercises his right in the following way. First i should choose a profession. Each choice determines a set of possible outcomes for i. (Clearly, the expected income depends on the choice of a profession.) Also, the workers in the same profession compete with each other. Thus, i's future income will be determined by competition with his peers, and may depend on factors that are not controlled by him. Hence, the 'right to work' does not determine i's profession and income directly; these are determined by i's decision and efforts that may be guided by signals of the labour market. Thus, in a capitalistic state the connection between the basic 'right to work' and the actual state of the labour force is highly indeterminate. This indeterminacy reflects the 'freedom of choice' that is embodied in a free market system (for a recent discussion of the problems of freedom of choice see, e.g., Puppe (1994)). We should add that Israeli governments also try to regulate the distribution of the labour force in Israel by other ways: massive support of higher education and vocational training, direct subsidies to exporting industries, and other means (which affect the attractivity of various sectors). The estimation of an 'optimal' degree of freedom may be very difficult. However, a system without freedom at all (people are assigned to jobs by the government) may be highly inefficient. We conclude from this example that the freedom aspect of a constitution is reflected, in our model, by the assumption that γ is a set-valued function (see Kanger and Kanger (1972) for a different approach to the concept of freedom).

Now we give an example where $|\rho| = \ell > 1$. (If D is a finite set, then $|D|$ denotes the number of elements in D.)

Example 3   This example of a society S also is taken from Gibbard (1974) (see also Hammond (1994)). N consists of three individuals: A (Angelina), E (Edwin), and J (the male Judge). There are three social states: $0, e, j$, where 0 indicates that Angelina remains single, e that she marries Edwin, and j that she marries the judge. The set of rights is $\rho = \{\rho_1, \rho_2\}$, where ρ_1 is the right to remain single, and ρ_2 is the right to marry. In Gibbard's example the assignment of rights is given by: $\alpha(\emptyset) = \emptyset, \alpha(A) = \alpha(E) = \alpha(J) = \rho_1, \alpha(\{A, E\}) = \alpha(\{A, J\}) = \rho, \alpha(\{E, J\}) = \rho_1$, and $\alpha(N) = \rho$. Using the usual interpretation of the foregoing data we may compute the access function γ in the following way. For each $B \subset \{0, e, j\}$ let $B^+ = \{\hat{B} \subset \{0, e, j\} | \hat{B} \supset B\}$. Then $\gamma(\emptyset, \theta) = \{0, e, j\}$ for all $\theta \subset \rho$, and $\gamma(S, \emptyset) = \{0, e, j\}$ for each $S \subset N$. The other values of γ are given by:

$$\gamma(A, \rho_1) = \gamma(A, \rho) = \{0\}^+, \text{ and } \gamma(A, \rho_2) = \{0, e, j\};$$

$$\gamma(E, \rho_1) = \gamma(E, \rho) = \{0, j\}^+, \text{ and } \gamma(E, \rho_2) = \{0, e, j\};$$

$$\gamma(J, \rho_1) = \gamma(J, \rho) = \{0, e\}^+, \text{ and } \gamma(J, \rho_2) = \{0, e, j\};$$

$$\gamma(\{A, E\}, \rho_1) = \{0\}^+, \gamma(\{A, E\}, \rho_2) = \{e\}^+, \text{ and } \gamma(\{A, E\}, \rho) = \{0\}^+ \cup \{e\}^+;$$

$$\gamma(\{A, J\}, \rho_1) = \{0\}^+, \gamma(\{A, J\}, \rho_2) = \{j\}^+, \text{ and } \gamma(\{A, J\}, \rho) = \{0\}^+ \cup \{j\}^+;$$

$$\gamma(\{E, J\}, \rho_1) = \{0\}^+, \gamma(\{E, J\}, \rho_2) = \{0, e, j\}, \text{ and } \gamma(\{E, J\}, \rho) = \{0\}^+;$$

$$\gamma(N, \rho_1) = \{0\}^+, \gamma(N, \rho_2) = \{e\}^+ \cup \{j\}^+, \text{ and}$$

$$\gamma(N, \rho) = \{0\}^+ \cup \{e\}^+ \cup \{j\}^+.$$

REPRESENTATION BY GAME FORMS

Let $S = \langle N, A, \rho, \alpha, \gamma \rangle$ be a society. An effectivity function (EF) is a correspondence $E : 2^N \twoheadrightarrow 2^A$ that satisfies the following conditions: (i) $E(\emptyset) = A$; (ii) $E(N) = 2^A \setminus \{\emptyset\}$; (iii) $\emptyset \notin E(S)$ for all $S \subset N$; and (iv) $A \in E(S)$ for all $S \subset N$. Under very mild conditions the constitution $\langle \rho, \alpha, \gamma \rangle$ defines an EF $E = E(\bullet; \alpha, \gamma)$ in the following way

$$E(S; \alpha, \gamma) = E(S) = \gamma(S, \alpha(S)) \tag{9.1}$$

Condition (i) above is satisfied as $\gamma(\emptyset, \alpha(\emptyset)) = A$. The next condition $\gamma(N, \alpha(N)) = 2^A \setminus \{\emptyset\}$ is the familiar condition of citizen's sovereignty (or non-imposition) for EF's (see Peleg (1984, Remark 6.1.3)). Condition (iii) is obvious: There is always some social state that prevails. The same (trivial) argument also justifies (iv). In summary, under the assumption of non-imposition (9.1) defines an EF. We shall now define some basic properties of α and γ. α satisfies monotonicity if

$$S \subset T \Rightarrow \alpha(S) \subset \alpha(T) \text{ for all } S, T \subset N \tag{9.2}$$

$\gamma : 2^N \times 2^\rho \twoheadrightarrow 2^A$ is monotonic with respect to (w.r.t.) the alternatives if for all $S \in 2^N$ and all $\theta \in 2^\rho$

$$[B \in \gamma(S, \theta) \text{ and } B^* \supset B] \Rightarrow [B^* \in \gamma(S, \theta)] \tag{9.3}$$

γ is monotonic w.r.t. rights if for all $S \subset N$ and $\theta, \theta^* \subset \rho$

$$[\theta^* \supset \theta] \Rightarrow [\gamma(S, \theta^*) \supset \gamma(S, \theta)] \tag{9.4}$$

Finally, γ is monotonic w.r.t. coalitions if for all $\theta \in 2^\rho$ and $S, S^* \in 2^N$

$$[S^* \supset S] \Rightarrow [\gamma(S^*, \theta) \supset \gamma(S, \theta)] \tag{9.5}$$

(9.2) is intuitively acceptable: Usually larger groups have more rights. Essentially, it follows from the usual interpretation of rights.

(9.3) is always satisfied if the constitution is coherent, that is E (see (9.1)) can be represented by a game form (see Definition 5, below). In this case $B \in \gamma(S, \theta)$ can be represented by a game form (see Definition 5, below). In this case $B \in \gamma(S, \theta)$ may be interpreted as follows: If S has the set of rights θ, then, by exercising its rights 'properly', S may force the social outcome to be an element of B. This argument will be precisely formulated when we shall discuss in the sequel representations of EFs.

(9.4) generally does not hold. As rights in our model include also obligations, having more rights may diminish the set of possible outcomes. Also, (9.5) may not be true. The members of $S^* \setminus S$ may have rights conflicting with those of the members of S and thereby excluding some of the outcomes in $\gamma(S, \theta)$. For example, a taxi driver has the right to smoke when he is alone in his car. However, passengers may prevent him from smoking by objecting (or by law) (see also Example 2). Nevertheless, we consider such conflicts as being 'marginal', and we shall usually assume (9.5).

Definition 2 An EF $E: 2^N \to \to 2^A$ is superadditive if for all $S_1, S_2 \in 2^N$, $B_1 \in E(S_1)$ and $B_2 \in E(S_2)$

$$[S_1 \cap S_2 = \emptyset] \Rightarrow [B_1 \cap B_2 \in E(S_1 \cup S_2)] \qquad (9.6)$$

A superadditive EF is monotonic w.r.t. coalitions, that is, if $S \subset T \subset N$ then $E(S) \subset E(T)$ (the proof is straightforward). Hence, an EF that is derived from a constitution by (9.1) might not be superadditive. Nevertheless, we shall deal with EF's that correspond to constitutions and are superadditive, because superadditivity is satisfied quite often.

In order to exercise their rights the members of S use (legal) strategies. These strategies must be, in addition, compatible with the constitution. The formulation of this compatibility condition is achieved in the following way.

Definition 3 A game form (GF) is a list $\Gamma = \langle N; \Sigma^1, \ldots, \Sigma^n; g; A \rangle$ where N is the set of members of the society; Σ^i is the non-empty set of strategies of $i \in N; g: \Sigma^1 \times \ldots \times \Sigma^n \to A$, is the outcome function; and A is the set of social states.

A GF Γ is legal if for each $i \in N$ every strategy $\sigma^i \in \Sigma^i$ does not contradict the assignment of rights $\alpha(\bullet)$. For example, if Adam has the obligation to support his family, and stealing is forbidden by rule (i.e. by the assignment $\alpha(\text{Adam})$), then Adam cannot support his family by stealing. Henceforth, we shall only consider legal GF's. Moreover, we shall assume that also coalitions cannot break the law (by coordination of strategies).

Definition 4 Let $\Gamma = \langle N; \Sigma^1, \ldots, \Sigma^n; g; A \rangle$ be a GF, let $S \subset N$, $S \neq \emptyset$, and let $B \subset A$. S is α-effective for B if there exists $\sigma_0^S \in \Sigma^S = \times_{i \in S} \Sigma^i$ such that for all $\sigma^{M \backslash S} \in \Sigma^{M \backslash S} g(\sigma_0^S, \sigma^{M \backslash S}) \in B$. Now assume that g is surjective (onto A), and denote for each $S \subset N, S \neq \emptyset$,

$$E_\alpha(S; \Gamma) = \{B \subset S | S \text{ is } \alpha\text{-effective for } B\}$$

and $E_\alpha(\emptyset; \Gamma) = A$. Then $E_\alpha(\bullet; \Gamma)$ is the $\alpha\text{-}EF$ of Γ (in particular, it is an EF).

A GF Γ is compatible with the constitution $\langle \rho, \alpha, \gamma \rangle$ if it has the following property.

Definition 5 A (legal) GF Γ is a representation of the constitution $\langle \rho, \alpha, \gamma \rangle$ if $E_\alpha(\bullet; \Gamma) = E(\bullet)$, where E is defined by (9.1).

123

A representation of the constitution may be considered as a permissible mechanism that enables all the members of the society to exercise their rights simultaneously. The basic EF E, which is defined by (9.1), may be represented by many GFs. Each representation may be considered as a (legal) translation of the constitution into strategic behaviour. If the society S is, for example, geographically divided into several communities, then each community may choose its own representation of the constitution.

The main result on existence of representations is the following theorem.

Theorem 1 Let $E: 2^N \rightarrow\rightarrow 2^A$ be the EF which is derived by (9.1). Then there exists a GF $\Gamma = \langle N; \Sigma^1, \ldots, \Sigma^n; g; A \rangle$ such that $E_\alpha(S; \Gamma) = E(S)$ for all $S \in 2^N$ if the following two conditions hold:

(i) γ is monotonic w.r.t. the alternatives;
(ii) E is superadditive.

The proof is given in the appendix. For a proof when A is finite see Moulin (1983).

Example 4 Consider the society of Example 1. (9.1) yields the following EF $E: E(\emptyset) = A$ and $E(S) = \gamma(S, \rho_1)$ for $S \neq \emptyset$. Let $\hat{w}(\hat{b})$ be the strategy 'choose a white (blue) shirt'. Then the GF $\Gamma = \langle N; \{\hat{w}, \hat{b}\}, \{\hat{w}, \hat{b}\}; g; A \rangle$, where g is given by $g(\hat{x}^1, \hat{x}^2) = (x^1, x^2)$ for all $x^1, x^2 \in \{w, b\}$ is a representation of E. According to Γ, the two members choose their shirt simultaneously.

Example 5 Let $\Sigma^1 = \{\hat{w}, \hat{b}\}$ (see Example 4), and let $\Sigma^2 = \{f | f: \Sigma^1 \rightarrow \{w, b\}\}$. Further define $g: \Sigma^1 \times \Sigma^2 \rightarrow A$ by $g(\hat{x}, f) = (x, f(\hat{x}))$. The GF $\Gamma_0 = \langle N; \Sigma^1, \Sigma^2; g, A \rangle$ describes the following sequential procedure.

Step 1 1 chooses her shirt.
Step 2 2 chooses her shirt after observing 1's choice.

Γ_0 is *not* a representation of E (see, again, Example 4). Indeed, by choosing the strategy $f(\hat{x}) = x \, 2$ can force the outcome to be in the set $B = \{(w, w), (b, b)\}$. However, $B \notin E(2)$.

Example 6 Now we compute the EF of the society of Example 3 by means of (9.1): $E(\emptyset) = \{0, e, j\}$; $E(A) = \gamma(A, \rho_1) = \{0\}^+$ (see Example 3); $E(E) = \gamma(E, \rho_1) = \{0, j\}^+$; $E(J) = \gamma(J, \rho_1) = \{0, e\}^+$; $E(\{A, E\}) = \gamma(\{A, E\}, \rho) = \{0\}^+ \cup \{e\}^+$; $E(\{A, J\}) = \gamma(\{A, J\}, \rho) = \{0\}^+ \cup \{j\}^+$; $E(\{E, J\}) = \gamma(\{E, J\}, \rho_1) = \{0\}^+$, and $E(N) = \gamma(N, \rho) = \{0\}^+ \cup \{e\}^+ \cup \{j\}^+$. As the reader may easily verify, $E(\bullet)$ is superadditive and monotonic w.r.t. the alternatives. Hence, by Theorem 1, E is representable. Also, if A is finite then

124

the proof of Theorem 1 is constructive and, therefore, may be used to obtain representations of E.

GAMES AND RIGHTS

Let $S = \langle N, A, \rho, \alpha, \gamma \rangle$ be a society, let the EFE be derived by (9.1), and let $\Gamma = \langle N; \Sigma^1, \ldots, \Sigma^n; g; A \rangle$ be a representation of E. If $i \in N$ then a preference ordering of i is a complete and transitive binary relation on A. Let Q be the set of all preference orderings on A. Then, Q^N is the set of all preference profiles. If $R^N \in Q^N$ then the pair $\langle \Gamma, R^N \rangle$ determines an (ordinary) game in strategic form $G(\Gamma, R^N) = \langle N; \Sigma^1, \ldots, \Sigma^n; g; A; R^N \rangle$ (in the usual way). Every situation of simultaneous exercising of rights by the members of S is a play of a game of the foregoing type (i.e., a play of a game $G(\Gamma, R^N)$ where Γ is a representation of E and $R^N \in Q^N$).

Example 7   Consider the $GF\ \Gamma$ of Example 4. The set $\{G(\Gamma, R^N)|R^N \in Q^N\}$ is isomorphic to the set of all ordinal types of 2×2 (two-person) games. (Two 2×2 (two-person) games with numerical payoffs are ordinally equivalent if one can be obtained from the other by strictly increasing (individual) transformations of the payoffs.) In particular, we can obtain the game of 'matching pennies', which is Gibbard's first paradox, and the 'prisoner's dilemma', which is Gibbard's second paradox. This observation is not new (see, e.g., Gaertner (1993) for the same observation and a list of references for earlier discussions of this example).

Remark 7   Let us consider 'matching pennies' in the framework of Example 7. The effectivity function E is given by $E(\emptyset) = A$, $E(1) = \{\{(w, w), (w, b)\}, \{(b, w), (b, b)\}\}$, $E(2) = \{\{(w, w), (b, w)\}, \{(w, b), (b, b)\}\}$, and $E(\{1, 2\}) = 2^A \setminus \{\emptyset\}$ (see examples 1 and 4). A profile of 'matching pennies' is given by:

R^1	R^2
b, w	w, w
w, b	b, b
w, w	b, w
b, b	w, b

The following claim is true:

If $\Gamma = \langle N; \Sigma^1, \Sigma^2; g; A \rangle$ is a representation of E, then the game

$G(\Gamma, R^N)$ has no Nash equilibrium (NE).

Proof   Let $\Gamma = \langle N; \Sigma^1, \Sigma^2; g; A \rangle$ be a representation of E. Assume, on the contrary, that $\sigma_0 = (\sigma_0^1, \sigma_0^2)$ is a NE of $G(\Gamma, R^N)$. We have four possible

125

values for $g(\sigma_0)$. We only will consider the case $g(\sigma_0) = (w, w)$. By assumption, 2 is not α-effective for $\{(w, w), (b, b)\}$. Hence, 1 has a strategy $\mu^1 \in \Sigma^1$ such that $g(\mu^1, \sigma_0^2) \in \{(w, b), (b, w)\}$, contradicting our assumption that σ_0 is an *NE*. QED.

Remark 8 Is the game which is considered in Remark 7 a paradox? Not according to game theory. In order to solve it we have to introduce mixed strategies. In our model we have to consider lotteries over A. If this is not possible, then the society may modify the constitution in order to avoid such inconsistent behaviour (see Remark 5).

Remark 9 Let $\Gamma = \langle N; \Sigma^1, \ldots, \Sigma^n; g; A \rangle$ be a *GF* and let $R^N \in Q^N$. $\sigma^N \in \Sigma^N$ is a strong Nash equilibrium (*SNE*) of $G(\Gamma, R^N)$ if for every $S \subset N$, $S \neq \emptyset$, and for every $\mu^S \in \Sigma^S$ there exists $i \in S$ such that $g(\sigma^N)R^i g(\mu^S, \sigma^{N\setminus S})$. Γ is strongly consistent if for every $R^N \in Q^N$ $G(\Gamma, R^N)$ has an *SNE*. The following class of *EF*s have strongly consistent representations. An *EF* $E: 2^N \to\to 2^A$ is maximal if for every $S \subset N$, and for every $B \subset A$

$$B \notin E(S) \Leftrightarrow A \setminus B \in E(N \setminus S).$$

E is convex if E is superadditive and for all $S_1, S_2 \subset N$ and all $B_1 \in E(S_1)$ and $B_2 \in E(S_2)$,

$$B_1 \cup B_2 \in E(S_1 \cap S_2) \text{ or } B_1 \cap B_2 \in E(S_1 \cup S_2).$$

If E is maximal and convex and A is finite, then E has a strongly consistent representation (see Peleg (1984, Theorems 6.A.7 and 6.4.2)). Thus, a strongly consistent behaviour is possible for the class of societies which yield, according to (9.1), a maximal and convex *EF*. Finally, we remark that the result of Peleg (1984) has been generalized to infinite sets of social states by Abdou and Keiding in several papers (see, e.g., Abdou (1987) and Keiding (1986)).

Remark 10 A *GF* $\Gamma = \langle N; \Sigma^1, \ldots, \Sigma^N; g; A \rangle$ is Nash-consistent if for every $R^N \in Q^N$ $G(\Gamma, R^N)$ has an *NE*. Clearly, we are interested in the *EF*'s of Nash-consistent *GF*'s. If $|N| = 2$, then a complete characterization of Nash-consistent *GF*'s in terms of their *EF* is given by Gurvich (1989) and Abdou (1993a, b). Also, a *GF* Γ is acceptable if: (i) It is Nash consistent; and (ii) for every $R^N \in Q^N$ and for every *NE* σ of $G(\Gamma, R^N)$, the outcome $g(\sigma)$ is Pareto-optimal (w.r.t. the profile R^N). Acceptable *GF*'s are constructed and characterized in Hurwicz and Schmeidler (1978) and Dutta (1984). They may also be useful in our framework.

IMPLEMENTATION AND SEN'S LIBERAL PARADOX

_et $S = \langle N, A, \rho, \alpha, \gamma \rangle$ be a society. A social choice rule (SCR) is a func-ion $C : 2^A \times Q^N \to 2^A$ that satisfies $C(B, R^N) \subset B$ and $C(B, R^N) \neq \emptyset$ for all $B \neq \emptyset$, $B \subset A$, and $R^N \in Q^N$, and $C(\emptyset, R^N) = \emptyset$ for all $R^N \in Q^N$. _et C be an SCR, let $i \in N$, and $x, y \in A, x \neq y$. i is decisive for x over y f for all $R^N \in Q^N$, and all $B \subset A$, the following condition is satisfied: If x $P^i y$, $x \in B$, and $x \notin C(B, R^N)$, then $y \notin C(B, R^N)$ (here $xP^i y$ if $xR^i y$ and not $yR^i x$). Sen's (weakest) condition of liberalism is: (ML) there are at least two persons i and j and two ordered pairs of alternatives (x, y) and (z, w), with $x \neq z$ and $y \neq w$, and such that i is decisive for x over y and j is decisive for z over w (see Sen (1970, p. 88)).

Now we shall recall Maskin's definition of implementability (see Maskin (1977)). Again let C be an SCR and let $B \subset A$, $B \neq \emptyset$. A GF $\Gamma_B = \langle N; \Sigma_B^1, \ldots, \Sigma_B^n; g_B; A \rangle$ implements the social choice correspondence $C_B(\bullet): Q^N \to 2^A$ (defined by $C_B(R^N) = C(B, R^N)$ for all $R^N \in Q^N$), if for every $R^N \in Q^N$ the following condition is satisfied: $x \in C_B(R^N)$ iff there is an NE $\sigma \in \Sigma_B^N$ of the game $G(\Gamma_B, R^N) = \langle N; \Sigma_B^1, \ldots, \Sigma_B^n; g_B; A; R^N \rangle$ such that $g_B(\sigma) = x$. C is implementable if for every $B \subset A$, $B \neq \emptyset$, there exists a GF Γ_B that implements $C_B(\bullet)$.

Also, we recall that an SCR C satisfies unanimity if for every $B \subset A$, $B \neq \emptyset$, $x \in B$, and $R^N \in Q^N$ such that $xP^i y$ for all $y \in B \setminus \{x\}$ and $i \in N$, $C(B, R^N) = \{x\}$. Now we may formulate the following result.

Theorem 2 If an SCR C satisfies ML and unanimity, then it is not imple-mentable.

Proof Assume, on the contrary, that C is implementable. Let $B_0 = \{x, y\} \cup \{z, w\}$ where (x, y) and (z, w) satisfy (ML). Then the social choice correspondence $C_{B_0}(\bullet)$ satisfies unanimity and it is implementable. Hence, by Masking (1977), $C_{B_0}(\bullet)$ is strongly monotonic (see also Defini-tion 2.3.15, Lemma 2.3.25, and Lemma 6.5.1 of Peleg (1984)). Now, it fol-lows from Lemma 3.2.12 of Peleg (1984) that $C_{B_0}(\bullet)$ satisfies the Pareto criterion. Therefore, by Sen (1970, Theorem 6*3), we have obtained the desired contradiction. QED.

Remark 11 The reader may easily construct SCRs that satisfy both unanimity and ML.

Remark 12 In Arrow (1967) constitutions are defined as social welfare functions. (A social welfare function is a function $F: Q^N \to Q$.) However, it seems to us that this approach might face some difficulties. The reader is referred to Gardenfors (1981) for criticism of Sen's definition of liberal-ism. Sen's model is based on the foregoing definition of Arrow.

DISCUSSION

The connection with Gardenfors's model

Let N be a society and A a set of social states. A right, according to Gardenfors (1981), is the possibility of a group S, $S \subset N$, to restrict the choice of a social state to a subset B of A. His main concept is the rights system, which is a subset of $2^N \times 2^A$; that is, a rights system is a set of pairs (S, B), $S \in 2^N$ and $B \in 2^A$ essentially, an EF (see above). Therefore, Gardenfors's starting point is our Definition 9.1. Because our analysis has been based mainly on (9.1), we see that our model is similar to that of Gardenfors. However, there are some important differences.

1 Unlike Gardenfors, we do not distinguish between rights and obligations. Now, in a constitution rights are usually supported by obligations (e.g., to maintain property rights we should forbid stealing). Hence, our model is more general.
2 We explicitly model the set of rights and the assignment of rights to groups of members of society. This may enable (future) analysis of the dynamics of systems of rights (see Remark 5).
3 Our notion of representation of an EF (see Definition 5) allows us to immediately apply quite a few results on strategic games to our model. In Gardenfors (1981) the connection between a rights system and the associated strategic games is much more complicated; in particular, the preferences of the players must be extended to 2^A.

Relationships with other works on game forms

In a series of recent papers rights are (formally) modelled via use of game forms (see, e.g., Deb (1994), Gaertner, Pattanaik and Suzumura (1992), and Hammond (1994)). As far as we could check, only Hammond (1994) contains a formal definition of systems of rights in terms of sets of alternatives. Therefore, all the works on game forms (except Hammond's) are not directly comparable with our work. Briefly, the main difference is as follows. We, essentially, endorse Gardenfors's definition of rights (because most of our work is based on the EF given by (9.1)). Other authors consider the mere availability of strategies in a GF to be equivalent to the existence of rights (see, e.g., Deb, Pattanaik and Razzolini (1993, p. 7)). We do not wish at this point to enter a debate on which approach is more suitable. Hence we only point out the main difference.

Hammond's model is different from our model in two respects: (a) his definition of rights profile which describes the distribution of rights among coalitions (i.e., groups of members of the society), is not an effectivity function; and (b) as a result of (a), Hammond lacks the notion of 'representation' of a rights system by a game form. Therefore, his analysis of coherent rights does not seem to be directly linked to known existence results for strategic equilibrium (see our results above).

Our main contribution to the literature on modelling rights via game forms is as follows. First, we generalize Gardenfors's work and reformulate his definition of rights system by means of effectivity functions. Secondly, by introducing representations of effectivity functions we are able to obtain a rich (formal) theory of rights exercising in a society. The use of representations also considerably limits the set of game forms that are consistent with a given constitution.

Minimal liberalism

Let $S = \langle N, A, \rho, \alpha, \gamma \rangle$ be a society and let the EF E be given by (9.1). The constitution $\langle \rho, \alpha, \gamma \rangle$ satisfies minimal liberalism if there exist $i, j \in N, i \neq j$, and $B_i, B_j \in 2^A \setminus \{A\}$ such that $B_i \in E(i)$ and $B_j \in E(j)$. This definition is related to Definition 2.3 of Deb, Pattanaik and Razzolini (1993) in the following (straightforward) way. Let $\Gamma = \langle N; \Sigma^1, \ldots, \Sigma^n; g; A \rangle$ be a GF, let $i \in N$, and let $a \in A$. i vetoes a if there exists $\sigma_0^i \in \Sigma^i$ such that for all $\sigma^{N\setminus\{i\}} \in \Sigma^{N\setminus\{i\}} g(\sigma_0^i, \sigma^{N\setminus\{i\}}) \neq a$. Denote by $V(i)$ the set of all the alternatives that are vetoed by i. Γ satisfies minimal liberalism if there exist $i, j \in N$, $i \neq j$, such that $V(k) \neq \emptyset$, $k = i, j$ (see Definition 2.3 of Deb, Pattanaik and Razzolini (1993)).

The following claim is true.

Claim 1 E satisfies minimal liberalism iff every representation of E (see Definition 5) satisfies minimal liberalism.

The proof of Claim 1 is left to the reader. For an analysis of the relationship between strategic equilbirium, liberalism, and Pareto-optimality the reader is referred to the beautiful paper by Deb, Pattanaik and Razzolini (1993). The following (weak) Liberal Paradox for game forms is a corollary of their Proposition 4.2.

Corollary 1 Let $\Gamma = \langle N; \Sigma^1, \ldots, \Sigma^n; g; A \rangle$ be a GF, let $i, j \in N, i \neq j$, and let $V(i) \cap V(j) \neq \emptyset$. Then there exists $R^N \in Q^N$ such that the game $G(\Gamma, R^N)$ has a Nash equilibrium whose outcome is Pareto dominated.

CONCLUSION

Our work generalizes the model of Gardenfors in three respects:

1 By explicitly introducing the set of rights and the assignment of rights we allow time-dependent constitutions that may change as a result of the legislative process.

129

2 We do not distinguish between rights and obligations to society. Hence our definition of constitution is similar to the ordinary concept.

3 By introducing the notion of representation of a rights system we can easily apply results on strategic games to our model. In particular, we do not have to extend the preferences of the players.

Our contribution to the literature on the analysis of rights by means of game forms consists of two parts:

1 the concise description of each constitution by means of an effectivity function; and

2 the use of representations of effectivity functions by game forms in order to model simultaneous exercising of rights by all members of a society. The use of representations (by *GFs*) allows the theory of strategic equilibrium to be applied to constitutions.

APPENDIX: REPRESENTATIONS OF EFFECTIVITY FUNCTIONS

We now shall prove a generalization of Theorem 1. Let $N = \{1, \ldots, n\}$, $n \geq 2$, be a set of players and let A be a set of alternatives. A may be finite or infinite. However, $|A| \geq 2$ if A is finite. Let $B \subset 2^A$ such that $A \in B$. (Such a set B is called a structure on A). An *EF* $E : 2^N \twoheadrightarrow 2^A$ is compatible with B if $E(S) \subset B \setminus \{\emptyset\}$ for all $S \in 2^N$; $E(\emptyset) = A$; $A \in E(S)$ for all $S \in 2^N$; and $E(N) = B \setminus \{\emptyset\}$. B is closed under finite intersections (*CFI*) if $B_1, \ldots, B_k \in B$ imply that $\bigcap_{i=1}^{k} B_i \in B$. If (A, B) is a measurable space or a topological space, then B is closed under finite intersections. Now let $B \subset 2^A$ satisfy $A \in B$ and *CFI*.

Theorem 1* Let $E : 2^N \twoheadrightarrow 2^A$ be an *EF* that is compatible with B. The following two conditions are equivalent:

E is superadditive and monotonic w.r.t. the alternatives

(i.e. $S \in 2^N, B \in E(S), C \in B$, and $C \supset B$ imply that $C \in E(S)$). (9.7)

There exists a *GF* $\Gamma = \langle N; \Sigma^1, \ldots, \Sigma^n; g; A \rangle$ such that

$$E_\alpha(S; \Gamma) \cap B = E(S) \text{ for all } S \in 2^N. \tag{9.8}$$

Proof (9.8) $\Rightarrow$ (9.7) To prove monotonicity w.r.t. the alternatives let $S \in 2^N$, $B \in E(S)$, $C \supset B$ and $C \in B$. Then $B \in E_\alpha(\Gamma; S)$. Hence $C \in E_\alpha(\Gamma; S)$. Thus $C \in E_\alpha(\Gamma; S) \cap B = E(S)$. Now let $S_i \in 2^N i = 1, 2$, $S_1 \cap S_2 = \emptyset$, and $B_i \in E(S_i)$, $i = 1, 2$. Then $B_1 \cap B_2 \in B$ by *CFI* and, also, $B_1 \cap B_2 \in E_\alpha(\Gamma; S_1 \cup S_2)$. Therefore $B_1 \cap B_2 \in E(S_1 \cup S_2)$. Thus E is superadditive.

$(9.7) \Rightarrow (9.8)$. For $i \in N$ let

$$F^i = \{(S, B)|i \in S \subset N \text{ and } B \in E(S)\}.$$

Further let $B^* = B \setminus \{\emptyset\}$ and

$$\Phi = \{\varphi: B^* \to A|\varphi(B) \in B \text{ for all } B \in B^*\}.$$

Now we define Γ in the following way. $\Sigma^i = F^i \times N \times \Phi$ for all $i \in N$. Let $\sigma^N = (f^i, t^i, \varphi^i)_{i \in N}$. A coalition $S \subset N$, $S \neq \emptyset$, is σ^N-consistent if there is $B \in E(S)$ such that $f^i = (S, B)$ for all $i \in S$. Denote by $S_1(\sigma^N) = S_1, \ldots, S_r(\sigma^N) = S_r$ the coalitions which are σ^N-consistent. Further, denote $S_0 = N \setminus \bigcup_{j=1}^{r} S_j$. Then $P(\sigma^N) = (S_0, S_1, \ldots, S_r)$ is a partition of N. Now let $i_0 \equiv \sum_{i=1}^{n} t^i(n)$, and $f^i = (S_j, B_j)$ for $i \in S_j, j = 1, \ldots, r$. So we may define

$$g(\sigma^N) = \varphi^{i_0}\left(\bigcap_{j=1}^{r} B_j\right).$$

Because E is superadditive $\bigcap_{j=1}^{r} B_j \in E\left(\bigcup_{j=1}^{r} S_j\right)$, and therefore $\bigcap_{j=1}^{r} B_j \neq \emptyset$ and g is well defined. (If $j = 0$, i.e., there are no σ^N-consistent coalitions, then, by definition, $g(\sigma^N) = \varphi^{i_0}(A)$.) Denote $\Gamma = \langle N; \Sigma^1, \ldots, \Sigma^n; g; A \rangle$.

It is obvious that for each $S \subset N$ $E_\alpha(\Gamma, S) \cap B \supset E(S)$. To prove the converse inclusion, let $S \subset N$, $S \neq \emptyset$, and let $C \in B$, $C \neq \emptyset$ and $C \notin E(S)$. Then $N \neq S$ and for every $B \in E(S)$, $B \setminus C \neq \emptyset$ (because E is monotonic w.r.t. the alternatives). Now let $\sigma^S = (f^i, t^i, \varphi^i)_{i \in S}$ be a member of Σ^S. Consider the following strategy $\sigma_0^{N \setminus S}$ of $N \setminus S$. $f_0^i = (N \setminus S, A)$ for all $i \in N \setminus S$. Let $j_0 \in N \setminus S$. Then we choose $t^i = 1$ for $i \in N \setminus S$, $j_0 \neq i$, and we choose t^{j_0} such that $t^{j_0} + \sum_{i \neq j_0} t^i \equiv j_0(n)$. Let $P(\sigma^S, \sigma_0^{N \setminus S}) = (S_0, N \setminus S, S_1, \ldots, S_r)$. Then $S_j \subset S, j = 1, \ldots, r$. For $i \in S_j$ left $f^i = (S_j, B_j)$, $j = 1, \ldots, r$. Then, by the super-additivity of E, $B = \bigcap_{j=1}^{r} B_j \in E(S)$. Hence $B \setminus C \neq \emptyset$ and j_0 can choose $\varphi^{j_0} \in \Phi$ such that $\varphi^{j_0}(B) \notin C$. Thus $g(\sigma^S, \sigma_0^{N \setminus S}) \notin C$. QED.

ACKNOWLEDGEMENTS

I am grateful to R. Deb, P.J. Hammond, P.K. Pattanaik, and A.K. Sen for several helpful conversations. I am also indebted to K. Basu for an important remark. I would like to thank the Center for Analytic Economics at Cornell University.

REFERENCES

Abdou, J. (1987), 'Stable Effectivity Functions with an Infinity of Players and Alternatives,' *Journal of Mathematical Economics*, 16, 291–295.

Abdou, J. (1993a), 'Nash and Strongly Consistent Two-Player Game Forms,' mimeo.

Abdou, J. (1993b), 'Solvability of Two-Player Game Forms with Infinite Sets of Strategies,' to appear in *Mathematics of Operations Research*.

Arrow, K.J. (1967), 'Values and Collective Decision-Making,' in *Philosophy, Politics, and Society, Third Series*, P. Laslett and W.G. Runciman (eds), Basil Blackwell, Oxford, 215–232.

Deb, R. (1994), 'Waiver, Effectivity and Rights as Game Forms,' *Economica*, 61, 167–178.

Deb, R., Pattanaik, P.K. and Razzolini, L. (1993), 'Game Forms, Rights, and the Efficiency of Social Outcomes,' mimeo.

Dutta, B. (1984), 'Effectivity Functions and Acceptable Game Forms,' *Econometrica*, 52, 1151–1166.

Gaertner, W. (1993), 'Rights and Games Forms, Types of Preference Orderings, and Pareto Inefficiency,' in W.E. Diewert, K. Sparemann, and F. Stehling (eds), *Mathematical Modelling in Economics*, Essays in Honor of Wolfgang Eichhorn, Springer-Verlag, Berlin, 177–187.

Gaertner, W., Pattanaik, P.K. and Suzumura, K. (1992), 'Individual Rights Revisited,' *Economica*, 59, 161–177.

Gardenfors, P. (1981), 'Rights, Games, and Social Choice,' *Noûs*, 15, 341–356.

Gibbard, A. (1974), 'A Pareto-Consistent Libertarian Claim,' *Journal of Economic Theory*, 7, 388–410.

Gurvich, V.A. (1989), 'Equilibrium in Pure Strategies,' *Soviet Math. Dokl.*, 38, 597–602.

Hammond, P.J. (1994), 'Games Forms versus Social Choice Rules as Models of Rights,' Department of Economics, Stanford University, mimeo.

Hurwicz, L. and Schmeidler, D. (1978), 'Construction of Outcome Functions Guaranteeing Existence and Pareto-Optimality of Nash Equilibria,' *Econometrica*, 46, 1447–1474.

Kanger, S. and Kanger, H. (1972), 'Rights and Parliamentarism,' in *Contemporary Philosophy in Scandinavia*, R.E. Olson and A.M. Paul (eds), The Johns Hopkins Press, Baltimore, 213–236.

Keiding, H. (1986), 'Stability of Effectivity Functions with an Infinite Set of Alternatives,' *Methods of Operations Research*, 50, 519–530.

Maskin, E. (1977), 'Nash Equilibrium and Welfare Optimality,' mimeo.

Moulin, H. (1983), *The Strategy of Social Choice*, North-Holland, Amsterdam.

Peleg, B. (1984), *Game Theoretic Analysis of Voting in Committees*, Cambridge University Press, Cambridge.

Puppe, C. (1994), 'Freedom of Choice and Rational Decisions,' mimeo.

Sen, A.K. (1970), *Collective Choice and Social Welfare*, Holden Day, San Francisco.

Sen, A.K. (1994), 'Individual Preference as the Basis of Social Choice,' mimeo.

10

RIGHTS AND POWERS
Reflections on Bezalel Peleg's theory of
effectivity functions, game forms,
games and rights

Emmanuel Picavet

Rights and liberties are part of the basic structure of society, and should
figure prominently in any ethical study of the desirable properties of
social arrangements. This is one of the lessons to be drawn from some of
the significant contributions to moral philosophy in recent times, as evi-
denced by the emphasis on personal autonomy in John Rawls's *A Theory
of Justice* and in Stanley Benn's *A Theory of Freedom*, and by Serge-
Christophe Kolm's normative discussion of property rights in *Le Contrat
social libéral*. Moreover, rights, liberties and obligations have an intimate
connection with the distribution of power in society.

Their properties can be appraised in the light of substantial moral or
religious values or criteria, and this is not always incompatible with a
reasonable, restricted assumption of pluralism. For example, in Thomas
Pogge's description of a conceivable new world order, in which mutual
obligations and national rights would involve certain morally accepted
and permanently protected 'value clusters', the shared institutional
scheme is 'based not upon a fickle power equilibrium but upon a firm
core of values'[1]. But sometimes it is sufficient to offer a purely political
normative evaluation of the prevailing system of rights and obligations,
and this may appear desirable indeed when we attempt to uphold by
rational argument a given system of rights and obligations, in a society
where peaceful life under common rules is possible, although there is no
agreement on ultimate moral or spiritual values. This is clearly brought
out in Attracta Ingram's description of the political foundations of any
modern democratic regime:

> citizens of such a regime have different, sometimes incommensurable,
> moral, religious, and philosophical views and associated modes of
> justification. Lacking agreement on such matters, citizens can share
> a scheme of rights only if they are prepared to forgo the conflicting

deliverances of their independent moralities in favour of a scheme they all agree.[2]

A political argument, then, may focus on such key notions as the rule o. law (as opposed to discretionary powers conferred upon particular bodie: or individuals), institutional stability, economic efficiency, internationa: prestige, alleviation of social unrest. Equally relevant is the ability of the normative system to solve interpersonal (or inter-community) conflicts with little or no active interpersonal coercion.[3] The argument may also focus on the ability of fundamental (human) rights to place constraints on the system of (legal) rights and obligations in a way which warrants that the law will perform its function of solving a number of important interpersonal conflicts, the guarantee being sold at not too high a cost (i.e. without unnecessary encroachments on the Legislator's ability to leave acts or attitudes unconstrained by the law).[4]

The analysis of power, coercion and the structure of action is thus central to the political understanding of rights. It should allow us to make sense of the particular ethical conceptions of a 'good' or 'just' scheme of rights in an uncompromising pluralistic spirit, and appreciate their respective merits from a political point of view. For example, the libertarian defence of traditional, so-called 'negative' fundamental rights may be understood as illustrating a political thesis concerning the structure of power: (i) the distribution of power should be decentralized rather than centralized, unless there are compelling reasons for the reverse, and (ii) although there might exist good reasons for some delegation or renunciation of power on the part of the individuals, it is illegitimate to deprive them of the faculty of exercising the powers associated with the right not to be interfered with in certain pursuits of life at least (as required by the seemingly weak condition of 'liberalism' which is responsible for the Paretian Liberal paradox).[5] Some interesting questions can be raised concerning the application of such principles: which sets of individual rights is it possible to grant, if their simultaneous exercise must always be possible? Given a certain set of individual rights, how acceptable are the constraints the individuals place on one another's lives through the exercise of these rights? Is it possible to assume that such constraints will be respected as a result of the existing interests of the individuals (hence the connection with game theory)? Such questions can play an important part in the search for politically desirable properties of systems of rights and obligations, and the acceptance of a rights-based, libertarian moral theory is clearly not a prerequisite.

The systematic analysis of the connections between rights, the exercising of rights, and the distribution of power in society may thus prove essential to both the justification of rights and the engineering of normative systems. These are some of the reasons one may give to explain and justify

Bezalel Peleg's line of inquiry, which exemplifies the promising game-form theoretic research programme in the philosophy of law, in sharp contrast with both the traditional social-choice format (which provided the background for Amartya Sen's discovery of the Paretian Liberal dilemma) and the extreme libertarian view which presupposes that the normative political analysis of interpersonal systems of norms should proceed entirely from the philosopher's intuitive grasp of the so-called 'native rights' or 'birthright' of man, i.e. from the nature of individuals (normally including their moral or religious destiny and their ability to enjoy freedom).[6]

Peleg's analysis is based on an original concept of 'constitution': a constitution consists of a set of rights, an assignment of rights to groups of individuals, and a specification of each coalition's set of attainable sets of outcomes. This differs from the Arrovian social welfare function or 'constitution', and also from the Kelsenian legal theorist's notion of a system of norms with implications for lawmaking (and, more generally, for the creation of new legal norms). Peleg's notion is more akin to the political philosopher's concept of 'constitution' in the sense of the basic features of the distribution of power in a given state.[7]

Like other recent contributions to the theory of law, beginning with Peter Gärdenfors's [1981] and Robert Sugden's [1985] seminal articles, Peleg's work focuses on the praxeological properties of the simultaneous exercising of rights.[8] In addition to the standard view that the Arrow [1951], Gibbard [1974] and Sen [1970] paradoxes should be disposed of in order to restore the intelligibility of the institutions of contemporary, democratic political structure (in which 'rights' and 'human rights' figure prominently), one of the arguments which can be adduced to uphold this research programme is that some of the desirable features of systems of rights and obligations can be thought of as properties of the sets of joint strategies that enable the individuals to exercise those rights and obligations, or else, as properties of the behavioural legal constraints which are necessary to ensure the possibility (or the probability) of the simultaneous exercising of the rights and obligations.[9]

Peleg's analysis might be interpreted as a retreat from the social choice programme of a universal framework for social, political and economic evaluation based on the study of the way in which individual preferences are taken into account. A. Sen [1991] has forcefully defended the view that individual preferences are crucial to the proper understanding of the importance of freedom, and this is also the lesson to be drawn from Bertrand Saint-Sernin's subtle analysis of the relevance of ends and goals (and their connection with personal powers) for individual freedom.[10] In his [1992], A. Sen further argues that one of the merits of the social choice format is its interpretative versatility. Social choice theory is able to go beyond the logic of choice, as it creates room for the normative study of the relationship between acts, outcomes and desire fulfilment (or individual hapiness). Liberty should not be seen as a choice problem only. Other thinkers, however, take a wholly different picture of the situation. They consider that the normative theory of law has mainly to do with external conduct, the objective geometry of personal agency and interpersonal external constraint, and the very idea of life under the rule of law.[11] Following this path, it is certainly worthwhile to elucidate the problems of simultaneous action, as in Peleg's article.

But Peleg's framework does not oblige us to ignore the fact that some substantial ethical requirements are commonly called 'rights'. On the contrary, his framework can accommodate for two levels of rights: rights as contraints on behaviour (as embodied in the sets of available individual strategies in the game form), and rights as distributed through the alpha function. This is clearly a great advantage, since it allows us to deal specifically with higher-level rights (such as moral rights or human rights) which provide criteria for evaluating what the legal system of rights and obligations says concerning legal or illegal conduct. In particular, we can examine higher-level rights which have no obvious translation in the language of restrictions on available individual strategies, such as the right to work, the right to housing or the right to a healthy environment. Then we can examine the existence of a legal game form which permits the simultaneous exercising of the higher-level rights.

Peleg's framework makes it necessary to give a precise content to the 'exercising' of rights, and hence to rights themselves. The 'right to work', for instance, is reinterpreted as meaning that the citizen can choose a type of activity, and that this choice (together with natural events and the actions of other people) results in certain possible outcomes, including the fact of being unemployed and earning a certain minimal income. But it must be emphasized that this model is a constructive definition of a certain 'right to work'. It is actually an acceptable model of the choice element in the functioning of the job market. But this is quite remote from the usual concepts of the right to work as either (i) the availability of a 'normative resource' (in S. Benn's phrase) that allows any conflict between myself and someone who would like to prevent me from working to be adjudicated in my favour, or (ii) the certainty that the social process will result in the fact that I work if I so decide.

Thus, unlike the usual social-choice formulations of rights, which would favour the second interpretation, Peleg's modelling incorporates none of the requirements which are able to give to the vocabulary of rights its normative appeal. It leaves room for various conceptions of rights, but it favours none. Hence it cannot be understood as the study of the 'contents' and 'rationale' of a substantial ethical conception of rights, which according to A. Sen [1992] would be the desirable direction for future game-form theoretic analyses of rights. What it does make possible is to

136

compare the implications and the merits of various systems of rights on the basis of the properties of their simultaneous exercise.

NOTES

1 T. Pogge [1989], ch. 5 (p. 231).
2 A. Ingram [1994], ch. 9 (p.195).
3 This argument plays an important role in the libertarian thesis according to which property rights should be viewed as a model or foundation for rights and obligations generally speaking. This has been emphasized by Bertrand Lemennicier [1995].
4 The 'purely political argument' in favour of human rights in my [1996] follows from the last suggestion.
5 A.K. Sen [1970].
6 For a critical discussion of the contrast between game forms and social choice in the study of rights, see A.K. Sen [1992].
7 This notion of 'constitution' as a basic, unwritten scheme of powers has had a long history in legal and political philosophy. See Paulette Carrive [1994].
8 On the history of this theoretical trend, see W. Gaertner, P. Pattanaik and K. Suzumura [1992]. Note that B. Peleg's formal framework allows us to study rights and obligations in a unified manner.
9 Such properties include, for instance, the absence of arbitrary or useless restrictions on the set of strategies the law-abiding agents can choose, and the efficiency or welfare consequences of the legal joint strategies.
10 See B. Saint-Sernin [1994], ch. VII ('La liberté comme pouvoir').
11 This is well documented in Simone Goyard-Fabre's [1996] study of the principles of Kant's legal philosophy (particularly pp. 35–38). Needless to say, external constaint is not an end in itself, and one should not overlook the moral and political dimension of Kantian legal theory. See Alexis Philonenko [1988] and Thomas Pogge [1988].

REFERENCES

Arrow, K.J., 1951, Social Choice and Individual Values, New York, Wiley.
Benn, S.I., 1988, A Theory of Freedom, Cambridge, Cambridge University Press.
Carrive, P., 1994, La Pensée politique anglaise de Hooker à Hume, Paris, Presses Universitaires de France.
Gaertner, W., Pattanaik, P. and K. Suzumura, 1992, 'Individual Rights Revisited', Economica, 59, 161–178.
Gärdenfors, P., 1981, 'Rights, Games and Social Choice', Noûs, 15, 341–356.
Gibbard, A., 1974, 'A Pareto-Consistent Libertarian Claim', Journal of Economic Theory, 7, 338–410.
Goyard-Fabre, S., 1996, La Philosophie du droit de Kant, Paris, Vrin.
Ingram, A., 1994, A Political Theory of Rights, Oxford, Clarendon Press.
Kolm, S.-C., 1985, Le Contrat social libéral, Paris, Presses Universitaires de France.
Lemennicier, B., 1995, 'A Property Right Approach to Morality and Liberty', mimeo., Université Paris II.
Philonenko, A., 1988, Théorie et praxis dans la philosophie morale et politique de Kant et de Fichte en 1793, 3rd edn, Paris, Vrin (1st edn 1968).
Picavet, E., 1996, 'Sur la justification des droits de l'homme', Archives de philosophie, 59, 249–271.

PICAVET

Pogge, T., 1988, 'Kant's Theory of Justice', *Kant-Studien*, 79, 407–433.
—— 1989, *Realizing Rawls*, Ithaca and London, Cornell University Press.
Rawls, J., 1971, *A Theory of Justice*, Cambridge, Massachusetts, Harvard University Press.
Saint-Sernin, B., 1994, *Parcours de l'ombre. Les trois indécidables*, Brussels, Paris and Basel, Editions des archives contemporaines.
Sen, A.K., 1970, 'The Impossibility of a Paretian Liberal', *Journal of Political Economy*, 72, 152–157.
—— 1991, 'Welfare, Preference and Freedom', *Journal of Econometrics*, 50, 15–29.
—— 1992, 'Minimal Liberty', *Economica*, 59, 139–159.
Sugden, R., 1985, 'Liberty, Preference and Choice', *Economics and Philosophy*, 1, 213–229.

138

11

RIGHTS, FREE EXCHANGE AND WIDESPREAD EXTERNALITIES

Peter J. Hammond

ABSTRACT

Sen's libertarian paradox is ascribed to the inevitable conflict between the Pareto criterion and individuals' rights to create negative externalities. Finite coalitions can effect exchanges of rights through Coaseian bargains in order to resolve inefficiencies due to local externalities. With a continuum of agents, however, finite coalitions are powerless to affect widespread externalities, except those that are regulated by policies such as inefficiently allocated quotas. Then finite coalitions may gain by exchanging such quotas, but Pareto improvements may require originally unused quotas to be confiscated. Thus, the voluntary exchange of rights may exacerbate widespread externalities.

RIGHTS, EXCHANGE AND EXTERNALITIES

Again, if he would give us Nuts for a piece of Metal, pleased with its colour; or exchanged his Sheep for Shells, or Wool for a sparkling Pebble or a Diamond, and keep those by him all his Life, he invaded not the Right of others, he might heap up as much of these durable things as he pleased; the *exceeding of the bounds of his* just *Property* not lying in the largeness of his Possession, but the perishing of any thing uselessly in it.

(John Locke *Second Treatise of Government* (1689/90), Section 46)

If an exchange of property rights can be made to mutual benefit, why forbid it? The answer is, to induce a pattern of exchanges that is better on the whole.

(Gibbard, 1985, p. 25)

INTRODUCTION

Most economists do not explicitly consider rights at all, except perhaps property rights. Accordingly, they are unable to justify free exchange except by noting the efficiency gains to which it may or may not give rise.

Yet to the lay person, the right to exchange might seem to be one of the most important economic freedoms, well worth the attention of economists – perhaps even of modern economic theorists. Of course, there are a few exceptions to this general neglect, especially the discussion of economic freedoms by Rowley and Peacock (1975, pp. 87–90) and by Peacock (1987). Also relevant are parts of the chapter by Cowan and Rizzo (1995).

Above all, one should not forget the many economists of the 'Austrian' school, who have certainly emphasized the importance, in their view, of doing as little as possible to interfere in a *laissez faire* economy of complete freedom to exchange. Indeed, Cordato (1992) tries to rescue this Austrian approach from its apparent inability to discuss externalities, public goods, or most other issues of public policy by using a notion of 'catallactic efficiency'. This follows 'the distinction that [von] Mises (1949, 1966) and Hayek (1976) have drawn between "economy" and "catallaxy"' (Cordato, 1992, p. 11).[1]

Apart from a few surviving 'Austrians', most recent writers on free exchange as a right have been philosophers or lawyers. Among these, the most noteworthy would seem to be Nozick (1974) as a proponent and Gibbard (1985) as an opponent. Nozick explicitly includes voluntary exchange among those activities justified by his 'principle of justice in transfer'. Previously, similar rights were included in Honoré's (1961) discussion of ownership. Gibbard is careful to distinguish between 'intuitionistic' and 'pragmatic' defences of free exchange, citing Nozick as the main reference for the former. On the other hand, a prominent pragmatic defence is that free exchange leads to Pareto efficient outcomes in the absence of externalities. Later, Gauthier (1986, p. 13 and ch. IV) goes so far as to declare that the perfectly competitive market is a 'morally free zone'. However, it is not entirely clear whether Gauthier wishes to invoke a pragmatic or an intuitionistic defence of free exchange. For recent insightful criticism of the claims by Nozick and others, see Hausman (1992). Also very relevant are the discussions by Satz (1992, 1995) of two particular kinds of transaction that many regard as morally reprehensible – indeed, so reprehensible that many intuitionists might want to prohibit them.

The well-known opposing Marxist view is that what many defenders of capitalism regard as free exchange often gives rise to unacceptable exploitation in practice. For a logically coherent discussion of exploitation, using modern economic terminology, see Roemer (1988) and also Arnold (1990).

On the other hand, there is also an extensive literature on libertarian social choice. In fact, the example of *Lady Chatterley's Lover* which drives Sen's (1970a, b) classic libertarian paradox illustrates how Pareto inefficiency arises from giving individuals the right to create externalities – as has been suggested, at least implicitly, by Hillinger and Lapham (1971) or Fine (1975). One example of this important conflict between rights and externalities is driving private cars, especially on congested roads. Other examples that are more remote from economics include the abuse of religious freedom by those who preach intolerance, or the abuse of freedom of speech by those who disseminate hate.

Yet social choice theory has largely treated rights as inalienable. In particular, there can be no right to exchange rights. Thus, a social choice rule respects rights if and only if it always gives the owner of each right absolute power to decide the corresponding issue. In a game form representation of rights, individuals enjoy unconditional rights to choose whatever strategies they want from a specified set. Of course, the early contribution by Gibbard (1974) on waiving rights was a significant departure. Important later elaborations of this idea are due to Suzumura (1983), Deb (1994) and others. Nevertheless, the possibility that there are conditions under which individuals might benefit from forgoing their rights voluntarily has not received much attention, especially in recent work.

As already pointed out, standard welfare economics suggests that individuals may gain from exchange. In the most obvious case, such exchanges are of property rights. Indeed, property rights are often best exercised by selling some property in exchange for other property of equal market value which is more desired. Advantageous exchanges, however, might well involve forgoing rights other than property rights – in particular, rights to create externalities. Furthermore, individuals may well be able to gain from trading their rights of any kind in exchange for money – i.e., quantities of a *numéraire* commodity – or more generally, for ordinary economic commodity bundles.

Of course, there are many rights, especially property rights, whose use or exchange does not create any externalities. If such rights were to be distributed equitably, it would be hard to justify the denial of any rights that fail to create externalities. After all, such rights do not conflict with the Pareto criterion. In fact, as shown by Coughlin (1986) and Hammond (1995b), when preferences are 'privately oriented', Pareto efficiency actually requires all individual rights to be exercised in full. In this sense, rights like property rights which create no externalities pose no ethical challenge except the important one of arranging their equitable distribution. Since this paper is about potential Pareto improvements from exchanging general rights, and especially about how these differ from the usual potential Pareto improvements from exchange, it naturally focuses on the rights to create externalities.

It is well known that externalities generally give rise to Pareto inefficient equilibrium allocations. Actually, for some economists, this is virtually the definition of externality. Not surprisingly, therefore, full Pareto efficiency requires making the rights to create negative externalities suitably scarce, and allocating these rights appropriately. Then it is natural to ask whether

141

free exchange of the rights to create externalities has the useful role to play that economists expect of free exchange of property rights. In fact, as argued below in connection with Sen's original example, there can indeed be gains from exchanging rights even in the face of negative externalities. After all, such exchanges are little more than an instance of that kind of Coaseian bargaining whose outcome is, by definition, a Pareto efficient allocation. Furthermore, a standard remedy for externalities is to create new property rights ensuring appropriate control of the activities causing externalities, as a way of internalizing them. For this property rights remedy to work, in the sense of yielding a Pareto efficient allocation, the rights must typically be freely exchangeable. Otherwise a Pareto improving redistribution of rights may be possible. For example, it is commonly claimed that many externalities could be resolved, and the overall allocation of resources made Pareto efficient, by allowing free trade in pollution permits or licences to create other kinds of externality.[2]

Another often suggested remedy for the inefficiencies that arise because of externalities is to allow unrestricted bargaining between those who create and those who experience each externality. Following ideas emanating from the work of Coase, it is then usually assumed that such bargaining will continue until no further Pareto improvements are possible because a Pareto efficient set of arrangements has been reached. This second remedy is clearly closely related to the first: property rights can be the subject of a bargain, and the outcome of any bargaining process is likely to be affected by pre-existing property rights.

The unrestricted bargaining remedy can be expected to work well in economies with not too many agents. Markets, however, typically require many participants in order to remove any monopoly power that might impede Pareto efficiency. This paper treats the case when there are many agents, so that markets can be expected to function reasonably well. It also allows only coalitions of bounded size to form and rearrange the externality-creating activities of their members.

The paper discusses what finite coalitions can achieve in continuum economies of the kind considered in the important work of Aumann (1964, 1966) and Hildenbrand (1974). In such economies, any finite coalition is of measure zero – i.e., a null set. The bulk of the paper then concentrates upon the special case of widespread externalities, defined as those that remain unaffected if any agents in a null set change their respective externality creating activities. Such externalities have been considered by Kaneko and Wooders (1986, 1989), Hammond, Kaneko and Wooders (1989), and also Hammond (1995a, c). They have the special feature that, if any merely finite coalition exchanges property rights and/or the rights to create widespread externalities, this has no effect upon either equilibrium prices or the externalities. If any non-null set of agents exchanges rights, however, the result could be deleterious changes in the externalities, perhaps combined with adverse price changes, which leave everybody worse off in the end. Such a possibility seems related to Hart's (1975) well-known example of how opening a market for a new security, unless it gives rise to a complete set of markets, can produce a Pareto inferior allocation. Then the issue is whether one can arrange compensation for both price and externality changes so as to ensure that each agent is better off.

This paper, however, asks whether finite coalitions can gain by exchanging rights. To address this question, it considers initially an economy with a continuum of agents but no widespread externalities. It argues that, while exchange does confer private benefits on the members of any finite trading coalition, unrestricted exchange is like adding new markets. Then, while there are always *potential* gains from exchange, achieving *actual* Pareto gains requires compensation for those who lose from adverse relative price movements, as in the usual results on the gains from trade in international economics.

Thereafter, this paper briefly sets out a general model of a continuum economy with widespread externalities. It recapitulates the definitions of Nash– and of Pigou–Walrasian equilibria that were given in Hammond (1995a). Then it argues that such equilibria are 'ƒ-externality constrained' Pareto efficient. This means that there is no scope left for finite coalitions to gain from exchanging rights. This is true even if no attempt is made to restrict the activities which create widespread externalities. Of course, large coalitions may still be able to improve the widespread externalities.

What this paper shows, in effect, is that gains from exchanging rights between members of a finite coalition can only occur when rights to create externalities are rationed in some way, other than through a 'Pigou' price mechanism. Accordingly, it considers what happens if initially there is direct rationing through quotas that each consumer is not allowed to exceed. It then discusses how to adapt the usual gains from trade results in order to show that there are benefits to exchanging these quotas, provided that widespread externalities are not altered as a result. An important limitation is that often there are some originally unused quotas, in which case there will be a deleterious increase in the widespread externalities as a result of exchanging these quotas.

The final section of this paper summarizes the main conclusions. It also discusses some other practical obstacles that add to the cost of allowing rights to be exchanged freely.

GAINS FROM EXCHANGE IN SEN'S EXAMPLE

The well-known example which drives Sen's (1970a, b) classic libertarian paradox involves two individuals, labelled Lewd and Prude respectively, and one copy of the book *Lady Chatterley's Lover*. Recall that this novel

143

by D.H. Lawrence had been the subject of a rather sensational court case in England some years before. In order to allow gains from exchanging rights, I shall expand Sen's example to include an extra *numéraire* commodity called 'money' that can be transferred in order to compensate for giving up the right to read or not to read the novel. Unlike Sen, I shall also assume that it is feasible for both individuals to read the novel, one after the other.

Let m^L and m^P denote the non-negative amounts of money allocated to Lewd and Prude respectively. Also, for $i \in \{L, P\}$, let $r^i \in \{0, 1\}$ be an indicator variable whose value is 0 if i does not read the novel, but is 1 if i does read it. Thus, the example involves a simple two-person economy in which feasible allocations are described by combinations $(m^L, m^P, r^L, r^P) \in \Re_+^2 \times \{0, 1\} \times \{0, 1\}$.

Assume next that Lewd's and Prude's preferences can be represented by utility functions $u^L(m^L, r^L, r^P)$ and $u^P(m^P, r^L, r^P)$, and that these functions are continuous in the variables m^L and m^P respectively. Also, for all fixed non-negative values of m^L and m^P, assume that u^L and u^P satisfy the following conditions:

$$u^L(m^L, 1, 1) > u^L(m^L, 0, 1) > u^L(m^L, 1, 0) > u^L(m^L, 0, 0)$$

$$u^P(m^P, 0, 0) > u^P(m^P, 0, 1) > u^P(m^P, 1, 0) > u^P(m^L, 1, 1).$$

Note how, if only one person is going to read the novel, both individuals prefer that it should be Prude. Otherwise these are the preferences that correspond in an obvious way to each individual's label, with each individual wanting the other to make the same decision as themselves regarding whether to read the book or not.

For each individual $i \in \{L, P\}$ and pair $(r^L, r^P) \in \{0, 1\} \times \{0, 1\}$, let $e^i(r^L, r^P; u)$ denote the minimum amount of money which i needs in order to reach the feasible utility level u. Thus, $e^i(r^L, r^P; u)$ is defined implicitly by $u^i(e^i(r^L, r^P; u), r^L, r^P) = u$ when this equation has a (finite) solution; otherwise $e^i(r^L, r^P; u) = +\infty$.

Suppose that, in the absence of any exchange of rights, both individuals simply exercise their free choice to read the book or not, as they wish. Suppose too that they have fixed endowments of money equal to $\bar{m}^L$ and $\bar{m}^P$ respectively. Then the resulting allocation will be $(\bar{m}^L, \bar{m}^P, 1, 0)$, with only Lewd choosing to read the novel. Let $\bar{u}^L := u^L(\bar{m}^L, 1, 0)$ and $\bar{u}^P := u^P(\bar{m}^P, 1, 0)$ denote the resulting utility levels of the two individuals.

One way in which gains from exchanging rights will be possible is if there exists a transfer $\tau_{PL} > 0$ from Prude to Lewd with the property that

$$u^L(\bar{m}^L + \tau_{PL}, 0, 0) > \bar{u}^L \text{ and } u^P(\bar{m}^P - \tau_{PL}, 0, 0) > \bar{u}^P$$

and so

144

$$\bar{m}^P - e^P(0, 0; \bar{u}^P) > \tau_{PL} > e^L(0, 0; \bar{u}^L) - \bar{m}^L > 0.$$

n this case Lewd can renounce any right to read the novel in exchange for he transfer τ_{PL}, in which case both agents will benefit. Such an exchange s possible if and only if the compensation $e^L(0, 0; \bar{u}^L) - \bar{m}^L$ which Lewd eeds for being denied the chance to read the novel is less than the mount $\bar{m}^P - e^P(0, 0; \bar{u}^P)$ which Prude is willing to pay in order to avoid he externality that would arise if Lewd were to read the novel.

A second way in which there can be gains from exchanging rights is f there exists a transfer $\tau_{LP} > 0$ from Lewd to Prude satisfying the inequalities

$$u^L(\bar{m}^L - \tau_{LP}, 1, 1) > \bar{u}^L \text{ and } u^P(\bar{m}^P + \tau_{LP}, 1, 1) > \bar{u}^P$$

and so

$$\bar{m}^L - e^L(1, 1; \bar{u}^L) > \tau_{LP} > e^P(1, 1; \bar{u}^P) - \bar{m}^P > 0.$$

In this case Prude can agree to read the novel and then take an examination based upon it. Lewd agrees to make the transfer τ_{LP} immediately after an independent assessor certifies that Prude has passed the examination. Once again, both agents benefit. Such an exchange is possible if and only if the compensation $e^P(1, 1; \bar{u}^P) - \bar{m}^P$ which Prude needs for reading the novel and taking the examination is less than the amount $\bar{m}^L - e^L(1, 1; \bar{u}^L)$ which Lewd is willing to pay in order to ensure that Prude does read the novel.

Both the above exchanges were of rights against money. Neither exchange will benefit the two individuals simultaneously if it happens that both $e^L(0, 0; \bar{u}^L) + e^P(0, 0; \bar{u}^P)$ and $e^L(1, 1; \bar{u}^L) + e^P(1, 1; \bar{u}^P)$ exceed $\bar{m}^L + \bar{m}^P$. Then appropriate compensation is impossible because both individuals value their rights too highly relative to the externality. Even in this case, however, the fact that both $u^L(\bar{m}^L, 0, 1) > u^L(\bar{m}^L, 1, 0)$ and $u^P(\bar{m}^P, 0, 1) > u^P(\bar{m}^P, 1, 0)$ makes a direct exchange of rights possible. Lewd agrees to postpone reading the novel at least until after Prude has had the opportunity to read it, and also never to read it at all if, before a date specified in the agreement, Prude passes an examination based on its content. In this exchange, no money changes hands. Moreover, provided it can actually be arranged, such an exchange is always mutually beneficial.

In fact, as Gibbard (1974) originally propounded, it is always possible in principle for any finite set of individuals to agree which rights should be exercised and which should be waived in a way that guarantees Pareto efficiency. This is just another instance of the tautology that, if groups of individuals always find some Pareto improvement whenever at least one is available, the allocation that results in the end is bound to be Pareto efficient. Of course, many people associate this tautology, perhaps rather misleadingly, with Coase.

FINITE EXCHANGES IN A CONTINUUM ECONOMY

The rest of the paper will consider an economy with a continuum of agents, as described by Aumann (1964, 1966), and then more fully by Hildenbrand (1974). The space of agents will be (I, B, α) where I is the unit interval $[0, 1]$ of the real line, the family B of measurable sets is the Borel σ-algebra generated by the open sets, and α is Lebesgue measure defined on those sets. For later reference, recall the following standard terminology from measure theory. A measurable set of agents $I^0 \subset I$ is null whenever $\alpha(I^0) = 0$, and a statement S_i about each agent is true for almost all $i \in I$ if S_i is false for at most a null set of agents.

Assume that there is a finite set G of exchangeable private goods. In this section, suppose that G is partitioned into the set T of goods that are traded initially, complemented by the disjoint set $N = G \setminus T$ of goods that cannot be traded until after new markets have been allowed to open. For each individual $i \in I$, let $x^i = (x^i_T, x^i_N) \in \Re^G = \Re^T \times \Re^N$ denote i's net trade vector of exchangeable goods, expressed as the combination of the vector x^i_T of initially traded goods, together with the vector x^i_N of goods that cannot be traded initially.

Next, each individual $i \in I$ is assumed to have a feasible set $X^i \subset \Re^G$ of net trade vectors x^i, over which is defined a (complete and transitive) preference ordering R^i. Let P^i denote the corresponding strict preference relation. For technical reasons, assume that the two correspondences $i \longmapsto\!\!\!\!\rightarrow X^i$ and $i \longmapsto\!\!\!\!\rightarrow \text{Graph } R^i$ both have closed values for every $i \in I$ and also graphs which are measurable subsets of $I \times \Re^G$ and of $I \times \Re^G \times \Re^G$ respectively, when both these Cartesian products are given their natural product σ-algebras. Assume too that each individual's preference ordering R^i is locally non-satiated w.r.t. the set T of traded goods in the sense that, given any $x^i = (x^i_T, x^i_N) \in X^i$ and any open neighbourhood $V \subset \Re^T$ of x^i_T, there exists some $\tilde{x}^i_T \in V$ with $(\tilde{x}^i_T, x^i_N) \in X^i$ for which $(\tilde{x}^i_T, x^i_N) P^i x^i$.

In this economy, a feasible allocation $\mathbf{x}$ is a measurable mapping $\mathbf{x}: I \to \Re^G$ such that:

1 $x^i \in X^i$ for almost all $i \in I$;
2 $\int_I x^i \, d\alpha = 0$.

Suppose that initially traded goods are exchanged at a non-zero *price vector* $p_T \in \Re^T$, which each individual $i \in I$ is forced to take as given. In addition, each individual is prevented from exchanging goods in the set N, and so $x^i_N = 0$. Hence, i faces the constrained budget set.

$$B^i(p_T) := \{x^i \in X^i | x^i_N = 0; p_T x^i_T \leq 0\}.$$

146

Given this constrained budget set, say that i is in *individual equilibrium* at $\hat{x}^i \in B^i(p_T)$ provided that $p_T x_T^i > 0$ whenever $(x_T^i, 0)$ P^i $(\hat{x}_T^i, 0)$. Obviously, this is equivalent to preference maximization over the set $B^i(p_T)$. Provided that the preference relation R^i is locally non-satiated as regards traded goods in the set T, it must then be true that $p_T \hat{x}_T^i = 0$.

Also, say that i is in *individual compensated equilibrium* at $\hat{x}^i \in B^i(p_T)$ provided that $p_T x_T^i \geq 0$ whenever $(x_T^i, 0)$ R^i $(\hat{x}_T^i, 0)$. Obviously, this is equivalent to expenditure minimization over the *upper contour set* $\{x^i \in X^i \mid (x_T^i, 0) \ R^i \ (\hat{x}_T^i, 0)\}$. Once again, local non-satiation of R^i w.r.t. goods in the set T implies that $p_T \hat{x}_T^i = 0$.

A Walrasian equilibrium is then a pair $(\hat{x}, p_T)$ consisting of a feasible allocation $\hat{x}$ which satisfies $\hat{x}_N^i = 0$ for almost all $i \in I$, together with a price vector p_T, such that almost every $i \in I$ is in individual equilibrium at $\hat{x}^i$. Note that feasibility implies market clearing for all traded goods.

Similarly, a *compensated Walrasian equilibrium* is a pair $(\hat{x}, p_T)$ consisting of a feasible allocation $\hat{x}$ which satisfies $\hat{x}_N^i = 0$ for almost all $i \in I$, together with a price vector p_T, such that almost every $i \in I$ is in individual compensated equilibrium at $\hat{x}^i$.

Consider a *status quo* Walrasian equilibrium $(\bar{x}, \bar{p}_T)$ which represents what will happen if no exchanges of goods in the set N are allowed. Suppose then that finite coalitions are allowed freely to exchange goods in the set N as they wish. Any allocation $\hat{x}$ which ultimately results from such a process of free exchange must have the property that, except for a null set of exceptional agents $I^0 \subset I$, no finite coalition $C \subset I \setminus I^0$ can block by reallocating its own resources in order to reach an allocation $x^i \in X^i$ to each member $i \in C$ such that $\sum_{i \in C} x^i = 0$ and $x^i P^i \bar{x}^i$ for all $i \in C$. Hence, only finite coalitions C that include members of the negligible set I^0 remain able to gain from further exchange. This implies that the allocation $\hat{x}$ meets the requirements to be a member of the *f-core* of the economy. Arguing as in Hammond, Kaneko and Wooders (1989), or in the more general model of Hammond (1995c), there must then exist prices $(\hat{p}_T, \hat{p}_N)$ at which $\hat{x}$ is a compensated Walrasian equilibrium. Under well-known standard sufficient conditions, or some generalizations which are extensively discussed in Hammond (1993), this compensated Walrasian equilibrium will actually be a Walrasian equilibrium.

In this sense, even exchange which is limited to finite coalitions results in a new Walrasian equilibrium, with a larger set of traded goods. Nevertheless, this extended trade may not benefit all, or even almost all, individuals. Initially, each individual i's net trade vector is $(\bar{x}_T^i, 0)$, satisfying the budget constraint $\bar{p}_T \bar{x}_T^i = 0$. After free exchange, almost every individual $i \in I$ has a new net trade vector $(\hat{x}_T^i, \hat{x}_N^i)$, satisfying the new budget constraint $\hat{p}_T \hat{x}_T^i + \hat{p}_N \hat{x}_N^i = 0$. In order to use a revealed preference argument to show that, even if i has not benefited from trade, at least he is no worse off, the condition $\hat{p}_T \bar{x}_T^i \leq 0$ must be met, implying that i can afford the old net trade vector $(\bar{x}_T^i, 0)$ at the new prices $(\hat{p}_T, \hat{p}_N)$. But in fact $\hat{p}_T \bar{x}_T^i$ may well be positive, indicating that the terms of trade in the old markets have turned against i as a result of all the new exchanges of goods in the set N. Then, if $\hat{p}_T \bar{x}_T^i$ is large enough, individual i may have been made worse off.

To ensure that nobody loses from free exchange in this way, it is well known that lump-sum compensation of those who suffer from adverse relative price changes is generally required. Specifically, suppose that each individual i receives a net lump-sum transfer $m^i(p_T, p_N)$, as a function of the price vector (p_T, p_N), that is equal to $p_T \bar{x}_T^i$. Hence, each individual faces the new budget constraint $p_T x_T^i + p_N x_N^i \leq p_T \bar{x}_T^i$. Note that the transfers $m^i(p_T, p_N)$ balance because $\int_I \bar{x}_T^i \, d\alpha = 0$ and so

$$\int_I m^i(p_T, p_N) \, d\alpha = \int_I p_T \bar{x}_T^i \, d\alpha = 0$$

for every possible price vector (p_T, p_N). Thus, those who gain from trade are being required to compensate those who lose.

Now, standard techniques for demonstrating existence of Walrasian equilibrium in a continuum economy apply in this new situation. Suppose that $(\hat{x}, \hat{p}_T, \hat{p}_N)$ is a Walrasian equilibrium. Because $\hat{p}_T \bar{x}_T^i = m^i(\hat{p}_T, \hat{p}_N)$ by construction, each individual $i \in I$ can afford the *status quo* net trade vector $(\bar{x}_T^i, 0)$, and so the revealed preference argument does apply. At least almost nobody loses from free exchange.

Grandmont and McFadden (1972) propose a different rule for compensating losers which ensures that, when any non-null set of agents gain from free exchange, then almost all will. To state this rule, first define

$$E^i(p, \bar{x}^i) := E^i(p_T, p_N, \bar{x}^i) := \min_{x^i} \{ p_T x_T^i + p_N x_N^i \mid x^i \in X^i; \ x^i \, R^i \, \bar{x}^i \}$$

as the mininum net transfer which i needs at prices $p = (p_T, p_N) \in \Re^G$ in order to be no worse off than at $\bar{x}^i = (\bar{x}_T^i, 0)$. Note that $E^i(p_T, p_N, \bar{x}^i) \leq p_T \bar{x}_T^i$ for all $i \in I$ and all price vectors p. Then define $\bar{E}(p) := \int_I E^i(p, \bar{x}^i) \, d\alpha$ as the population mean of the net transfers $E^i(p, \bar{x}^i)$. Of course,

$$\bar{E}(p) \leq \int_I p_T \bar{x}_T^i \, d\alpha = 0$$

for all price vectors p. When $\bar{E}(p) = 0$, giving almost all the losers compensation for the relative price changes induced by expanded free exchange leaves no surplus, and there are no strict gains to almost everybody. But when $\bar{E}(p) < 0$, suppose that each individual i receives the net transfer $m^i(p) = E^i(p, \bar{x}^i) - \theta^i \bar{E}(p)$ as a function of the price vector p, where θ^i is some positive constant for each i. Furthermore, suppose that the asso-

148

ciated function $\theta : I \to \Re_+$ is measurable and also satisfies $\int_I \theta^i \, d\alpha = 1$. Then the transfers will evidently balance. Once again, standard techniques for demonstrating existence of Walrasian equilibrium in a continuum economy apply. Finally, whenever $\bar{E}(\hat{p}) < 0$ in the new equilibrium, it will be true that $m^i(\hat{p}) > E^i(\hat{p}, \bar{x}^i)$ for all $i \in I$, implying that almost all individuals are better off as a result of the exchanges of goods in the set N.

Hence, allowing goods in the set N to be freely exchanged among members of finite coalitions will typically benefit some individuals. In the absence of appropriate compensation, however, some others may well be made worse off. In this sense, free exchange of goods in the set N is itself a form of widespread externality, though of a purely redistributive kind that does not involve any Pareto inefficiency. Indeed, it seems to be another instance of what some economists such as Shubik (1971) have called a 'pecuniary externality' – see also Hausman (1992). These conclusions should be remembered when discussing the free exchange of rights later on.

EQUILIBRIUM WITH WIDESPREAD EXTERNALITIES

Widespread externalities will now be introduced into the continuum economy, following the formulation in Hammond (1995a) rather closely. Specifically, assume that in addition to the finite set G of exchangeable private goods, there is a disjoint finite set E of externalities. As before, for each individual $i \in I$, let $x^i \in \Re^G$ denote i's net trade vector of exchangeable goods. But now let $e^i \in \Re^E$ denote the vector of externalities that i creates. Also, suppose that each agent $i \in I$ is affected by the mean externality vector $z = \int_I e^i \, d\alpha \in \Re^E$. Specifically, conditional on z, each individual $i \in I$ is assumed to have a feasible set $F^i(z) \subset \Re^G \times \Re^E$ of pairs (x^i, e^i). Assume too that a (complete and transitive) conditional preference ordering $R^i(z)$ is defined on $F^i(z)$. Let $P^i(z)$ denote the corresponding strict preference relation.

In this model, a feasible allocation (x, e, z) consists of measurable mappings $x: I \to \Re^G$ and $e: I \to \Re^E$ such that:

1 $(x^i, e^i) \in F^i(z)$ for almost all $i \in I$;
2 $z = \int_I e^i \, d\alpha$;
3 $\int_I x^i \, d\alpha = 0$.

Throughout this section it is assumed that all exchangeable goods are freely traded at a non-zero price vector $p \in \Re^G$ so that the losers from free exchange can be appropriately compensated by the gainers. Suppose too that there are lump-sum transfers given by a measurable mapping $\mathbf{m}$: $I \to \Re$ satisfying $\int_I m^i \, d\alpha = 0$. Each individual $i \in I$ is forced to take the price vector $p \in \mathfrak{R}^G$, the mean externality vector $z \in \mathfrak{R}^E$, and i's own transfer m^i all as given. Hence i faces the conditional budget set

$$B_C^i(p, m^i; z) := \{(x^i, e^i) \in F^i(z) \mid p \, x^i \leq m^i\}.$$

Given this conditional budget set, say that i is in *individual equilibrium* at $(\hat{x}^i, \hat{e}^i) \in B_C^i(p, m^i; z)$ provided that $p \, x^i > m^i$ whenever $(x^i, e^i) \, P^i(\hat{z})$ $(\hat{x}^i, \hat{e}^i)$. Obviously, this is equivalent to conditional preference maximization over the set $B_C^i(p, m^i; \hat{z})$.

A Nash–Walrasian equilibrium with lump-sum transfers (or NWELT) is then a collection $(\hat{x}, \hat{e}, \hat{z}, p, \mathbf{m})$ consisting of a feasible allocation $(\hat{x}, \hat{e}, \hat{z})$, a price vector p, and transfers $\mathbf{m}$, such that almost every $i \in I$ is in individual equilibrium at $(\hat{x}^i, \hat{e}^i)$ given $\hat{z}$. Note that once again feasibility implies market clearing for private goods. Also, conditional on $\hat{z}$, each individual i chooses e^i without any restriction beyond individual feasibility and the choice of an x^i satisfying the budget constraint $p \, x^i \leq m^i$. Thus, within the budget set $B_C^i(p, m^i; \hat{z})$, the choice $(\hat{x}^i, \hat{e}^i)$ can be regarded as a best response to the mean externality $\hat{z}$ resulting from the choices of all the other players. In this sense, there is a Nash equilibrium in the (generalized) game where each player $i \in I$ is restricted to choose some $(x^i, e^i) \in B_C^i(p, m^i; \hat{z})$.

The concept of Pigou–Walrasian equilibrium is an obvious and simple extension of the corresponding concept of Nash–Walrasian equilibrium. Indeed, consider price systems of the form $(p, t) \in \mathfrak{R}^G \times \mathfrak{R}^E$, where $t \in \mathfrak{R}^E$ is the Pigou price vector, together with lump-sum transfers m^i ($i \in I$), where $\mathbf{m}: I \to \mathfrak{R}$ is a measurable function. Thus, t could be a vector of net taxes imposed by the government with a view to allocating the total widespread externality vector z efficiently between different consumers. Alternatively, it could be the free market price vector for permits to create all the different kinds of widespread externality.

Accordingly, the budget constraint of each individual $i \in I$ becomes $p \, x^i + t \, e^i \leq m^i$. Given the mean externality vector z, each individual $i \in I$ will be confronted with the (conditional) Pigou–Walrasian budget set

$$B_{PW}^i(p, t, m^i; z) := \{(x^i, e^i) \in F^i(z) \mid p \, x^i + t \, e^i \leq m^i\}.$$

Evidently $B_{PW}^i(p, 0, m^i; z) = B_C^i(p, m^i; z)$, so that the Pigou–Walrasian budget set reduces to $B_C^i(p, m^i; z)$ when the Pigou price vector $t = 0$.

Then the combination $(\hat{x}, \hat{e}, \hat{z}, p, t, \mathbf{m})$ is a Pigou–Walrasian equilibrium with lump-sum transfers (or PWELT) if $(\hat{x}, \hat{e}, \hat{z})$ is a feasible allocation satisfying, for almost all $i \in I$, both $(\hat{x}^i, \hat{e}^i) \in B_{PW}^i(p, t, m^i; \hat{z})$ and also $p \, x^i + t \, e^i > m^i$ whenever $(x^i, e^i) \in F_C^i(\hat{z})$ with $(x^i, e^i) \, P^i(\hat{z}) \, (\hat{x}^i, \hat{e}^i)$. Thus, $(\hat{x}, \hat{e}, p, t, \mathbf{m})$ is effectively a Walrasian equilibrium with lump-sum transfers in the economy with complete competitive markets in both private goods and externalities, but with the mean externality vector $\hat{z}$ fixed.

150

Also, a NWELT is effectively just a PWELT for which the Pigou price vector t happens to be 0.

As in Hammond (1995a), a feasible allocation $(\hat{x}, \hat{e}, \hat{z})$ is said to be f-externality constrained Pareto efficient if, except for a null set $I^0 \subset I$ of exceptional agents, no finite coalition $C \subset I \setminus I^0$ can find an alternative allocation $(x^i, e^i) \in F_C^i(\hat{z})$ ($i \in C$) to its members which satisfies the three conditions that: (i) $\sum_{i \in C} x^i = \sum_{i \in C} \hat{x}^i$; (ii) $\sum_{i \in C} e^i = \sum_{i \in C} \hat{e}^i$; and (iii) $(x^i, e^i) P^i(\hat{z}) (\hat{x}^i, \hat{e}^i)$ for all $i \in C$. Hence, only finite coalitions C that include members of the negligible set I^0 are able to gain from exchanging combinations of goods and externalities. In fact, it is easy to prove, in an entirely standard way, that any PWELT allocation is f-externality constrained Pareto efficient. Pareto improvements can only result from changes made by (large) coalitions of positive measure which affect the widespread externalities in a beneficial way. Since an NWELT is a particular instance of a PWELT, the same is true for those externalities which are not controlled at all.

THE GAINS FROM EXCHANGING QUOTAS

Now suppose that rights to create externalities are limited by some sort of quota scheme instead of Pigou prices. Suppose too that there are no lump-sum transfers. So, in addition to the usual conditional budget constraint $(x^i, e^i) \in B_C^i(p, 0; z)$ when $m^i = 0$, each individual $i \in I$ faces the additional constraint $e^i \leq q^i$ for some vector of quotas $q^i \in \Re^E$. Here, the choice of sign in each constraint $e_k^i \leq q_k^i$ reflects what is probably the usual case, which is when quotas limit the external diseconomies that individuals are allowed to create. But if k is an external economy and the quota q_k^i requires a minimum contribution toward creating k, this can also be accommodated if one thinks of $-e_k^i$ as representing the magnitude of this contribution. For then the kth constraint of the vector inequality $e^i \leq q^i$ can be expressed equivalently as $-e_k^i \geq -q_k^i$. Also, note that if $k \in E$ is such that $q_k^i = +\infty$, then i's right to create e_k^i units of externality k is totally uncontrolled. On the other hand, if $e_k^i \geq 0$ is required for feasibility and if $q_k^i = 0$, then there is total prohibition.

Let $B_Q^i(p, q^i; z)$ denote the subset of $B_C^i(p, 0; z)$ that results when the extra constraints $e^i \leq q^i$ are imposed. It is easy to modify the earlier definitions of Nash–Walrasian equilibrium and of compensated Nash–Walrasian equilibrium to reflect these quota constraints simply by replacing $B_C^i(p, 0; z)$ with $B_Q^i(p, q^i; z)$ throughout.

Suppose now that, if the exchange of quotas were to remain prohibited, the economy would reach a status quo Nash–Walrasian equilibrium without lump-sum transfers, but with quota constraints, of the form $(\bar{x}, \bar{e}, \bar{q}, \bar{z}, \bar{p})$. Arguing as above, if free exchange of quotas were allowed, the result would be an allocation in the f-core. In fact, this will be a Walrasian equilibrium without lump-sum transfers of the form $(\hat{x}, \hat{e}, \hat{z}, \hat{p}, \hat{t})$. Here, for each externality $k \in E$, the price $\hat{t}_k$ that each individual pays is really the price of the corresponding quota rather than the Pigou price of the externality itself. Nevertheless, whenever $\hat{t}_k > 0$, individuals who buy quotas will use them all – that is, they will choose $\hat{e}_k^i = \hat{q}_k^i$. On the other hand, if $\hat{t}_k = 0$, then individuals will buy as many quotas as they need in order to accommodate their unconstrained levels $\hat{e}_k^i$ of the externality k. Hence, it loses no generality to impose the requirement that $\hat{e}_k^i = \hat{q}_k^i$. Therefore, in equilibrium we can assume that $\hat{e}^i = \hat{q}^i$ for almost all $i \in I$. In this sense, there is no real difference after all between buying quotas and buying the rights to create externalities. Thus, $(\hat{x}, \hat{e}, \hat{z}, \hat{p}, \hat{t})$ can be regarded as a Pigou–Walrasian equilibrium.

Of course, many rights are inherently indivisible. It might be thought that this creates problems for the existence of a Walrasian equilibrium. Indeed, similar problems can already arise in the economy described earlier, since there it was not assumed that individuals' preference orderings R^i or even their feasible sets X^i were convex. But as discussed in Yamazaki (1978, 1981), Hammond (1993), and Coles and Hammond (1995), such existence problems tend to disappear if there is a continuum of individuals with dispersed characteristics – see also Sondermann (1975) and Trockel (1984).

Assume moreover that the total availability of quotas per head remains fixed. Then one will have

$$\hat{z} = \int_I \hat{e}^i \, d\alpha = \int_I \hat{q}^i \, d\alpha = \int_I \bar{q}^i \, d\alpha \geq \int_I \bar{e}^i \, d\alpha = \bar{z}.$$

Were it also true that $\hat{z} = \bar{z}$, the arguments set out earlier could now be applied to the conditional continuum economy with $\bar{z}$ fixed. The set T of initially traded goods would be replaced by G, and the set N of non-traded goods by E, the set of externalities. Then there would be potential gains from free exchange within finite coalitions, but actual Pareto gains would require suitable lump-sum compensation of any losers from relative price changes.

However, now there is the new feature that $\hat{z} = \bar{z}$ only when $\bar{q}^i = \bar{e}^i$ for almost all $i \in I$. That is, potential gains occur when there were almost no unused quotas in the status quo. Otherwise, for at least one of the externalities $k \in E$, it will be true that $\bar{e}_k^i < \bar{q}_k^i$ for a non-null set of individuals, implying that $\hat{z}_k > \bar{z}_k$. Then this change in externality k could well rule out even potential Pareto gains. Indeed, a strictly Pareto inferior allocation could easily result. Only by confiscating quotas that were unused in the status quo can this possibility be avoided, in general.

HOW FREE EXCHANGE CAN BE COSTLY

As shown earlier, even in the absence of other externalities, giving individuals the right to exchange a larger set of goods can create redistributive externalities. As usual, the potential gains from exchange do not become actual Pareto gains, in general, unless those who would otherwise lose from relative price movements receive suitable compensation from those who gain. When there are widespread externalities whose creation is controlled by quotas, the free exchange of those quotas may fail to produce even potential gains. This is because quotas that would otherwise have gone unused are likely to be transferred to those who will wish to use them. Hence, the level of the widespread externality is likely to change in an adverse way.

None of this discussion has dealt with other important obstacles to the achievement of Pareto gains from expanded free exchange. In particular, when individuals have private information determining what they would have transacted in the absence of expanded free exchange, proper compensation for adverse relative price movements is generally impossible. The second-best schemes devised in Hammond and Sempere (1995), with their frozen consumer prices and markets which get cleared by adjusting commodity taxes, are hardly more practicable.

Essentially this paper has been about limits to the economic gains from free exchange, not only of goods and services in the usual sense, but also of the rights or duties to create externalities. It should not be forgotten, however, that there can be other costs, possibly much larger, to expanded free exchange in certain goods and services. For example, evading taxes by participating in the undergound economy is in some obvious sense promoting free exchange, but at the cost of undermining a society's ability to provide public goods that benefit everybody, including tax evaders. Similar illegal activites such as smuggling or bribing public officials or politicians are often even worse than tax evasion because of the negative externalities they cause.

Examples where the costs are less evident include transactions that are judged by many not to be worth trying to suppress, yet are currently either illegal or else involve contracts that courts are unlikely to enforce. A rather dramatic example of the second category was the surrogate motherhood case in the USA concerning Mary Beth Whitehead – see also Satz (1992). The first category of 'marginally' illegal transactions might include some 'victimless crimes' such as prostitution (Satz, 1995), supplying drugs to adult addicts, or selling alcohol during the Prohibition era in the USA. Another case where the alleged costs are particularly difficult to discern concerns the freedom to exchange labour internationally – i.e., 'economic' migration.[3]

Nevertheless, it is important to understand how expanded freedom to exchange can provide new opportunities for the criminal or the merely unscrupulous. The reported development of an unofficial market in India for human kidneys destined for use in transplant surgery has led not only to some poor people selling one of their kidneys voluntarily, especially when they need to repay a burdensome debt. There have also been reports of people being kidnapped and waking up to find that one of their kidneys has been removed against their will. Similar outrages have been linked to the international traffic that supplies babies born in poor countries for adoption by people in rich countries. Also, of course, many people object to drug dealing or prostitution, especially near where they live or work, because such activities tend to attract more violent forms of crime. In all these cases, any gains from allowing voluntary exchange must be balanced against the need to prevent greedy people from arranging coerced exchange involving, quite possibly, outright theft or even murder.

The above objections to expanded free exchange admittedly concern only some cases which may be rather special. They do not deny that freer exchange may often be beneficial. They also fail to address directly the intuitionist argument that freedom to exchange should be valued for its own sake – but that task has been undertaken most capably by Gibbard (1985, especially p. 25). At most, it has been shown here that there may be economic costs to set against any benefits from freedom *per se*. Sometimes, however, these costs can be very large.

ACKNOWLEDGEMENTS

An incomplete first draft of this paper was written during a fruitful visit to THEMA during June 1995 arranged by Marc Fleurbaey, Serge Kolm, Jean-François Laslier, and Alain Trannoy. It has also benefited from helpful discussions with Frank Hahn and Robert Waldmann, and useful information from Debra Satz. My gratitude to all of these without implicating them in any errors or deficiencies in the paper.

NOTES

1 In this connection, I should perhaps report that the *Oxford English Dictionary* does contain the related word 'catallactic', meaning 'pertaining to exchange', which was derived from a Greek root apparently artificially. Also, during the nineteenth century 'catallactics' was suggested as an alternative subject name intended to be more accurately descriptive than 'political economy'.

2 In Hammond (1995a), I have discussed some of the limitations of this common claim.

3 For some recent discussions of the economic costs and benefits of international migration, see Brecher and Choudhri (1990), Freeman (1993), Kemp (1993), Wildasin (1994), and also Hammond and Sempere (1996), amongst others.

REFERENCES

Arnold, N.S. (1990) *Marx's Radical Critique of Capitalist Society*, New York: Oxford University Press.

Aumann, R.J. (1964) 'Markets with a Continuum of Traders', *Econometrica*, vol. 32, pp. 39–50.

Aumann, R.J. (1966) 'Existence of Competitive Equilibria in Markets with a Continuum of Traders', *Econometrica*, vol. 34, pp. 1–17.

Brecher, R.A. and E.U. Choudhri (1990) 'Gains from International Factor Movements without Lump-sum Compensation: Taxation by Location versus Nationality', *Canadian Journal of Economics*, vol. 23, pp. 44–59.

Coles, J.L. and P.J. Hammond (1995) 'Walrasian Equilibrium without Survival: Equilibrium, Efficiency, and Remedial Policy', in K. Basu, P.K. Pattanaik, and K. Suzumura (eds), *Choice, Welfare and Development: A Festschrift in Honour of Amartya K. Sen*, Oxford: Oxford University Press, ch. 3, pp. 32–64.

Cordato, R.E. (1992) *Welfare Economics and Externalities in an Open Ended Universe: A Modern Austrian Perspective*, Boston: Kluwer Academic Publishers.

Coughlin, P.J. (1986) 'Rights and the Private Pareto Principle', *Economica*, vol. 53, pp. 303–320.

Cowan, R. and M.J. Rizzo (1995) 'Fundamental Issues in the Justification of Profits', in R. Cowan and M.J. Rizzo (eds), *Profits and Morality*, Chicago: University of Chicago Press ch. 1, pp. 1–21.

Deb, R. (1994) 'Waiver, Effectivity, and Rights as Game Forms,' *Economica*, vol. 61, pp. 167–178.

Fine, B. (1975) 'Individual Liberalism in a Paretian Society', *Journal of Political Economy*, vol. 83, pp. 1277–1281.

Freeman, R.B. (1993) 'Immigration from Poor to Wealthy Countries: Experience of the United States', *European Economic Review*, vol. 37, pp. 443–451.

Gauthier, D. (1986) *Morals by Agreement*, Oxford: Clarendon Press.

Gibbard, A. (1974) 'A Pareto-Consistent Libertarian Claim', *Journal of Economic Theory*, vol. 7, pp. 388–410.

Gibbard, A. (1985) 'What's Morally Special about Free Exchange?', in E.F. Paul, F.D. Miller, and J. Paul (eds), 'Ethics and Economics', Oxford: Basil Blackwell, pp. 20–28.

Grandmont, J.-M. and D. McFadden (1972) 'A Technical Note on Classical Gains from Trade', *Journal of International Economics*, vol. 2, pp. 109–25.

Hammond, P.J. (1993) 'Irreducibility, Resource Relatedness, and Survival in Equilibrium with Individual Non-Convexities', in R. Becker, M. Boldrin, R. Jones, and W. Thomson (eds), *General Equilibrium, Growth, and Trade II: The Legacy of Lionel W. McKenzie*, San Diego: Academic Press ch. 4, pp. 73–115.

Hammond, P.J. (1995a) 'Four Characterizations of Constrained Pareto Efficiency in Continuum Economies with Widespread Externalities', *The Japanese Economic Review*, vol. 46, pp. 103–124.

Hammond, P.J. (1995b) 'Social Choice of Individual and Group Rights', in W.A. Barnett, H. Moulin, M. Salles, and N. Schofield (eds), *Social Choice, Welfare, and Ethics*, Cambridge: Cambridge University Press ch. 3, pp. 55–77.

Hammond, P.J. (1995c) 'On f-Core Equivalence in a General Continuum Economy with Widespread Externalities', Department of Economics, Stanford University, Working Paper 95-004.

Hammond, P.J. and J. Sempere (1995) 'Limits to the Potential Gains from Economic Integration and Other Supply-Side Policies', *The Economic Journal*, vol. 105, pp. 1180–1204.

Hammond, P.J. and J. Sempere (1996) 'On the Contrast between Policies toward Trade and Migration', preprint, Department of Economics, Stanford University.

Hammond, P.J., Kaneko, M. and M.H. Wooders (1989) 'Continuum Economies with Finite Coalitions: Core, Equilibrium and Widespread Externalities', *Journal of Economic Theory*, vol. 49, pp. 113–134.

Hart, O.D. (1975) 'On the Optimality of Equilibrium when the Market Structure is Incomplete', *Journal of Economic Theory*, vol. 11, pp. 418–443.

Hausman, D.M. (1992) 'When Jack and Jill Make a Deal', *Social Philosophy and Policy*, vol. 9, pp. 95–113.

Hayek, F.A. (1976) *Law, Legislation and Liberty, Volume 2*, Chicago: University of Chicago Press.

Hildenbrand, W. (1974) *Core and Equilibria of a Large Economy*, Princeton: Princeton University Press.

Hillinger, C. and V. Lapham (1971) 'The Impossibility of a Paretian Liberal: Comment by Two Who Are Unreconstructed', *Journal of Political Economy*, vol. 79, pp. 1403–1405.

Honoré, A.M. (1961) 'Ownership', in A.G. Guest (ed.), *Oxford Essays in Jurisprudence*, Oxford: Oxford University Press.

Kaneko, M. and M.H. Wooders (1986) 'The Core of a Game with a Continuum of Players and Finite Coalitions: The Model and Some Results', *Mathematical Social Sciences*, vol. 12, pp. 105–137.

Kaneko, M. and M.H. Wooders (1989) 'The Core of a Continuum Economy with Widespread Externalities and Finite Coalitions: From Finite to Continuum Economies', *Journal of Economic Theory*, vol. 49, pp. 135–168.

Kaneko, M. and M.H. Wooders (1994) 'Widespread Externalities and Perfectly Competitive Markets: Examples', in R.P. Gilles and P.H.M. Ruys (eds), *Imperfections and Behavior in Economic Organizations*, Boston: Kluwer Academic Publishers ch. 4, pp. 71–87.

Kemp, M.C. (1993) 'The Welfare Gains from International Migration', *Keio Economic Studies*, vol. 30, pp. 1–5.

Nozick, R. (1974) *Anarchy, State and Utopia*, New York: Basic Books.

Peacock, A. (1987) 'Economic Freedom', in J. Eatwell, M. Milgate and P. Newman (eds), *The New Palgrave: A Dictionary of Economics*, London: Macmillan.

Roemer, J.E. (1988) *Free to Lose: An Introduction to Marxist Economic Philosophy*, Cambridge, Massachusetts: Harvard University Press.

Rowley, C.K. and A.T. Peacock (1975) *Welfare Economics: A Liberal Restatement*, London: Martin Robertson.

Satz, D. (1992) 'Markets in Women's Reproductive Labor', *Philosophy and Public Affairs*, vol. 21, pp. 107–131.

Satz, D. (1995) 'Markets in Women's Sexual Labor', *Ethics*, vol. 106, pp. 63–85.

Sen, A.K. (1970a) 'The Impossibility of a Paretian Liberal', *Journal of Political Economy*, vol. 78, pp. 152–157.

Sen, A.K. (1970b) *Collective Choice and Social Welfare*, San Francisco: Holden Day.

Shubik, M. (1971) 'Pecuniary Externalities: A Game Theoretic Analysis', *American Economic Review*, vol. 61, pp. 713–8.

Sondermann, D. (1975) 'Smoothing Demand by Aggregation', *Journal of Mathematical Economics*, vol. 2, pp. 201–224.

Suzumura, K. (1983) *Rational Choice, Collective Decisions, and Social Welfare*, Cambridge: Cambridge University Press.

Trockel, W. (1984) *Market Demand: An Analysis of Large Economies with Non-Convex Preferences*, Berlin: Springer Verlag.

von Mises, L. (1949, 1966) *Human Action*, Chicago: Contemporary Books, Inc.
Wildasin, D.E. (1994) 'Income Redistribution and Migration', *Canadian Journal of Economics*, vol. 27, pp. 637–59.
Yamazaki, A. (1978) 'An Equilibrium Existence Theorem Without Convexity Assumptions', *Econometrica*, vol. 46, pp. 541–555.
Yamazaki, A. (1981) 'Diversified Consumption Characteristics and Conditionally Dispersed Endowment Distribution: Regularizing Effect and Existence of Equilibria', *Econometrica*, vol. 49, pp. 639–654.

12

A COMMENT ON 'RIGHTS, EXCHANGE AND EXTERNALITIES'

Antonio Villar

INTRODUCTION

It is well known that the presence of externalities in market economies bring inefficiencies in the allocation of resources, but also that a suitable combination of markets and transfers can restore the efficiency of equilibrium outcomes (indeed the second welfare theorem can be applied to very general environments, including those with externalities, public goods and nonconvexities). Different market-like solutions (the creation of markets for externalities, bargaining procedures, the imposition of quotas) and the introduction of personalized prices or sophisticated tax systems have been proposed in order to implement the necessary transfers that lead to Pareto optimal allocations in these economies. Peter Hammond's contribution refers to the 'limits to the economic gains from free exchange, not only for goods and services in the usual sense, but also of the rights or duties to create externalities'. The key issue in his discussion concerns the achievement of efficient allocation by means of market-like solutions in the presence of widespread externalities (to be associated with rights), in an economy with a continuum of agents. The discussion of the Pareto principle itself as way of evaluating rights and opportunities, however, remains hidden in the background.

I would like to comment on Peter Hammond's story by rephrasing it as a finite world tale. So I shall first try to translate his main conclusions to the case of an economy with a finite number of agents, and will consider the moral derived from this later on.

WIDESPREAD EXTERNALITIES IN A FINITE WORLD

Following the formulation in Debreu (1952), let us consider a society made of h agents. The kth agent's choice set is given by $A_k \subset \mathbb{R}^\ell$, whose members will be denoted by $\mathbf{a}_k$. The behaviour of this agent can be defined as the maximization of a real-valued payoff function U_k, taken into account the restrictions she faces (summarized in a correspondence β_k, to be specified

158

later). A social system is given by $[A_k, U_k, \beta_k]_{k=1}^h$. Let now $A = \prod_{k=1}^h A_k$ and let $a = (a_1, \ldots, a_h)$ stand for an element of A. We can define, for each $k = 1, 2, \ldots, h$, the correspondence $\beta_k : A \to A_k$ that tells us the elements in A_k that are feasible for the kth agent when the remaining agents choose $a_{-k} = (a_1, \ldots, a_{k-1}, a_{k+1}, \ldots, a_h)$. Hence, for each a in A, $\beta_k(a)$ is the kth agent's opportunity set.

In order to allow for each individual agent's payoff function to depend on other agents actions, we define $U_k : A \to \mathbb{R}$. We write $U_k(a) = U_k(a_k, a_{-k})$, in order to distinguish the dependence on the different variables (those chosen by the kth agent, and those chosen by the others). The kth agent's rational behaviour can now be described by a correspondence $\mu_k : A \to A_k$ given by:

$$\mu_k(a) = \{a'_k \in \beta_k(a) \mid U_k(a'_k, a_{-k}) \geq U_k(a)\}$$

A **social equilibrium** for a social system $[A_k, U_k, \beta_k]_{k=1}^h$, is a point $a^* \in A$ such that, for all $k = 1, 2, \ldots, h$, one has:

$$U_k(a^*_k, a^*_{-k}) \geq U_k(a_k, a^*_{-k}), \quad \forall \, a_k \in \beta_k(a^*).$$

In other words, a^* is a social equilibrium if and only if $a^*_k \in \mu_k(a^*)$ for all k. Then, by letting $\mu : A \to A$ be defined by $\mu(a) = \prod_{k=1}^h \mu_k(a)$, a^* turns out to be a social equilibrium if and only if $a^* \in \mu(a^*)$ (i.e., if and only if a^* is a fixpoint of the correspondence μ). Under suitable convexity and continuity conditions, a social equilibrium can be shown to exist.

This abstract model easily accommodates the standard competitive market economy, but also more complex worlds. In particular the case of an economy with all kind of externalities fits into this framework (one can think of the fictitious auctioneer as one of the agents, whose only purpose is to find prices that clear the markets). Existence of market equilibrium in economies with externalities derives from the existence of social equilibria mentioned above. These equilibria will typically fail to be Pareto optimal (competitive behaviour implies that individual agents ignore the external effects they produce, contrary to what optimality prescribes).

Externalities can be of many types, and this is by no means irrelevant in order to discuss the remedies for the inefficiencies they create. From the point of view of depletability, one can distinguish between those externalities that are **private** and those that are **public**. Private externalities are those that can be identified with additional private commodities (i.e., the consumption of an externality by an agent reduces the global externality in the amount consumed). Public externalities are like public goods: their consumption by an agent does not affect the amount available, and they are typically multilateral (i.e., they affect all agents simultaneously). Air pollution is a more than familiar example of public externality: the inconveniences experienced by an agent are not affected by the inconveniences experienced by other agents. More generally, those externalities that depend on the aggregate actions of all agents as well as the public goods themselves can be considered as public externalities.

Market-like solutions for externalities work well when externalities are private (and multilateral, if you wish also to avoid the presence of monopoly power). Hence the creation of competitive markets for externalities (or the imposition of appropriate levels of quotas) can ensure efficient outcomes. Yet this is not the case for public externalities, where free-riding may also be present.[1] Indeed, market-like solutions for this case correspond to the voluntary subscription model for pure public goods, that is known to produce inefficiencies. In particular, if we consider a constrained walrasian equilibrium in which there are quotas that limit the individual contributions to public externalities, and allow people to freely exchange these quotas in competitive markets, the outcome can be a Pareto inferior allocation rather than a Pareto improvement (this will be the case when there are some unused quotas in the constrained equilibrium).

One can thus interpret Peter Hammond's results as an expression of this phenomenon: there is no equivalence between creating markets (or imposing tradable quotas) for externalities when externalities are private and when they are public. Only via Lindahl-like solutions can efficiency be achieved in the context of public externalities (and this involves the bunch of difficulties associated with the revelation of agents' true characteristics).

When there is a continuum of agents, widespread externalities are defined as 'those that remain unaffected if agents in a null set change their respective externality creating activities'. This notion may be associated in our framework to the case of public externalities, and applies nicely to the case of creating markets for untraded commodities that was discussed. Opening a new market implies introducing a new commodity that affects all agents simultaneously (here the externality is the availability of a market for trading a new commodity, and not the commodity itself).

I believe that most of Hammond's analysis on widespread externalities can be carried out along these lines. His work can thus be interpreted as extending these ideas to the continuum case: going to a continuum of agents does not help for the public externality problem, if one insists on market-like solutions. Taking for granted the Pareto principle as the proper way of evaluating the allocations (in an enlarged commodity space that may include rights as public externalities), he provides a model that can be thought of as an allegory of the limits of market-like solutions to achieve the good (as a situation in which no agent can propose further Pareto improvements).

THE PARETO PRINCIPLE

The preceding discussion can be summarized by saying that market-like solutions for externalities can fail to achieve efficiency when externalities are public (or widespread in the continuum case). The point under discussion now is the Pareto principle itself, which becomes particularly weak when externalities are subjective (i.e., externalities that only affect agents' utilities U_k, by contrast with those that affect the choice sets A_k or $\beta_k(.)$ that can be called objective).

The Pareto principle is an efficiency criterion difficult to object in the standard competitive world with a well-defined commodity space of tradable goods, and an externally given set of property rights and moral principles. The Pareto criterion may be seen as a mild expression of John Stuart Mill's ideal of 'the greatest good for the greatest number'. When externalities are present, however, things get much more complex very quickly. Even if externalities are objective (what we can consider as a genuine economic problem), to restore efficiency requires taking distributional decisions (and optimality gives no guidelines for this). But the Pareto principle lacks most of its appeal in other circumstances, as when externalities are subjective (should we pay to appease meddlers?), or when we expand the commodity space to cover also moral principles, rights, liberties or opportunities (especially if one keeps a welfarist approach). Sen has produced clever examples showing the limits of this framework, the libertarian paradox being just one of them.

Let us consider Sen's libertarian paradox, for the sake of absolute certainty. The issue here is that of a conflict between personal rights and the Pareto principle when there are subjective externalities. Whenever I put this problem to my undergraduate students I have a hard time to convince them that this is a problem at all. And for good reasons: they tend to conclude that one should not take these interrelationships as inefficiencies worth considering (this is probably what Sen tries to tell us anyway). The thing gets even worse when I explain to them that when one agent feels worse off because another agent is consuming more, *ceteris paribus*, efficiency requires him to be compensated. And the more envious she is, the bigger the compensation. Some of them actually laugh at this conclusion.

Rights and liberties might probably be modelled as public externalities in an enlarged commodity space. We know that market-like solutions may fail to achieve Pareto optimality in this context (this is the subject of Hammond's work). But there is still the question of whether the Pareto principle is *the* way to evaluate the allocation of rights and opportunities. My answer would be no, if preferences are the only information to be taken into account.

The big issue behind this is, of course, how to combine the allocation of rights by a social choice type of procedure (that is, a decision rule that makes the outcome dependent on agents' preferences, so that rights are essentially relative), with the existence of what some may consider as unalienable (or absolute) rights such as life, freedom, etc. In the first case the Pareto criterion seems appropriate (e.g., the exchange of previously allotted property rights in classical economies), whereas the second amounts to give veto power to agents on specific issues (e.g., when primary goods are involved). And this is far from being a classification. Many of the relevant problems lie somehow in between (e.g., the allocation of property rights itself). Peter Hammond does not discuss these questions here, even though they are relevant to the point. Let us not blame him for that, as he already did it elsewhere (see Hammond (1995)).

NOTE

1 See the discusion in Mas-Colell, Whinston and Green (1995, 11D).

REFERENCES

Debreu, G. (1952), 'A Social Equilibrium Existence Theorem', *Proceedings of the National Academy of Sciences*, 38: 886–893.

Hammond, P. (1995), 'Social Choice of Individual and Group Rights', in A. Barnett, H. Moulin, M. Salles, and N. Schofield (eds), *Social Choice, Welfare and Ethics*, Cambridge University Press, Cambridge.

Mas-Colell, A., Whinston, M.D. and Green, J.R. (1995), *Microeconomic Theory*, Oxford University Press, New York.

Part III
OPPORTUNITIES

Part III

OPPORTUNITIES

13

REAL FREEDOM AND DISTRIBUTIVE JUSTICE

Richard Arneson

Here is a picture of a society that one might suppose to be ideally just in its distributive practices: all members of the society are equally free to live in any way that they might choose, and institutions are arranged so that the equal freedom available to all is at the highest feasible level. What, if anything, is wrong with this picture? One might object to the insistence on equal freedom for all, and propose that freedom should instead be maximinned, or leximinned, or maximized, or distributed according to some alternative norm. In this essay I wish to set aside the choice of distributive norm. The question for this essay is whether freedom in any sense is the aspect of people's condition that is the right basis of interpersonal comparison for a theory of distributive justice. I approach this question by analysing some rival conceptions of freedom.

NEGATIVE AND POSITIVE FREEDOM

Concepts of freedom are notoriously various and tricky. The distinction between negative and positive freedom has been drawn in many different ways. Here I intend simply to pick out a distinction in this region that will help us to understand contemporary writers on distributive justice who take principles of freedom to be primary and foundational for their subject. Philippe Van Parijs contrasts what he calls 'real freedom' with non-genuine varieties and urges that a just society is concerned above all with the distribution of real freedom (Van Parijs, 1995). Real, substantive, or positive freedom is to be contrasted with formal or negative freedom. Let us say I am formally free to travel to the South Pole if no law forbids me and no one will interfere in certain ways if I attempt to go there. Interfering 'in certain ways' covers two types of intervention: my freedom to travel to the South Pole is reduced by interference if some one wrongfully violates my rights in ways that either prevent me from making the trip or menace my travel plans. On the other hand, my freedom to travel to the South Pole is also reduced by interference if you prevent me from even making a significant attempt but without violating my rights. If I am imprisoned after a fair trial, I am not formally free to travel to the South Pole, but neither have my rights been violated. I can be free in the negative sense to do something even though I lack the ability or the means to do that thing. I can be free in the negative sense to travel to the South Pole even though I cannot actually get there because I lack the ability to swim there and the means to charter any other mode of transport that would get me there. In contrast, whatever I have the positive freedom to do I can do if I choose to try. My abilities and talents and the resources at my disposal affect the extent of my positive freedom but not the extent of my negative freedom. Generally, if I am positively free to do X I am also negatively free to do X, but not always. If someone tries to coerce me or places obstacles in my path, but the obstacles are not completely effective, so that I can still get X if I try to get X, then I am positively free with respect to X but not completely negatively free.

FREEDOM AS HAVING CHOICES

Consider what I will call the simple notion of positive freedom – namely, that to be free is to have a choice, and the more choices one has, the more free one is. A choice is an opportunity to choose; if I have a choice between A and B, then if I choose A, I get A, and if I choose B, I get B.[1]

In order to have a choice, there must be at least two items in my choice set. If the choice set consists just of A, then I get A whatever I choose, so I am forced to get A. Of course it is still true in the latter case that if I choose A, I get A, so isn't there some choice available to the agent in this case after all? I would say No, which indicates that the opportunity to choose must be more fully characterized: if I have the opportunity to choose among the items in a set, then if I choose any item in that set, I get it because I choose it, where this last clause implies that if I did not choose it, I would not get it. When confronted by a one-item choice set, I do not have the opportunity to choose as just described, and in the absence of genuine opportunity to choose there is no freedom (from here on I usually will omit the qualifiers 'positive' and 'positively'). According to the simple view, having more choices means more freedom, whether the choices are goods or evils. A person who has to choose a physical hell of flames, a hell in which the pain consists of psychological torture, or a hell in which the pain is absence of spiritual satisfaction is more free than another person who must choose among just two of these hells. Furthermore, the simple view holds that a person who must choose from a very small set of options has very little freedom even if one of the options, the one she actually chooses, is very attractive. If I have just two choices, one that yields misery and one that provides ecstatic bliss, I have hardly any freedom of choice. We can readily imagine a person who

166

ranks option sets just by comparing the top-ranked option in each set and ranks as best the set with the single best option regardless of the number or qualitative characteristics of the less than best options. Such a person does not place any value on freedom according to its simple construal.

According to the simple notion, if one person's choice set dominates another's, because the first set contains everything in the second set, plus more, then the person facing the dominating choice set has more freedom than a person facing the dominated choice set. A powerful though controversial intuition supports the view that at least in this special case, more choice means more freedom. The dominance condition is a strong one, however. If adding an extra option alters the character of some previously existing options, then the new choice set does not dominate the old choice set, because if one subtracts the extra option from the new set, the two sets are not identical and the first set does not contain everything in the second set, plus more.

Where no choice set in a comparison class is dominant, the simple view still identifies the extent of a person's freedom with the number of choices she has: the more choices, the more freedom. Where the application of the simple view yields the judgement that a choice set that one person faces is larger than the choice set another faces, a strong assumption is being made that one can non-arbitrarily count options. If this assumption did not hold, the judgement that the set A contains more choices than the set B could always be reversed by redescribing some of the options in B so that the count of choices is changed and the number of choices in B exceeds the number in A.

One might well query whether non-arbitrary counting of options is really possible. But the simple view is vulnerable to a strong challenge even if the possibility of nonarbitrary counting is taken for granted.

Suppose that Smith has a choice among three options that she regards as highly desirable and Jones has a choice among three options that she regards as worthless. The simple view says that they enjoy equal freedom. An alternative view holds that the extent to which an option enhances its possessor's freedom depends on its valuation. Amartya Sen's illuminating writings on freedom elaborate and defend this alternate view. He writes that 'we find it absurd to dissociate the extent of our freedom from our preferences over the alternatives. A set of three alternatives that we see as "bad," "awful" and "dismal" cannot, we think, give us as much real freedom as a set of three others that we prefer a great deal more and see as "great," "terrific" and "wonderful"' (Sen, 1990, p. 469). There are at least two significantly different conceptions of freedom in competition here, and the contrast is worth exploration.

Notice first of all that some examples can challenge Sen's intuition. Suppose that freedom of religion is severely limited in a society. Only

Buddhism and Islam may be practised. Smith, a Buddhist, finds he is free to practice his chosen religion, whereas Jones, a Christian, is not. Surely in an unproblematic sense both have equal religious freedom, though they benefit very unequally from it.[2]

If we are wondering whether the extent of one's freedom varies with the valuation of the choices in one's opportunity set, we should distinguish the judgement on the choices that is made by (a) the consensus valuation (if any exists) of the agent's society, (b) the valuation that 'we', outside observers, make, (c) the valuation of the agent herself whose freedom is in question, and (d) the true valuation that would be made by an ideal observer. We most confidently suppose that valuation affects freedom when valuations (a) to (d) coincide – or when we think this is so. But the components should be examined separately. Regarding (a), one may wonder why the valuations of persons other than the agent in question should be thought to have a bearing on the amount of freedom enjoyed by that agent. The agent's valuations may be idiosyncratic, different from the consensus of society. If the consensus of society valuation affects the amount of freedom the agent possesses, then all of Smith's circumstances can stay exactly the same, yet if enough people change their valuation of Smith's choices to alter the consensus, we must say that Smith's freedom has increased or decreased even though nothing whatsoever has altered except the opinions of people other than Smith. Why should the extent of Smith's freedom depend on alterations of cultural fashions in which she does not share? Note also that Smith's evaluation might be reasonable, while the consensus valuation is unreasonable. This same objection applies to the claim that the (b) valuation is the determiner of an agent's freedom in a situation, unless we blur the distinction between (b) and (d).

No doubt evaluation (d) would be nice to have, but some might doubt its availability. Others might suppose that even if (d) is accessible to those charged with deciding on social policy, the extent of a person's freedom varies with her own valuation of her options, not the true valuation (which may have no bearing on her choice among options).

Consider the perfectionist proposal that the measure of an individual's real freedom is the extent to which the options available to her provide opportunities for living in ways that are truly valuable. Suppose that Fred's present options constitute a rich array of opportunities for living in ways that are truly valuable, but which Fred happens to despise without good reason. He would much prefer an option that is not currently available to him – the way of life consisting of eating potato crisps, lying on the sofa and watching mindless television programmes. Adding this low-life option to his set of available options increases his real freedom not at all, according to the perfectionist measure, but surely this indicates that this measure is defective. Adding the option that he strongly desires and values, however misguidedly, significantly expands Fred's freedom.

What then of (c), the agent's own valuation? This can also yield counter-intuitive judgements. The members of society may have sacrificed much to provide Smith with a wide range of options, but if the true measure of Smith's freedom is the extent to which he values these options on being confronted with this particular array of them, then nothing in Smith's circumstances need shift except that he swings erratically from one ill-informed and unreasoned valuation of his options to another that is just as unreflective, yet the conclusion must be that Smith's freedom has greatly increased or decreased just by virtue of his change of opinion. This point could perhaps be met by the stipulation that the more stable and fixed the agent's valuations, the more it is the case that adding options that are currently highly valued by the agent increases his freedom.

A greater difficulty perhaps is that Smith might assess her options on the basis of an evaluative perspective that prereflectively we would judge to be averse to freedom. Suppose that Smith prefers to follow commands issued by others when she is deciding how to live her own life, and prefers fewer options to more because choice among options fills her with nameless dread. Smith then values at naught the many rich options that are open to her in a modern city in a democratic and tolerant society and prefers the simple uncluttered life of a patriarchal village with a council of elders rigidly constraining her options by coercive fiat. If 'the idea of effective freedom cannot be dissociated from our preferences', as Sen asserts, then Smith's few options in the patriarchal village give her more freedom than the many options at her disposal in the tolerant city. An alternative view would be that in this example Smith's valuations and preferences indicate that she places a low valuation on having freedom and do not provide a good measure of the amount of freedom she actually would enjoy in city and village.

The objection here is not that Smith might espouse an idiosyncratically low (or high) valuation on freedom as opposed to other goods. If this were the objection, it could be met by stipulation that the extent of an agent's freedom is determined by the valuation of her options that would be made on the average by persons in her society. At least this latter valuation would not be idiosyncratic. Or one could insist that in principle the extent of a person's freedom is determined by the true value of the choices available to her, whether or not anyone is actually in a position to know this true value. This true valuation, if we could gain access to it, would also not be vulnerable to the objection that it is arbitrary or idiosyncratic.

The objection might also be construed in this way: It is natural to suppose that the question 'What is freedom?' is distinct from the question 'What value does freedom have?' The value of freedom might well fluctuate with changing circumstances and be different for different individuals with distinctive and reasonable evaluative perspectives. If my preferences change, the value of the options open to me shifts, but if nothing changes except my preferences, and the situation is otherwise unchanged, it is odd to say that prior to my preference change I was more free than at present. Freedom as understood in the positive freedom tradition is *inter alia* a benefit that society confers on individuals. The nature of the good that is conferred does not change just because the recipient's valuation of it changes, any more than the nature of the purple shirt my mother gave me for my birthday changes if I suddenly develop an intense liking for the colour purple or intense loathing of it.

So construed, the objection is not decisive. According to the evaluative conception of freedom, how free one is depends *inter alia* on the value of the options among which one is free to choose. The objection just flatly denies what the evaluative conception assumes.

The preliminary considerations canvassed in this section indicate that we need to explore further.

INELIGIBLE OPTIONS

Peter Jones and Robert Sugden (1982) have proposed what is in effect a way of responding to Sen's argument for the evaluative conception that does not reaffirm the simple view.

Imagine that Freda now has the option of travelling by train or car, and to this option set is added the option of crawling about on one's belly with broken legs. Consider the position that the expanded option set contains no more real freedom than the original set. One might defend this position by taking Sen's line that 'we cannot dissociate the idea of effective freedom from our preferences.' On this view it is the presumption that Freda will never desire this third option nor choose it that supports the conviction that the crawling option does not increase her real freedom. An alternative suggested by Jones and Sugden is that it is not the fact that Freda herself has no desire to travel by crawling with broken legs, but rather the fact that no reasonable set of desires that anyone might have would value that extra option. They write:

> Suppose that this person's preferences are not known, but that from a general knowledge of human nature it is possible to say something about the sort of preferences that a person in his position might have. More precisely, it is possible to draw up a list of preference orderings, any one of which he might reasonably have. Then an option x can be said to be eligible in relation to a choice set S (where S contains x) if and only if x might reasonably be chosen from S.
>
> (Jones and Sugden, 1982, p. 56)

On the Jones and Sugden view, if one has a choice between a hell of fire and a hell of spiritual torment and is then offered the third option of a hell of ice, this extra option increases the agent's freedom, not in virtue of his own preferences with respect to it, because there are non-crazy preference orderings that someone in his situation might have, according to which hell-ice would be preferred to the other options. But if one had a choice between a green valley heaven and a tall skyscrapers heaven, and a hell of ice option was added to this choice set, it would not expand the agent's freedom, because it would not reasonably be chosen by anyone. And since any reasonable preference ordering a person might have would favour the option set with a great, a terrific, and a wonderful option to an alternative set with a dismal, an awful, and a bad option, the former set offers more freedom than the latter on their view. They see the extent of freedom provided by an option set as partially determined by evaluation, but not by the agent's evaluation of the options in the set.

They note quickly that the fact that someone might reasonably choose an option provided to an agent does not suffice to determine that the addition of the option expands the agent's freedom. Consider a choice set consisting of two identical cans of beans, which is then augmented by the addition of a third identical can of beans. One might reasonably pick the third option. But this is so because anyone with a non-crazy preference ordering will be indifferent between the three bean can options. Besides being eligible, an option must be distinguishable from others in the set, if its addition can be taken to augment the agent's freedom.

The Jones and Sugden response to Sen fails for a reason that does not vindicate the Sen approach they are criticizing. Return to the Freda example. Adding an option such as crawling about on one's belly with broken legs is not eligible (as Jones and Sugden interpret eligibility), but might significantly increase Freda's freedom nonetheless, provided that she strongly desires to exercise this option, even though her desire is unreasonable. She may have bizarre and unreasonable beliefs that lead her to the conclusion that crawling about in this way is the most appropriate response to her circumstances. I believe this point holds whatever the nature of her unreasonableness. She might hold unreasonable beliefs about morality or about what sort of life is choiceworthy or valuable for her. She might also be ignorant or in error about matters of fact in circumstances that would mislead no reasonable person. But freedom surely includes freedom to make one's own mistakes and act on unreasonable beliefs and convictions. I conclude that augmenting one's choice set by an ineligible option can increase an agent's freedom provided she desires it.

SIGNIFICANTLY DIFFERENT ALTERNATIVES

As stated, the simple view is implausible quite aside from the issue of whether or not the extent to which having an option contributes to an agent's freedom depends on the valuation of the option. The simple view holds that the more choices one has, the more freedom one has. But not all choices are created equal. If Smith is free to choose among twelve nearly identical brands of toothpaste (we can stipulate that each brand is valuable, choiceworthy) whereas Jones is free to choose among one brand of toothpaste, dental floss, eggs, beer, chocolate and salad greens, it is counter-intuitive to hold that Smith has more freedom with respect to consumer choice than Jones on the ground that Smith has more choices, because the alternatives among which he can choose are only trivially different. Adding trivially different options to one's opportunity set only trivially expands one's freedom. The simple view must be amended to say that to be free is to have a choice, and the more options one has, and the more these options are significantly different, the more free one is. A more precise statement of the amended simple view would have to specify the comparative weight to be assigned the two factors of 'more choice' and 'more significantly different choice' in determining how free an individual is. The suspicion may arise that talk of 'significant differences among options' reintroduces by the back door the acknowledgement that the value of options affects the extent to which they contribute to freedom that I had resisted at the front door. But at least in many cases the two ideas are readily distinguishable. I might regard a set of options as very close to one another in their value for me, whether this value is high or low, negative or positive, and yet be sure that these options are very different from one another. My vacation options might include sunbathing on the beach and climbing mountains, I might hold these vacation options to be just about equally attractive, yet they impress me as significantly different. The same point holds in the other direction: I might regard a set of occupational options as very similar in character even though just one of them happens to suit me and elicit my high valuation. An individual's similarity metric and her valuation metric will not in fact coincide. Being similar and being valuable are different. But things are similar to one another, and fail to be similar, in many different respects, and it is unclear either that there is just one sort of similarity involved in assessments of a person's freedom or what the relevant dimensions of similarity are.

Moreover, whether options strike us as saliently different or similar sometimes does depend on our interests and values. Not being an aficionado of fly-fishing, one tied lure looks about the same to me as any other, whereas the differences among them may appear enormous to a knowledgeable expert. What strikes the knowledgeable expert as a salient difference is a difference that matters to those who are participants in the activity.

The upshot of this discussion is that the degree to which options are similarly valuable and the degree to which options are similar are distinct issues. But the issues are connected. To an extent, what counts as a significant difference is relative to our interests.

SEN'S COUNTER-FACTUAL ANALYSIS

The amended simple proposal is that the more options an individual has, and the more significantly different from each other these options are, the more freedom he possesses. This proposal is challenged by the thought that the value of the options that are accessible to an individual significantly affects the extent to which having the options increases her freedom. This thought is part of the rationale of Amartya Sen's view that whether or not the addition of an option to one's choice set increases one's freedom depends on the answer to the further question, if one had the choice to have this extra option or not, would one choose to have it? According to Sen (1992), if the answer to the further question is affirmative, the option enhances one's freedom, if negative, then having the extra option decreases one's freedom. Consider a disadvantageous option, having which makes its possessor worse off because when faced with the option one must spend time and energy deciding how to respond to it. For example, a consumer who already is free to choose among several brands of toothpaste now is faced with an expanded choice set that includes the option of an additional brand of toothpaste. Sen notes that such an amplification of one's choice set is accompanied by the 'loss of option of leading a peaceful and unbothered life.' Sen adds, 'It is easy to think of circumstances when given the choice of having to make these particular choices, one would have good reason to say no. This indicates that the expansion of those particular obligations and choices need not be seen as a valued expansion of freedom (Sen, 1992, p. 63). But the question is not whether the extra option is a valued increase in freedom but whether it increases one's freedom. The question at issue is supposed to be whether having more freedom can be disadvantageous to its possessor. Sen prefers to see the example as indicating that there are different types of freedom and that more of one type (expansion of trivial choices) may mean less of another type (freedom to live as one would like).

We should distinguish between a case in which gaining an extra option is accompanied by the loss of formerly available options – this will diminish freedom according to the simple view – and a case in which gaining an extra option alters the character of some formerly available alternatives, perhaps for the worse, without reducing their number. In the latter case, there is an overall increase of options, hence an expansion of freedom.

Sen's counter-factual test suggests an alternative way of thinking about the measurement of freedom. The test is that in moving from one set of circumstances to another, whether the move increases or decreases the freedom of an individual affected by it depends on whether or not the person would choose the old or the new circumstances if she were presented with this choice. However, the test does not capture the intuitive idea of an increase compared to a decrease in someone's freedom. To see this, it suffices to note that the counter-factual test will register an increase in freedom when someone prefers to live with less rather than more freedom and if offered the choice between circumstances giving more freedom and circumstances giving less, would choose the latter circumstances precisely because they provide less freedom. This individual might fear that with more available choices, she will choose badly, to her detriment, whereas a restricted choice set will facilitate better choice, perhaps by deleting tempting but disadvantageous options. Or the individual might simply have a basic preference for choice among fewer options over choice among more options. The counter-factual test would be a good test for deciding under which among several alternative sets of circumstances an individual would have more freedom if the test were restricted so that the individual would be choosing with the aim of increasing her freedom. But of course in that restricted form the test presupposes a prior understanding of what constitutes more and less freedom and cannot be understood as determining what constitutes more and less freedom. The point is that what I would choose depends on my goals, and what I would choose indicates which choice gives more freedom only if my goal is more freedom. I borrow this last point from Cohen (1995).

This line of thought might seem flatly to beg the question as to whether Sen's counter-factual test analysis is adequate. If Sen is correct, what I would choose conceptually determines which choice offers more freedom, so there is no conceptual room for wondering, given that I would choose X over Y if offered either set of circumstances, would X or Y yield more freedom for me? My choice tells the answer, according to Sen. But at least I have identified a significant cost of accepting Sen's analysis. Prior to analysis of the concept of freedom, most of us would (I claim) suppose that it is coherent to suppose that an individual or a society might want to have less freedom rather than more. Sen's counter-factual test collapses the distinction, which we might well wish to retain, between believing that a condition best allows us to achieve our goals (so we would choose it over other conditions if offered a choice) and believing that a condition offers us the most freedom.

Sen's counter-factual test merits further exploration. Consider his helpful distinction between agency freedom and well-being freedom, illustrated by his example of the picnicker enjoying a lunch by a riverbank. As it happens, a man is drowning far away, but if the man were instead to be

174

bout to drown in the river near the picnicker, her agency freedom would be enhanced (she can save the drowning man's life) while her well-being reedom would be decreased (whatever she chose to do, her picnic would be spoiled). According to Sen, a 'person's "agency freedom" refers to what the person is free to do and achieve in pursuit of whatever goals or values he or she regards as important' (Sen, 1995, p. 203). We might say the person's agency freedom is greater, the greater is the contribution to her all-things-considered goals that would be made by the act available to her that is best in this respect. In contrast, a person's well-being freedom is greater, the greater the well-being she would reach in the condition, among those she could attain, that would give her most well-being. Sen notes that if it is the case that if the picnicker could choose between having the opportunity to save the drowning man and being able to finish her picnic lunch without interruption or distraction, then shifting to the former condition would increase her agency freedom. But since the opportunity to eat one's lunch in peace is more valuable than the opportunity to save a drowning man from the standpoint of one's own self-interest, in this example well-being freedom decreases when agency freedom increases.

The counter-factual test can also be shown to be flawed in this application. Consider a variant of the picnic example. In the actual setting, the man has ten options, any of which would make positive contributions to his agency goals if exercised. But if the option set was drastically reduced to two options, it would become more likely that the man would choose the option that would make the greatest contribution to his agency goals. Accordingly if he were presented with a choice between the wider and the narrower option set, if he were choosing to maximize the fulfilment of his agency goals he would pick the narrower option set. The Sen counter-factual test then yields the result that the person's agency freedom is increased if the narrower rather than the wider option set is made available to him. But how can narrowing one's options increase one's freedom, especially when the wider set contains all of the options in the narrower set, plus more? Here the counter-factual test yields what is intuitively the wrong result because the choice of circumstances that one would make in order to maximize the satisfaction of one's agency goals may not be the same as the choice one would make in order to attain the greatest extent of agency freedom.

MILL ON CHOICE-RESTRICTING EXPANSIONS OF FREEDOM

The issue that Sen engages – whether less choice can simultaneously be more freedom – is linked to an issue that puzzled Mill in *On Liberty*. Mill is arguing in a different context, so a bit of stage-setting is needed.

His immediate concern is whether acceptance of the principle of liberty would be compatible with refusal by the state to enforce a fully voluntary contract by which a person sells himself into slavery. The principle of liberty holds that the only good reason to interfere by way of coercion or compulsion with a person's voluntary act is to prevent harm to others (who do not voluntarily consent to share its costs and benefits). If a person's voluntary act is to sign away his future liberty, what then? Mill writes: 'The principle of freedom cannot require that he should be free not to be free. It is not freedom to be allowed to alienate his freedom' (Mill, 1978).

Leave aside the complex question, irrelevant for our purposes, of whether Mill's liberty principle allows or forbids non-enforcement of voluntary slavery contracts. (To my mind it forbids non-enforcement.) Consider the claim that 'it is not freedom to be allowed to alienate his freedom'. From the perspective of the amended simple view, the example suggests two different ways of calculating a person's freedom over the course of her life. First, notice that a person's freedom at the moment of choice is greater if besides all the other options among which she is free to choose, she also has an additional option, namely the option to alienate her future freedom by voluntary contract. The opportunity set that includes the option of contractual renunciation of future liberty dominates the option set that is identical except that it lacks that option. In this sense a person does have more freedom if she is allowed to alienate her freedom, Mill to the contrary notwithstanding. But a further question arises: over the course of the person's life, does she have more freedom if she (a) lacks the slavery option and chooses some non-slave mode of life or (b) chooses her mode of life from an expanded option set that includes the slavery option, and in fact chooses the slavery option? The answer is: it depends on how one is calculating freedom over the course of an individual's life. One might calculate an individual's freedom over the course of her life by counting the weighted sum of the number of options she faces and the degree to which they are significantly different at each moment in her life, and by summing the total. On the *total* view, the amount of freedom the individual has over the course of her life is the sum of her freedom scores at each moment of her life. On this way of counting, choices the individual makes that restrict her freedom from then on reduce her freedom over the course of her life. In contrast, on the *global* view, one counts all the options that an individual would face in all of the different lives that she might choose, and sums the total of the possible choices to which she has had access over the course of her life. On the global view, whatever life options an individual has, if to that set of options one adds another possible mode of life, the life of a slave, that extra option increases the total set of possible choices the individual might have made and hence her freedom over the course of her life, however the individual chooses. Mill's

176

comment that 'it is not freedom to be allowed to alienate his freedom' is correct if interpreted in this way: an individual's overall freedom in her life as a whole, on the total view (but not on the global view), is doubtless larger if she is denied the freedom-renouncing choice to be a slave than if she is allowed this option and to exercise it by choosing slavery, thus reducing her actual freedom available from then on.

DOES THE AGENT'S EVALUATIVE PERSPECTIVE AFFECT THE EXTENT OF HER FREEDOM?

More needs to be said about the issue of whether or not the amount of real freedom a person enjoys is determinable apart from that very person's evaluative perspective. On one side, the idea that how free you are depends on how much you want the options you have appears to have the troublesome implication that you can increase your freedom by learning to like the options you have even though your external circumstances do not change. This is the familiar 'contented slave' problem. It is resolved in the approach of Jones and Sugden by taking the amount of freedom one enjoys to be determined by the set of preference orderings that anyone reasonably might have in their position. No special weight is given to the agent's own particular preferences and evaluations.

But as we have seen in discussing the problem of measuring the diversity of an option set, the agent's evaluative perspective tends to sneak back into the account. The problem with the Jones and Sugden approach is that the idea of reasonable preference ordering needs further clarification. Some constraint must be imposed on what counts as a reasonable preference ordering, but what sort of constraint? One natural idea is to fix the notion of what it would be reasonable for someone to want to the agent's situation, with the agent's evaluative perspective included as part of her situation. A preference ordering would then be more reasonable, the more likely it is that it might become the preference ordering of the agent (or perhaps, the more it is likely it would become the preference ordering of the agent if she was to engage in careful reflection on the matter). On this way of elaborating the idea of a reasonable preference ordering, the limit case of an unreasonable preference ordering is one such that there is nil probability it will ever become the agent's (or would after careful reflection). Moreover, the agent's actual preference ordering has a special status; the preference ordering I am overwhelmingly most likely to have in the next moment is the one I now have. This construal of the idea is not in the spirit of the Jones and Sugden proposal.

So let's explore the idea of a reasonable preference ordering that someone in the agent's position might have, construed without any privileging of that very agent's evaluative perspective. Giving me the option of having a large iron sword within arm's reach leaves me cold, but this

177

option would be highly valued by Genghis Khan. Some of us might balk at the idea that Genghis's evaluative perspective on the options that I might face is relevant to the measurement of the extent of my freedom. This resistance seems to stem from the thought that the agent's own perspective has special weight for the determination of the agent's own freedom. If Genghis were placed in the position of a middle-class college professor, he would look for opportunities to display fierce warrior virtues. But his psychological type is so different from mine that what it would be reasonable for him to prefer, in my position, strikes us as irrelevant to the assessment of my freedom. We might then offer a friendly amendment to the Jones and Sugden approach: it is the preferences that a reasonable person might have in my position whose psychological type is the same as mine that determines the extent to which the options I have or might have would affect the extent of my freedom. But this friendly amendment turns out to be unfriendly. We might start with a broad classification of types, but we seem to be on a slippery slope: if someone proposes that a more fine-grained individuation of psychological types would yield a more fine-grained identification of possible reasonable persons whose preferences would determine the extent of my freedom , it would be arbitrary to resist an ever more fine-grained specification, and the limit of this process is to individuate types so finely that one person exemplifies each type. Either we allow the reasonable preferences of any type of person, however alien from me, to count in determining the value for freedom of the options I face, which is unacceptable, or we hold that it is the reasonable preferences of persons of my type in my position that determine the freedom value of the options I face, which is to give up the Jones and Sugden approach.

To motivate the thought that the preferences that a reasonable person in my position might have, rather than my own actual preferences, are the ones that determine whether the addition of an option to my choice set would render me more free, Pattanaik and Xu consider the example of a woman who knows with certainty that she will never wish to join the armed forces, but regards herself as significantly more free if women are allowed to enter the armed forces. What explains this judgement is supposed to be the thought that a reasonable person in her position, even if not she, might prefer above all to embark on a military career (Pattanaik and Xu, 1997).

The example can be interpreted differently. Having an option available can influence the process of preference and value formation in a desirable way, a way that the agent desires. This can be so whether or not there is any chance that this option will ever be the top-ranked option of the agent. The woman in the example might know in advance she will never choose the life of a soldier, but nonetheless worry that her career and life goal choices are selected from a too narrow set of culturally approved

178

options, and that the actual availability of unconventional options might liberate her imagination in ways she desires and judges valuable. Choosing from a wider option set might improve preference selection even if the added options are not selected and this is known in advance. In other words, one might desire to have an option without desiring to exercise it. One might think that just reflecting in thought about the possibility of becoming a soldier should suffice to improve the quality of one's reflection about choiceworthy careers whether or not that option is available in fact. But this might or might not be so. Maybe for some of us with respect to some types of choices, actual availability of the option improves the quality of our deliberation concerning it.

The question also arises, what counts as a position in this measurement endeavour. One might suppose that valuations of options that would not be reasonable or at least likely in one's exact circumstances might become reasonable or likely if one's circumstances were perturbed somewhat, and that the valuation of an option from this altered position can be relevant to the impact of the option on the extent of one's freedom. Jones and Sugden present as an example of an insignificant option (which would not increase one's freedom if added to one's choice set) the choice of size 10 shoes offered to someone who has size 8 feet and already has the option of shoes that fit. But if one's foot were to become enlarged by disease, the size 8 person would choose a size 10 shoe, and if wearing over-sized shoes became as immensely fashionable as wearing oversized trousers has in certain communities in the US in the 1990s, then again the size 8 individual might well choose a size 10 shoe. These alterations in one's circumstances are possible but extremely improbable.

The measurement of the extent of an agent's freedom by reference to the preferences regarding the options in her choice set that any reasonable person in her position might have thus strikes me as unsatisfactory.

OPTIONS AND VALUE

So far I have mainly been trying to offer a very limited defence of the amended simple conception of positive freedom by discrediting some attacks on it. Leaving behind the amended simple conception, I turn now to explore the other branch of this fork in the road, namely the evaluative conception – the idea that the contribution of an option to our freedom depends on its value.

I don't believe that conceptions of political concepts such as freedom can be literally correct or incorrect. A proposed conception may be revisionary with respect to ordinary usage, and this must be reckoned a cost. But whether the cost is worth paying depends on what it is we wish to do with a conception, what role it is to play in our theories. Since we are considering the use of some notion of freedom as the fundamental basis of interpersonal comparison in a theory of distributive justice, the merits and weaknesses of proposed notions must be weighed with this project in mind.

One central component of the reasons we care about the extent of the freedom our circumstances provide us is that freedom is a tool for satisfying our important goals over the course of our lives in a world of uncertainty. To the extent that I can be confident that the goals I affirm now I will continue to affirm in the future, I am still often ignorant of future contingencies that will determine what in the future will enable me to reach my goals to the greatest possible extent. If I know I will want a dinner tomorrow that gives me pleasure, but I don't now know whether fish or chicken will taste best at dinner tomorrow, I am well advised to ensure that I will have a choice then between fish and chicken. To the extent that my preferences and values, and hence my goals, may change in the future and I am confident that I will identify with these future values and want them to be satisfied, to that extent it is reasonable for me to act now to ensure that in the future I will be able to choose among options that will enable me to satisfy my future desires, whatever they might be (Kreps, 1979).

Both my present uncertainty about my future circumstances and my uncertainty about my future goals and preferences render it reasonable for me to ensure that I have wide freedom in the future. But from this standpoint, not all options are created equal. To the extent that I am simply trying to predict what values I will embrace in the future, and thus to predict what options will enable me to fulfil these values, it is usually overwhelmingly more likely that I will come to embrace values that are commonly affirmed by other members of my society, especially those whom I regard as wise and knowledgeable about the good life and its requisites. Moreover, my own present values are likely to resemble the values I will come to affirm in the future, especially if my present considered identification with my values is strong. So the agent's own valuation of options now available and the valuation of options by the consensus of the agent's society are both good indicators of the sorts of options that one would be well advised to ensure are available to the agent in the future because they are likely to be reasonably deemed choiceworthy by her in the future. In short, given what freedom is for, the estimation of the contribution of options to an agent's freedom in terms of their value makes good sense.

Now consider uncertainty of another sort. Suppose I want my life to be oriented to the successful pursuit of correct values, but at present I recognize I am woefully ignorant of what those values are. I have beliefs about values, but I affirm them weakly, because I suspect they are based on ignorance, lack of relevant experience of the ways of the world, emotional immaturity, lack of adequate reflection, and my inherent cognitive limit-

180

ations. My doubts about my present values do not *per se* provide me with guidance as to the sorts of options I should ensure I will be free to choose among in the future, given my overriding aim to achieve correct values. But a third party acting on my behalf now would be well advised to provide me with options in the future that will enable me to achieve correct values. Of course, nothing guarantees that I will in fact happen upon correct values in the future, but if truly valuable options are made available to me, at least it is the case that if I come to affirm better values, I will be able to satisfy them. Moreover, freedom may act as a desirable preference and value formation mechanism. Having the option to achieve X may help me to come to appreciate the value of X, which I would never notice if X were entirely beyond my reach. This train of thought also supports the idea that we should rank the contribution of options to a person's freedom by their value to that person. Here the relevant notion of valuation is objective: we want to provide options to Smith that are genuinely valuable, in part because the valuable options will be most beneficial to Smith in the event he does come to affirm them, and in part because having options available to an agent may be conducive to desirable value and preference formation, so making good options available leads to good options embraced and genuine values achieved.[3]

For the purposes of distributive justice, freedom may also be thought to be desirable in view of its interaction with responsibility. That is, if we believe in individual responsibility, we should not aim to arrange matters so as to guarantee that individuals achieve any particular level of well-being. The idea of individual responsibility in play here is that to some degree each individual is able to exercise choice and act in ways that partially determine the quality of her life, and to this same degree the individual should be responsible for the outcome of her choices of how to live in the sense that society is not obligated to make good any deficits in individual well-being that were avoidable through reasonable individual choice. On the personal responsibility view, if the options society has provided an individual are good enough (and if the individual is capable of acting responsibly), then if the individual comes to a bad end as a result of unfortunate choices or poor implementation of her choices, this state of affairs is the responsibility of the individual, not the responsibility of society.

A large family of principles of distributive justice agrees in holding that society is responsible for providing options to the individual that ensure that she has the real freedom to achieve a good life, a life that includes a fair share of the good that society can make available to persons (see Arneson, 1989, and Cohen, 1989; and for criticism, Fleurbaey, 1995). Obviously from the standpoint of theories of justice of this type, it does not suffice that the society provide wide freedom as the amended simple view conceives of it. For I can have a lot of freedom on the amended

181

simple view without having any prospect whatsoever of leading a good, rich, satisfying life. I may be blessed with numerous and significantly different options, but none that is choiceworthy. Having freedom of this sort does not suffice for distributive justice. Having wide freedom renders it plausible to hold that I am responsible for the subsequent quality of my life only if I have not just many options, but good, valuable options. A plausible division of responsibility between individual and society assigns society the responsibility for providing each individual wide freedom to lead a kind of life that she has reason to value. The freedom that is owed the individual on distributive justice views that accept as fundamental this division of responsibility is freedom according to the evaluative conception.

MIXED VIEWS

The simple view and the evaluative view can be combined in an attempt to avoid the implausible implications of both of these positions. For example, one mixed position consists of the following stipulations:

1 No choice, no freedom. If an agent is confronted with a choice set containing just a single option, which she cannot reject, she has no freedom, however attractive or unattractive the single option might be.[4]
2 The more choice, the more freedom. Other things being equal, one has more freedom if one faces a choice set with more rather than fewer options.
3 The more diverse the choices, the more freedom. Other things being equal, one has more freedom if one faces a choice set that contains options that are more rather than less significantly different from one another.
4 The more valuable the choices, the more freedom. Other things being equal, one has more freedom to the degree that the options one faces are valuable. Options that have nil value or less still increase one's freedom, but to a lesser extent than more valuable options.
5 The more desired by the agent are the choices, the more freedom. Other things being equal, one has more freedom to the degree that the options one faces are desired by oneself. (Note: other things are not equal if the choice set is a singleton.)

The *ceteris paribus* clause in each stipulation incorporates other factors asserted to be significant in the other stipulations. Nothing else renders things unequal.

Stipulation 4 determines that if Smith faces three worthy options and Jones faces three worthless options, Smith is more free (unless Jones's options are more diverse). Stipulation 1 determines that if Smith and Jones each face just one option, neither has any freedom, no matter how much more valuable Smith's option is than Jones's. If Smith faces more options than Jones, but Jones's options are more valuable or more diverse or both, then Jones may or may not be more free than Smith. This would depend on the comparative weight that is attached to the value, diversity, and number of options in the agent's choice set.

The most I would claim for the mixed view is that it accommodates the various criticisms made of different interpretations of the idea of positive freedom canvassed in this essay. Whether it is satisfactory, all things considered, is a topic I do not claim to address. And one difficulty already considered may still press against the mixed view. Recall the worry that according to the evaluative view, Smith and Jones, each enjoying the same religious options in a society that does not allow full freedom of religion, might be free to different degrees depending on whether or not the options allowed happen to coincide with their religious preferences. And according to the evaluative view, Smith can become more free or less free even though nothing significant in his circumstances alters and all that changes is his own assessment of the options available to him. I make no attempt to resolve this puzzle. I suspect its source is that genuinely different political ideals have marched under the single banner of 'freedom' as understood in the positive freedom tradition. No single proposal will encompass all of these.

The mixed view aims to reconcile two apparently incompatible claims about the nature of positive freedom. One claim is that being given a more valuable option augments one's freedom to a greater degree than being given a less valuable option. The counter-claim is that the valuation of an option cannot be the measure of the amount of freedom its availability creates, because an option might have negative value, yet more choice is always more freedom, not less. I acknowledge that my response has an *ad hoc* flavour. My suggestion is that we simply stipulate that in the positive range, a more valuable option increases freedom more than a less valuable option, but any addition of an option increases freedom, even the addition of a negatively valued option. This is the heart of the mixed view as so far presented.

Leaving aside its *ad hoc* quality, I fear the response offered so far is inadequate for a more fundamental reason. If we compare disparate choice sets A and B, we may evaluate the options in A as better precisely because they are fewer. Going to church on Sunday in the presence of few alternative options, which A offers, might be deemed more valuable than going to church on Sunday in the presence of many alternative options, which B offers. In the same vein, someone might prefer the choices in choice set A precisely because they are more alike, less significantly different than the choices in set B. Valuing circumstances A over circumstances B on the ground that there is less freedom in A than in B can hardly establish that there is more freedom in A than in B. Perhaps

183

another *ad hoc* response will suffice. Let us say that options that are valued on the ground that they are few in number or on the ground that they are not significantly different from one another are valued because they are restricted. We then amend the mixed view by adding a sixth stipulation:

6 Options that are valued because restricted do not augment freedom. To whatever degree options are valuable or desired because they are restricted, to that degree these options do not increase the freedom of an agent to whom they are made available.

The rationale of stipulation 6 is that we wish to respect two claims that might seem to be in tension but which are in fact compatible. On the one hand, we wish to allow with the evaluative view that if, for example, one has a choice of any one of three steaks, and steak is better than hamburger, the three-steaks choice set provides more freedom than the three-hamburgers choice set, provided the set of steaks is just as diverse as the set of hamburgers. On the other hand, against the evaluative view, we wish to deny that if, for example, one has a choice of any one of three steaks, all choiceworthy, and this choice set is then augmented by adding the option of a less desirable hamburger, the larger choice set might offer less freedom than the smaller and dominated choice set, if it is the case that the agent fears that she might choose hamburger against her better interests and places a negative value on the hamburger choice and a lower value overall on the three-steaks-plus-hamburger choice set than on the three-steaks choice set. Of course, recalling the lesson of the Mill discussion, we should add that if one has the metachoice of choosing either the three-steaks choice set or the three-hamburgers-plus-steak choice set, one has more freedom in that metachoice than one would if the three-steaks choice were not an option. Other things being equal, a more highly valued option increases one's freedom to a greater extent than a less highly valued option unless the preferred option is valued more highly because it offers less choice or less diverse choice.

CAPABILITIES

One powerful interpretation of freedom as a norm of distributive justice is the capabilities approach developed by Amartya Sen. This approach begins with the idea of a 'functioning', explained as follows:

> Living may be seen as consisting of a set of interrelated 'functionings', consisting of beings and doings. A person's achievement in this respect can be seen as the vector of his or her functionings. The relevant functionings can vary from such elementary things as being adequately nourished, being in good health, avoiding escapable morbidity and premature mortality, etc., to more complex achievements

such as being happy, having self-respect, taking part in the life of the community, and so on.

(Sen, 1992, p. 39)

A person's capability to function consists of 'the various combinations of functionings (beings and doings) that the person can achieve. Capability is, thus, a set of vectors of functionings, reflecting the person's freedom to lead one type of life or another (Sen, 1992, p. 40). Sen argues that we should conceive of well-being, the good for a person, as constituted by the functionings that the person attains over the course of her life, and well-being freedom as the capability for functionings that the person has (Sen, 1985, p. 203).

The chief rivals to the functionings and capability approach to well-being singled out for attack in Sen's analysis are (i) resources or means to freedom and (ii) utility understood as pleasure or desire satisfaction or some other mental state. At issue here is the appropriate basis of interpersonal comparison for the theory of distributive justice. Against each of the rival measures of interpersonal comparison Sen has an elegant and simple argument.

The resources alternative is elaborated in the writings of John Rawls (1971).[5] The core of the idea is that social justice should be concerned with the distribution of general purpose resources such as fundamental liberties and money, goods that will be useful for implementing any of a wide range of plans of life, hence resources that a rational person who recognizes that her present goals and values might shift over the course of her life and wishes to preserve her ability to fulfil her important goals over the course of her life will want to have. The core of Sen's objection against this proposal is that individuals differ in their capacities to transform resources into desirable achievements. But people's native talents and traits are doled out in arbitrary lotteries of genetic inheritance and early childhood socialization. The same level of resource may well provide two different individuals with very different levels of real freedom to lead lives they have reason to find valuable. Hence at the fundamental level principles of justice should rate people's condition in terms of what they are actually able to be and do with the resources they have.

The utility approach to interpersonal comparison as Sen conceives it takes some aspect of an individual's mental state such as pleasure or desire satisfaction to be the appropriate basis of interpersonal comparison for purposes of deciding our fundamental moral obligations to one another. Sen's objection to these subjectivist welfare conceptions of well-being is that individuals may adapt to adverse and oppressive conditions by adjusting their aspirations and by refining their abilities to savour little benefits. The person may then suffer from deprivations that are not registered in measurements of the individual's desire satisfaction level. Perhaps this objection does not apply to the interpretation of well-being as pleasure or enjoyment. But the hedonistic proposal excludes as irrelevant to the good life much that we take to be important. Sen urges that there is more to leading a fulfilling life than being happy, which may count as one valuable functioning, but surely is not the only one that matters.

Sen's objection against a resource conception of well-being is decisive, in my judgement. The objections against the interpretation of well-being as utility require comment. One objection is that there is more to leading a good life than being in any type of mental state. Notice that a desire satisfaction measure of well-being accommodates this point. People standardly desire not simply to have certain beliefs or feelings but that the world should meet certain specifications. The desire to write a good novel or to have a faithful spouse is not satisfied by experiencing a perfect illusion of writing a good novel or having a faithful spouse. The desires are satisfied only if one actually does write a novel and it is good, and only if one actually has a spouse who is faithful. But Sen's central and more powerful objection appeals to the widely shared intuition that the good life must include achievement of a number of distinct goods (e.g., love, friendship, intense and various enjoyments, cultural and work achievement, success in carrying out plans reasonably regarded as significant by oneself and by others, etc.) and that if one somehow comes not to desire these goods, their loss is still a significant deprivation even though it would not register as lack of desire satisfaction.

Sen's objection against subjectivist conceptions of well-being does not show that functionings and capabilities in general are the right way to measure well-being. The appeal is to the judgement that some particular doings and beings are important for well-being. This is an argument against a subjectivist conception of well-being and for an 'objective list' conception of well-being (Parfit, 1984). Any individual's capabilities for functioning at a time are legion in number, and a great many of them will be absolutely trivial and unimportant (e.g., my capability to touch my nose any number of times in an infinite array of slightly different ways). Still other functionings available to an individual at a time will be important to her, but will not plausibly be regarded as functionings the achievement of which advances her well-being. It may be very important to Smith that she should have the capability to give a sizeable sum of money, constituting her entire material wealth, to Oxfam. This capability is an important part of her present ability to achieve goals she regards as important, but not an important part of her ability to enhance her own well-being. Although Sen explicitly identifies functionings and capability with well-being and well-being freedom, the general characterization he gives does not in fact provide a way of picking that subset of the things I can do and be that constitutes my well-being capability. If he did provide a convincing test for distinguishing well-being functionings from others, he would have succeeded in specifying an objective criterion of human welfare or well-being.

Sen himself stresses the diversity of conceptions of human good. Part of the attraction of the functionings and capability account is that its generality and abstractness provide a way of thinking about the good that proponents of different views of the good can use without denying or ignoring their differences. Moreover, the objection against hedonistic and desire-satisfaction accounts of the good does not presuppose full knowledge of the human good. The objection appeals rather to a partial knowledge: Human good, whatever it might be, includes more than happiness or desire satisfaction among its important elements. Sen's account is epistemically modest and does not presuppose more agreement about what is choiceworthy than exists in fact.

But if Sen's objection is sound, it's not enough for him to claim that there is more to the good life than pleasure or desire satisfaction. He must claim that the other aspects left out of the subjectivist reckonings are important, so that we can plausibly claim to know that an impoverished peasant who lacks basic civil liberties and cannot feed or house his family even by backbreaking hard work year in and year out is not leading a good life no matter what heights his enjoyment and desire satisfaction levels reach. If we accept Sen's objection, we are committed to claiming some knowledge of what components of the good life are most important for fulfilment – or at any rate, important enough to take lexical priority over happiness and desire satisfaction. And if we are to take the functionings and capability approach as Sen wishes us to take it, as providing the most defensible answer to the question 'Equality of what?', then we have to know when people's functioning achievements overall are the same; and likewise for their capability freedoms. Sen suggests that we can often make reasonable comparative judgements about individuals' well-being in capability terms by an 'intersection approach' to measurement. The intersection method says that if everyone agrees within a certain range on the numerical importance of functionings, then we can make quantitative judgements within the range. For example, if everyone accepts that functioning A is worth between two and four units on a scale on which functioning B is worth five to nine units, then other things being equal, if Smith has A and Jones has B, Jones is better off. But the fact that everyone agrees that the importance of a functioning falls within a certain range gives us reason to use this range for purposes of quantitative assessment of well-being only if we accept that the true value of the functioning lies within the range of people's judgements. Otherwise what people happen to think is inconsequential.

I have argued that Sen's objection against the use of subjectivist measures of well-being in distributive justice theory is an argument for an objective measure of well-being as a basis for interpersonal comparison.

The basis of interpersonal comparison is not functionings and capabilities but truly valuable functionings and capabilities. Sen is coy on the question whether or not one can credibly claim objectivity in judgements of well being, but if we cannot, the proposal to use functionings and capabilties as interpersonal measures collapses.

If the interpretation of well-being as functionings is the same as an objective list conception of well-being, the question still remains whether having (i) a life of value or (ii) freedom to have a life of value should be the basis of interpersonal comparison for distributive justice.

STATUS OF FREEDOM IN THE THEORY OF DISTRIBUTIVE JUSTICE

What role do the various conceptions of positive freedom so far canvassed play in the theory of distributive justice? Is some version of positive freedom fit to be a foundational value, so that a society is just in its distributional practices just in case the distribution of freedom is fair? My answer is that freedom is an instrumental, not a fundamental value.

If freedom is having more choice, a rational person seeking her own advantage will not always prefer more choice to less. The example of the amplification of a person's freedom by provision to her of access to thousands of nearly identical tubes of toothpaste illustrates that more freedom can be valueless to the person who gains it (Dworkin, 1988, pp. 62–81). But even when, other things being equal, one would prefer more freedom to less, other things are usually not equal. In particular, the provision of a larger rather than a smaller menu of options from which to choose is costly, and the resources devoted to provision of more options might instead be devoted to enhancing the value of the most preferred option that is anyway going to be chosen. As we saw, there need be nothing irrational in ranking sets of options solely in terms of the value of the best option in each set. But when a person evaluates sets of options in this way, then any resources expended on increasing the variety of options and the attractiveness of options that are less than best are wasted resources if the goal of resource provision is to help the rational person attain her goals. Health care policy provides examples of social choice that involves trade-offs between providing more options for individuals and providing fewer but better options.

Of course, there is also nothing intrinsically irrational in valuing more choice for its own sake. One might simply prefer choosing from a rich array of options rather than from a more crimped set, quite independently of any further gains that might be achieved from enjoyment of wider freedom. When more freedom is preferred, all things considered, by some members of society, and less freedom is preferred, all things considered, by others, the problem of choosing a just policy that is fair to all parties

188

can be complicated and delicate. Often positive freedom has the marks of a public good; once it is made available to some, it is then available, or can be made available at slight extra cost, to many others, and in some cases, once a quantity of positive freedom has been made available to some members of a group, that same quantity is automatically provided to all group members, so that one level of the good must be selected for the entire group. But in this sort of case, in which freedom enters as a constituent of people's final welfare and is variously a great good, a small good, or no good at all for different individuals, no challenge is posed to an outcome-oriented principle that ranks the condition of individuals for purposes of deciding fair distribution entirely in terms of the welfare levels they actually reach.

Positive freedom also has value as a preference formation mechanism (as mentioned above). In *On Liberty* John Stuart Mill suggests that the same reasons that justify freedom of expression also 'require that men should be free to act upon their opinions' (Mill, 1978, p. 53). Mill's idea is that just as exposure to free discussion improves one's beliefs and desires, exposure to a wide variety of experiments in living can do the same. Both the individual's own freedom to try out experiments in living and the opportunity to observe and learn from the experiments undertaken by others contribute to rational preference formation.

Positive freedom is also a hedge against uncertainty and against the unavailability now of information that will be relevant to determining what course of action it will be reasonable to follow later.

A society that accepts an obligation to help people achieve good lives will accept an obligation to cater to each individual's rationally prudent preferences for the course of her life, which will include provision of positive freedom. But none of this gainsays the simple point that freedom is a means to well-being as well as a means to the achievement of non-well-being goals that individuals have reason to value. Often it is a vital means, but sometimes efficient action to assist individuals in reaching their goals bypasses freedom for other means, and in some contexts freedom is an obstacle to goal realization. The theory of justice should prize freedom but not make a fetish of it.

Moreover, the ideal theory of justice for human beings as they are will reflect the limited cognitive abilities of individuals and the wide variation in cognitive abilities among persons. A theory of justice in the 'real freedom' tradition which endorses special assistance to those with lesser talents is already working at a level of abstraction at which the limited cognitive abilities and different cognitive abilities among persons must be addressed. Individuals vary in their ability to gather information that is relevant to their decisions about how they wish to live. Individuals also vary in their ability to make good use of the information they have when making such decisions. Finally, besides varying in cognitive abilities,

189

individuals vary in their possession of native 'willpower' talent that enables one to carry on with what one has decided is best to do. The lack of this talent is sometimes denoted 'weakness of will'. A theory of justice must treat with respect and fairness all individuals, not merely those who are most competent at decision-making and decision-implementation. Whether freedom is understood according to the amended simple construal, the evaluative conception, or some mixed variation, freedom will be differentially valuable to persons depending on their differing abilities to make good decisions. The correct theory of distributive justice must appropriately balance the well-being of the less competent and the well-being of the more competent. If the fundamental basis of interpersonal comparison is 'real freedom' in any of the ways it has been interpreted in this essay, this conflict of interests between better choosers and worse choosers is resolved one-sidedly in favour of the good choosers. More freedom will always help me achieve my goals if I choose well and am never confused by additional options, and if my cognitive abilities are such that facing a richer array of options never strains my decision-making ability in a way I dislike. If my decision-making abilities are limited, more freedom is usually a benefit, and sometimes a great benefit, but is sometimes inimical to my life prospects. Hence freedom is an important secondary value, but not suitable for the role of fundamental basis of interpersonal comparison for the purposes of determining fair treatment of persons.

FREEDOM AND INDIVIDUAL RESPONSIBILITY

A widespread and entrenched moral opinion in contemporary societies holds that individual adults by their voluntary choices assume personal responsibility for the quality of their own lives in so far as their choices affect their lives. The idea that society has a responsibility to help its citizens gain good lives probably makes no sense if all claims of personal responsibility are abjured. For the responsibility of society in this regard must surely decompose into the responsibility of individual members of society to act in ways that steer institutions and practices toward the obligatory helping behaviour. At any rate, I have no quarrel with this claim: the obligation of society to help its individual members attain good lives is limited by the personal responsibility of each individual to help herself in this respect.

If society has given Smith a fair share of help, and Smith squanders the resources available to her and ends up living badly, Smith's unfortunate plight does not trigger further obligations on the part of society. The obligations of society specified by justice will be, on anyone's account, limited. It might seem an easy step from this assertion, which I do not challenge, to the further claim that what society owes the individual is to be specified in terms of some notion of positive freedom, resources, or opportunities. Society, following principles of justice, does not guarantee that individuals will reach any particular outcomes such as a minimal acceptable level of well-being. Society, in order to fulfil requirements of justice, must guarantee individuals resources that suffice to provide every individual the freedom or opportunity to lead a life of value.

In fact it is a mistake to infer from the premise (a) that the obligations of society to help the individual lead a good life are limited to the conclusion (b) that the obligation of society is to provide freedom. To say that an obligation is limited in the demands it places on the persons who are obligated is not to say that the content of the obligation is to provide opportunities to the persons to whom the obligation is owed. The limited strength or stringency of the obligations of justice to help individuals attain the good is compatible with those obligations being resolutely outcome-oriented. Suppose one maintains that what matters morally is well-being and how it is distributed. Freedoms matter not for their own sakes but for the contributions they make to promoting well-being and its fair distribution. Indeed, if provision of real freedom or opportunities to individuals was the fundamental aim mandated by justice, then provision of opportunities would still be mandated even in a special situation in which it is known for certain that the provision of opportunities has no prospect of increasing anyone's well-being. If I know for certain that provision of opportunities would be pointlesss or counter-productive, then any moral obligation I might be under to provide those opportunities lapses. This means that even in the normal case where provision of opportunities raises the expectation that the beneficiary will put the opportunities to good use, the opportunities and resultant freedoms are properly regarded as means to a further goal, morally significant not for their own sakes but as means to individual good.

The limitation of social obligation by personal responsibility can be accommodated in a theory of justice without making positive freedom the fundamental basis of interpersonal comparison. For example, one might regard failures of individuals to behave responsibly as decreasing their deservingness, and hold that the goal of social justice is to maximin (or maximize, or leximin, or equalize, or whatever) the well-being of the individuals who are most deserving, with lesser priority being assigned to helping the less deserving as well as to helping those who already are well off.

Another possibility is to argue from the assumed great value of real freedom to the necessity of letting stand the outcome that is reached by the free and voluntary choices of many individuals, even if that outcome departs from a socially preferred distribution of value across individuals. If we are going to provide genuine, real freedom to individuals, these individuals will then have the power to make foolish or wise choices, and we cannot undo the distributions that result from the exercise of free choice by many individuals without curtailing their freedom.

But from the fact that freedom has great value, meaning that it contributes significantly to individuals' prospects for well-being, nothing follows about giving primacy to individual responsibility as described above. Freedom is a good that is characterized by this fact: if one provides freedom to people, this results in some dispersion of well-being among individuals (who exercise their freedom in ways that are better and worse for their well-being). This characteristic does not belong uniquely to freedom. It quite likely applies to other constituents of the good life as well. If one tries to make the good of appreciation of culture available to individuals, this may result in some dispersion of well-being among persons, because people differ in their ability to appreciate culture and in their tastes for exercising such ability as they have. In the same way, if society tries to increase the degree to which individuals gain the great good of romantic love (say by providing privacy to young persons), this also may increase the dispersion of well-being among persons, as the privacy will be differentially useful to persons depending on their physical attractiveness. All that these examples show is that with respect to many important human goods, principles of justice must balance the goals of increasing their aggregate incidence and improving their distribution across persons, so that the less well off become better off. In this respect at least there is nothing special about freedom.

AGENCY FREEDOM, WELL-BEING FREEDOM, AND JUSTICE

Sen is non-committal on the question, should principles of justice use a measure of freedom or outcomes (or both) as the fundamental basis of interpersonal comparisons. But he is adamant that principles of justice must attend to both the agency and well-being aspects of persons: neither can be reduced to the other; neither can be ignored. If outcomes are fundamental, then both agency and well-being outcomes are fundamental; if freedoms are fundamental, then both agency and well-being freedoms are fundamental. So says Sen. The insistence on the moral importance of both agency and well-being is part of Sen's emphasis on the need to accept plural sources of information for moral judgement.

If one accepts that agency and well-being characterizations of an individual's condition are both important for deciding what constitutes fair treatment of the person, this might well be taken as a reason for holding that the freedom to choose between agency and well-being pursuits should be a fundamental concern of justice. One is pushed along the path from the acceptance to the conclusion by the further thought that within broad limits it is morally optional whether one pursues well-being goals or agency goals not concerned with well-being. An important way that individuals give shape to their lives is by picking a mix of these two types of aspirations, so having the freedom to select one's own mix is important, and society owes each individual wide freedom of choice in this respect.

I doubt that the agency aspect of persons should be a fundamental basis of interpersonal comparison for principles of distributive justice. I also reject the idea that the freedom to choose between well-being pursuits and agency pursuits not aimed at well-being should be a fundamental distributive justice concern.

'A person's agency achievement refers to the realization of goals and values she has reasons to pursue, whether or not they are connected with her own well-being', writes Sen (1992, p. 56). An important further distinction is drawn between what he calls 'realized agency success' and 'instrumental agency success'. The latter refers to the extent to which the goals an agent has reason to promote are achieved by her own acts directed toward those goals. The former refers to the extent to which the goals an agent wishes to achieve are in fact achieved, regardless of whether this is done through this agent's acts or in some other way. (In passing, I wonder whether the achievement of goals I wish to achieve that comes about through no doings of my own should count as part of my agency achievement. If I form the wish that cancer shall be cured and medical researchers in China find a successful cure for cancer even though I have not in fact had occasion to lift a finger toward this goal and none of my activities has contributed in the slightest to the achievement of the goal, is this cure to be counted part of my agency success on the ground that I would have helped if I could have helped?)

Consider the totality of my considered goals other than those that are part of my well-being. Call these the pure agency goals, just to have a label for them. Let us further divide these pure agency goals into the morally required and the morally optional. If Smith is pursuing a morally required pure agency goal, the reasons that render this pursuit morally required may apply to others or apply to Smith alone. If there are strong moral reasons for others to pursue the goal, it is these reasons, I submit, not the extra fact that Smith happens to be following them, that may indicate that the others should provide resources to further the achievement of the goal. The point is to achieve X because X is morally required, not because Smith wants the morally required X.

Sen's example of an individual who finds her agency freedom increased when she can interrupt her picnic to save a drowning person illustrates the point. If others should help Smith in this situation, they should do so because it is morally important that the drowning person be saved. Enhancing Smith's agency freedom or agency achievement is beside the point. If instead we suppose that Smith's reasons are what is called agent-relative, and render pursuit of the goal morally required for Smith and not others, again it is unclear why respect for Smith's agency requires that others should provide resources to help Smith achieve the goal. Smith will be required to pursue the goal to the extent that it lies within her power to achieve it, and if others fail to supply resources to boost Smith's pursuit, this fact does not reflect badly on the quality of Smith's will, which may be oriented correctly toward the morally required agent-relative goals whatever the others do. In this case also it does not seem that social justice requires the members of society to devote resources to helping Smith achieve his pure agency goals.

Consider now the other fork of the disjunct: the pure agency goal X that Smith pursues is not morally required. If its pursuit is optional for Smith, but morally required for others, the reasons for the others to devote resources to it surely do not involve the consideration of Smith's agency. If its pursuit is morally optional for Smith and for others, once again it is far from obvious that others are bound in justice to make sacrifices to aid Smith in satisfying this goal. Suppose Smith wants to save the snail darter and that this is a morally optional pure agency goal. Here there is if anything less reason for others to help Smith than in the case where Smith is pursuing a goal that is morally required for him but not for the others. And insofar as there is reason for others to assist Smith in seeking his goal, the reason derives from the desirability of preserving the snail darter, not from the additional fact that Smith happens to be interested in this project.

Next, consider the possibility that Smith's aim is an agency goal in a strict sense, that his aim is not that X be achieved but rather that X be achieved through his agency. In Sen's terminology, Smith is seeking an instrumental agency aim not merely a realized agency aim. Let's suppose that if Smith were to be seeking X, in the realized agency mode, X would be a pure agency aim. The achievement of X does not advance Smith's achievement of well-being. The question now arises whether social justice should incorporate a concern for Smith's instrumental agency success in cases of this sort. There are three cases to consider. One is that Smith's instrumental agency aim is in fact best construed as a well-being aim. A second possibility is that Smith's instrumental agency aim is an agent-relative aim generated by agent-relative reasons that apply to Smith and not to others. A third possibility is that Smith's aim is an agent-relative aim generated by reasons that are agent-neutral, applying to everyone. To illustrate the differences, suppose that Smith's aim is that his child prosper through his activity on behalf of his child. This might be an element of Smith's well-being: His own flourishing requires that he act effectively as a parent. Or it might be the case that there are moral reasons that apply to each parent and only each parent, instructing that very parent to bring about her child's prosperity by her efforts. The third possibility is that it might be deemed good in general that children should prosper through the agency of their parents. In the first case, the agent's self-interested aim does generate a reason for society (all of us regarded collectively) to help the agent satisfy the aim. A well-being-oriented theory of justice must balance the interest of the parent in being a successful parent and the interests of the child, which may in some cases conflict with parental self-interest. (In many cases, an individual's instrumental agency aim that figures in her well-being aspirations will be an expensive preference.) In the second and third cases, the point made previously applies again. If the agent's reasons to act are moral reasons, the proper weight that these reasons should have in the decision-making of others depends entirely on their moral force, not the fact that they happen to apply to the agent. In the third case, where there are agent-neutral moral reasons to bring it about that parents help their children, society will have moral reason to help Smith (and all other parents) be a successful parent. In the second case, again it would seem that if there are moral reasons that apply to the agent and not to others, it is not the responsibility of the others to bring it about that the agent can fulfil the moral demand.

Here there may be a difference between negative and positive freedom. If your strong conscientious belief is that you as parent should bring about the flourishing of your child, your conscientious belief *per se* does not oblige me to provide you the means you may need to follow your conscience. But in many cases it does seem wrongful to violate your negative liberty in this respect: to block you from acting on your conscientious belief. Whether what seems so here is really so is a topic for another occasion.

NOTES

1 The idea of measuring freedom by counting the number of choices available to the agent is discussed and criticized in Pattanaik and Xu (1990).
2 Van Parijs explicates this unproblematic sense as follows: an individual enjoys freedom to the extent that she has the 'opportunity to do whatever she might want to do' (Van Parijs, 1992, p. 467). The idea is that freedom is understood so that the amount of it I have is independent of my desires, preferences, and values – my conception of the good.
3 Notice that it is an empirical conjecture that providing valuable options is a better influence on preference formation than provision of other options. If a person was counter-suggestible, and tended to form preferences and values opposed to those that society suggests are worthwhile by making available to him even at some cost, then for this person provision of worthless options would be a better preference formation mechanism.
4 This assumption is made in Pattanaik and Xu (1990) and attacked in Sen (1990).
5 See also Dworkin (1981). But since Dworkin incorporates personal talents into the calculation of a person's resource share in a complex way, the Sen objection

against primary goods is not obviously decisive against Dworkin's conception of resources. See also Van Parijs (1990).

REFERENCES

Arneson, Richard 1989. 'Equality and Equal Opportunity for Welfare', *Philosophical Studies* 56, no. 1, 77–93.
Cohen, Joshua 1995. 'Amartya Sen: *Inequality Reexamined*', *Journal of Philosophy* 92, no. 5, 275–288.
Cohen, G. A. 1989. 'On the Currency of Egalitarian Justice', *Ethics* 99, no. 3, 906–944.
Dworkin, Gerald 1988. 'Is More Choice Better than Less?', in his *The Theory and Practice of Autonomy*, Cambridge: Cambridge University Press, 62–81.
Dworkin, Ronald 1981. 'What Is Equality? Part 2: Equality of Resources', *Philosophy and Public Affairs* 10, no. 4, 283–345.
Fleurbaey, Marc 1995. 'Equal Opportunity or Equal Social Outcome?', *Economics and Philosophy* 11, 25–55.
Jones, Peter, and Sugden, Robert 1982. 'Evaluating Choice', *International Review of Law and Economics* 2, 47–65.
Kreps, D.M. 1979. 'A Representation Theorem for "Preference for Flexibility"', *Econometrica*, 47, no. 3, 565–577.
Mill, J.S. 1978. *On Liberty* Elizabeth Rapaport (ed.), Indianapolis: Hackett Publishing. (Originally published 1859).
Parfit, Derek 1984. *Reasons and Persons*, Oxford: Oxford University Press.
Pattanaik, Prasanta, and Xu, Yongsheng 1990. 'On Ranking Opportunity Sets in Terms of Freedom of Choice', *Récherches Economiques de Louvain* 56, no. 3–4, 383–390.
— 1995. 'On Preference and Freedom', mimeograph.
Rawls, John 1971. *A Theory of Justice*, Cambridge, Massachusetts: Harvard University Press.
Sen, Amartya 1985. 'Well-being, Agency and Freedom: The Dewey Lectures 1984', *Journal of Philosophy* 87, no. 4, 169–220.
— 1990. 'Welfare, Freedom, and Social Choice: A Reply', *Récherches Economiques de Louvain* 56, no. 3–4, 465–484.
— 1992. *Inequality Reexamined*, Cambridge, Massachusetts: Harvard University Press.
Van Parijs, Philippe 1990. 'Equal Endowments as Undominated Diversity', *Récherches Economiques de Louvain* 56, no. 3–4, 327–355.
— 1992. 'Basic Income Capitalism', *Ethics* 103, no. 3, 464–465.
— 1995. *Real Freedom for All: What (if Anything) Is Wrong with Capitalism?*, Oxford: Oxford University Press.

14

JUSTICE AS THE FAIR DISTRIBUTION OF FREEDOM

Fetishism or stoicism?

Philippe Van Parijs

There are very few political philosophers whose work I find as congenial as Richard Arneson's. In some of his recent writings, however, including the one which I have been asked to comment on here, I believe he is moving in the wrong direction. Before characterizing this move and explaining why I think it is wrong-headed, let me briefly describe the relevant philosophical landscape.[1]

DISTRIVUTIVE JUSTICE: OUTCOME-ORIENTED VERSUS FREEDOM-ORIENTED

Contemporary theories of distributive justice can conveniently be partitioned into entitlement conceptions, such as Robert Nozick's (1974) but also David Gauthier's (1986), and equal-concern conceptions, such as John Rawls's (1971) but also all variants of utilitarianism. According to the former, implementing distributive justice basically consists in designing institutions that respect and enforce pre-institutional individual entitlements. According to the latter conceptions, the implementation of distributive justice basically consists in designing institutions that attend equally to the interests of all. Equal-concern theories can usefully be further partitioned using two other distinctions. Depending on the criterion they select, they can be purely distributive (as when they require maximal equality, whatever the cost), purely aggregative (as when they require the sum total or the average to be maximized) or intermediate (as when they require the maximization of the minimum score). Depending on what they take to be the distribuendum, i.e. the variable whose distribution matters to justice as such, not as a proxy or a causal factor, they can be either outcome-oriented – if what counts is people's achievements, what they end up with – or opportunity-oriented – if what counts is people's real freedom, their potential.[2]

As regards the first of these three distinctions, Arneson's contribution to this volume takes for granted that what we need is an equal-concern theory. As regards the second one, I suspect that he would go for an intermediate conception, even though his references to Mill and Dworkin indicate that he intends his argument to apply to purely aggregative and purely distributive conceptions too. As regards the third distinction, Arneson opts unambiguously for a (not fully specified) outcome-oriented conception against opportunity-oriented ones, including the one he presented and defended himself in a sequence of influential articles (Arneson 1990, 1991, 1992).

Before scrutinizing the main arguments behind Arneson's conversion – and, by the same token, behind the emerging disagreement between us – let me dwell a little on the diversity of the conceptions that populate the two sets that the third distinction generates. Outcome-oriented conceptions include all welfarist conceptions, from Mill's (1861) classical utilitarianism to Tinbergen's (1943) welfare egalitarianism, from conceptions that interpret welfare as the experience of pleasure (and the absence of pain) to those that construe it abstractly as rational goal achievement. They also include conceptions of justice that take income, or consumption, or income-leisure bundles, or functionings in Sen's (1985) sense as the distribuendum. They even include perfectionistic conceptions of justice that take as their distribuendum a particular conception of what is good for people, irrespective of whether these people attach any importance to it.

Opportunity-oriented (or real-freedom-oriented) conceptions, on the other hand, can be further differentiated along three dimensions. For the sake of simplicity, I shall list them using (maximum) equality as the relevant criterion. But analogous distinctions apply if more aggregative criteria are used, such as maximin. First, what should be the relevant time span? Should opportunities be equalized 'at the start', as people enter adult life, or throughout life at regular intervals?

Secondly, how broadly should one conceive the obstacles that need to be removed for opportunities to be equal? Does the equalization of opportunities reduce to abolishing all forms of discrimination on grounds of gender or race, religion or sexual preference, height, looks or age? Does it involve the equalization of the external endowments people are granted by bequests and gifts? Does it involve further the equalization of the internal endowments they derive from their genetic make up and their social background?

Thirdly, what metric should be used? Should opportunities (on the appropriate time-scale and in the appropriate range) be equalized, for example, in the sense that the extent of the freedom they afford should be the same for all? If so, does this mean that they should be able to do the same things, or the same number of things, or the same number of significantly different things, or sets of things which are, in some sense, of the same spatio-temporal size? Or is it rather the subjective value of people's freedom that is to be equalized? If so, should this value be understood as he welfare that can be achieved by making the best possible use of one's opportunities, i.e. the level of utility associated with the optimal element in the option set, or rather as the welfare directly associated with the set of opportunities as a whole (which will depend on the value of the best option, but may also be affected by the size of the set)? Or should one equalize the objective value of people's opportunities, understood for example as their access to a number of functionings whose nature and weight are determined in the light of a certain conception of man's objective needs, not of each individual's subjective wishes? Or finally, should one not instead equalize the social value of people's opportunities, understood as the opportunity cost to others of the appropriation of the resources these opportunities require and approximated by the competitive value of these resources?[3]

THE SIMPLE CASE FOR REAL FREEDOM

On this background, one can easily state the central intuition behind the choice for an opportunity-oriented (or real-freedom-oriented) conception of distributive justice, well expressed by Arneson (pp. 182, 190) himself in terms of an ethical division of labour between society and its individual members. It is not society's business to make people happy, let alone equally happy, or to make them achieve any other outcome one may wish to attach special importance to.[4] But it is society's business, perhaps even its primary business, to secure to its members an equal (or at least fair) distribution of opportunities to achieve whatever outcomes they may care about. The fact that equal opportunities will not lead to equal happiness, or equal achievement along any other dimension, is not an imperfection of this conception of social justice, but a reflection of the requirement that people should bear the cost of their actions and preferences.

This same fundamental intuition is sometimes expressed in a more roundabout way, by starting from a typical outcome-oriented conception, say equality of welfare. Such a conception gives rise to the standard objection that it is unfairly generous to people with expensive tastes – people with preferences whose satisfaction at any given level requires more resources than those of the average person – and unfairly mean to people with adaptive tastes – people whose preferences can be satisfied more cheaply than average because they adjusted to the meagre resources at their disposal. Now, one can attempt to accommodate this twofold objection while sticking to an outcome-oriented approach. For example, one might think of requiring equality of income rather than of welfare. But by focusing on one particular dimension (among the many that get amalgamated into welfare measures), one would have become unacceptably narrow: think of the people who work harder than others and could legitimately claim, on grounds of justice, a higher income. Or one might think of requiring equality along a number of dimensions, say income leisure, health, etc. But by requiring such multidimensional equality (without trade-offs across dimensions), one would have clearly become unacceptably rigid. Faced with such difficulties, it is tempting to leave aside marginal modifications and give up altogether the project of defining distributive justice as equal achievement or equal success and move on to the task of characterizing it as equal (or fair) opportunity.

But it is precisely this temptation that Arneson now wants to resist. He does not challenge that 'if society has given Smith a fair share of help, and Smith squanders the resources available to her and ends up living badly, Smith's unfortunate plight does not trigger further obligations on the part of society'. But he does challenge what 'might seem an easy step from this assertion . . . to the further claim that what society owes the individual is to be specified in terms of some notion of positive freedom, resources, or opportunities' (p. 190). What are his arguments?

First objection: freedom as fetish

One argument derives directly from the central claim of his contribution: 'Is some version of positive (i.e. real) freedom fit to be a foundational value, so that a society is just in its distributional practices just in case the distribution of freedom is fair? My answer is that freedom is an instrumental, not a fundamental value' (p. 188). Admittedly, 'some people may value freedom for its own sake' (p. 188), but the main reason why people care about freedom lies elsewhere: 'both my present uncertainty about my future circumstances and my uncertainty about my goals and preferences render it reasonable for me that I have wide freedom in the future' (pp. 180, 189). Moreover, freedom can be supported by straightforward consequentialist considerations, such as Mill's argument to the effect that freedom is important for the sake of fostering experiments (p. 189). Hence 'freedom is a means to well-being as well as a means to the achievement of non-well-being goals that individuals have reason to value . . . The theory of justice should prize freedom but not make a fetish of it' (p. 189).

Fair enough. But I cannot see anything here that could shake the intuitive case sketched above in favour of an opportunity-oriented approach. For the choice of opportunities as the locus of distributive justice does not commit one to denying that it is outcomes that ultimately matter to people. It is not based on the belief that people care about freedom for its own sake. As presented in the previous paragraph, the rationale behind this choice holds just as much if freedom does not matter as such to any of them. It holds just as much if welfare is the only 'foundational value', in the sense that the value to each person of anything else, including freedom, is derived from the value they ascribe to welfare. It is not because outcomes are what people care about that justice or injustice can be read from the distribution of these outcomes, rather than from the distribution of the opportunities to reach them.

Second objection: tough luck for bad choosers

However, Arneson presents a second argument that is not vulnerable to this objection. Freedom, he rightly points out,

> will be differentially valuable to persons depending on their differing abilities to make good decisions. The correct theory of distributive justice must appropriately balance the well-being of the less competent and the well-being of the more competent [whether they are better at gathering or processing information or endowed with a stronger will]. If the fundamental basis of interpersonal comparison is 'real freedom' . . . , this conflict of interest between better choosers and worse choosers is resolved one-sidedly in favour of the good choosers. . . . If my decision-making abilities are limited, more freedom is usually a benefit . . . but is sometimes inimical to my life prospects.
>
> (p. 190)

It is of course not enough to argue that adopting one metric ('real freedom') will turn out to be better for some people and worse for others than if another metric ('outcome') had been adopted. This is only an objection if one can show, using a different argument, that justice is a matter of equalizing success rather than opportunities. But Arneson's second argument against opportunity-based conceptions can precisely be understood as bringing out the uncomfortable implication that the incompetent, those who, for any reason, are bad choosers, are given an unfairly bad deal.

Those who insist, as I do, that talent-based opportunities should also be equalized, are unlikely to be moved by this argument. For they can fully share Arneson's moral intuitions and simply respond that the unequal ability to gather and process information and even the unequal strength of people's will constitute, according to their view too, unfair states of affairs which their conception of justice requires them to correct. In fact, I cannot imagine any situation that could be construed as unjust according to an outcome-oriented approach that makes adequate room for individual responsibility, while not being interpretable as unjust according to an opportunity-oriented approach that construes opportunities so broadly that it encompasses the ability to turn opportunities into desired outcomes.

Might the outcome-oriented approach then not have the advantage of accommodating these moral intuitions in a simpler or less problematic way? Arneson himself is hardly explicit on how his responsibility-sensitive variant of the outcome-oriented approach should be formulated:

The limitation of social obligation by personal responsibility can be accommodated in a theory of justice without making positive freedom the fundamental basis of interpersonal comparison. For example, one might regard failures of individuals to behave responsibly as decreasing their deservingness, and hold that the goal of social justice is to maximin (or maximize, or leximin, or equalize, or whatever) the well-being of individuals who are most deserving, with lesser priority being assigned to helping the less deserving as well as those who already are well off.

(p. 191)

Arneson is probably planning to spell this out more fully elsewhere. He may even have done so by now.[5] But I cannot see how he can get around the powerful challenge to this project that stems from the following difficulty: in pluralistic societies such as ours, there is no homogeneous conception of what counts either as deserving behaviour or as a reward. In such a context, it seems so much simpler to forget about trying to fine-tune desert and reward and to focus instead on equalizing (or whatever) people's real freedom, their opportunities. I am not denying that finding a suitably unbiased metric for these opportunities is a tricky business. Indeed, a large portion of *Real Freedom for All* (Van Parijs 1995a) is devoted to precisely this task. But in the absence of an explicit alternative, I remain convinced that spelling out what a fair distribution of opportunities or real freedom involves is the simplest, least problematic way of acknowledging the importance 'responsibility' and 'deservingness' can claim, in a pluralistic society, on the strength of considered judgements I fully share with Arneson.[6]

AN EMBARRASSING AFTERTHOUGHT: STOICISM AND THE PREFERENCE FOR FREEDOM

While scrutinizing the reasons behind my instinctive dislike for Arneson's recent move, I came to suspect that there was more involved than this conviction about how most conveniently to accommodate our shared intuitions about solidarity and responsibility, equality and desert. Perhaps the strongest and deepest reason for my dislike had something to do with some of my beliefs about the nature of a good life and hence with an aspect of my ethical views which I, as a professed liberal, was committed to keeping tightly separate from my conception of justice.[7] Let me explain what prompts this potentially embarrassing afterthought.

One can doubtlessly imagine that a tractable (responsibility-sensitive) version of equality of outcomes could be characterized so as to be abstractly equivalent to the most appropriate version of equality of (broadly construed) opportunities. Yet, this would not make the two approaches interchangeable. For the institutions each inspires will arguably generate different distributive patterns because of a difference in the initial presumption, and hence in the location of the burden of proof. An outcome-oriented approach starts with the requirement that everyone should reach the same outcome (somehow measured). If someone gets less than others, the natural response will be to shift resources so as to bring her up to the same level – unless it can be shown that her lower success was her fault. An opportunity-oriented approach, on the other hand, starts off by requiring an equal division of what doubtlessly counts as opportunities. If on this basis some turn out to achieve (what they regard as) poorer outcomes than others, they will be invited to make a better use of their opportunities, including possibly their opportunity to change their preferences – unless it can be shown that their freedom is, possibly in a subtle way, more limited than that enjoyed by others. Under appropriate specifications of outcomes and responsibilities, opportunities and choices, the two approaches will no doubt display a great deal of convergence: what one cannot plausibly be held responsible for will approximate what uncontroversially belongs to one's opportunities.

Because of the different points of departure, however, the burden of proof is naturally located on opposite sides. The convergence process will therefore tend to get stranded in the mud of unavoidably controversial factual claims, typically about how much of a person's poor achievement is due to a lack of capacity she cannot be held responsible for rather than to a lack of will. On the side of the outcome-oriented, a move (further) away from equal outcomes is required only if a lack of will can be demonstrated. On the side of the opportunity-oriented, a move in the direction of more equal outcomes is required only if a lack of opportunity can be exposed. Given the uncertainty surrounding many of the relevant facts, a sizeable gap is therefore most likely to persist between the distributive patterns that would emerge even from the closest variants of the two approaches.

This is the point at which one's conception of a good life may come to play a role. For how little one minds being stuck on the equal-opportunity side of the persistent gap is likely to be correlated with how much one is attracted by a stoic approach to life. Some of us find it comparatively more praiseworthy, or less strenuous, in their personal lives, to adjust their ambitions to the circumstances that happen to be theirs. For them, being stuck in the mud on the equal-opportunity side of the gap, conceding less than justice requires to the weakness of human nature, asking people to pull themselves together even in cases in which they could not, does not seem such a terrible thing. Not terrible enough, at any rate, to join Arneson on the other side of the gap – where some of the weak-willed are getting more than justice requires – and to assist him in the attempt to work out a responsibility-corrected equal-outcome conception of justice.

Here may well lie the deepest source of my instinctive resistance to Arneson's conversion. Recognizing this does not undermine my earlier rebuttals of the two arguments he gives for making the move. But perhaps it should make me accept that one's conception of the good life may, after all, legitimately affect one's conception of social justice?

NOTES

1 Earlier versions of this chapter were presented at the conference 'The ethics and economics of liberty' (Cergy-Pontoise, 21 June 1995) and at the 1996 meeting of the September group (New York, 7 September 1996). I am particularly grateful to Dick Arneson and Jerry Cohen for useful reactions.

2 Note that opting for an outcome-oriented conception does not prevent one from giving great importance to opportunities, as classically illustrated by Mill's utilitarian defence of liberty. Nor does opting for an opportunity-oriented conception prevent one from granting a key role to the satisfaction of people's preferences. The latter are of crucial importance, for example, if opportunities are assessed in terms of how high a level of welfare they give access to, or in terms of the competitive value of the resources they require (see below).

3 Typical 'extent metrics' are defended, for example, by Pattanaik and Xu (1990), Steiner (1994) and Carter (1995); typical 'subjective value' metrics by Musgrave (1974) and Arneson (1990); a typical 'objective value' metric by Sen (1985, 1992); and a typical 'social value' metric in the treatment of external endowments by Dworkin (1981) and Van Parijs (1995a). Undominated diversity, which I propose as the criterion that should apply to internal-endowment-based freedom (ibid., chapter 3), can be assimilated to an extremely modest version of the 'subjective value' metric. Note that none of the three types of 'value metric' (as opposed to the 'extent metrics') entails an 'evaluative conception of freedom' in the sense in which Arneson op. cit. (p. 9) uses this expression. According to each of them, the value of one's freedom is not what defines how much of it one has, but what determines how much of it one should get.

4 Making opportunities, rather than outcomes, the locus of distributive justice does not prevent one from talking about a fair or unfair distribution of outcomes, but only in the derivative sense that it came about as the result of a fair or unfair distribution of opportunities.

5 See Arneson (1996). See also in a related perspective, some of Marc Fleurbaey's (1995a, 1995b) recent work.

6 This is argued at more length in section 5.6 of Van Parijs (1995a) on the background of the metric of real freedom I develop in chapters 2 to 4.

7 In Van Parijs (1995b), I uncompromisingly defend against continental critics the liberal 'neutrality' shared by most contemporary Anglo-American conceptions of justice. The possible interference pointed out below is therefore something that should leave me uncomfortable.

REFERENCES

Arneson, Richard J. 1990. 'Liberalism, Distributive Subjectivism, and Equal Opportunity for Welfare', *Philosophy and Public Affairs* 19, 158–194.

Arneson, Richard J. 1991. 'A Defense of Equal Opportunity for Welfare', *Philosophical Studies* 62 (2), 187–195.

Arneson, Richard J. 1992. 'Property Rights in Persons', *Social Philosophy and Policy* 9, 201–230.

Arneson, Richard J. 1996. 'Should Swifers be Fed?', *The Good Society* 6(2), 38–42.

Arneson, Richard J. 1997. 'Real Freedom and Distributive Justice', this volume, chapter 13.

Carter, Ian 1995. 'Interpersonal Comparisons of Freedom', *Economics and Philosophy* 105, 819–845.

Dworkin, Ronald 1981. 'What is equality? Part II. Equality of resources', *Philosophy and Public Affairs* 10, 283–345.

Fleurbaey, Marc 1995a. 'Equal Opportunity or Equal Social Outcome', *Economics and Philosophy* 11, 25–56.

Fleurbaey, Marc 1995b. 'Equality and Responsibility', *European Economic Review* 39, 683–689.

Gauthier, David 1986. *Morals by Agreement*, Oxford: Oxford University Press.

Musgrave, Richard A. 1974. 'Maximin, Uncertainty, and the Leisure Trade-Off', *Quarterly Journal of Economics* 88, 625–632.

Nozick, Robert 1974. *Anarchy, State and Utopia*, Oxford: Blackwell.

Pattanaik, Prasanta and Xu, Yongsheng 1990. 'On Ranking Opportunity Sets in Terms of Freedom of Choice', *Recherches Economiques de Louvain* 56 (3–4), 383–390.

Rawls, John 1971. *A Theory of Justice*, Oxford: Oxford University Press.

Sen, Amartya 1985. *Commodities and Capabilities*. Amsterdam: North-Holland.

Sen, Amartya 1992. *Inequality Re-examined*. Oxford: Oxford University Press.

Steiner, Hillel 1994. *An Essay on Rights*. Oxford: Blackwell.

Tinbergen, Jan 1943. *Redelijke Inkomensverdeling*, Haarlem: De Gulden Pers.

Van Parijs, Philippe 1995a. *Real Freedom for All. What (if Anything) Can Justify Capitalism?*, Oxford: Oxford University Press.

Van Parijs, Philippe 1995b. 'The proof is in the pudding. Réponse à de Stexhe et Maesschalck', *Revue Philosophique de Louvain* 93, 555–566.

15

EQUALITY AMONG RESPONSIBLE INDIVIDUALS

Marc Fleurbaey

ABSTRACT

This paper analyses the concept of responsibility and the way it appears in economic theory and in egalitarian theories of justice. It identifies two general principles (natural reward, and compensation) which inspire many arguments and axioms in theories based on responsibility. The main results obtained in models where responsibility plays a central part are summed up and presented in the light of the two principles. The main criteria put forth by philosophers who combine an egalitarian concern with the idea of personal responsibility are also described, and their performance with respect to the two principles are compared.

INTRODUCTION

Economists have long since understood that, unless one is willing to accept big efficiency losses, equality cannot be achieved because the agents have some influence over their own outcomes. But political philosophers argue that equality is not desirable in the first place, for exactly the same reason. Equality would remove most of the expression of agency by free agents; and/or it would unduly relieve them from the burden of the consequences of their choices. In other words, full equality would deny responsibility. It is therefore important for the definition of social goals which guide public policies to better understand what responsibility means, and how it can be taken into account.

Responsibility is a difficult notion, and this paper proposes a few concepts in order to clarify and organize the various arguments which may appear, in economics or in theories of justice, in relation to this notion. The analysis is very tentative, and is certainly not exhaustive.[1]

This paper defines some basic concepts, which help characterize the various ways in which responsibility can be attributed to agents and taken into account in redistribution schemes. In particular, one can distinguish a general principle of 'natural reward', according to which agents must bear the direct consequences of their responsible behaviour, and a general (egalitarian) principle of 'compensation', according to which equality of outcomes should prevail wherever responsibility is absent.

Recent contributions to the economic theory of distributive justice which directly import some features of responsibility are reviewed, and models of compensation for handicaps in economic environments are discussed. Social welfare functions embodying principles of equal opportunities are examined and social rankings of distributions of opportunity sefs are considered. The various axioms and properties studied in these contributions may be related to the two general principles mentioned above, and shed light on the various facets and meanings of these principles. The results suggest that there is a general trade-off between the two principles, and interesting allocation rules emerge at the feasibility frontier of this trade-off.

Theories of justice which combine responsibility with an egalitarian concern, in particular the contributions by Rawls, Dworkin, van Parijs, Arneson, Cohen and Sen, are described. The two general principles are again useful to compare the performance of the various criteria put forth in these theories.

In order to give the analysis a more precise formulation, and to put in perspective the various approaches to the general issue of responsibility, we will often refer to the same general model. The following model encompasses most particular cases which will be described in the sequel.

A (finite or infinite) set N of individuals represents the population. Borrowing from Sen's theory,[2] any individual i in N is said to have a vector of 'functionings' f_i, which describes all his doings and beings. The vector f_i is causally determined by external resources alloted to individual i, denoted z_i, and by personal characteristics θ_i, through a given function φ which is identical for all individuals:

$$f_i = \varphi(z_i, \theta_i).$$

Nothing is assumed to be random, but components of z_i and θ_i may denote the value taken by random factors, and with a slight abuse of language we may consider that the choice of a gamble by an agent is equivalent to the choice of the value taken by the random factor for this agent.

The profile of characteristics in the economy is the mapping $\theta : i \mapsto \theta_i$. The economy also features a variable representing global (unproduced and/or productive) resources, Ω. An economy is then fully defined by the data $\mathcal{E} = (N, \theta, \varphi, \Omega)$. In the economy, an allocation of resources is denoted z and is a mapping defined on N by $z : i \mapsto z_i$. The set of feasible allocations in the economy $\mathcal{E}$ is denoted $Z(\mathcal{E})$. One can view Z as a correspondence defining sets of feasible allocations in a given domain of economies.

There are two possible social problems. One is to choose an allocation rule, that is, a correspondence S which, for each economy $\mathcal{E}$ in a given domain, selects a subset of feasible allocations $S(\mathcal{E}) \subset Z(\mathcal{E})$. Another social problem is to form a social ranking, that is, a function R which, for each economy $\mathcal{E}$ in a given domain, selects a preordering $R(\mathcal{E})$ over the set of feasible allocations $Z(\mathcal{E})$. The two problems are formally similar. An allocation rule defines a two-tier preordering, while a preordering induces an allocation rule by taking the best choice in every economy. In practice, allocation rules are appropriate for first-best analysis, whereas preorderings are preferred in second-best analysis.

In the sequel, general discussion will focus on allocation rules, in order to avoid a too lengthy presentation. We restrict our attention to allocation rules satisfying anonymity, that is, rules such that

$$\forall \mathcal{E} = (N, \theta, \varphi, \Omega), \forall \pi : N \rightarrow N \text{ bijective, } S(\mathcal{E})o\pi = S(N, \theta o\pi, \varphi, \Omega).$$

Unless otherwise stated, we also consider only rules satisfying equal treatment of equals, that is, rules such that

$$\forall \mathcal{E}, \forall z \in S(\mathcal{E}), \forall i, j, \ \theta_i = \theta_j \Rightarrow \varphi(z_i, \theta_i) = \varphi(z_j, \theta_j).$$

THE CONCEPT OF RESPONSIBILITY

Responsibility is a complex notion, and it may be defined in various ways, which correspond to different philosophical approaches. In this section the main distinctions needed for the argument of the paper are briefly sketched.

First, responsibility may be attributed either on the basis of control, or of delegation.[3] Responsibility by control is assigned to an agent on a particular variable when this agent has full control over the value of this variable. In this approach, responsibility is simply the necessary consequence of the fact that individual i controls variable v, but social institutions may alter the sphere of responsibility by modifying the domain of individual control. Responsibility by delegation, on the contrary, is assigned to an agent on a particular variable when the rest of society decides not to spend any resource on the value obtained by the individual for this variable. This does not mean that social interventions do not interfere with the fate of this variable, but only that this fate is not a part of any direct social objective. The individual is left to his own means if he decides to drive this variable to a better level. Responsibility by delegation can be given quite independently of the actual degree of control of the individual over the variable.

When responsibility is based on control, the notion of control may be defined in a compatibilist or incompatibilist way. The incompatibilist view considers that there is control only when the only factor which determines the considered variable is the agent's will, with no interference by any other causal factor or deterministic mechanism. This proviso also excludes causal influence over the agent's will itself, so that there is control

208

only when the agent's pure free will is the sole determining factor of the variable. The compatibilist view, on the other hand, considers that there is control even when causal factors interfere with the agent's will, but requires certain conditions over the exercise of the agent's will and decision-making power. For instance, it may require that there was enough deliberation, that a sufficient variety of alternative options were available, etc.

Responsibility is related in several ways to the ideal of freedom. Now, these various approaches to responsibility are related to different views on freedom. Under responsibility by control, responsibility is a consequence of freedom, and freedom is viewed as the free exercise of will (in a compatibilist or incompatibilist sense). In the incompatibilist approach, the only thing society can do is to interfere more or less with the consequences of the agent's free will, and that raises the ethical issue of determining the extent to which the agent must bear the consequences of her choices. For instance, the agent may freely choose her utility function, but society may intervene to influence her utility level. Authors like Arneson and Cohen seem to argue in favour of letting the largest set of consequences be borne by the agent, a stance which is related to the 'principle of natural reward' defined below: when agents choose their utility functions, for instance, society need not interfere with their utility levels directly. In the compatibilist approach to control, society can also interfere more or less with the consequences of the agents' decisions, but in addition it can intervene directly with the quality of decision-making by the agents, by providing them with the means and conditions that define free control in the compatibilist sense. For instance, improving the education level of the population may enhance its freedom of the will, in the compatibilist sense.

Under responsibility by delegation, the attribution of responsibility is by itself the definition of a liberty, and such liberty is less related to the exercise of will than to the existence of a personal sphere, which is not subject to a coordinated intervention by social organizations. Freedom in this approach has little to do with personal control and decision-making, even in a compatibilist sense, but is rather related to social interactions and pressure. This still permits different views. One is the well-known Millian definition of the private sphere, based on independence of the individual from social intervention. Another view is proposed by Schoeman (1992), and relates the existence of a free personal sphere to the connection of the individual to various overlapping social networks (as opposed to one all-purpose social group). It should be stressed that a theory based on responsibility by delegation need not be indifferent to the individuals' freedom in terms of choice and will, and may want to promote it; but it will not base responsibility on that ground.

The next important distinction is between responsibility over factors vs. responsibility over outcomes. The distinction between factors and outcomes is not completely obvious itself. When an individual's situation is assessed, there is some overlapping between the outcomes she obtains and the ultimate factors which explain such outcomes: some factors can be retained as relevant outcomes. But some factors (e.g. the weather) are not personal outcomes, while some outcomes (e.g. satisfaction) are not ultimate factors. In the model proposed in the introduction, the outcomes are the functionings f_i, and the factors are the arguments of the function φ: (z_i, θ_i). When responsibility is construed as a responsibility over factors, the agent is deemed responsible over the evolution of some factors which determine her personal outcomes. In our model, that can only concern some of the personal characteristics θ_i, since z_i is allotted by a social mechanism. Then, the vector θ_i is split into two subvectors $\theta_i = (\bar{\theta}_i, \hat{\theta}_i)$, where $\hat{\theta}_i$ denotes the components of θ_i whose value is assigned to the agent's responsibility, while $\bar{\theta}_i$ represents those characteristics for which the agent is not responsible. When responsibility is defined as responsibility over outcomes, it bears directly on the outcomes obtained by the individual, independently of the factors explaining them. In our model, this approach amounts to splitting the vector f_i into two subvectors $f_i = (\bar{f}_i, \hat{f}_i)$, the latter denoting the responsible part, and the former the part for which the agent is not responsible.

These distinctions pave the way to various combinations. Responsibility by control is most naturally given over factors, because usually the agents have only a partial control over outcomes (although under a compatibilist construal of control this may be less problematic). Responsibility by delegation, on the other hand, can be assigned over factors as well as over outcomes. Examples of theories choosing these various options are provided in the next sections.

RESPONSIBILITY AND REWARD

Responsibility is a recurrent theme in the theory of incentive compatibility. It often appears in the following, typical way. The agent has control over some variable, and is driven by particular interests, which may be viewed as a 'natural reward scheme' (for instance, making less effort is less tiring). But the principal's objectives diverge from those interests, so that she sets up an 'artificial reward scheme' to induce the appropriate exercise of control by the agent. The ideal solution would actually be to remove control from the agent altogether.

The ethics of responsibility heads toward a quite different approach. The general idea is that society (or the so-called 'social planner') should let the agents exercise their responsibility and bear the consequences of such exercise, without trying to distort their outcomes in a particular way and with particular incentives. If there is some 'natural reward scheme', it should, according to this view, operate as freely as possible, and the agents should benefit from it by making appropriate decisions or by having favourable characteristics. And there would be a loss if responsibility were removed from the agent.[4]

I propose calling this idea the principle of natural reward. It works slightly differently with responsibility over factors or over outcomes.

When responsibility is assigned over some factor, the principal wants the agent to bear all consequences of his decisions over this factor. In our model, this can be interpreted in various ways. Some of them will be illustrated in particular frameworks, in the next section. The strongest axiom which may be derived from this principle is probably the requirement that the allocation rule should not depend on $\hat{\theta}$:

Independence of responsibility characteristics (IRC)

$$\forall \hat{\theta}, \hat{\theta}', \quad S(N, \bar{\theta}, \hat{\theta}', \varphi, \Omega) = S(N, \bar{\theta}, \hat{\theta}, \varphi, \Omega).$$

This entails that when an agent changes $\hat{\theta}_i$, he alone bears the consequences, and these consequences are determined by the shape of φ, which is given and unalterable:

$$f_i' - f_i = \varphi(z_i, \bar{\theta}_i, \hat{\theta}_i') - \varphi(z_i, \bar{\theta}_i, \hat{\theta}_i).$$

Notice that the solution S adopted still influences $f_i' - f_i$ (unless φ is additive in z_i), so that the principle of natural reward should not be confused with the (absurd) principle that the consequences of exercise of responsibility should be completely independent of the surrounding institutions.[5]

Another expression of the same principle can be given by the following axiom, which requires equal resources for individuals who differ only in their responsibility characteristics:

Equal resource for equal non-responsibility characteristics (ERENRC)

$$\forall \mathcal{E}, \forall z \in S(\mathcal{E}), \forall i, j, \quad \bar{\theta}_i = \bar{\theta}_j \Rightarrow z_i = z_j.$$

Lemma 1 Assume that on the relevant domain φ satisfies the following condition:

$$[\forall \hat{\theta}, \varphi(z, \bar{\theta}, \hat{\theta}) = \varphi(z', \bar{\theta}, \hat{\theta})] \Rightarrow z = z'.$$

Then IRC implies ERENRC. The easy proof (which relies on equal treatment of equals) is omitted.

The relationship between natural reward and incentive compatibility is not always so negative as the introduction of this section may suggest. Consider the situation in which one wants to implement an allocation rule S when $\bar{\theta}$ is known but $\hat{\theta}$ is unknown. First, it is clear that satisfying the principle of natural reward is likely to make implementation easier. For instance, the axiom IRC entails full implementability (there is no need to make the agents reveal their $\hat{\theta}_i$). The more surprising fact is that conversely, under the equal treatment of equals condition, implementability itself requires to follow the principle of natural reward significantly. This will be illustrated in particular frameworks, below.

Consider now the case when responsibility is assigned over some outcome (presumably by delegation). The principle of natural reward is then *ipso facto* satisfied if this outcome is nowhere an argument of social objectives. Here again, this does not mean that the outcome is not influenced by the allocation rule. In our model, the principle can be immediately understood as stipulating that the social objective must deal with $\bar{f}$ only.

There is an idea of neutrality in the principle of natural reward. To distort the 'natural reward scheme' would oblige society to make a decision about the direction of exercise of responsibility which should be rewarded. The principle of natural reward allows society to shun such a decision. This is, however, only partially true, since there is in general some influence of the allocation rule over the consequences of responsibility, as explained above. One may imagine cases in which two allocation rules are almost equivalent as far as the social goal (including responsibility) is concerned, but have very different consequences over the exercise of responsibility (e.g., $f_i' - f_i$ widely differs).

Although the principle of natural reward is defended, more or less explicitly, by the philosophers who introduced responsibility into distributive justice, there may be good reasons to depart from it in some cases. The first reason is that it may sometimes be incompatible with other values one may want to promote. Efficiency is an example. In a model where agents are responsible for their preferences (viewed as factors of well-being), the principle of natural reward, by the above axiom of independence, would require the allocation to be independent of their preferences, and the allocation rule could not then be Pareto-efficient. In some cases, as in this example, it is not very difficult to find weaker versions of the principle which are compatible with the other imposed values (the equal budget allocation rule, in this example, seemingly guarantees any agent equal 'resources' for any profile of preferences). Gaspart (1996) proposes adding to the IRC axiom the proviso that it applies only when the selected allocation remains Pareto-efficient after the change in $\hat{\theta}$. Fleurbaey and Maniquet (1996) weaken the equality conclusion in the ERENRC axiom into a no-envy condition (which makes sense mainly when φ is one-dimensional): $\varphi(z_i, \bar{\theta}_i, \hat{\theta}_i) \geq \varphi(z_j, \bar{\theta}_i, \hat{\theta}_i)$.

A second potential reason to abandon the principle of natural reward is that the 'natural reward scheme' may be judged too harsh, when the slope of punishment and reward is very steep (for instance, you suffer death for the slightest mistake). This is particularly true for lotteries. Under responsibility by control, and the principle of natural reward, an agent who deliberately chooses a particular gamble must bear its consequences whatever the outcome, and this may induce huge gaps *ex post* between agents who took the same risks.[6]

These reasons are likely to lead to a weakening or softening of the principle of natural reward, and do not suggest to abandon it altogether. If the principle of natural reward were completely dropped, the way in which the exercise of responsibility by the agents is rewarded would become arbitrary because the idea of responsibility by itself provides no other guideline. An example will illustrate this point later. One might then try to find other ethical principles to justify the reward scheme. For instance, some paternalistic views about how the individuals should exercise their responsibility may lead the 'social planner' to devise artificial reward schemes representing such paternalistic views as well as inducing the agents to follow them.

RESPONSIBILITY AND COMPENSATION

Assume that responsibility is assigned to agents over some factor or outcome, and that the principle of natural reward is more or less satisfied in this respect. This fact, in itself, tells nothing about the way society deals with differentials in factors or outcomes for which the agents are *not* responsible. In particular, it tells nothing about the inequality aversion in social objectives. It may very well be the case that only the aggregate outcome, in its non-responsible part, is maximized, which leads society to give more resources to agents with outcome-enhancing non-responsible characteristics, or favourable ability to develop non-responsible outcomes.

But assume that equality is retained as a basic principle concerning the non-responsible part of the individuals' fate. How can this principle be embodied in more precise requirements, in view of the ethics of responsibility?

To begin with, consider responsibility over factors, retaining the notation $\theta_i = (\bar{\theta}_i, \hat{\theta}_i)$. Egalitarians then want the influence of differentials in $\bar{\theta}_i$ to be counter-balanced by the allocation rule S. A handicap in non-responsible characteristics elicits a bonus in resources, and an advantage calls for a penalty in resources. I propose calling this general idea the principle of compensation. Like the principle of natural reward, it can be given various expressions in axiomatic language. The prominent axiom might be the following one. It requires that two agents who display the same responsible characteristics should end up with equal outcomes. Their possible differences in $\bar{\theta}_i$ then do not prevent them from achieving equal outcomes, which clearly reflects the principle of compensation.

213

Equal outcome for equal responsibility (EOER)

$$\forall \mathcal{E}, \forall z \in S(\mathcal{E}), \forall i, j \in N, \text{ if } \hat{\theta}_i = \hat{\theta}_j \text{ then } \varphi(z_i, \theta_i) = \varphi(z_j, \theta_j).$$

A maximin version of this axiom is more appropriate in cases where this version is empty. The principle of compensation can also be expressed by solidarity between individuals w.r.t. changes in $\bar{\theta}$. Indeed, since differentials in $\bar{\theta}_i$ should be fully compensated, the cost or benefit of a change in the profile $\bar{\theta}$, even if the change happens only to a few agents, should be borne by the whole community. This suggests the following axiom:

Solidarity w.r.t. non-responsibility characteristics (SNRC)

$$\forall z \in S(N, \bar{\theta}, \hat{\theta}, \varphi, \Omega), z' \in S(N, \bar{\theta}', \hat{\theta}, \varphi, \Omega), \forall i, \ \varphi(z_i, \theta_i) \geq \varphi(z'_i, \bar{\theta}'_i, \hat{\theta}_i) \text{ or}$$

$$\forall i, \ \varphi(z_i, \theta_i) \leq \varphi(z'_i, \bar{\theta}'_i, \hat{\theta}_i).$$

There is again a logical link between the two axioms.

Lemma 2 SNRC implies EOER. The easy proof (which relies on anonymity) is omitted.

When there is no responsibility over factors ($\theta = \bar{\theta}$), one may view the principle of compensation as simply advocating equality of outcomes. When there is full responsibility over factors ($\theta = \hat{\theta}$), one may consider that the principle of compensation vanishes (the above axiom then boils down to an equal treatment of equals condition).

When responsibility bears over outcomes, egalitarianism simply advocates equality over $\bar{f}_i$ across the agents (it may be over the vectors or over an aggregate index of the components of $\bar{f}_i$). Again, a maximin formulation is more compatible with feasibility (and efficiency).

Let me emphasize again that the principle of natural reward and the principle of compensation are logically independent. This independence has often been overlooked in the literature on equal opportunity, in which they are not even clearly distinguished. One may find allocation rules which apply some natural reward scheme in the responsible sphere, but are not egalitarian at all concerning the non-responsible sphere. Symmetrically, some allocation rules do not follow the principle of natural reward while fully compensating for differentials in the non-responsible sphere.

RESPONSIBILITY IN ECONOMIC THEORY

This section reviews a recent literature which explicitly studies applications of the idea of responsibility. Responsibility was not, however, totally absent from previous approaches.

Of course, the traditional welfarist approach cannot easily take account of responsibility.[7] It retains utility as the only relevant functioning, and since utility may be viewed as the most comprehensive index of subjective assessment of the goodness or success of a life, this means that if there is responsibility (by delegation) over other functionings, it has little value. And responsibility over factors of the utility level is essentially absent since vectors of utilities themselves are ranked.

The literature on fair allocations too retains utility as the only relevant functioning, but the fact that it considers only purely ordinal (non-comparable) information over utilities means that the principle of natural reward (as expressed by the IRC axiom) is fully satisfied as far as utility functions (as distinct from preferences) are concerned.[8] This means in particular that the ordinal approach of this literature may be justified not only in the classical Robbinsian way, but also on grounds of responsibility for utilities, a kind of responsibility which some philosophers advocate (see below).

Fair compensation

Models of fair allocation can easily be adapted to the study of responsibility by adding personal characteristics representing non-responsible variables. Only three models, representing a small sample of possible situations, have been studied so far. The first two are in a pure exchange context, the third one considers production of a private good.

In model 1, utility is the relevant outcome: $\bar{f}_i = f_i^u$. This model describes a fair division problem in which non-transferable resources exist, and agents have preferences over bundles of extended (transferable plus non-transferable) resources. The responsible characteristic is $\hat{\theta}_i = u_i$, a utility function. The non-responsible characteristic is $\bar{\theta}_i \in \bar{\Theta}$, where $\bar{\Theta}$ is some set containing at least $\bar{\theta}_1, \ldots, \bar{\theta}_n$. A given, unproduced amount of transferable resource has to be shared among the agents. The external resource is one-dimensional and can be consumed in any non-negative amount: $z_i \in I\!R_+$. The total amount available is ω. The utility function is a mapping from $I\!R_+ \times \bar{\Theta}$ to $I\!R$, assumed to be increasing in its first argument. The function φ is defined by:

$$\varphi(z_i, \bar{\theta}_i, u_i) = u_i(z_i, \bar{\theta}_i).$$

The feasible set is $Z(\mathcal{E}) = \{z \in I\!R_+^n | \sum_i z_i = \omega\}$. It coincides with the set of efficient allocations.[9]

In model 2, disposable income is the relevant outcome.[10] Let it be noted $\bar{f}_i$ simply. Pre-tax incomes are determined by two kinds of characteristics, and a redistribution of income may be carried out. It is assumed that the profile of characteristics is given, and therefore that pre-tax incomes are not altered by the redistribution scheme. The responsible characteristic $\hat{\theta}_i$ belongs to $\hat{\Theta}$, a subset of euclidean space. And the non-responsible characteristic $\bar{\theta}_i$ belongs to $\bar{\Theta}$, a subset of euclidean space. Pre-tax income of agent i equals $g(\bar{\theta}_i, \hat{\theta}_i)$, where g is the same function (from $\bar{\Theta} \times \hat{\Theta}$ to $I\!R$) for all agents. An income transfer is $z_i \in I\!R$, and may be positive or negative. The function φ is defined by:

$$\varphi(z_i, \theta_i) = z_i + g(\theta_i).$$

The set of feasible allocations is, for all economies, $Z = \{z \in I\!R^n \mid \sum_i z_i = 0\}$, and coincides with the set of efficient allocations. Notice that, from a mathematical standpoint, this model is essentially the quasi-linear subcase of the previous one.

In model 3, utility is the relevant outcome. A production technology is available, and agents have unequal productivity parameters. But we want to restrict responsibility to the utility function only, and compensate any differential in productivity. One then has $\hat{\theta}_i = u_i$, the utility function, and $\bar{\theta}_i \in I\!R_+$ is a productivity parameter. The consumption of external resources is $z_i = (x_i, y_i) \in [0, \bar{x}] \times I\!R_+$, where x_i is the input contribution (bounded above by $\bar{x}$), and y_i the output share. Utility functions are mappings from $[0, \bar{x}] \times I\!R_+$ to $I\!R$, assumed to be non-increasing in the first argument, increasing in the second one, and quasi-concave. The function φ is defined by:

$$\varphi(z_i, \bar{\theta}_i, u_i) = u_i(z_i).$$

Notice that it does not depend on $\bar{\theta}_i$. The set of feasible allocations is $Z(\mathcal{E}) = \{z \in ([0, \bar{x}] \times I\!R_+)^n \mid \sum_i y_i \leq f(\sum_i \bar{\theta}_i x_i)\}$, where f is a non-decreasing continuous production function from $I\!R_+$ to $I\!R_+$.

We only briefly and informally summarize the main results obtained so far, distinguishing three points. First, a more precise understanding of conditions expressing the principles of natural reward and compensation. Second, a trade-off between satisfaction of the two principles. Third, identification of interesting allocation rules.

With respect to the first point, many axioms have been considered in these models, which add to the four main axioms presented above. In order to obtain compatibility with Pareto-efficiency, IRC can be weakened into Pareto-preserving independence (Gaspart 1996), stipulating that if a change in $\hat{\theta}$ does not break the Pareto-efficiency of the selected allocation, it remains selected after the change. A further weakening is support-preserving independence (Nagahisa 1991), stipulating that if a change in $\hat{\theta}$ leaves the selected allocation Pareto-efficient with the initial support, it remains selected after the change. A further weakening is the well-known Maskin monotonicity, stipulating that a change in $\hat{\theta}$ which increases the ower-contour sets at the selected allocation leaves the allocation still selected.

In models 1 and 2, these four axioms are equivalent, and they imply ERENRC (by Lemma 1). In model 3, the implications are strict, and Maskin Monotonicity implies the no-envy version of ERENRC (Fleurbaey and Maniquet 1996), while for a Pareto-efficient allocation rule, support-preserving independence implies an equal budget version of ERENRC (the agents must have equal shadow budgets; see Maniquet 1994b). In this model, Pareto-preserving independence is unfortunately incompatible with equal treatment of equals.

Weakenings of ERENRC are readily obtained by applying it only when all individuals have identical $\bar{\theta}$ (call it uniform ERENRC), or even when all individuals have $\bar{\theta}$ equal to a particular benchmark value (call it benchmark ERENRC).[11] In model 2, Sprumont (1995) considers an axiom logically between ERENRC and uniform ERENRC, namely, requiring z_i and z_j to have the same sign (call it sign ERENRC).

In model 2 SNRC can be strengthened into an axiom (call it additive SNRC) stipulating that individual after-tax incomes vary by the same amount after a change in $\bar{\theta}$ (Bossert 1995). It can similarly be strengthened into an axiom (call it multiplicative SNRC) stipulating that individual after-tax incomes vary in the same proportion (Iturbe-Ormaetxe 1996). In model 2, an axiom (call it fixed SNRC) which is logically in between SNRC and EOER says that when total income does not change, a change in $\bar{\theta}$ does not affect after-tax incomes (Iturbe-Ormaetxe 1996).

Weakenings of EOER are obtained by applying it only when all individuals have identical $\hat{\theta}$ (call it uniform EOER), or even when all individuals have $\hat{\theta}$ equal to a particular benchmark value (call it benchmark EOER).

Other axioms have been proposed which enforce some amount of natural reward and of compensation at the same time. In model 3, Gaspart (1996) applies Pareto-preserving independence to changes of θ (call it total Pareto-preserving independence). A change of skills which is combined to a change in preferences so as to preserve Pareto-efficiency of the initial allocation makes it still acceptable. The part of independence relative to changes in skills conveys some idea of compensation. In the same model, Maniquet (1994a) proposes what he calls an 'Equal Right', namely a minimal guarantee of welfare to all agents, in the form of an opportunity set which is the same for all agents, whatever their skill. An Equal Right is all the more valuable as it is larger. It then carries more compensation for the agents with low skills. But it is also closer to the feasibility frontier, so that the agents do not obtain much more than what is guaranteed by the Equal Right. Therefore the situation is not much different from a natural reward scheme in which every agent chooses from an opportunity set which does not depend on her preferences. In

217

brief, it seems that an Equal Right simultaneously conveys an idea o natural reward and an idea of compensation.

The general dilemma between the principle of natural reward and the principle of compensation can now be stated. It takes the form of incompatibilities between pairs of axioms, the first one from the natural reward side, the second one from the compensation side. In model 1, the axioms IRC and uniform-EOER are incompatible, as well as ERENRC and EOER (see Fleurbaey 1994), and as well as uniform ERENRC and SNRC. This holds in model 2 (consider additive SNRC) if and only if g is not additively separable (see Bossert 1995). In model 3, under Pareto-efficiency, Maskin monotonicity and uniform EOER are incompatible, as well as ERENRC (no-envy version) and EOER, and as well as uniform ERENRC (no-envy version) and SNRC (see Fleurbaey and Maniquet 1994, 1996).

Such a trade-off between the two principles gives a perspective to compare various allocation rules. Some of them can even be characterized by reference to this trade-off. Here is a sample of such solutions.

Undominated diversity (van Parijs 1990) $z \in S(\mathcal{E})$ iff z is Pareto-efficient and for no pair i, j one has: $\forall k, \varphi(z_i, \bar{\theta}_i, \hat{\theta}_k) > \varphi(z_j, \bar{\theta}_j, \hat{\theta}_k)$.[12]

This solution satisfies ERENRC in models 1 and 2, and uniform EOER in general.

$\hat{\theta}^*$-Conditional equality (Roemer 1993) $z \in S(\mathcal{E})$ iff z maximizes $\min_i \varphi(z_i, \bar{\theta}_i, \hat{\theta}^*)$.

This allocation rule satisfies IRC on the natural reward side, but only benchmark EOER on the compensation side. In its equality version, it is obviously characterized by these two axioms, and Fleurbaey (1995d) characterizes it on the basis of uniform ERENRC and benchmark EOER.[13] It is not efficient in model 3, where two adaptations have been proposed (the first one making sense only in convex economies).

u^*-Equivalent budgets (Fleurbaey and Maniquet 1996) $z \in S(\mathcal{E})$ iff z is a competitive equilibrium and, B_i denoting the budget set allotted to agent i, $\forall i, j, \max\{u^*(t) | t \in B_i\} = \max\{u^*(t) | t \in B_j\}$.

u^*-Equivalent bundles (Gaspart 1996) $z \in S(\mathcal{E})$ iff z is Pareto-efficient and $\forall i, j, u^*(z_i) = u^*(z_j)$.

The former satisfies support-preserving independence, the latter satisfies Pareto-preserving independence.[14] Fleurbaey and Maniquet (1996) characterize the former on the basis of Maskin monotonicity and benchmark

218

EOER, while Gaspart (1996) characterizes the latter on the basis of total Pareto-preserving independence and benchmark EOER.

In Fleurbaey (1995d) and Bossert and Fleurbaey (1996) an averaging version of this solution is proposed for models 1 and 2. Namely, take each individual's $\hat{\theta}_i$ as the benchmark value successively, and compute the average allocation. This solution satisfies uniform EOER but no longer IRC (it satisfies ERENRC). They characterize it on the basis of uniform EOER (and an axiom stronger than ERENRC, in the case of Bossert and Fleurbaey).

Another interesting solution for models 1 and 2 is the following one, which satisfies only benchmark ERENRC on the natural reward side, but satisfies SNRC (and even Additive SNRC in model 2) on the compensation side.

$\bar{\theta}^*$-Egalitarian-equivalent (Pazner and Schmeidler 1978): $z \in S(\mathcal{E})$ iff z is efficient and $\exists z^*, \forall i, \ \varphi(z_i, \theta_i) = \varphi(z^*, \bar{\theta}^*, \hat{\theta}_i)$.

This solution is characterized in model 1 by Fleurbaey (1995d) on the basis of benchmark ERENRC and uniform EOER, and in model 2 by Bossert and Fleurbaey (1996) on the basis of benchmark ERENRC and Additive SNRC.

Fleurbaey and Maniquet (1994) and Maniquet (1994a) propose two adaptations of this solution to model 3, which they characterize on the basis of SNRC (and Equal Right in the case of Maniquet 1994a). Moulin (1994) and Bossert and Fleurbaey (1996) propose an averaging version of this solution for models 1 and 2, by taking each individual's $\hat{\theta}_i$ as the benchmark successively. Bossert and Fleurbaey characterize it by uniform ERENRC and an axiom stronger than EOER. Sprumont (1995), in a version of model 2 in which $\bar{\theta}_i$ is one-dimensional, considers taking $\bar{\theta}^*$ to be the value such that $\sum_i g(\bar{\theta}^*, \hat{\theta}_i) = \sum_i g(\theta_i)$. He characterizes it by SNRC and uniform ERENRC, and in a version of the model with a continuum of agents, by EOER and sign ERENRC. Bossert (1995) and Iturbe-Ormaetxe (1996) present two other allocation rules for model 2. Iturbe's rule reads $\varphi(z_i, \theta_i) = \gamma g(\bar{\theta}^*, \hat{\theta}_i)$, where γ is a coefficient adjusted to make the allocation feasible. He characterizes it by Multiplicative SNRC and benchmark ERENRC. Bossert's rule is another kind of averaging of this rule and has $\varphi(z_i, \theta_i) = \gamma \sum_j g(\bar{\theta}_j, \hat{\theta}_i)$. He characterizes it by uniform ERENRC and an axiom somewhat similar to SNRC.

Social welfare functions

The previous section deals with allocation rules but, as stated in the introduction, it may be useful (especially in second-best applications) to have more fine-grained social rankings of allocations. For the moment this

FLEURBAEY

latter issue has been tackled in an even less comprehensive way than the former, but it is marked by the rather sophisticated scheme proposed by Roemer (1993, 1996, 1997).

Roemer's proposal is inspired by Arneson's and Cohen's theories of equality of opportunities (see below), but is aimed at being directly applicable in real-life contexts, with imperfect information and any constraint on the set of available policy instruments. Assume that $(\bar{\theta}_i, \hat{\theta}_i)$ is not directly observable, and that one can only observe two variables (a_i, e_i), where a_i denotes some traits which, for simplicity, will be assumed to belong to $\bar{\theta}_i$, and e_i is a real number representing an effort variable, which is chosen by the individual, although possibly under the influence of circumstances.[15] The choice of e_i may or may not be determined by the maximization of utility by rational individuals, but it is typically influenced by incentives set up by the allocation rule S, as well as by θ_i. The allocation rule S can only depend on the profile (a, e), and assuming a large economy and anonymity, what individual i receives may be written as depending only on (a_i, e_i): $z_i = S(a_i, e_i)$. Another important assumption is that there exists a function u such that $\varphi(z_i, \theta_i) = u(z_i, a_i, e_i)$. In other words, the individual outcome is fully determined by observable variables (although e_i does not represent full responsibility, in contrast with $\hat{\theta}_i$). The function u is known to the planner.

The proposal then goes as follows. First, society is supposed to draw a finite partition of the population, and individuals are then sorted out into different 'types' t, on the basis of their similarity in a_i. Let t_i denote individual i's type. The planner is assumed to know the conditional distribution of e by type, whose CDF is denoted $F(e|t; S)$. Let $e(\pi|t; S)$ be the level of effort corresponding to percentile π for F: $F(e(\pi|t; S)|t; S) = \pi$.

To formulate the social objective function, one must be able to define an indirect outcome function $v(S, t, \pi)$. This is not feasible in general, unless there is only one value of a_i by type, or at least a_i is unambiguously determined by π within a type. Assume then that the latter condition holds, so that there is such a function $v(S, t, \pi) = u(S(a_i, e(\pi|t; S)), a_i, e(\pi|t; S))$.

Then, Roemer proposes that society choose S so as to maximize either objective 1:

$$\min_t v(S, t, .5)$$

or objective 2:

$$\int_0^1 \min_t v(S, t, \pi)d\pi.$$

Objective 1 applies to maximin criterion to all agents with median effort in their respective types, while objective 2 aggregates the worst off across

220

types, for all (comparable) levels of effort. These two objectives define new kinds of social welfare functions.[16]

It seems that in this proposal the partition device, and the restriction to a finite number of types, is inessential to the main argument. If the planner knows the CDF $G(e|a; S)$, then using a function $e(\pi|a; S)$ similar to the previous one, one could define $v(S, a, \pi) = u(S(a, e(\pi|a; S)), a, e(\pi|a; S))$, and proceed similarly. The partition seems to be meant to reflect the intuition that as it goes thinner and thinner, society assigns less and less responsibility to individuals. In the limit one gets full equality of welfare.[17] But in general individuals in a type will have differences in a_i (and *a fortiori* in $\bar{\theta}_i$) as well as in $\hat{\theta}_i$. It is troubling for this proposal to grant society the right to assign (partial) responsibility over a_i to individuals, while it is admitted that individuals do not control a_i, which is observable.

Even if one drops the arbitrary social partition, the social objectives 1 and 2 may be far from equalizing opportunities. Two individuals i and j with, for instance, median effort in their respective subgroups of a_i, a_j may have displayed very different degrees of responsibility $\hat{\theta}_i$ and $\hat{\theta}_j$. To try to equalize their outcomes would then contradict the ethics of responsibility. This difficulty is avoided only if one makes the crucial assumption:[18]

Assumption R $\forall i, j$, $G(e_i|a_i; S) = G(e_j|a_j; S) \Rightarrow \hat{\theta}_i = \hat{\theta}_j$.

In order to understand this assumption, it is useful to represent the underlying determination of effort. One may safely think that e_i is determined by a function $e_i = f(S, \theta_i)$. Then one can easily show that Assumption R is implied by the following four assumptions: 1) There is only one value of $\bar{\theta}_i$ for each value of a_i; 2) $\hat{\theta}_i$ is a real number (or can be ordered on the line so that assumption 3 hereafter is satisfied w.r.t. this order); 3) f is increasing in $\hat{\theta}_i$; 4) The distributions of a_i and $\hat{\theta}_i$ are independent. The last assumption is natural, because responsibility for $\hat{\theta}_i$ would be dubious if it were correlated with a_i, but the first three assumptions are quite heroic, and illustrate how strong assumption R may be. These four assumptions are sufficient and not necessary, although relaxing each one of them enables one to find examples in which Assumption R is not true.

Let us now examine these objectives in the light of the principles of reward and compensation. Objective 1 tends to equalize only the welfare of agents who have exerted a particular level of responsibility (under assumption R). But if all individuals have uniform responsibility, it tends to equalize welfare, which is akin to the uniform EOER axiom of the compensation family. As mentioned above, Objective 1 is reminiscent of the conditional equality rule, except that the reference effort depends on the actual profile of the population, which is quite reasonable. There is, however, another interesting difference. The principle of natural reward is well implemented by the conditional equality rule, but Objective 1 does not reproduce this feature very well. Consider for instance the case when all agents have uniform $\bar{\theta}_i$ (hence a_i). Then there is essentially no need for redistribution of resources between individuals, but with Objective 1 which focuses on agents with median effort, a substantial tax is likely to be chosen in order to enhance median agents' outcomes. This may be viewed as problematic.[19] Notice, however, that in an economy with a continuum of agents, with an anonymous allocation rule all individuals in a given type a_i (under all assumptions made above) face the same opportunities, that is, have access to the same pairs $(\varphi(S(a_i, e_i), \theta_i), \hat{\theta}_i)$. In second-best applications, it is generally true that individuals of the same type face the same budget.

Objective 2 is much better as far as compensation is concerned, as it tends to equalize welfare between any two agents who have the same responsibility (under assumption R), which is akin to axiom equal outcome for equal responsibility. On the side of natural reward, however, it enforces a utilitarian-like reward scheme, which is quite questionable. In particular, if individuals have a uniform a_i, then it is equivalent to utilitarianism, and will thus reward individuals with outcome-enhancing effort variables. For instance, agents with expensive tastes are likely to receive less income than others under such a scheme, a rather severe penalty. Now, as above, one can try to correct this drawback by adding constraints to the objective. For instance, if a constraint of equal budget for equal a_i is introduced, natural reward will be somewhat satisfied in some cases. In some recent examples, Roemer (1997) introduces an ERENRC constraint. But in a production economy with equally skilled individuals, a utilitarian income tax would respect the equal budget constraint while clearly violating the natural reward principle.

A similar proposal has been made by Van de Gaer (1993). For brevity, we will not examine the details of the definition of variables, and just examine the social objective, retaining Roemer's framework. Let $H(a_i)$ denote the CDF of the distribution of a_i in the population, and A the support of a_i. Then the objective is to maximize:

$$\int_A w \left(\int_0^1 v(S, a, \pi) d\pi \right) dH(a)$$

where w is a concave function reflecting a social aversion to inequality.

This objective is not very good at compensation, since it simply aggregates individuals with different efforts and identical talents. When all agents have the same degree of responsibility, however it does tend to equalize welfare, when inequality aversion in w tends to infinity. It does not contain more of the principle of natural reward than Roemer's proposals: like Objective 2, it is equivalent to utilitarianism when all agents have uniform a_i.

222

Bossert, Fleurbaey and Van de Gaer (1996) examine how social order-ings can be derived from the allocation rules studied in the first-best litera-ture. They concentrate mainly on the adaptation of conditional equality, which leads to a slight generalization of Roemer's Objective 1, and of the egalitarian-equivalent rules, which are easily transformed into orderings. Indeed, it is immediate that allocations can be compared on the basis of $\min_i \lambda_i$, where λ_i is the solution of

$$\varphi(z_i, \theta_i) = \varphi(z_{\lambda_i}, \bar{\theta}^*, \hat{\theta}_i),$$

for some appropriate parameterization of reference bundles z_λ. This point was already noticed in Pazner and Schmeidler (1978).[20] Bossert *et al.* then make a comparison, in a simple example of a production economy borrowed from Roemer (1996), between these various orderings, including Roemer's and Van de Gaer's ones.

RANKING DISTRIBUTIONS OF OPPORTUNITY SETS

The social orderings described in the previous subsection are devised to rank economic allocations, but one can also view them as ranking distribu-tions of opportunity sets. For instance, Roemer's Objective 2 is based on the area of the intersection of the opportunity sets for each type, $\cap_t C(t)$, where $C(t) = \{(v, \pi) | v \leq v(S, t, \pi)\}$. Indeed, one has $\cap_t C(t) = \{(v, \pi) | v \leq \min_t v(S, t, \pi)\}$. Van de Gaer's social welfare function, in its maximin version (w infinitely concave), is based on the minimum area of $C(t)$ across types. Conditional equality (Roemer's Objective 1) evaluates $C(t)$ on the basis of $\max\{v | (v, \pi^*) \in C(t)\}$ where π^* is the benchmark level (.5 in Roemer's Objective 1). Egalitarian equivalent orderings can be viewed as relying on nested opportunity sets which are not individuals' actual oppor-tunity sets, but from which individuals would be indifferent to choose. These sets being nested, the application of the maximin criterion to distri-butions of these sets is unambiguous.

In this setting, one sees that the principle of compensation advocates equality of opportunity sets for individuals whatever their $\bar{\theta}_i$. And it is interesting to notice that equality of sets is more demanding than equality of values of sets. In this respect, a criterion based on the intersection of individual opportunity sets seems quite appealing. The principle of natural reward has more to do with the shape of the opportunity sets, and cannot be really studied in the framework of the literature reviewed hereafter.

The axiomatic analysis of social rankings of distributions of sets is a recent branch of the literature. We briefly summarize a few results obtained in this area. Let $(O_1, \ldots, O_n)$ be the general notation for a distri-bution of sets, each set O_i belonging to some abstract set $\mathcal{O}$. The problem is to rank all distributions $(O_1, \ldots, O_n) \in \mathcal{O}^n$.

Kranich has initiated this literature by focussing on how to measure inequalities between sets. In Kranich (1994) he characterizes measures based on the differences of cardinals between individual (finite) sets, and generalizes this to a topological framework in Kranich (1995a), in which differences in cardinals are replaced with general advantage functions, namely, functions $a_i : \mathcal{O}^n \to \mathbb{R}$ such that $\sum_i a_i(O_1, \ldots, O_n) = 0$ and $a_i(O_1, \ldots, O_n) < a_j(O_1, \ldots, O_n)$ whenever O_i is poor (for some given definition) compared to O_j. One then has the ranking $\succeq$ defined by

$$(O_1, \ldots, O_n) \succeq (O'_1, \ldots, O'_n)$$

$$\Leftrightarrow \sum_i \left| a_i(O_1, \ldots, O_n) \right| \leq \sum_i \left| a_i(O'_1, \ldots, O'_n) \right|.$$

For instance, $a_i(O_1, \ldots, O_n)$ may be the difference between the value of set O_i and the average value of sets $O_1, \ldots, O_n$ (this is reminiscent of the Kuznets inequality index). Kranich and Ok (1995) study the application to this setting of the criterion of Lorenz dominance, and show that the main results do extend to this new framework, while Kranich (1995b) characterizes a criterion of envy-freeness.

Herrero, Iturbe-Ormaetxe and Nieto (1995) extend this analysis in order to combine inequality aversion with a Pareto principle in the evaluation of distributions $(O_1, \ldots, O_n)$. In a framework with finite sets and only two individuals, they characterize social rankings based on the intersection of sets (as in Roemer's Objective 2). In particular, the most interesting ordering they characterize seems to be the one which applies the leximin criterion to the $n + 1$-vector of cardinals ($\sharp \cap_i O_i, \sharp O_1, \ldots, \sharp O_n$).

Bossert, Fleurbaey and Van de Gaer (1996) and Herrero (1996b) consider an abstract setting in which $\mathcal{O}$ has no particular structure, but they assume that there is a given valuation function $\varphi : \mathcal{O} \to \mathbb{R}$ which enables one to compare individual opportunity sets. Using variants of the Hammond Equity axiom, Bossert et al. characterize the ordering based on $\min_i \varphi(O_i)$, and the ordering based on $\varphi(\cap_i O_i)$. Herrero characterizes an inequality ordering based on $\min_i \varphi(O_i) - \max_i \varphi(O_i)$.

One may also mention here related works on capabilities and primary goods. Herrero (1996a) analyses the notion of capability set, the definition of a capability index that would evaluate individual capability sets, and she characterizes the leximin criterion applied to distributions of capability indices. Roemer (1996) studies the allocation of primary goods, viewed as necessary goods, and shows how one can make use of the fact that individuals consume (luxury) secondary goods to assess how equitable the allocation is. Villar (1996) constructs an inequality measure of the distribution of primary goods, which embodies the idea that the distribution of each good should be as egalitarian as possible.

EQUALITY AND RESPONSIBILITY IN THEORIES OF JUSTICE

Egalitarian theories of justice, after Rawls' influential work, now take into account the individuals' responsibility in determining their own well-being. Two main approaches have to be distinguished: the first one advocates 'equality of resources', and the second one 'equality of opportunity'. A brief discussion is proposed here, in which the kind of responsibility assigned in these theories is analysed, and the extent to which they satisfy the principles of natural reward and compensation is assessed.

Equality of resources

The three main representatives of this approach are Rawls, Dworkin and van Parijs. To some extent, one can consider that the relevant outcome selected by these authors is well-being, or success in life.[21] Therefore responsibility over outcomes is not important in this approach. Responsibility over factors is, in contrast, central.

Let us begin with Rawls' theory. A rough picture of his approach to responsibility can be drawn as follows.[22] Responsibility is assigned by delegation over a part $\hat{\theta}_i$ of personal characteristics, $\hat{\theta}_i$ denoting preferences and conceptions of the good life which the individual may adopt.[23] The non-responsibility characteristics are split into two parts $\bar{\theta}_i = (\bar{\theta}_i^c, \bar{\theta}_i^p)$, such that φ depends only on the first one, which denotes consumptive talents, $f_i = \varphi(z_i, \bar{\theta}_i^c, \hat{\theta}_i)$, while the second one represents productive talents. Now, Rawls assumes that all agents are identical in $\bar{\theta}_i^c$, so as to avoid the difficult issue of compensation by differential resources z_i, and simply proposes to apply the maximin criterion to a social index of resources or 'primary goods', $I(z_i)$.[24] Rawls argues that only when a fully satisfactory theory is devised in the case of uniform $\bar{\theta}_i^c$ can the issue of differential $\bar{\theta}_i^c$ be tackled.

In Dworkin's theory (Dworkin 1981), responsibility is also attributed by delegation over preferences and conceptions of life which the individual identifies with. The remaining personal characteristics are considered as internal resources, and Dworkin does not shun the problem of compensation for handicaps in internal resources. Equality of resources, in Dworkin's construal, means equality of the composite bundles $(z_i, \bar{\theta}_i)$. Since there is no obvious way in which such an equality may be assessed, Dworkin proposes a sophisticated mechanism to define it. Taxation policy, according to him, should try to approximate the virtual outcome of an insurance market in which, with equal budgets, the individuals would be able to insure themselves against $\bar{\theta}_i$, before knowing it, while already knowing their preference parameters $\hat{\theta}_i$. This partial veil of ignorance would, for instance, enable the individual who would like to become a musician to insure against the possibility of having a bad ear. As a consequence, the individual who regrets to have a bad ear because she would have liked to play music would receive a compensation equal to the virtual indemnity of this imaginary insurance market.

This idea is probably worth being studied more than it has been in the literature. But it suffers from a few important drawbacks. An obvious one is that the equilibrium prices of a virtual market are very difficult to compute, all the more as the relevant preferences (comparing bundles (z_i, θ_i)) are not observable by revealed choices. A second drawback is that although individuals must have definite preferences if the virtual market is to have a determinate outcome, it is problematic that preferences and life plans are commonly influenced by personal talents. If the taste for music comes from a good ear, does it make sense to let the individual insure on the basis of such preferences? The consequence is likely to be an insufficient compensation for handicaps, because by a well-known process of reduction of cognitive dissonance, preferences tend to adapt to potentialities.[25]

One of the weak conditions expressing the principle of compensation requires that when all utility functions are exactly identical, all individuals should end up with equal well-being. Such a condition is likely to be entirely violated by Dworkin's insurance scheme, as noticed by Roemer (1985). When all individuals have identical preferences, the outcome of the insurance market will be the contract which maximizes the expected utility of the typical individual, and by a well-known Harsanyian argument, this coincides with the outcome of the utilitarian criterion, where utility functions are taken to be the Von Neumann-Morgenstern utility functions of the population. Now, the utilitarian criterion does not lead to equal well-beings, but, on the contrary, it is likely to yield substantial inequalities in favour of individuals with high consumptive talents and low productive talents. People with low consumptive talents may then be even worse off under the insurance mechanism than without it! And people with high productive talents may be worse off than people with low productive talents. Dworkin actually seems to think of a rough insurance system, which would cover only unanimously admitted personal disasters. This would not satisfy the axiom equal outcome for uniform responsibility either, but would at least perform some compensation in its direction. Van Parijs (1990) notices that if individuals are sufficiently risk-averse, they tend to apply the maximin criterion, and equality of welfare would then approximately obtain in this case.

The insurance scheme does not fare much better as far as the principle of natural reward is concerned. Indeed, Dworkin insists that individuals with expensive tastes (who need more resources to obtain the same well-being as others) should not receive a higher income, which is reminiscent of the ERENRC axiom. This axiom, however, will not be satisfied because

226

two individuals with equal $\bar{\theta}_i$ may have different preferences and would thus have chosen different insurance contracts, leading to unequal indemnities for the same talent. We can only hope to satisfy the uniform ERENRC axiom. In this case indeed, there is no uncertainty about the talent obtained, so that no insurance contract will be signed, and since equal budgets are granted under the veil of ignorance, they should remain equal after the veil is lifted.

Van Parijs's theory (1995) is quite complex and involves several institutions (a basic income funded by different kinds of taxes), but the main idea related to the issue of equal extended resources is the undominated diversity scheme already described in the previous section. In general, this scheme satisfies ERENRC (provided external resources are defined as the budget set) and uniform EOER.

Equality of opportunity

The idea of equal opportunity has been put forth by several authors under different labels and with a few variations.[26] The main differences within this school deal with the selected outcome $\bar{f}_i$. Arneson proposes to retain utility (appropriately 'laundered'), while Cohen and Sen prefer a composite index in which objective outcomes are taken into account in addition to utility. In both cases, responsibility over outcomes is of little interest, so that this divergence need not be further analysed here, and we will concentrate on responsibility over factors.

In this approach, responsibility over factors is based on control. Notice, however, that Sen proposes equality of capabilities as a way to promote freedom, not on the ground that agents who waste opportunities should suffer the consequences. $\hat{\theta}_i$ are the characteristics individual i fully controls, while $\bar{\theta}_i$ are those characteristics which are given to her. When a personal parameter is only 'partially' controlled, the analysis should be able to split it into two parameters, one fully controlled and the other one out of control. When a fully controlled parameter $\hat{\theta}_i^k$ can be taken from a set $\hat{\Theta}_i^k$ which is not the same for all individuals, we will assume again that with additional parameters it can always be the case that all controlled parameters can be taken from the same sets, with equal access to the various levels of such parameters (i.e., a given level of $\hat{\theta}_i$ represents the same effort to everybody). Let $\hat{\Theta}$ denote the set from which $\hat{\theta}_i$ can be drawn.

In this subsection, we can assume that the profile θ is the only argument of the allocation rule S: $S(\theta)$, considering that the other features of the economy are fixed. In addition, we will restrict the attention to allocation rules which are single-valued.

In an immediate reading of these theories, one might think that there is equality of opportunity (or, rather, 'equality of capabilities') when the set of functionings an individual can attain is the same for all:

227

$$\forall i, j, \quad \varphi(S_i(\bar{\theta}_i, \hat{\Theta}, \theta_{-i}), \bar{\theta}_i, \hat{\Theta}) = \varphi(S_j(\bar{\theta}_j, \hat{\Theta}, \theta_{-j}), \bar{\theta}_j, \hat{\Theta}).$$

This definition is criticized by Arneson and Cohen as insufficient. It may very well be the case that two individuals can attain the same set of outcomes, while to get the same outcome requires a different effort from each one.[27] Therefore, one must add to the above definition the condition that with equal controlled parameters equal outcomes are attained by the individuals:[28]

$$\forall i, j, \quad \varphi(S_i(\bar{\theta}_i, ., \theta_{-i}), \bar{\theta}_i, .) = \varphi(S_j(\bar{\theta}_j, ., \theta_{-j}), \bar{\theta}_j, .).$$

Several difficulties with this approach are studied in Fleurbaey (1995b,c). Some of them are briefly summed up here.

A first difficulty lies in the fact that in the above formula, $\hat{\theta}_i$ is at the same time the blind argument of a function in the left-hand member, and a fixed parameter determining the function in the right-hand member. This makes it impossible to define the *ex ante* opportunities of the individuals: i's opportunities depend on j's choices, and conversely. This difficulty is, however, alleviated in large economies, where the profile of characteristics θ_{-i} may be viewed as essentially independent of θ_j.[29] And it is radically eliminated if the principle of natural reward is fully satisfied, i.e. if S does not depend on $\hat{\theta}$. Kolm (1993) proposes another solution, namely, to weaken the equal opportunity condition into a condition of 'equal liberty potentials', which says that for all i, j and all profiles θ, θ', if $\bar{\theta}' = \bar{\theta}, \hat{\theta}'_i = \hat{\theta}_j, \hat{\theta}'_j = \hat{\theta}_i$, and $\forall k \neq i, j, \hat{\theta}'_k = \hat{\theta}_k$, then $\varphi(S_i(\theta), \theta_i) = \varphi(S_j(\theta'), \theta'_j)$. The outcome i obtains is equal to what j would obtain if they exchanged their responsibility characteristics.

The principle of natural reward leads to the second difficulty. If the IRC axiom can be satisfied, that is, if there exist feasible S which do not depend on $\hat{\theta}$, it is likely that none of them will be able to satisfy the above equality of opportunity. The reason is simple. The above equality obviously entails that the EOER axiom is satisfied, and under some efficiency conditions, the SNRC axiom is also satisfied. Therefore the principle of compensation is substantially satisfied under equality of opportunity. The conflict between the principles of natural reward and compensation is likely to lead to an impossibility, and in Fleurbaey (1995c) it is shown that, in a simple model similar to model 1, the impossibility can be avoided only if φ is separable in $(z_i, \bar{\theta}_i)$, a condition which has no reason to hold in general.

Now, given this incompatibility, if the principle of natural reward is dropped, another difficulty arises with the fact that many allocation rules are then likely to equalize opportunities, with widely different reward schemes. This subdetermination problem has already been touched upon. A simple example can be given here. Consider an economy where $\varphi(z_i, \bar{\theta}_i, \hat{\theta}_i) = z_i + \bar{\theta}_i\hat{\theta}_i$, all three variables being real numbers. Assume that there is a continuum of individuals, 50 per cent of which have $\bar{\theta}_i = 1$ and 50 per cent have $\bar{\theta}_i = 2$. In the two categories, $\hat{\theta}_i$ is uniformly distributed over [0, 1]. Given that this is a large economy, and under a natural anonymity condition, the allocation rule may just make every agent face a function $S(\theta_i)$ which is the same for all. Assume that the feasibility constraint is $\int_0^1 S(1, t) + S(2, t)dt = 0$. One then obtains the result that any S satisfying $\int_0^1 S(2, t)dt = -1/4$ and $S(1, t) = S(2, t) + t$ fulfils equal opportunities. A large class of allocation rules satisfy these conditions, and give rise to many opposite reward schemes. For instance, one may give the agents the (equal) opportunities defined by $\varphi(S(\theta_i), \theta_i) = 2\hat{\theta}_i - \frac{n}{4}\hat{\theta}_i^{n-1}$, for any $n \geq 1$. For $n = 2$, this gives $\varphi(.) = \frac{3}{2}\hat{\theta}_i$, a linear increasing function, while for $n = 10$, this function starts at 0, increases until $\hat{\theta}_i \approx .74$, then decreases to end up at $-1/2$. The criterion of equal opportunities is then quite incomplete.

Equality of selected functionings

In a previous paper (Fleurbaey 1995b), I proposed to drop responsibility over factors, to restrict responsibility to outcomes, and to grant it by delegation. Society should decide on a bundle of functionings $\bar{f}_i$ it considers as important enough to be taken in charge collectively, and try to equalize (maximin) an index $I(\bar{f}_i)$ across individuals.

This proposal is very similar to Rawls' approach, except that it replaces primary goods with 'primary functionings'. This enables the redistribution scheme to take account of consumptive talents and handicaps.[30]

This proposal leads to substantial differences with criteria based on responsibility over factors, especially by control. First, this criterion will perform compensation even when individuals are causally responsible. For instance, if health is retained in $\bar{f}_i$, all individuals who have car accidents will receive the same help and medical assistance, whatever their responsibility in the accident; similarly, all patients with lung cancer would be treated regardless of their smoking behaviour in the past. If something like career or social integration is retained in $\bar{f}_i$, an individual who is unstable in jobs and is often on the dole will receive some assistance independently of the degree of his responsibility in this situation.

Symetrically, there will be no compensation even in the absence of causal responsibility, for outcomes which belong to $\hat{f}_i$. Suppose subjective satisfaction is put into $\hat{f}_i$. Consider a person who has always dreamt of becoming a flight assistant, because her father was one, but turns out to be too tall for this job. Under Dworkin's equality of resources, she would receive compensation. Under Arneson's equality of opportunity, she will probably receive compensation, especially because her preferences have been influenced by family background. With my own proposal, she will

229

receive compensation only insofar as this affects her social integration, career failures, or health (or any other selected functioning), but not on the basis of loss of satisfaction.

Advocates of equal opportunity argue that if individuals had no ultimate control over their own fate, if hard determinism were true, for instance, then full equality of outcome should be the social goal. This point is or would be rejected by all authors who propose to assign responsibility only by delegation. It is indeed highly questionable. The existence of a private sphere in which the individual can form plans, conceptions of life, and realize them to a variable extent is fundamental to the kind of society desired by many people nowadays. The mere project to evaluate life achievements of individuals, at a centralized level, in a comprehensive way covering satisfaction and other intimate functionings, and moreover to equalize these achievements, seems in deep contradiction with the widespread conception of a liberal society mentioned above. Whatever the actual degree of freedom of the will enjoyed by individuals, it is unreasonable to consider social equality going beyond the few basic functionings which are significant in social interactions. If individuals are not free from deterministic causation, at least should they be free from social scrutiny and interference in intimate functionings such as satisfaction, lifestyle, etc. In spite of their focus on responsibility, the theories based on responsibility over factors (except Rawls' one) never get rid of this basic flaw of utilitarian ethics.

A usual objection to this proposal is that compensating individuals who deliberately waste opportunities, as far as selected functionings are concerned, contradicts a basic moral intuition. Moral intuitions may be misleading, but I suspect that in the present case intuition supports equality of selected functionings rather than equality of opportunities. Because when a functioning is selected, that should mean that preserving some equality for this functioning (probably in combination with other functionings, and under a maximin criterion) is more important than letting the individuals bear the consequences of their actions. Preserving some degree of equality (under all qualifications mentioned above) in wealth or health, for instance, may be a more appealing social goal than leaving losing gamblers in dire straits, and reckless smokers in poor shape.

ACKNOWLEDGEMENTS

This paper has benefited from remarks by participants at the Conference, in particular P. Hammond, and by N. Gravel, F. Maniquet and A. Trannoy. I alone am responsible for the remaining shortcomings.

230

NOTES

1 This paper is an expanded version of Fleurbaey (1995a). A related attempt at a synthesis about egalitarianism with responsibility is made by Kolm (1993, 1996).
2 See Sen (1985, 1987).
3 This distinction was proposed, with a different terminology, in Fleurbaey (1995b). The distinction made by Kolm (1996) between 'responsibility' and 'accountability' is similar.
4 This latter point does not hold for theories based on responsibility by control, in an incompatibilist sense. Responsibility is then given by Nature, and no value judgement needs to be made about its extent.
5 Gaspart (1996) has shown that when a particular characteristic is not an argument of φ but is an argument of Z, then independence w.r.t. this characteristic conveys an idea of compensation rather than responsibility. Independence in effect comes close to solidarity in this case, and solidarity entails compensation (see below). Notice that independence cannot then be simply formulated by an axiom like IRC, since after the change in characteristic the selected allocation may no longer be feasible. Gaspart proposes an axiom stipulating that after a change in all characteristics θ, if the selected allocation remains Pareto-efficient, it is still selected (see below). This axiom simultaneously enforces responsibility for characteristics influencing φ but not Z, and compensation for characteristics influencing Z but not φ. The case of characteristics which influence both φ and Z is not addressed by Gaspart.
6 See examples of these two points in Fleurbaey (1995b).
7 See the surveys by Blackorby, Donaldson and Weymark (1984), d'Aspremont (1985) and Sen (1986).
8 See the surveys by Thomson and Varian (1985), Thomson (1994), Arnsperger (1992) and Moulin (1990, 1996).
9 This model has some similarity with Roemer's model (Roemer 1986). The reasons why Roemer's model and axioms have to be modified for the study of compensation are briefly explained in Fleurbaey (1994).
10 This model is due to Bossert (1995).
11 Notice, however, that using a reference productivity parameter $\bar{\theta}^*$ in model 3 does not make sense, since it is not realistic to distinguish between the units of measurement of skills and the units of measurement of the production function.
12 This solution has been refined in Fleurbaey (1994) and Iturbe-Ormaetxe and Nieto (1995).
13 In order to save space, I will not mention the other axioms used in characterizations, which are not related to the responsibility issue.
14 The latter therefore violates equal treatment of equals, and it does not satisfy the no-envy version of ERENRC.
15 The case of multi-dimensional e_i is also examined in Roemer (1997).
16 In the previous section, the Conditional Equality allocation rule was attributed to Roemer in view of its close formal similarity with Objective 1.
17 Notice that this limit result requires the partition to be made on the population, not on the set of traits.
18 This assumption is explicitly made by Roemer.
19 This point, which stems from the difference between first-best and second-best efficiency, is developed in Bossert, Fleurbaey and Van de Gaer (1996). In order to avoid having non-median agents severely taxed, Roemer (1993) adds a constraint of monotonicity of outcome w.r.t. effort. But this does not prevent a penalty for submedian agents.

20 I thank F. Maniquet for having drawn my attention to this historical point.
21 Rawls argues that such a functioning is incommensurable across individuals, but that is mainly an argument in favour of primary goods, and is not essential to the main structure of the theory.
22 We refer here to Rawls (1971, 1982).
23 Some ambiguity in Rawls' argument makes another interpretation plausible. Responsibility might be viewed as assigned by control, in a compatibilist sense, over preferences, provided the social institutions are set up so as to put individuals in good conditions to master their preferences and conception of life. This is still not full responsibility by control, since a particular domain, i.e. preferences, is chosen *a priori*. A full theory of responsibility by control first defines control, and the sphere of responsibility is then decided by the amount of control, not by the philosopher.
24 The framework is then very close to model 3 described in the previous section, except that Rawls thinks of a second-best context. Notice that the social index may refer to prices, for instance, so that I may depend on the profile θ. If I were independent of the profile, then the approach would be akin to the 'objective egalitarianism' studied by Gaspart (1994).
25 Dworkin notices this problem, and tackles it with a variant of the insurance mechanism. See van Parijs (1990) and Roemer (1996) for a criticism.
26 The main references are Arneson (1989, 1990), Cohen (1989, 1990), Sen (1985, 1987).
27 A game with non-anonymous rules may produce such a situation, and that is commonly viewed as scandalously unfair.
28 This issue, to my knowledge, is not directly addressed by Sen, but can be solved in his framework by considering $\hat{\theta}_i$ as a functioning. Then equality of accessible functionings means the same thing as 'equality of opportunity' in Arneson's theory and 'equality of access' in Cohen's one.
29 This argument is not fully convincing, because θ_{-i} in S may represent vicinity influences: even in a large economy, one may strongly depend on a particular brother's attitude.
30 This move is actually suggested by Rawls (1982).

REFERENCES

Arneson R. J. 1989, 'Equality and Equal Opportunity for Welfare', *Philosophical Studies* 56: 77–93.
Arneson R. J. 1990, 'Liberalism, Distributive Subjectivism, and Equal Opportunity for Welfare', *Philosophy and Public Affairs* 19: 158–194.
Arnsperger C. 1992, 'Envy-freeness and distributive justice', *Journal of Economic Surveys* 8: 155–186.
Blackorby C., D. Donaldson and J. A. Weymark 1984, 'Social choice with interpersonal utility comparisons: a diagrammatic introduction', *International Economic Review* 25: 327–356.
Bossert W. 1995, 'Redistribution mechanisms based on individual characteristics', *Mathematical Social Sciences* 29: 1–17.
Bossert W. and M. Fleurbaey 1996, 'Redistribution and compensation', *Social Choice and Welfare* 13: 343–355.
Bossert W., M. Fleurbaey and D. Van de gaer 1996, 'On Second-Best Compensation', *Cahiers du THEMA* 9607.
Cohen G. A. 1989, 'On the Currency of Egalitarian Justice', *Ethics* 99: 906–944.

232

EQUALITY AMONG INDIVIDUALS

Cohen G. A. 1990, 'Equality of What? On Welfare, Goods and Capabilities', *Récherches Economiques de Louvain* 56: 357–382.
D'Aspremont C. 1985, 'Axioms for social welfare orderings', in L. Hurwicz, D. Schmeidler and H. Sonnenschein (eds), *Social goals and social organization*, Cambridge: Cambridge University Press.
Dworkin R. 1981, 'What is Equality? Part 1: Equality of Welfare, Part 2: Equality of Resources', *Philosophy and Public Affairs* 10: 185–246 and 283–345.
Fleurbaey M. 1994, 'On Fair Compensation', *Theory and Decision* 36: 277–307.
Fleurbaey M. 1995a, 'Equality and Responsibility', *European Economic Review* 39: 683–689.
Fleurbaey M. 1995b, 'Equal opportunity or equal social outcome?', *Economics and Philosophy* 11: 25–55.
Fleurbaey M. 1995c, 'The requisites of equal opportunity', *Advances in Social Choice Theory and Cooperative Games*, W. A. Barnett, H. Moulin, M. Salles and W. Schofield (eds), Cambridge: Cambridge University Press.
Fleurbaey M. 1995d, 'Three solutions for the compensation problem', *Journal of Economic Theory* 65: 505–521.
Fleurbaey M. and F. Maniquet 1994, 'Fair allocation with unequal production skills: The solidarity approach to compensation', Cahiers du THEMA 9419.
Fleurbaey M. and F. Maniquet 1996, 'Fair allocation with unequal production skills: The no-envy approach to compensation', *Mathematical Social Sciences* 32: 71–93.
Gaspart F. 1994, 'Objective Well-Being in the Cooperative Production Problem', forthcoming in *Social Choice and Welfare*.
Gaspart F. 1996, 'Independence Axioms in Economic Environments', mimeo FUNDP, Namur.
Gevers L. 1986, 'Walrasian Social Choice: Some Simple Axiomatic Approaches', in W. Heller *et al.* (eds), *Social Choice and Public Decision Making*, vol. 1, Cambridge: Cambridge University Press.
Herrero C. 1996a, 'Capabilities and Utilities', *Economic Design* 2: 69–88.
Herrero C. 1996b, 'Equitable Opportunities: An Extension', mimeo, University of Alicante.
Herrero C., I. Iturbe-Ormaetxe and J. Nieto 1995, 'Ranking Social Decisions without Individual Preferences on the basis of Opportunities', IVIE WP-AD 95–23.
Iturbe-Ormaetxe I. 1996, 'Redistribution and Individual Characteristics', *Economic Theory* 7: 125–138.
Iturbe-Ormaetxe I. and J. Nieto 1995, 'On Fair Allocations and Monetary Compensations', *Economic Theory* 7: 125–138.
Kolm S. C. 1993, 'Equal Freedom', mimeo CGPC, Paris.
Kolm S. C. 1996, *Modern Theories of Justice*, Cambridge: MIT Press.
Kranich L. 1994, 'Equitable Opportunities: An Axiomatic Approach', forthcoming in *Journal of Economic Theory*.
Kranich L. 1995a, 'Equitable Opportunities in Economic Environments', forthcoming in *Social Choice and Welfare*.
Kranich L. 1995b, 'The Distribution of Opportunities: A Normative Theory', Carlos III University of Madrid, W. P. 95–19.
Kranich L. and E. A. Ok 1995, 'The Measurement of Opportunity Inequality: A Cardinality-Based Approach', Carlos III University of Madrid, W. P. 95–137.
Maniquet F. 1994a, 'Fair allocation with unequal production skills: The equal right approach to compensation', publication forthcoming in *Mathematical Social Sciences*.

Maniquet F. 1994b, 'On Equity and Implementation in Economic Environments', Ph.D. Thesis, FUNDP, Namur.

Moulin H. 1990, 'Fair Division under Joint Ownership: Recent Results and Open Problems', Social Choice and Welfare 7: 149–170.

Moulin H. 1994, 'La présence d'envie: comment s'en accommoder?', Récherches Economiques de Louvain 60: 63–72.

Moulin H. 1996, Cooperative Microeconomics: A Game-Theoretic Introduction, London: Prentice Hall.

Nagahisa R. 1991, 'A Local Independence Condition for Characterization of Walrasian Allocations Rule', Journal of Economic Theory 54: 106–123.

Pazner E. and D. Schmeidler 1978, 'Egalitarian-Equivalent Allocations: A New Concept of Economic Equity', Quarterly Journal of Economics 92: 671–687.

Rawls J. 1971, Theory of Justice, Cambridge: Harvard University Press.

Rawls J. 1982, 'Social Unity and Primary Goods', in A. Sen, B. Williams (eds), Utilitarianism and Beyond, Cambridge: Cambridge University Press.

Roemer J. E. 1985, 'Equality of Talent', Economics and Philosophy 1: 151–187.

Roemer J.E. 1986, 'Equality of Resources Implies Equality of Welfare', Quarterly Journal of Economics 101: 751–784.

Roemer J. E. 1993, 'A Pragmatic Theory of Responsibility for the Egalitarian Planner', Philosophy and Public Affairs 22: 146–166.

Roemer J. E. 1996, Theories of Distributive Justice, Cambridge: Harvard University Press.

Roemer J. E. 1997, Equality of Opportunity: A Theory and Examples, forthcoming.

Schoeman F. D. 1992, Privacy and Social Freedom, Cambridge: Cambridge University Press.

Sen A. K. 1985, Commodities and Capabilities, Amsterdam: North-Holland.

Sen A. K. 1986, 'Social choice theory', in K. J. Arrow and M. D. Intriligator (eds), Handbook of mathematical economics, North-Holland, vol. 3.

Sen A. K. 1987, On Ethics and Economics, Oxford: Blackwell.

Sprumont Y. 1995, 'Balanced Egalitarian Distribution of Income', forthcoming in Mathematical Social Sciences.

Thomson W. 1994, 'The Theory of Fair Allocation', mimeo, University of Rochester.

Thomson W. and H. Varian 1985, 'Theories of Justice Based on Symmetry', in L. Hurwicz, D. Schmeidler, H. Sonnenschein (eds), Social Goals and Social Organization, Cambridge: Cambridge University Press.

Van de gaer D. 1993, 'Equality of opportunity and investment in human capital', Doct. dissertation, K. U. Leuven.

Van Parijs P. 1990, 'Equal Endowments as Undominated Diversity', Récherches Economiques de Louvain 56: 327–355.

Van Parijs P. 1995, Real Freedom for All. What if Anything Can Justify Capitalism?, Oxford: Clarendon Press.

Villar A. 1996, 'The Welfare Evaluation of Primary Goods', mimeo, University of Alicante.

16

EQUALITY VERSUS WHAT?

Louis Gevers

The study of the incidence of taxation on the distribution of income and consumption is quite central to public economics. In particular, it is interesting to know the shape of the fiscal authority's option set in income or allocation space before proceeding to the next logical question, viz. which tax rule will actually be selected? These studies are positive or explanatory in nature. They require a full specification of the economy under scrutiny and the political economy question further requires a full specification of the political constitution.

Of course, these matters can hardly be conjured up without raising thorny normative problems. What tax rules should be considered just? At a deeper level, one must also question from a normative viewpoint the choice of a political constitution, as it has a bearing on the choice of the actual tax rule. These are two independent questions; however it is not uncommon to find citizens who endorse their country's democratic constitution, while considering unjust its democratically chosen tax rules.

All these questions, be they positive or normative, were first studied with one specific economy in mind. In particular, productive skills, individual preferences and initial property rights were thought of as fixed. If all goods are private, if agents behave competitively and elastically and if individual lump sums transfers cannot be used adequately, then redistributive taxation generally implies an efficiency loss because individual incentives get distorted. This is the well-known equality-efficiency trade-off, a description of the Pareto set as one moves away from the no-tax no-transfer equilibrium and one attempts to redistribute income more equally.

The normative question of which tax rules may be considered just in a particular economic context was often answered by invoking the utilitarian doctrine. In the late thirties, the more general Bergson-Samuelson social welfare function was found persuasive by many economists. In either case, the equality-efficiency trade-off was felt important because the actual cost of transferring income from one agent to another is higher than the amount received by the beneficiary, due to the distortion of

235

market incentives, and this must be appreciated if we want to compare or equalize the welfare loss of the losers with the welfare gain of the beneficiaries.

In the late forties, K. J. Arrow (1950) reconsidered the problem of social choice in an abstract framework and he realized that it was more natural to drop the single individual preference profile assumption and to adopt the multiprofile approach. Arrow's contribution was the founding stone of a rich literature that developed in many directions. The latter contain several results revealing a tension between the equality requirement and various other social values.

In the comments which follow, we plan to imbed Fleurbaey's contribution in a selection of existing results and to show that the tension we just mentioned has much the same origin as the efficiency-equality trade-off observed in public economics. It is well known that the formal language of social choice theory is often susceptible of more than one interpretation. We would like to warn the reader that the interpretation offered below is not unanimously accepted.

We shall start our summary review with Arrow's (1950) seminal contribution. His method became standard in social choice theory and it is worth recalling. If no obvious solution can be found to a particular social conflict, it is a sound practice to drop insignificant details and to consider the stripped-down version of the original problem as a member of a family of problematic situations that share the same essential features. One hopes to solve easily a member problem while meeting a set of desirable properties or axioms. This approach is quite useful if nice transition rules for adapting the solution to the original member problem can be invoked.

But how are we to define the domain of our investigation? Anyone interested in the solution of social conflicts would of course dream to get a recipe for solving all of them adequately. This would require consideration of the broadest domain of abstract conflicts. Arrow's pioneering theorem operates in this universal domain. It is a sobering result, revealing a general incompatibility between political equality and Pareto efficiency. This clash cannot be avoided if the social decision-maker is assumed to have the highest degree of rationality (a transitive social preference relation) and to use parsimoniously local information in the transition rule, in case of change of individual preferences.

Many research paths radiate from Arrow's negative result. The one followed by Marc Fleurbaey involves narrowing the definition of the domain under study. Giving it a simple but strong economic structure makes it possible to move from the constitutional problem to the question of what allocation of income and consumption we must consider just. Such properties as equality of individual consumption and effort level can now be defined, while retaining an Arrow-like assumption of a rich

236

domain of individual preference profiles. Let us for instance consider the two-good model of an artisans' economy (Fleurbaey's model 3), the constant returns to scale version of which was used by Mirrlees (1971) in his study of optimal income taxation. If individual preferences vary, it is immediately obvious that equality of outcome clashes with Pareto efficiency. Thus, one needs to relax the definition of equality and the weaker concept of envy-freeness has been found acceptable until Pazner and Schmeidler (1974) showed that it is also incompatible with Pareto efficiency when artisans differ in innate skill level, in the context of model 3. In an as yet unpublished paper about a standard exchange economy with non-convex preferences, Maniquet (1996) shows that Pareto efficiency is incompatible with the even weaker notion of no domination. Thomson (1995) gets the same negative results in an economy with convex individual preferences and a non-convex production set.

As to Pareto efficiency itself, it is perhaps too little questioned by economists who see themselves as its professional missionaries. Indeed, it has immediate normative appeal if one thinks of the social decision-maker as a benevolent dictator. Further justifications are nevertheless welcome and I surmise that one can be found in the concept of responsibility. Since the main source of the latter is man's autonomy or agency capacity, society must be respectful of individual preference when it happens to be shared unanimously.

In conclusion, the incompatibility results I have been sketching can be reinterpreted as already revealing a tension between the two social values of equality and responsibility. Marc Fleurbaey's contribution adds a new depth to the picture: it gets much closer to capturing the distinction between man's innate characteristics and those for which he is responsible. In model 3 for instance, artisans are assumed to have innate skills, whereas they are individually responsible for their choice of preference. In this set-up, equality could require that all artisans end up on the same indifference curve, at least when all of them happen to have chosen the same indifference map. Among other things, Fleurbaey's Proposition 1 tells us that this requirement is not compatible with Pareto efficiency together with another responsibility enhancing requirement: viz. Maskin monotonicity. This is a transition rule which says that a just social decision must not be altered when an agent decides to change his or her indifference map in a way that makes him or her less regretful than before the change.

Monotonicity is obtained by weakening Fleurbaey's axiom of independence of responsibility characteristics, according to which the allocation does not depend on individual preferences. Another weakening of the same axiom is proposed by Gaspart (1996): it requires independence only when Pareto efficiency is not violated. Gaspart further weakens the equality requirement as follows: there exists an *a priori* determined preference relation and if all agents choose to espouse it, they end up on the same

237

indifference curve. Together with Pareto efficiency, the last two axioms are sufficient to characterise the efficient solution which is egalitarian in terms of reference preferences.

Rather than adding more comments on the equality-responsibility dilemma, I would like to consider yet another interpretation of Pareto efficiency, monotonicity and independence of responsibility characteristics. This is their instrumental value for implementing social decision rules by means of game forms. The equilibrium concept used in implementing matters itself a lot and it needs further justification, that hinges on agents' information levels and commitment opportunities. As Maskin (1977) has shown, monotonicity is implied by Nash equilibrium, a concept relying on complete information and lack of commitment possibilities with respect to strategic cooperation. When the latter possibilities exist, the concept of strong Nash equilibrium introduced by Aumann (1959) seems quite worthwhile if existence is warranted and it requires Pareto efficiency. In total contrast, the concept of dominant strategy equilibrium requires neither Pareto efficiency nor complete information. This concept is in turn implied by independence of responsibility characteristics.

If the reader agrees with this reinterpretation in the context of implementation theory, Fleurbaey's results can be compared not only with incompatibility results involving Pareto efficiency, as we have done above, but they can also be compared with the Gibbard (1973)-Satterthwaite (1975) fundamental theorem which operates in the universal domain and says that dominant strategy equilibrium is incompatible with political equality. Together with Pareto efficiency, the same equilibrium implies dictatorship in standard two-person exchange economics on various relevant convex preference domains, as Zhou (1991) and Schummer (1997) have shown.

I would like to conclude these comments by suggesting that the implementation reading of Fleurbaey's dilemma links with the well known equality-efficiency dilemma which public economists consider fundamental in taxation theory. Let us study the latter more closely.

Let us consider again a particular version of model 3 with constant returns to scale, diverging individual skill levels and fixed individual preferences, and let us suppose that we are interested in various redistributive schemes. If individual lump-sum transfers can be used the Pareto set is maximal. Under horizontal equity (equal treatment of equals), the Pareto set contracts but this is not ethically significant and we shall therefore maintain this assumption.

Suppose we consider a nested sequence of sets of anonymous tax functions, each one of which being interpreted as a pure redistributive scheme. If the sequence is decreasing in the sense of inclusion, so is of course the corresponding sequence of Pareto sets. This remark becomes interesting if we add two more assumptions, viz.:

238

1 taxpayers' behaviour is more or less elastic; and

2 the no tax–no transfer, or *laissez-faire*, scheme is an element of all sets of tax functions.

Then, we can assert that the corresponding nested sequence of Pareto sets has in common the *laissez-faire* allocation, which may be regarded as a natural reward scheme because artisans do not exchange anything in this particular instance. Now, this allocation may lie very far from an egalitarian allocation and any attempt by the tax authority to get closer to it, will in general involve a loss by comparison with the larger Pareto sets in the sequence.

First of all, I would like to suggest that this relative efficiency loss has itself little ethical significance. Rather I would consider it as a challenge for the imagination of tax authorities, who often seem to believe in the dictum 'an old tax is a good tax'.

More to the point is the observation that designing a redistributive tax scheme is an exercise in contract theory, where the tax authority acts as the principal (the leader) whereas the taxpayers are the agents (the followers). Thus, in order to build appropriate sequences of tax functions, we can again refer to fundamental game-theoretic distinctions pertaining to observability and *a priori* information of the principal and agents and also to the number of stages in the game. The latter are at the root of the dilemma of public economics. The reader is referred to the work by Hammond (1979), Guesnerie (1981) and Piketty (1993).

In conclusion, game theoretic considerations of observability, information, number of stages in the game, possibility to commit to cooperate offer nice opportunities to connect a reinterpretation of Fleurbaey's dilemma with the public economics literature. Social choice theorists will have noticed that the implementation viewpoint is essentially multiprofile whereas the contract theory viewpoint is single profile. Further clarification of the relation between the two approaches would be an interesting exercise.

ACKNOWLEDGEMENTS

I am indebted to François Maniquet and Alain Trannoy for clarifying discussions on these comments. Responsibility for errors rests with the author.

REFERENCES

Arrow, K.J. (1950), 'A difficulty in the concept of social welfare', *Journal of Political Economy* 58, 328–346.

Aumann, R. (1959), 'Acceptable points in general cooperative n-person games', *Contributions to the theory of games IV*, Princeton University Press, Princeton.

Gaspart, F. (1996), 'Independence axioms in economic environments', FUNDP working paper.

Gibbard, A. (1973), 'Manipulation of voting schemes', *Econometrica* 41, 587–601.

Guesnerie, R. (1981), 'On taxation and incentives: further remarks on the limits to redistribution', Bonn working paper.

Hammond, P. (1979), 'Straightforward incentive compatibility in large economies', *Review of Economic Studies* 46, 263–282.

Maniquet, F. (1996), 'A strong incompatibility between efficiency and equity in non-convex economies', mimeo, FUNDP.

Maskin, E. (1977), 'Nash equilibrium and welfare optimality', MIT working paper.

Mirrlees, J. (1971), 'An exploration in the theory of optimum income taxation', *Review of Economic Studies* 38, 175–208.

Pazner, E. and S. Schmeidler (1974), 'A difficulty in the concept of fairness', *Review of Economic Studies* 41, 441–443.

Piketty, T. (1993), 'Implementation of first-best allocations via generalised tax schedules', *Journal of Economic Theory* 61, 23–41.

Satterthwaite, M.A. (1975), 'Strategy-proofness and Arrow's conditions', *Journal of Economic Theory* 10, 187–217.

Schummer, J. (1997), 'Strategy-proofness versus efficiency on restricted domains of exchange economies', *Social Choice Welfare* 14, 1–22.

Thomson, W. (1995), 'The theory of fair allocation', University of Rochester, mimeo.

Zhou, L. (1991), 'Inefficiency of strategy proof allocation mechanisms in pure exchange economies', *Social Choice Welfare* 8, 247–254.

17

EQUAL OPPORTUNITY FOR HEALTH

Paying the costs of smoking-induced
lung cancer[1]

John E. Roemer

A THEORY OF EQUAL OPPORTUNITY

In this section, I shall briefly review a general theory of equal opportunity that I have explained in detail elsewhere (Roemer, 1996, chapter 8; Roemer (in press)). In the next section, I apply the theory to determine the assessment of health insurance premiums on smokers, which shall be used to pay the costs of treating their smoking-induced lung cancer.

In the general theory, there is a set of individuals who choose actions that affect their future welfare. Their choice of actions is determined both by circumstances beyond their control and by autonomous choice, viewed as within the realm of their personal responsibility. Their welfare is, in turn, a function, in general, of circumstances, choices, and some resource endowment. I shall call the choice a person makes his effort, and this shall be a unidimensional variable (such as years she chooses to abstain from smoking).

Individuals are initially partitioned into a set of types, where a type consists of all persons with the same vector of circumstances. Circumstances, in the smoking case, are aspects of the person's environment which influence his smoking behaviour and which we deem he should not be held accountable for: for instance his sex, age, level of education, and perhaps occupation. (An individual's occupation is to some extent within his control, but we may decide that, nevertheless, it is wrong to hold a person accountable for not taking into account the effect his occupational choice will have on his smoking behaviour.) A type consists of all persons, then, who are similarly situated in respect to these circumstances.

Suppose we impose a health insurance premium, abstractly represented as $f^t(y)$ on members of type t, where y is the number of years the person has smoked. I shall assume, for the duration, that y is observable (perhaps to a physician). Let the measure of (expected) welfare for type t be $u^t(M, y)$, where M is his disposable income. I emphasize that the function

241

u^t is chosen by the Ministry of Health, which is concerned with the person's health, and so u^t is a decreasing function of y (that is, the probability of contracting lung cancer is an increasing function of y). Facing a premium policy f^t, members of type t will respond with a certain distribution of smoking behavior: let $F_{f^t}^t$ be the probability measure (on the positive reals) characterizing the distribution of years smoked by members of type t, when facing the premium f^t. In particular, we can speak of the person at the πth centile of that distribution, and the years smoked by the person at that centile, $y(\pi)$. We can define the indirect advantage function v^t as $v^t(\pi, f^t) = u^t(M - f^t(y(\pi)), y(\pi))$; that is, $v^t(\pi, f^t)$ is the advantage accruing to the individual at the πth centile of the smoking distribution of type t persons, when facing the premium function f^t.

In our analysis, we take the probability measures $\{F_{f^t}^t\}$ as data of the problem. We also know (as data) the cost of treating a case of lung cancer and the fraction of people who will contract the disease, as a function of type and years smoked. Thus, we can speak of a set of premium function vectors $f = (f^1, \ldots, f^T)$ which are self-financing, in the sense that the income they raise is precisely sufficient to treat the cases of lung cancer that ensue. Call this set of balanced-budget profiles of premium functions, Φ. We may wish also, for reasons of tractability, to require that all premium functions be linear, say, in y. The equality-of-opportunity premium function profile solves the following maximization problem:

$$\max_{f \in \Phi} \int_0^1 \min_t v(\pi, f^t) \, d\pi. \tag{17.1}$$

In constrast, the Rawlsian premium functon solves:

$$\max_{f \in \Phi} \min_{t, \pi} v(\pi, f^t). \tag{17.2}$$

The utilitarian premium profile solves:

$$\max_{f \in \Phi} \sum_t p^t \int_0^1 v(\pi, f^t) \, d\pi, \tag{17.3}$$

where p^t is the fraction of type t individuals in the population.

As I have explained in the writings referred to above, the equal opportunity policy (EOp for short) holds individuals responsible for their degree of effort (in this case, abstention from smoking), but not for their circumstances; the Rawlsian policy holds individuals responsible for neither their circumstances nor their effort, and the utilitarian policy holds invidivuals responsible for both their effort and their circumstances.

THE CALCULATION OF THE EOp POLICY

People in our society have been intensively exposed to warnings about the dangers of smoking, yet many persist, and of those, a fraction develop lung cancer or other serious ailments that require costly medical care. Suppose we hold an equality-of-opportunity-for-health ethic. To what extent should the necessary medical care be financed by society at large, and to what extent should the individual have to pay? If, indeed, we decided that an individual were entirely responsible for his choice to smoke – that society had provided a level playing field by the various restrictions on cigarette advertising it had implemented and by the warnings it had broadcast – then an equality-of-opportunity-for-health view would hold that the individual should pay the costs of medical care sustained due to his smoking, perhaps through insurance whose premiums were an increasing function of the intensity with which the insured had smoked.

Here, the relevant effort is the degree to which the person refrains from smoking. The choice with regard to smoking that a person makes is in part determined by his circumstances – say, his economic class, his ethnicity, whether his parents smoked, and his level of education – and is in part a matter of autonomous choice. One might question whether 'economic class' and 'level of education' should properly be 'circumstances', since there is an aspect of autonomous choice in determining them. Here is an example where, even though a characteristic is not beyond a person's control, it might well be included as a component of circumstance. Society might well decide that a person should not be accountable for not having considered the effect of his choice of occupation on his smoking behaviour. Thus, if the list of circumstantial factors for smoking is taken to be gender, ethnicity, occupation, age, then one type might consist of all sixty-year-old white, female college professors, and another of all sixty-year-old black, male steelworkers.

Here, the social policy will consist in the health insurance premiums that different persons should pay, where the premium will, in principle, be a function both of one's type and one's 'effort'; alternatively, medical services for lung cancer could be financed by taxes on tobacco consumption. These premiums or taxes, of course, are being determined by a government agency whose job is to equalize opportunities for health, not by a profit-maximizing insurance company.

We might specify the problem, for purposes of illustration, in the following way. Suppose the fraction of people who contract lung cancer in a given year among those who have smoked for y years is θy, for some constant θ. As postulated earlier, the advantage a person enjoys is given by a function $u(M, y)$, where M, now, is the annual health insurance premium the person pays and y is the number of years smoked. I will specify

243

$$u(M, y) = -M + (1 - \alpha\theta y)\sigma, \qquad (17.4)$$

where σ is the 'value of life lived for a year' and α is the probability of dying once lung cancer is diagnosed, assuming that it is treated. Thus, θy is the probability of contracting the disease during a given year conditional upon having smoked for y years, $\alpha\theta y$ is the probability of dying from lung cancer conditional upon having smoked for y years, and so $(1 - \alpha\theta y)\sigma$ is the expected value of life for a year, conditional upon having smoked for y years.

Let us suppose that the Ministry of Health designs an insurance policy under which everyone who contracts the disease will be treated; the question is how to assess insurance premiums on the population in question. Suppose the ministry, for the sake of simplicity, assigns premiums which are linear functions of the number of years persons have smoked.[2] Thus, the annual premium for an individual of type t who has smoked for y years will be $b^t + a^t y$, where the constants b^t and a^t are to be determined.

Suppose that the 'effort' response of individuals to the insurance premium is as follows: persons of type t, who face a premium schedule $b + ay$, will smoke some number of years between y^t and $y^t - \beta a$, where y^t and β are constants, and further suppose that the years smoked, among individuals of type t, is uniformly distributed on that interval. Thus, the higher the 'marginal premium', a, of smoking for a year, the fewer years people smoke, in general: but the most dedicated smokers of type t always smoke y^t years, independent of the insurance premium. Suppose the cost of treating a case of lung cancer is c, independent of type and years having smoked. Finally, suppose there are T types, where the fraction of individuals of type t is p^t, and let $y^1 > y^2 > \ldots > y^T$. Thus, type 1 is the most 'disadvantaged' type: its members tend to smoke longer than those of other types.

We now have all the data needed to compute the EOp, the Rawlsian, and the utilitarian policies. I shall assume, to avoid having to identify a person's type, that the Ministry of Health restricts itself to using the same allocation rule for every type: that is, it shall choose one pair of numbers (b, a), and announce that the insurance premium is $b + ay$, for all individuals. To make the problem more sensible, let us assume that the relevant population consists of individuals all of whom are sixty years old. Thus, a complete solution to the problem would involve solving the problem for each age cohort. The data given above are assumed, then, to apply just to the sixty-year-old cohort.

One can, of course, challenge the realism of some of the assumptions I have made in specifying the problem. It is highly unlikely, for instance, that the distribution of years smoked, within a type, would be a uniform distribution on an interval. These assumptions have been made in order

244

to make the following calculations simple. I shall have more to say presently about the specification of the advantage function u.

We first compute the EOp policy, that is, the solution to the maximization problem (17.1). I first specify the budget constraint. Facing an insurance premium (b, a), the average number of years smoked by individuals of type t will be $y^t - \beta\frac{a}{2}$; hence the average premium these persons will pay is $b + a(y^t - \beta\frac{a}{2})$; hence the average premium paid by the entire population involved will be

$$\sum_{t=1}^{T} p^t\left(b + a\left(y^t - \beta\frac{a}{2}\right)\right).$$ (17.5)

On the other hand, the fraction of persons of type t who will contract lung cancer is $\theta(y^t - \beta\frac{a}{2})$, and so the fraction of the population who will contract lung cancer is

$$\sum_{t=1}^{T} p^t\theta\left(y^t - \beta\frac{a}{2}\right).$$ (17.6)

Hence the cost per capita of treating lung cancer contracted in the population is the expression in (17.6) multiplied by c; so, from (17.5) and (17.6), the premiums collected will just pay for the costs of treating the population if

$$\sum_{1}^{T} p^t\left(b + a\left(y^t - \beta\frac{a}{2}\right)\right) = c\sum_{1}^{T} p^t\theta\left(y^t - \beta\frac{a}{2}\right).$$ (17.7)

This is the planner's budget constraint. We can solve equation (17.7) for the constant b:

$$b(a) = \theta c\left(\bar{y} - \frac{\beta a}{2}\right) + \frac{\beta a^2}{2} - a\bar{y},$$ (17.8)

where $\bar{y} = \sum p^t y^t$ is the average number of years smoked by the most dedicated smokers of the various types. Equation 17.8 tells the planner that the parameter b must be a certain function of the parameter a to satisfy the budget constraint. Hence, we may now think of the planner as choosing the single parameter a, where b is determined according to (17.8). Let us say that a must be greater than or equal to zero, and that there is a certain maximum premium, $\hat{M}$, that the planner can charge. Thus the largest possible 'marginal' premium, $\hat{a}$, the planner can charge is determined by the equation

$$\hat{b} + \hat{a}y^1 = \hat{M},$$ (17.9)

where $\hat{b} = b(\hat{a})$. Equation 17.9 can be solved for $\hat{a}$, once $\hat{M}$ is specified. Thus the planner's set of feasible policies consists of marginal premiums a drawn from the interval $[0, \hat{a}]$.

We must calculate the indirect advantage function $v^t(\pi, a)$, the advantage enjoyed by the individual at the πth quantile of the smoking distribution in type t facing the insurance policy a. π takes on all values between 0 and 1. Since the distribution of years smoked in type t is uniform on the interval $[y^t - \beta a, y^t]$, the individual at the πth quantile of that distribution smokes for $y^t - \beta a \pi$ years. That person also pays an annual premium of $b + a(y^t - \beta a \pi)$. Thus, substituting into (17.4), we derive that person's advantage level:

$$v^t(\pi, a) = -b(a) - a[y^t - \beta a \pi] + (1 - \alpha\theta(y^t - \beta a \pi))\sigma. \qquad (17.10)$$

We can now substitute the expression in (17.10) into (17.1): expression (17.1) allows us to find the value of a that solves

$$\max_a \int_0^1 \min_t (-b(a) - a[y^t - \beta a \pi] + (1 - \alpha\theta(y^t - \beta a \pi)\sigma)d\pi. \qquad (17.11)$$

In turn, for every π, the minimum of the argument in (17.11) is achieved at $t = 1$, so (17.11) becomes

$$\max_a \int (-b(a) - a(y^1 - \beta a \pi) + (1 - \alpha\theta(y^1 - \beta a \pi))\sigma)d\pi$$

which in turn can be rewritten:

$$\max_a \left\{ -b(a) - ay^1 - \alpha\sigma\theta y^1 + (a^2\beta + \alpha\sigma\theta\beta a) \int_0^1 \pi \, d\pi \right\}.$$

Integrating, we have

$$\max_a \left\{ -b(a) - ay^1 + \frac{a^2\beta + \alpha\sigma\theta\beta a}{2} \right\};$$

now, substituting from (17.8) for $b(a)$, we have

$$\max_a \left\{ \frac{\theta c \beta a}{2} - \frac{\beta a^2}{2} + a\bar{y} - ay^1 + \frac{a^2\beta + \alpha\sigma\theta\beta a}{2} \right\}$$

or

$$\max_a \left\{ \frac{\theta\beta}{2}(c + \alpha\sigma) + \bar{y} - y^1 \right\} a. \qquad (17.12)$$

The solution to (17.12) depends upon whether the term in brackets is positive or negative. If

$$\frac{\theta\beta}{2}(c + \alpha\sigma) + \bar{y} - y^1 < 0 \qquad (17.13)$$

then (17.12) is solved by setting $a = 0$. If

$$\frac{\theta\beta}{2}(c + \alpha\sigma) + \bar{y} - y^1 > 0, \qquad (17.14)$$

then (17.12) is solved by setting a equal to its maximum feasible value, $\hat{a}$. Thus, the equal-opportunity marginal premium is given by

$$a^{EOp} = \begin{cases} 0 & \text{if } \dfrac{\theta\beta}{2}(c + \alpha\sigma) < y^1 - \bar{y} \\[2mm] \hat{a} & \text{if } \dfrac{\theta\beta}{2}(c + \alpha\sigma) > y^1 - \bar{y}. \end{cases} \qquad (17.14)$$

Note that $y^1 - \bar{y}$ is the deviation of y^1 from the average of the $\{y^i\}$. What (17.14) says, qualitatively, is that if this deviation is sufficiently large, then the EOp policy charges everyone the same premium, regardless of the number of years smoked; on the other hand, if $y^1 - \bar{y}$ is sufficiently small, then the insurance policy applies the largest feasible marginal premium per year of smoking.

Let us make a rough calculation of what the EOp policy might be by assigning values to the various constants specifying the problem. Let us measure c and β in thousands of dollars. Let us say $c = 50$ (in thousands of dollars) and, rather arbitrarily, $\beta = 50$ (the value the planner puts on an extra year of life is $50,000). Further, suppose $\theta = 0.02$ and $\alpha = 0.5$ (smoking an extra year increases the probability of contracting lung cancer by 2 per cent, and the probability of dying in the year one contracts lung cancer is 50 per cent). Then we have

$$a^{EOp} = 0 \quad \text{if } y^1 - \bar{y} > 0.75\beta.$$

Let us suppose that $y^1 - \bar{y} = 10$: that is, the heaviest smokers in the 'worst' type smoke ten years more than the average numbers of years smoked by the heaviest smokers across types. Then we have

$$a^{EOp} = 0 \quad \text{if } \beta < 13.3.$$

Now β is the number of years by which, on average, people reduce their smoking when the marginal premium per year smoked is increased by $1,000. It seems very likely that $\beta < 13.3$; hence, if these values of the various parameters are reasonably accurate, then the EOp policy would entail charging everyone in the age cohort the same annual premium, regardless of years having smoked. Thus, due to the constraints we have placed on the planner, of using a linear policy and using the same policy for all types, it turns out that the EOp policy is just the 'egalitarian' policy – all individuals pay the same premium.

Suppose, however, that $y^1 - \bar{y} = 1$. Then

$$a^{EOp} = \hat{a} \quad \text{if} \quad \beta > 1.33.$$

Now it seems quite likely that $\beta > 1.33$, and so in this case, the EOp policy is highly inegalitarian: the premium is very sensitive to the number of years smoked.

We can understand these results in this way. The numbers $y^1, y^2, \ldots, y^T$ are characteristics of the types: thus, persons are not to be held accountable for their sizes. If $y^1 - \bar{y}$ is large, that means that a large part of the variation in smoking is due to circumstances, while if $y^1 - \bar{y}$ is small, then a large part of that variation is due to autonomous choice. In the first case, the EOp policy is, correspondingly, egalitarian, while in the second case it forces the individual to be accountable for her smoking behaviour. This makes sense.

We next calculate the Rawlsian policy. By substituting into (17.2), we deduce that the Rawlsian policy solves

$$\max_a \min_{\pi,t} \{-b(a) - y^t(a + \alpha\sigma\theta) + \pi(\beta a^2 + \alpha\sigma\theta\beta a)\}$$

which reduces to

$$\max_a \{-b(a) - y^1(a + \sigma\theta)\}$$

and then to

$$\max_a \left\{ \left(\frac{\theta\beta c}{2} + \bar{y} - y^1\right)a - \frac{\beta a^2}{2} \right\}. \tag{17.15}$$

The maximand in (17.15) is a concave function of a; it is maximized by setting its first derivative equal to zero, which yields:

$$a^R = \begin{cases} \dfrac{\theta}{2}c + \dfrac{\bar{y} - y^1}{\beta} & \text{if} \quad y^1 - \bar{y} < \dfrac{\beta\theta}{2}c \\ 0 & \text{if} \quad y^1 - \bar{y} > \dfrac{\beta\theta}{2}c. \end{cases} \tag{17.16}$$

Thus the Rawlsian policy has the same qualitative characteristic as the EOp policy: if $y^1 - \bar{y}$ is sufficiently large, then $a^R = 0$, and all members of population are charged a constant premium, whereas if $y^1 - \bar{y}$ is small, then the premium increases with years smoked. Note, however, that the Rawlsian policy is decidedly more egalitarian than the EOp policy, because the cut-off value of $y^1 - \bar{y}$ above which a constant premium is charged is much lower in the Rawlsian policy: indeed the Rawlsian cut-off value is $\frac{\beta\theta}{2} c$ while the EOp cut-off value is $\frac{\beta\theta}{2} (c + \alpha\theta)$. In particular, if $y^1 - \bar{y} = 1$, and $\theta = 0.02$, the Rawlsian policy would be egalitarian as long as $\beta < 100$, while we calculated, in this case, the EOp policy would be egalitarian only if $\beta < 1.33$. So, for example, if in actuality $\beta = 2$, then, given the value of the other parameters, the EOp policy would be highly inegalitarian (in premiums charged) while the Rawlsian policy would be completely egalitarian.

Finally we calculate the utilitarian policy. I shall spare the reader the details: this time, by substituting into (17.3) and simplifying, it turns out that the utilitarian policy solves

$$\max_{a} (c + \alpha\sigma)a, \qquad (17.17)$$

which is solved by setting a equal to its highest feasible value:

$$a^u = \hat{a}. \qquad (17.18)$$

Thus, the utilitarian policy is always as inegalitarian as is feasible with respect to premiums charged.

These computations illustrate a general fact, that the EOp policy generally takes a middling position *vis-à-vis* the Rawlsian and utilitarian policies. The utilitarian policy holds people maximally accountable for their behaviour, assigning all variations in effort to 'autonomous choice,' while the Rawlsian policy holds people minimally accountable for their behaviour, effectively assigning all variations in smoking to circumstances. The EOp policy implements a position in between these two solutions.

Note that the above computations were all performed under the restriction that the Health Ministry offer the same insurance schedule to all persons in the target population, independent of type. This restriction was imposed to reduce the costs of applying the policy – that is, costs that would otherwise be borne in identifying the types of individuals. This restriction also prevents backlash: no person can say that those in another type are receiving preferential treatment. Even with this restriction, we see that the EOp policy holds individuals more accountable than the Rawlsian policy and less accountable than the utilitarian policy. If, however, the ministry felt it were politically and financially feasible to offer different insurance schedules to different types (thus, choosing different values (b^t, a^t) for each t), then we could recompute the EOp policy (a more delicate computation, this time), and the resulting policy would be more fine-grained with respect to holding individuals accountable for their smoking behaviour. In particular, we would expect that those from more 'disadvantaged' types (i.e., lower values of t) would pay smaller premiums, holding constant the number of years smoked.

Finally, the promised comment on the advantage function, $u(M, y)$. As I have specified that function in (17.4), it is not the same as the traditional utility function that an economist would assign to the person, for most economists would say that people smoke because they derive some pleasure from doing so. Thus, the utility function should contain a positive term in y, reflecting the positive returns to smoking, and a negative term in y (like the second term in (17.4)) reflecting the risk of death from smoking. One might say that my planner is paternalistic: he is not computing the equality of opportunity for *welfare* policy, where welfare includes the positive effects people get from smoking, but rather, a policy to equalize opportunities for a certain kind of material advantage, where that advantage is the sum of the expected value of a year of life debited by the health insurance premium paid. Further, the planner uses his own valuation of a year of living (namely σ), not the individual's valuation, and he does not take account of the fact that individuals have different incomes or wealths. All these assumptions, I think, are justified by a view that the planner in question is concerned only with a slice of the lives of people, namely their relationship to the health-services system. Thus, if the planner took account of the fact that the wealth of individuals in some types is greater than of individuals in other types, and added the person's wealth or income to the advantage function, then these income effects might well swamp the effects of smoking behaviour: the EOp policy for that kind of advantage would tend to charge the highest premiums to those with high incomes. Many would consider this to be an unacceptable mixing of different issues: differential income, they would say, should be dealt with by the tax system, where an 'equality of opportunity for income' tax policy could be implemented, while equality of opportunity for health should not be concerned to equalize different incomes, but only with the costs and benefits associated with behavior pertaining to health.

In the problem as specified, the taxing authority is assumed to be able to determine the number of years an individual has smoked. In reality, this is private information, and it would be difficult to base a tax policy upon it. One can, nevertheless, imagine ways in which an estimate of smoking intensity could be made. At an annual examination, a physician could estimate the number of years the patient had smoked based on a measure of lung capacity; the patient and physician could then agree on a number of years the patient had smoked for purposes of tax policy.

Alternatively, a 'two-part tariff' could be levied on the purchase of cigarettes. The first time in a given month an individual purchases a pack of cigarettes, he would pay a fixed tax, receiving a receipt as proof of payment. In addition, a constant marginal tax per pack would be levied. This two-part tariff would give the Ministry of Health one degree of freedom in

250

its tax policy, just as the tax policy analysed above has one degree of freedom. The advantage of the two-part tariff is that smoking intensity need never be observed: for the tax levied on each pack of cigarettes automatically taxes people according to their intensity of smoking. The two-part tariff could be calculated to solve the EOp problem.

FINAL REMARK

A response is perhaps appropriate to those from the left, who would criticize taking the equal opportunity approach to health insurance. Many would argue that citizens should be fully indemnified against the costs of illness, with health insurance financed from general revenues. I am, in this article, disagreeing in principle with that stance. I ask these would-be critics: do you not think it appropriate that taxes on tobacco be used to finance the costs of tobacco-related disease? If so, then you, indeed, advocate a policy similar to the one in this paper. For such a policy would have smokers contribute more to the health insurance fund than non-smokers: it would, thereby, hold them in part accountable for their dangerous behaviour. The EOp policy is a refinement of that general principle, in which we only tax smokers to the extent that we feel their behaviour is not determined by factors beyond their control.

NOTES

1 This paper is based on a chapter from my forthcoming book, Roemer (In press).
2 I have chosen to set the problem up as one of determining insurance premiums. The effort variable in this case, years of smoking, is subject to problems of revelation. I shall assume, for the purposes of the example, that the insurance agency can verify years of smoking. Alternatively, had I set the problem up as one of determining taxes on tobacco, then no revelation problem would exist. A person would automatically pay into the medical care fund in proportion to the amount he smoked. Of course, this instrument limits the tax mechanism to one that is proportional to consumption, unless a two-part tariff is used, as described below.

REFERENCES

Roemer, J.E. 1996. *Theories of Distributive Justice*, Cambridge, Massachusetts: Harvard University Press.
—— In press. *Equality of Opportunity: A theory and applications*, Cambridge, Massachusetts: Harvard University Press.

18

SOME TRADE-OFFS IN ROEMER'S MECHANISM

Dirk Van de Gaer

Roemer's mechanism requires that the population is partitioned into types. Each type is characterized by a vector of socioeconomic and personal characteristics such as innate intelligence, race and sex. The set of characteristics reflects society's view of which factors affect a person's choices and over which one has no control. Given this partitioning into types, his mechanism can be seen as consisting of two parts: an objective function and a procedure to define comparable degrees of responsibility. People are said to have exercised a comparable degree of responsibility if they are at the same percentile of their type's distribution of the outcome under consideration, say welfare. The objective is to maximize a weighted average of minimum welfares across types of persons of the same degree of responsibility. The weight attached to the welfare of those at a given degree of responsibility is their population frequency. It is the combination of these two components which allows the mechanism to be applied to actual situations. Given that one can observe people's outcomes and types, no other information (such as counter-factual choices) is needed to implement the mechanism. From a practical point of view this is an enormous advantage.

Roemer's ideas have recently been compared to several alternatives that have been proposed in the literature – see, e.g., Bossert et al. (1996). His ideas have been discussed by several authors (Solow, Scanlon, Epstein, Hurley, Rosenblum, Fox-Genovese, Scheffler, Maskin, Ripstein) in a special issue of the Boston Review (1995). Among the issues discussed are the domain of the mechanism, the underlying notion of responsibility and the informational requirements of the scheme. I do not enter into this discussion. Instead I will focus on the trade-off between the two components of the mechanism and under what conditions a consensus can be established even when people have different opinions about how the population should be partitioned into types.

A TRADE-OFF BETWEEN THE TWO COMPONENTS OF THE MECHANISM

As was indicated above, the mechanism consists of a procedure to define comparable degrees of responsibility and an objective function. Many of the variables which can enter into the definition of a type are continuous, such as intelligence and parental background. For the identification procedure to work, we have to take discrete approximations to these variables. Otherwise each class will contain only one individual, and everyone will have exercised the same degree of responsibility. The fewer the discrete classes, the more observations we have for each type, and the finer we can define comparable degrees of responsibility. However, the less refined our grid, the more our practical definition of types differs from its true definition, and the more our approximate objective will deviate from the true objective defined over the continuous types. There is a direct trade-off between the goodness of the approximation of the objective and the identification power of the procedure to define comparable degrees of responsibility. It is not clear to me how this trade-off should be resolved.

The trade-off is a result of the interaction between the identification procedure and the objective. Most other contributions to the literature on equality of opportunity do not have an identification procedure, and simply assume that 'responsibility' can be somehow determined. In theoretical models this is often the case. If so, one can apply Roemer's objective and there is no need to resort to the identification procedure, such that no trade-off arises. It is a concern with situations where such *a priori* information is missing and the degree of responsibility has to be determined on the basis of observable information only which led to the identification procedure and the resulting trade-off.

STRIVING FOR A CONSENSUS IN A PLURALISTIC SOCIETY

In this section I want to see whether and how the mechanism works in a pluralistic society. It will be assumed throughout that everyone agrees that society's objective is given by Roemer's criterion but that people have different opinions about the exact partitioning in types. As is shown by the other contributions in this book, there are many other opinions about the right objective for society. I will abstract from this richness of opinions and assume that everyone agrees that Roemer's mechanism is the one to implement.

Roemer assumes that the partitioning in types is somehow decided by society. In any pluralistic society, there will be divergent views on the characteristics upon which the partitioning has to be based. This leads to some important questions about whether such a mechanism will work in a pluralistic society. Under what conditions is it possible that people who partition the population differently will agree on certain policy measures. These conditions will be mechanism-dependent, and the answer to the question is less straightforward than would appear at first sight.

To help us look for an answer to this question, let us suppose that the population can be divided into four groups on the basis of two characteristics: sex (F = female, M = male) and effort exercised (H = high, L = low). Each group contains one quarter of the total population. We compare four alternatives, A, B, C and D. The level of welfare which each group obtains under each alternative is given in the table below.

A		B		C		D	
F	M	F	M	F	M	F	M
L 1	5	L 2	4	L 2	6	L 2	5
H 5	7	H 6	6	H 4	6	H 6	7

The 'enlightened' partition the population on the basis of sex and use Roemer's criterion to evaluate the alternatives. As usual, R denotes 'is at least as good as', P is the corresponding strict preference relation and I expresses indifference. In each of the alternatives type F is worst off for each level of effort. Since the fraction of the population in each effort level equals one half, Roemer's criterion ranks the alternatives on the basis of the average value of the outcome for type F. Hence the enlightened rank the alternatives as follows:

$D I B P C I A.$

B and D are better than A and C. Note that D weakly Pareto dominates the other allocations, while B can be obtained out of A after a reallocation of outcomes in favour of the type which is worst off, at the expense of the outcomes of the other type. C contains the same outcomes as B, but the welfare levels of males which exert a low level of effort and women which put in a lot of effort have been switched. Given that people agree upon the partitioning in types, the ranking suggests two kinds of preference results. One is based on weak Pareto dominance and the other is based on transfers in favour of those who are worst off for a given level of effort. Note that in B the level of welfare of the males who exert a low level of effort could be further decreased without a change in the ranking. Thus, to a certain extent, 'leaky bucket transfers' are possible.

What happens when people disagree on the manner in which society should be partitioned into types? Suppose that a part of the population, the 'ignorant', think that the distinction between types is superfluous, and (erroneously) attribute all differences in outcomes to differences in effort level. Since in each alternative they observe four different outcomes, each with a relative frequency of 1/4, they believe there exist four different levels of effort, very low (VL), low (L), high (H) and very high (VH). The view that they have on the alternatives is given in the following table:

A		B		C		D	
VL	1	VL	2	VL	2	VL	2
L	5	L	4	L	4	L	5
H	5	H	6	H	6	H	6
VH	7	VH	6	VH	6	VH	7

The ignorant apply Roemer's criterion to this table. In the present case, where no types are distinguished, this is equivalent to the application of average utilitarianism. Therefore, they rank the alternatives as follows:

D *P* **A** *I* **B** *I* **C**.

If we now look for pairwise choices among the alternatives about which the enlightened and the ignorant can agree, we have the following:

C *I* **A**
D *R* **B**   and   **D** *P* **C**
B *R* **C**

This suggests that agreement between the enlightened and the ignorant is possible in three cases. First, when one alternative weakly Pareto dominates another with respect to the finest grid of types (in our example the grid of the enlightened), then this alternative will be at least as good as the other, irrespective of the way the population is divided into types. This is shown by the fact that **D** *R* **X** (**X** = A, B or C). Second, if, using the finest grid of types one allocation can be obtained out of another by a sequence of transfers within effort categories and these transfers favour those who are worst off, then the allocation obtained after the sequence of transfers is at least as good as the original allocation, irrespective of the way the population will be partitioned. The resulting allocation will be strictly better for some partitionings. This explains **B** *R* **A** and is an application of the Pigou-Dalton principle of transfers in the present framework, taking into account the fact that Roemer only looks at the types which for each level of effort are worst off. If one type is more numerous than another, then the size of the amount gained by the type which is worst off and the size of the amount lost by the other type have to be adjusted so as to keep aggregate welfare constant. Note that the transfers considered here, to establish the consensus result between the enlightened and the ignorant, are a subclass of the transfers which were allowed in the discussion of the preference ordering of the enlightened. No 'leaky bucket transfers' are possible. Third, consider the set of people who are worst off for a level of effort when we use the finest grid of types. Then the same kind of transfers within this group, going from a group with a higher outcome to a group with a lower outcome yields an allocation which is not worse than the original one. This is shown by C I A. If one considers more than two types it is easy to see that such a reallocation might actually be strictly preferred by those who use a less fine grid.

These examples show that even when people disagree about the way the population should be partitioned, agreement about the ranking of alternatives is possible in certain cases. Moreover, the strategy which tries to partition the population based on those characteristics about which people agree that they constitute the circumstances beyond the control of the individual (i.e. the intersection of the sets of characteristics which the citizens think that should be included in the definition of 'a type') is flawed. Indeed, applying Roemer's scheme to this partitioning will not lead to any consensus at all. Often, those who use a finer grid will disagree with the resulting ranking of alternatives. Note that this also implies that informational problems can be enormous. Stating the point differently, there exists another trade-off between the degree of consensus about the choice among alternatives and the amount of information necessary to reach this consensus.

ACKNOWLEDGMENT

Financial support through a grant from the Interuniversity Poles of Attraction initiated by the Belgian State, Prime Minister's Office, Science Policy Programming is gratefully acknowledged.

REFERENCES

Bossert, W., Fleurbaey, M. and Van de Gaer, D. (1996), On Second Best Compensation, THEMA Discussion paper.
Boston Review (1995), vol. 20, number 2.

19

THE EMPIRICAL ACCEPTANCE OF COMPENSATION AXIOMS*

Erik Schokkaert and Kurt Devooght

ABSTRACT

Many recent contributions on the definition of an equitable income distribution have suggested that people should only be compensated for these characteristics for which they cannot be held responsible. We present empirical results concerning the acceptance among Belgian undergraduates of some of the axioms proposed in this literature. When applied to a problem of distribution of subsidies for medical expenditures, the axioms 'full compensation' and 'strict compensation' are accepted by a majority of the respondents. However, this is not the case within a setting of income redistribution. We suggest that our respondents do not distinguish sufficiently between incentive and justice considerations.

INTRODUCTION

Many recent contributions on the definition of an equitable or just income distribution have proposed distinguishing between different characteristics of the economic agents. The idea is that income differences are acceptable when they are due to characteristics for which agents can be deemed responsible. If they are caused by characteristics for which these agents are not responsible, compensation is needed. Dworkin (1981) proposed to include preferences in the former category and resources (including personal resources) in the latter, but the discussion on the exact location of the cut between the two sets of characteristics is far from closed (see, e.g., Sen, 1985, 1992, Roemer, 1985, 1993, Arneson, 1989, Cohen, 1989, Fleurbaey, 1995b).

Even if there could be unanimous agreement on the location of the divide between the two sets of characteristics, the (first-best) distribution problem would not yet be solved. This has been shown by Fleurbaey (1994, 1995a, 1995b). In a series of papers he proposed an abstract framework, in which he tried to capture in simple formal axioms some of the philosophical ideas from the discussion about compensation. A quasi-linear version of that model has been discussed in Bossert (1995) and Bossert and Fleurbaey (1996).[1] They propose to call 'relevant' characteristics those characteristics for which the economic agents are deemed responsible. Characteristics for which the agents are not responsible and which entitle them therefore to a compensation are called 'irrelevant'. The analysis then centres around two axioms. The axiom of 'full compensation' states that two agents with identical relevant characteristics (but possibly different irrelevant characteristics) should get an identical income (or welfare level). The axiom of 'strict compensation' states that two agents with identical irrelevant characteristics (but possibly different relevant characteristics) should pay the same tax or get the same transfer. As argued by the authors, both axioms seem eminently plausible within a theory of compensation. Yet the analysis reveals a crucial finding: these two axioms are in general incompatible if there are four agents or more.

We therefore now face two questions. First, what are relevant and irrelevant characteristics in a specific setting? Second, how to 'solve' the inconsistency between the two basic axioms? While further theoretical work is certainly needed, we feel that there is also some scope for empirical research. This is fairly obvious for the first question, which has an important empirical component. It has even been suggested (Roemer, 1993) that the exact classification of variables for which individuals have to bear responsibility may be different in different societies, because it will be influenced by the dominant physiological, psychological or social theories of man. Empirical work may then be useful to discover these different opinions. In this paper we will not concentrate on that first question, however. Rather, we want to suggest that empirical work may also be relevant to help directing the research about the second question.

There is by now already some experience with research about the justice opinions of individuals. The most important contribution has undoubtedly been made by Yaari and Bar-Hillel (1984), whose work has been influential to strengthen the criticism on welfarism, but others have followed (e.g., Schokkaert and Overlaet, 1988, Gaertner, 1994). In the context of income inequality, Amiel and Cowell (1992) have presented equally striking results, e.g., on the Pigou-Dalton-criterion. We will apply a similar methodology to investigate the acceptance of the axioms of strict and full compensation. Our empirical results, obtained from a sample of 208 Belgian undergraduate students, will be used to shed some light on the theoretical approaches to compensation.

In this paper we briefly summarize the model of Bossert and Fleurbaey (1996) and give a loose formalization of the relevant axioms and distribution mechanisms. In addition to the income distribution problem analysed by Bossert and Fleurbaey (1996) we also suggest a (slight) reinterpretation to analyse the problem of the financing of health expenditure. The introduction of this health expenditure problem allows us to look for the relevance of the model across different settings. There is then a description of our empirical work which goes deeper into the construction of the questionnaire. Like in the work of Amiel and Cowell (1992), our questionnaire consisted of a numerical and a verbal part, allowing for both an indirect and a direct testing of the axioms. Results are then discussed and the paper concludes.

REDISTRIBUTION AND COMPENSATION

We will first give a short and mathematically loose summary of the compensation model, proposed by Bossert (1995) and Bossert and Fleurbaey (1996), following closely these two references. We first concentrate on their own preferred interpretation, the case of income redistribution. We then reinterpret their model slightly for the problem of dividing government subsidies for health expenditures.

Income redistribution

Assume there are n individuals in society, each characterised by a characteristics vector $a_i \in \mathfrak{R}^{r+s}$, determining their pre-tax income $f(a_i)$. This characteristics vector can be partitioned as $a_i = (a_i^R, a_i^S) \in \mathfrak{R}^{r+s}$, where a_i^R is an r-vector of 'relevant' characteristics and a_i^S an s-vector of 'irrelevant' characteristics. The former can be interpreted as the characteristics for which individual i is responsible, the latter as those for which he does not bear any responsibility. A characteristics profile is $\bar{a} = (a_1, \ldots, a_n) \in \mathfrak{R}^{n(r+s)}$.

A redistribution mechanism gives for each possible characteristics profile $\bar{a}$ the vector of post-tax ('just') income levels $F(\bar{a})$. A budget constraint has to be satisfied, such that, for all possible $\bar{a}$,

$$\sum_{i=1}^{n} F_i(\bar{a}) = \sum_{i=1}^{n} f(a_i). \tag{19.1}$$

The further analysis will be restricted to anonymous mechanisms, i.e., mechanisms giving the same post-tax income to individuals with the same characteristics.

The point of the exercise now is to define conditions which have to be satisfied by the redistribution mechanism. The idea is that the final after-tax ('just') income should reflect the influence of the 'relevant' characteristics, while compensating perfectly for the influence of the 'irrelevant' characteristics. This general intuition is translated into two easily understandable axioms. The first axiom is called EIER ('equal income for equal relevant characteristics' or 'full compensation') and states that two agents with identical relevant characteristics should end up with identical post-tax incomes. Indeed, if this were not the case, then the income inequality between the two would reflect an unacceptable influence of

259

irrelevant characteristics. More formally, EIER states that for all possible $\bar{a}$, for any two individuals, one should have

$$a_i^R = a_j^R \Rightarrow F_i(\bar{a}) = F_j(\bar{a}) \qquad \text{(EIER)}$$

The second axiom is in a certain sense dual to the first. It requires that two agents with identical irrelevant characteristics should be treated the same by the redistribution mechanism, i.e., should pay the same tax or receive the same transfer. This implies that the differences in pre-tax incomes which are due to the relevant characteristics remain intact in the post-tax income distribution. Bossert and Fleurbaey (1996) have baptized this axiom ETES ('equal transfer for equal S' or 'strict compensation'). Formalized, ETES states that for all possible $\bar{a}$, for any two individuals, one should have

$$a_i^S = a_j^S \Rightarrow F_i(\bar{a}) - f(a_i) = F_j(\bar{a}) - f(a_j). \qquad \text{(ETES)}$$

Both axioms seem to be a plausible formalization of basic insights from the philosophical literature on compensation. Therefore, it is an important result of Fleurbaey (1994) that they are in general incompatible if the number of individuals is four or more. In the context of the quasi-linear model, we can only find a redistribution mechanism respecting ETES and EIER, if the function f is additively separable in the relevant and irrelevant characteristics, i.e.,

$$f(a_i) = g(a_i^R) + h(a_i^S). \qquad (19.2)$$

In this additively separable case, a natural way to redistribute is given by the mechanism F^0, defined for all possible $\bar{a}$, and assigning to individual k the post-tax income

$$F_k^0(\bar{a}) = g(a_k^R) + \frac{1}{n} \sum_{i=1}^{n} h(a_i^S). \qquad (19.3)$$

This mechanism satisfies both ETES and EIER.

If the function f is not additively separable, no redistribution mechanism can satisfy both ETES and EIER. Bossert and Fleurbaey (1996) show what can be done after the weakening of one of both axioms. If one is willing to relax EIER, but keep ETES, one can choose within the class of conditionally egalitarian mechanisms F^{CE}, which define for all possible $\bar{a}$ the post-tax income of individual k as

$$F_k^{CE}(\bar{a}) = f(a_k) - f(\bar{a}^R, a_k^S) + \frac{1}{n} \sum_{i=1}^{n} f(\bar{a}^R, a_i^S) \qquad (19.4)$$

where $\bar{a}^R$ gives a 'reference' level of relevant characteristics.[2] With this mechanism each individual is guaranteed the average income level of a

260

ACCEPTANCE OF COMPENSATION AXIOMS

hypothetical economy in which all agents have relevant characteristics equal to $\tilde{a}^R$, provided that $a_k^R = \tilde{a}^R$. She bears the consequences of any deviation from this reference level (Bossert and Fleurbaey, 1996, p. 345). If the transfer to any agent is the average transfer obtained under F^{CE}, where the benchmark $\tilde{a}^R$ successively assumes all the agents' values, we find the average conditionally egalitarian mechanism F^{ACE}.

If on the other hand one is willing to relax ETES, but keep EIER, one can resort to the class of egalitarian-equivalent mechanisms F^{EE}, which define for all possible $\bar{a}$ the post-tax income of individual k as

$$F_k^{EE}(\bar{a}) = f(a_k^R, \tilde{a}^S) - \frac{1}{n} \sum_{i=1}^{n} [f(a_i^R, \tilde{a}^S) - f(a_i)] \tag{19.5}$$

where $\tilde{a}^S$ gives a 'reference' level of irrelevant characteristics.[3] With this mechanism each individual has a post-tax income equal to the pre-tax income she would earn if her irrelevant characteristics were $\tilde{a}^S$, plus a uniform transfer (Bossert and Fleurbaey, 1996, p.345). If each agent gets the average of his post-tax income under F^{EE}, where the benchmark $\tilde{a}^S$ successively assumes all the agents' values, we have the average egalitarian-equivalent mechanism F^{AEE}.

In our empirical research we wanted to test in the first place whether the axioms ETES and EIER are accepted by our respondents. Since we are working with the description of distribution cases, we will also be able to see whether the distributions chosen by the respondents are consistent with any of the distribution mechanisms described above. Note that the mechanisms F^{CE}, F^{ACE}, F^{EE} and F^{AEE} coincide with F^0, if the function f is additively separable in the relevant and irrelevant characteristics.

Health expenditures

The income redistribution context is the preferred interpretation in the Bossert/Fleurbaey (1996) paper. An analogous model can also be used to analyse other problems, however, and in the context of compensation the problem of financing health care seems to be especially important. In fact, it is an interesting empirical question whether the same model keeps its relevancy across different settings. Let us therefore reinterpret the model in the context of health expenditures.

The function $f(a_i^R, a_i^S)$ is now interpreted as giving the medical expenditures of individual i, where the interpretation in terms of relevant and irrelevant characteristics remains the same. This means that the individual is deemed partly responsible for his medical expenditures, but should be compensated for the part for which he is not responsible. For this compensation, the government divides a fixed budget of subsidies ω among the different individuals. The division mechanism now will specify the vector $(\omega_1(\bar{a}), \ldots, \omega_n(\bar{a}))$ of individual subsidies, such that $\sum_{i=1}^{n} \omega_i(\bar{a}) = \omega$. If the individual i gets a subsidy $\omega_i(\bar{a})$, it is obvious that her own contribution $c_i(\bar{a})$ is given by

$$c_i(\bar{a}) = f(a_i^R, a_i^S) - \omega_i(\bar{a}). \qquad (19.6)$$

Since all medical expenditures have to be covered, there is an overall budget constraint

$$\sum_{i=1}^{n} f(a_i^R, a_i^S) = \omega + \sum_{i=1}^{n} c_i(\bar{a}). \qquad (19.7)$$

Comparing the two settings (and especially the budget constraints (19.1) and (19.7), it will be clear that all the mechanisms defined before work for this reinterpretation if we calculate the own contributions as

$$c_i(\bar{a}) = F_i(\bar{a}) - \frac{\omega}{n}. \qquad (19.8)$$

The two axioms get a plausible interpretation in the context of health expenditures.[4] The axiom of full compensation can be reinterpreted as axiom EIER*:

$$a_i^R = a_j^R \Rightarrow c_i(\bar{a}) = c_j(\bar{a}) \qquad \text{(EIER*)}$$

stating that two agents with the same relevant characteristics should pay the same own contribution. The idea of strict compensation is translated as

$$a_i^S = a_j^S \Rightarrow \omega_i(\bar{a}) = \omega_j(\bar{a}) \qquad \text{(ETES*)}$$

which means in verbal terms that two agents with the same irrelevant characteristics should get the same government subsidy. The link between these formulations and the traditional ETES- and EIER-axioms is so close that we will drop the '*' in the sequel.

STRUCTURE OF THE EMPIRICAL WORK

To investigate the acceptance of the EIER and ETES axioms, we opted for a questionnaire setting inspired by the approach of Amiel and Cowell (1992). Like in their study, our questionnaire consisted of two interrelated parts.[5] The first part was numerical: it contained the description of various cases, for which we asked the respondents to pick from a list of possibilities the distribution or redistribution that they considered as 'just'. If they wanted, the respondents could add another preferred redistribution. The distributions were presented as vectors, without explicit currency units or references to living standards or welfare levels. Among the suggested answers, we included the results of some of the mechanisms described above. Other possible responses corresponded to views which appear in other literature (e.g. progressivity, proportionality, egalitarianism) or just seemed to us to have intuitive plausibility. Some suggested distributions satisfied one (or both) of the two axioms ETES and EIER and the acceptance of these axioms can therefore be tested in an indirect way.

The second part was verbal: here respondents were confronted with various general propositions about (re)distribution. These statements represented an attempt to translate ETES and EIER in plain language. The respondents simply had to report whether they agreed or not. This can be seen as a direct test of the acceptance of the axioms. The answers on these direct questions were then confronted with the choices made in the first part. If the respondents reported that they had made inconsistent choices, they got the opportunity to change their answer on the numerical case. If they did not want to alter their answer, they were asked to explain the reasoning behind their choices.

To allow for 'learning-by-doing' the first part of the questionnaire started with four easy and straightforward (re)distribution problems.[6] Thereafter came the cases which were of importance to us. There were four of these. The first two are designed as a distribution problem of government money in a health setting. In both cases, the amount of money to be divided is $\omega = 500$. In Case 1 the function f is additively separable, so that the axioms EIER and ETES can be satisfied at the same time. If we interpret a^S as a dummy variable, taking the value 1 for the genetically weak individuals, and a^R as a dummy taking the value 1 for the individuals choosing an expensive doctor, the case is constructed on the basis of

$$f(a) = 150 + 50a^S + 150a^R \qquad (19.9)$$

where we omit the subscript i for convenience. Case 2 is situated in a similar context, but now the function f is no longer additively separable, so that the respondents can no longer reconcile ETES and EIER. In fact, using similar definitions for a^S and a^R (now taking the value 1 for the individuals leading a wild life), case 2 started from

$$f(a) = 200 + 200a^S + 150a^R + 100a^R a^S. \qquad (19.10)$$

Cases three and four are designed in the same way, but relate to the original Bossert/Fleurbaey (1996) formulation of a pure income redistribution problem. The numbers are the same: in Case 3 the function f is additively separable, in Case 4 it is not. The variables a^S and a^R have now been concretized as being intelligent and working hard respectively.[7]

Remember that our main purpose was to test the acceptance of the axioms EIER and ETES. We therefore wanted to create as little confusion as possible by choosing variables which can safely be interpreted as a^R- and a^S-type respectively. In the health case this is *a priori* fairly obvious. In the distribution case there is by now plenty of evidence that effort definitely is an a^R variable for Flemish (and probably, more generally, western) respondents, but there is less certainty about the interpretation of intelligence as an a^S variable (see, e.g., Schokkaert and Lagrou, 1983, Schokkaert and Overlaet, 1988, Schokkaert and Capéau, 1991). We will return to that problem when we discuss our results.

The questionnaires were completed anonymously in April 1995 by 208 first-year (business school) undergraduates of the K.U. Leuven (Belgium). None of these students had been exposed to any teaching on formal theories of justice. The completion of the questionnaire took about one hour. Its purpose was explained to the respondents orally and also summarized on the first page.

RESULTS

For reasons that will be obvious afterwards, we will first describe the results for the health cases and then for the income distribution cases.

Health expenditures

Let us first present the results for the numerical part. Table 19.1A summarizes the choices of our respondents for case 1. Remember that this is the case where the f-function is additively separable. Therefore, all the mechanisms described in Bossert and Fleurbaey (1996)[8] coincide with the 'natural' mechanism F^0 (19.3), the results of which are given in row C. The most striking result in Table 19.1A is then immediately obvious: this option C is chosen by a majority of 56.3 per cent of our respondents.

This result is more surprising than may seem at first sight. After all, the numbers in row C do not look extremely self-evident for non-specialists. Previous empirical research (e.g. Schokkaert and Overlaet, 1988) has shown that very many respondents are attracted by easy solutions like the proportional or equal ones (rows E and B or G respectively). In this questionnaire only 20 per cent of the respondents chose one of these easy solutions.

While only F^0 satisfies both axioms EIER and ETES, many of the other proposed divisions satisfy one of the two. For the divisions, added by the respondents, we also checked whether they satisfied the axioms. All this information is summarized in Table 19.1B: it is fair to say that the empirical acceptance of EIER and ETES is substantial in our case 1. The strict compensation criterion ETES is slightly more popular than the full compensation criterion EIER.

264

Table 19.1A

Row	Axioms	Mechanisms	Results
A		Higher subsidy for normal doctor	7.3%
B	ETES	Equal distribution	14.6%
C	ETES+ EIER	$F(0) = F(EE) = F(CE) = F(AEE) = F(ACE)$	56.3%
D		Higher subsidy for expensive doctor	2.9%
E		Proportional distribution	4.8%
F	EIER	Progressity	5.3%
G	EIER	Egalitarian outcome	1.0%
H	ETES		1.0%
H	EIER		2.0%
H			4.8%

(206 valid responses)

Table 19.1B

	ETES	Not ETES
EIER	56.3%	8.3%
Not EIER	15.6%	19.8%

The fact that F^0 is chosen so often in case 1 makes it interesting to look at the results for the non-additively separable case 2 (see Table 19.2). Indeed, here it is no longer possible to reconcile ETES and EIER and our respondents have to choose between them. It is obvious that this makes for a much more difficult question and the picture of the answers is therefore less clear than in Table 19.1A. In fact, one third of the respondents now adds a solution which was not proposed by us in the questionnaire. Still, the most popular mechanism (selected by 31 per cent of the respondents) is the conditionally egalitarian mechanism F^{CE} (see 19.4), with $\tilde{a}^R = 0$ (row B). The average conditionally egalitarian mechanism F^{ACE} is almost never chosen (row G). The same is true for the egalitarian-equivalent outcomes, which is in line with the suggestion made before that ETES is more generally accepted than EIER.

This suggestion is corroborated in Table 19.2B where we summarize the results in terms of the axioms. For the non-additively separable case, this is probably the most interesting way of looking at the results. The acceptance of the strict compensation axiom ETES is striking: almost two thirds of our respondents chose a division respecting it. Full compensation is respected only by a small minority[9].

Of course, these interpretations are heavily dependent on the implicit hypothesis that the respondents treat genetic defects as an a^S-variable and

265

Table 19.2A

Row	Axioms		Mechanisms	Results
A		EIER	Egalitarian outcome	3.4%
B	ETES		F(CE) with $\tilde{a}^R = 0$	30.8%
C		EIER	F(AEE)	8.2%
D			Mild form of egalitarianism	2.4%
E		EIER	F(EE)	3.4%
F	ETES		Equal distribution	17.8%
G	ETES		F(ACE)	1.4%
H	ETES			14.9%
H		EIER		0.4%
H	——			17.3%

(208 valid responses)

Table 19.2B

	ETES	Not ETES
EIER	——	15.4%
Not EIER	64.9%	19.7%

the choice of an expensive doctor (or an extravagant lifestyle) as an a^R-variable. If they would consider people to be responsible for all the variables, axiom EIER would become empty for our cases and ETES would require the subsidies to be the same for everybody: this is one way to interpret the equal distributions (row B in Table 19.1A and row F in Table 19.2A). We can also investigate the consequences of treating people as not responsible at all: ETES then becomes empty and EIER requires equal own contributions for all the individuals in the cases. This possibility is hardly chosen.[10] We feel it is fair to say that both these interpretations are somewhat counter-intuitive.

We now turn to the *verbal* and direct testing of the axioms. It is perhaps interesting to give here the exact formulation chosen. For ETES we asked: 'Do you think that the government has to pay an equal subsidy to

Table 19.3

	ETES	Not ETES
EIER	44.4%	19.8%
Not EIER	20.8%	15.0%

(207 valid responses)

266

all people with the same genetic characteristics, i.e., people with the same innate inclination to become ill?' And EIER was operationalized as follows: 'Medical expenses are not only caused by the illness of individuals, but also by their lifestyle which they can choose to a certain extent themselves. Do you think that people who take the same decisions concerning their lifestyle should bear the same amount of medical expenses themselves?' The results are summarized in Table 19.3 and are not surprising. The acceptance of the ETES/EIER-combination in the explicit questions is high, although somewhat lower than in the numerical part. Here again it is necessary to point out the need for a cautious interpretation: respondents are not always consistent and the tables give only a broad indication of the pattern of the responses.

Income distribution

Let us now turn to the income distribution case, the preferred interpretation of Bossert (1995) and Bossert and Fleurbaey (1996). The numerical results for the additively separable case 3 are shown in Table 19.4. Again the mechanism F^0 yields a division respecting both the axioms ETES and EIER: row B in Table 19.4A. However, the difference with the health case is extremely striking: only a small minority (15 per cent) of the respondents chose this division. In fact, as shown in Table 19.4A and summarized in Table 19.4B, the problem with the compensation framework is worse than that. About 75 per cent of the respondents (indirectly) reject both the axioms ETES and EIER in this setting.

The question immediately arises whether this may have something to do with our interpretation in which individuals are not responsible for their genetic capacities (intelligence) but are responsible for their efforts. As noted before, the latter hypothesis rests on very firm empirical grounds. In fact, those respondents who applied F^0, while judging that individuals should not be remunerated for their efforts, should have chosen an egalitarian income distribution: this choice is made by only 1 per cent of the sample, in line with our hypothesis. But the idea that people have to bear themselves the consequences of differences in intelligence can be expected to occur more often. Such respondents should have kept to the status-quo, when applying F^0: this is done by about 10 per cent of the sample. By and large, while this second interpretation might increase the acceptance of F^0 somewhat, it is certainly not sufficient to 'save' the axioms.

It seems fair to conclude that in the income distribution context more is going on than can be captured in the Bossert/Fleurbaey (1996) approach. But what exactly is going on? Perhaps respondents think in terms of actual income tax systems, where in fact no distinction is made according to the sources of income. Indeed, 18 per cent of the respondents prefer division E, which can be interpreted as a kind of 'progressive' tax system,

Table 19.4A

Row	Axioms	Mechanisms	Results
A		EIER Egalitarian outcome	1.0%
B	ETES+	EIER $F(0) = F(EE) = F(CE) = F(AEE) = F(ACE)$	14.6%
C	ETES		—
D		Mild form of egalitarianism	5.4%
E		Progressivity	18.0%
F			39.0%
G	ETES		—
H	ETES		1.0%
H		EIER	—
H	ETES	No redistribution	9.3%
H	——		11.7%

(205 valid responses)

Table 19.4B

	ETES	Not ETES
EIER	14.6%	1.0%
Not EIER	10.3%	74.1%

where the tax (the amount of redistribution) is only dependent on the overall income level. But the most popular division (by far!) is the one given in row F: it is chosen by almost 40 per cent of the respondents. It is worth looking at this division somewhat more closely.

The division in row F satisfies none of the axioms (in our preferred interpretation of the variables) and it is not the result of a redistribution scheme appearing in the literature. This redistribution remunerates effort in such a way that less intelligent hard workers get a higher transfer than their more intelligent (and equally hard working) colleagues and it taxes the people who work (equally) less hard in such a way that the talented have to pay more tax than the less talented. What results is a widening of the income inequality, without however a reversal in the original ranking of the different individuals. Since the more talented for the same effort level always end up with a higher income, this can not really be seen as an example of 'slavery of the talented'. But nevertheless it is clear that we have an intricate mechanism at work here, where the amount of compensation (for the differences in a^R-variable) is codetermined by the level of the a^S-variable. A closer inspection shows that not only row F has this property, but that many of the added redistribution vectors (included in row H and not shown in the table) are of a similar nature.

Table 19.5A

Row	Axioms		Mechanisms	Results
A		EIER	Egalitarian outcome	0.5%
B	ETES		$F(CE)$ with $\bar{a}^R = 0$	9.8%
C		EIER	$F(AEE)$	5.9%
D				12.2%
E		EIER	$F(EE)$	4.9%
F				32.4%
G	ETES		$F(ACE)$	2.0%
H	ETES			0.5%
H		EIER		0.5%
H	ETES		No redistribution	6.8%
H	——			24.5%

(204 valid responses)

Table 19.5B

	ETES	Not ETES
EIER	——	11.8%
Not EIER	13.1%	69.1%

Given the non-acceptance of the axioms EIER and ETES in the additively separable case, the non-additively separable case loses most of its transparency. However, for the sake of completeness, we show the results in Table 19.5. Again, a large majority of the respondents chooses a division which does not satisfy any of the axioms. The most popular division (row F) does not respect ETES and EIER. It is necessary to be careful with the interpretation: this row F has different features from row F in Table 19.4A.[11] But what is similar to the previous case is the intricate interrelationship between effort and intelligence: again, the lazy but talented individual is punished quite heavily for his laziness.

All of this might perhaps suggest that our respondents introduce incentive considerations into their judgement. The talented are provided with more incentives to work hard than the less talented. Of course, this preliminary interpretation can hardly be justified by the description of the case, in which the absence of behavioural effects of the tax scheme was explicitly mentioned. On the other hand it may be an element for the explanation of the difference between the results in the health- and in the income-setting, since incentive effects surely play a lesser role in the former situation. While we are well aware of the *ad hoc* character of these *ex post* interpretations, one conclusion at least is obvious. The opinions of

269

our respondents concerning income (re)distribution cannot easily be captured into the simple Bossert/Fleurbaey (1996) framework.

The results for the verbal and direct testing of the axioms are summarized in Table 19.6. Here, the formulation chosen was as follows. To test the axiom ETES we asked: 'Do you think that the government should treat people with the same innate talents in the same way, i.e., that they should pay the same amount of taxes or receive the same subsidy?' And for EIER the question was: 'Do you think that people who perform the same effort can claim an equal income?' The results are not in contradiction with the answers on the numerical questions, although they are much less extreme. About half of the respondents rejected both axioms. Only 13 per cent accepted them both. Contrary to the health case the acceptance of the EIER-axiom is larger than the acceptance of ETES. Given the importance of the effort criterion in the commonsense conception of justice in the western world (Elster, 1992), this is hardly surprising.

Table 19.6

	ETES	Not ETES
EIER	12.7%	25.4%
Not EIER	13.2%	48.7%

(207 valid responses)

CONCLUSION

What can be concluded from this empirical work? It is obvious that this study constitutes only a first empirical application of the compensation framework and it remains to be seen whether the results presented here will be confirmed with other samples. Moreover, the results from simple survey questions can never act as a substitute for the refinement of the theoretical thinking. But perhaps they might be inspiring as to the direction which can be chosen for that theoretical work. Two conclusions then seem to stand out.

In the first place: the compensation framework, including the axioms ETES and EIER, has worked rather well for the health case. This is an encouraging finding, certainly when we compare it with the many negative results which have been found in previous empirical papers, including the most influential ones (Yaari and Bar-Hillel, 1984, Amiel and Cowell, 1992). Moreover, the case presented was not a trivial one. Despite the difficulty of the case, our respondents did not opt for easy solutions, such as the proportional or equal distributions. Apparently, the model remains rather close to the moral intuitions of a large part of our respondents.

270

In the second place: the compensation framework did not work well for the income distribution case. This confirms the well-known finding that similar justice considerations may act quite differently in different settings. This is an extremely open-ended conclusion and, although we are aware of the dangers attached to *ex post* interpretation of survey results, we want to go somewhat further. The answers of the respondents suggest that there is an intricate interrelationship between 'desert' criteria (effort) and compensation, which is not easily captured into the simple Bossert/Fleurbaey (1996) framework. Perhaps respondents do not make a clear distinction between 'first best' and 'second best' and are unable to disentangle incentive and compensation considerations. This could explain why the axioms work better in the health setting, for which it can be argued that incentives play a smaller role. If one could accept (at least partly) this interpretation, this surely does not constitute a criticism on the compensation framework as such. Rather it is an argument to go beyond the first-best world and start introducing incentives explicitly.

* A first version of this paper has been prepared for a conference on 'Ethics and Economics of Liberty' at the Université de Cergy-Pontoise (June 1995). The authors thank Lorelei Crisologo, André Watteyne and especially Bart Capéau for their useful suggestions.

NOTES

1 See also Moulin (1994).
2 Bossert and Fleurbaey (1996) give a complete characterization of conditionally egalitarian mechanisms with axioms constituting a weakening of EIER and a strengthening of ETES.
3 Again, Bossert and Fleurbaey (1996) give a complete characterization of egalitarian-equivalent mechanisms with axioms constituting a weakening of ETES and a strengthening of EIER.
4 Application of the mechanisms may lead to a solution with negative c_i's. However, this does not happen in our empirical cases.
5 The complete version of the questionnaire can be found in the appendix.
6 These have not been included in the appendix.
7 All respondents were confronted with all cases. We therefore depart from the 'quasi-experimental' setting in Yaari and Bar-Hillel (1984) and Schokkaert and Overlaet (1988). This choice immediately follows from our research question. We wanted to confront our respondents (as clearly as possible in the description of the numerical cases) with the dilemma of choosing between 'full' and 'strict' compensation in the non-additively separable case. This could best be done by first showing to all of them the additively separable formulation.
8 With the exception of a subset of the generalized average egalitarian-equivalent mechanisms and a subset of the generalized average conditionally egalitarian mechanisms.
9 Note that an easy comparison of Tables 19.1B and 19.2B is somewhat misleading: although in both cases about 20 per cent of the respondents respect neither

ETES nor EIER, these are not necessarily the same respondents! As can be expected, individual response patterns are not always consistent and our results give only the broad lines and should be interpreted cautiously.

10 Theoretically there is also the possibility that a respondent considers individuals to be responsible for their genetic defects, but not responsible for their choice of doctor or of lifestyle. In that case the interpretation of the axioms has to be reversed completely. But this clearly is *not* a plausible interpretation.

11 Since the popularity of row F in case 3 came as a complete surprise to us, we did not propose a similar mechanism in case 4. The exploration of these links is left for later research.

REFERENCES

Amiel, Y. and Cowell, F., 1992, Measurement of income inequality: experimental test by questionnaire, *Journal of Public Economics* 47, 3–26.

Arneson, R., 1989, Equality and equal opportunity for welfare, *Philosophical Studies* 56, 77–93.

Bossert, W., 1995, Redistribution mechanisms based on individual characteristics, *Mathematical Social Sciences* 29, 1–17.

Bossert, W. and Fleurbaey, M., 1996, Redistribution and Compensation, *Social Choice and Welfare* 13, 343–356.

Cohen, G., 1989, On the currency of egalitarian justice, *Ethics* 99, 906–944.

Dworkin, R., 1981, What is equality? Part 1: Equality of Welfare, Part 2: Equality of Resources, *Philosophy and Public Affairs* 10, 185–246 and 283–345.

Elster, J., 1992, *Local Justice* (Cambridge: Cambridge University Press).

Fleurbaey, M., 1994, On fair compensation, *Theory and Decision* 36, 277–307.

Fleurbaey, M., 1995a, Three solutions for the compensation problem, *Journal of Economic Theory* 65, 505–521.

Fleurbaey, M., 1995b, Equality and responsibility, *European Economic Review* 39, 683–689.

Gaertner, W., 1994, Distributive justice: theoretical foundations and empirical findings, *European Economic Review* 38, 711–720.

Moulin, H., 1994, La présence d'envie: comment s'en accomoder?, *Recherches Economiques de Louvain* 60, 63–72.

Roemer, J., 1985, Equality of Talent, *Economics and Philosophy* 1, 151–187.

Roemer, J., 1993, A pragmatic theory of responsibility for the egalitarian planner, *Philosophy and Public Affairs* 22, 146–166.

Schokkaert, E. and Capéau, B., 1991, Interindividual differences in opinions about distributive justice, *Kyklos* 44, 325–345.

Schokkaert, E. and Lagrou, L., 1983, An empirical approach to distributive justice, *Journal of Public Economics* 21, 33–52.

Schokkaert, E. and Overlaet, B., 1988, Moral intuitions and economic models of distributive justice, *Social Choice and Welfare* 6, 19–31.

Sen, A., 1985, *Commodities and Capabilities* (Amsterdam: North-Holland).

Sen, A., 1992, *Inequality Reexamined* (Oxford: Clarendon Press).

Yaari, M. and Bar-Hillel, M., 1984, On dividing justly, *Social Choice and Welfare* 1, 1–24.

APPENDIX: QUESTIONNAIRE

This questionnaire has two parts. Please complete part one before you look at part two. We ask you to change nothing in the first part after you have started part two. Your answers would become completely useless for us and you will not gain or lose anything by changing them.

This questionnaire will look at some attitudes towards justice and redistribution. We will do this at the hand of some hypothetical cases. We are interested in *your* insights! Because these cases deal with attitudes, there are no 'right' or 'wrong' answers. Your answers will clarify axioms which appear in the economic literature and of which we do not know if they prevail under the population. Please do not write your name on this questionnaire.

Part One

1 Chris, John, Tim and Tom suffer from similar effects of lung cancer. The total cost for a successful cure is 350 for Chris, 200 for John, 300 for Tim and 150 for Tom. The total costs are composed as follows. To help Tim and Tom the cost for the basic cure is 150 each. To help Chris and John the cost for the basic treatment is 200 each, due to their lower natural resistance against cancer. Chris and John have a genetic defect and therefore need additional treatment. This is not necessary for Tim and Tom. There is also a second reason for the difference in costs. Tim and Chris have chosen a very expensive doctor, which costs them each 150 extra. Tom and John have not chosen such an expensive doctor. We suppose that all treatments are effective. The government has to divide 500 for the treatments among these patients and wants to spend this amount completely. What would you consider to be a just division of this amount of money? Place an asterisk '*' in the box at the back of the row you prefer. In row H you can add your own distribution of the government money.

273

	Chris		John		Tim		Tom	
	Expensive doctor Genetically weak		Normal doctor Genetically weak		Expensive doctor Genetically strong		Normal doctor Genetically strong	
	Govern.	Chris	Govern.	John	Govern.	Tim	Govern.	Tom
A	100	250	150	50	100	200	150	0
B	125	225	125	75	125	175	125	25
C	150	200	150	50	100	200	100	50
D	150	200	100	100	150	150	100	50
E	175	175	100	100	150	150	75	75
F	200	150	100	100	150	150	50	100
G	225	125	75	125	175	125	25	125
H								

2 Bart, Bert, Hans and Henk suffer from similar effects of lung cancer. The total cost for a successful cure is 650 for Bart, 400 for Bert, 350 for Hans and 200 for Henk. The total costs are composed as follows. To help Bart and Bert the cost for a basic cure is 400 each, due to their lower natural resistance against cancer. Bart and Bert have a genetic defect and need additional treatment. Hans and Henk do not need such additional treatment. The cost of the basic treatment for Hans and Henk is 200 each. But there is a second reason for the difference in costs. Bart and Hans have a very extravagant lifestyle (long wild nights, smoking, drinking, exuberant meals, drugs). This lifestyle makes it more difficult to treat cancer especially if the natural resistance against lung cancer is already low. For this reason Bart's treatment costs an additional 250. The treatment for Hans only costs an additional 150. Bert and Henk do not have such a lifestyle. They do not need additional treatment and therefore have no extra costs. We suppose that all treatments are effective. The government has to divide 500 for the treatments among these patients and wants to spend this amount completely. What would you consider to be a just division of this amount of money? Place an asterisk '*' in the box at the back of the row you prefer. In row H you can add your own distribution of the government money.

	Bart (Wild Genetically weak)		Bert (Normal Genetically weak)		Hans (Wild Genetically strong)		Henk (Normal Genetically strong)		
	Govern.	Bart	Govern.	Bert	Govern.	Hans	Govern.	Henk	
A	375	275	125	275	75	275	−75	275	
B	225	425	225	175	25	325	25	175	
C	275	375	225	175	−25	375	25	175	
D	325	325	125	275	75	275	−25	225	
E	300	350	200	200	0	350	0	200	
F	125	525	125	275	125	225	125	75	
G	250	400	250	150	0	350	0	200	
H									

3 Ann, Anna, Barbara and Babette are employed in a similar job. The total labour income is 350 for Barbara, 200 for Babette, 300 for Ann and 150 for Anna. The individual labour income is composed as follows. Barbara and Babette receive a basic income of 200 each for their labour. Due to their lower productivity Ann and Anna receive a lower basic income of 150 per person. These differences in productivity result from differences in innate intelligence: Barbara and Babette are more intelligent than Ann and Anna. The situation is complicated by the fact that Barbara and Ann are hard workers and therefore have a higher productivity. This extra productivity is remunerated with an extra income of 150 each. Babette and Anna are lazy and do not have this extra productivity. They do not receive an extra income. The government wants to redistribute the income of these four people. The knowledge that there will be a redistribution does not change the behaviour of the individuals. What would you consider to be a just redistribution? The given numbers are the received subsidy (+) or the paid tax (−). The numbers between brackets stand for the post-redistribution income. Please place an asterisk '*' in the box of your choice. In row H you can add your own redistribution.

	Barbara		Babette		Ann		Anna	
	Effort Intelligent		Less effort Intelligent		Effort Not intelligent		Less effort Not intelligent	
A	−100	(250)	+50	(250)	−50	(250)	+100	(250)
B	−25	(325)	−25	(175)	+25	(325)	+25	(175)
C	−50	(300)	−50	(150)	+50	(350)	+50	(200)
D	−75	(275)	+50	(250)	−25	(275)	+50	(200)
E	−50	(300)	+25	(225)	−25	(275)	+50	(200)
F	+25	(375)	−50	(150)	+50	(350)	−25	(125)
G	−100	(250)	−100	(100)	+100	(400)	+100	(250)
H								

4 Paul, Peter, Jan and Karel are employed in a similar job. The total labour income is 650 for Paul, 400 for Peter, 350 for Jan and 200 for Karel. The individual labour income is composed as follows. Paul and Peter receive a basic income of 400 each for their labour. Due to their lower productivity Jan and Karel receive a lower basic income of 200 per person. These differences in productivity result from differences in innate intelligence: Paul and Peter are more intelligent than Jan and Karel. The situation is complicated by the fact that Paul and Jan are motivated and hard workers. Each week, they work 5 hours more than Peter and Karel. For these additional hours Paul receives 250 extra. Due to his lower productivity Jan only earns 150 extra for his additional effort. Peter and Karel are lazy and do not work additional hours. They do not receive an extra income. The government wants to redistribute the income of these four people. The knowledge that there will be a redistribution does not change the behaviour of the individuals. What would you consider to be a just redistribution? The given numbers are the received subsidy (+) or the paid tax (−). The numbers between brackets stand for the post-redistribution income. Please place an asterisk '*' in the box of your choice. In row H you can add your own redistribution.

ACCEPTANCE OF COMPENSATION AXIOMS

	Paul		Peter		Jan		Karel		
	Effort Intelligent		Less effort Intelligent		Effort Not intelligent		Less effort Not intelligent		
A	−250	(400)	0	(400)	+50	(400)	+200	(400)	
B	−100	(550)	−100	(300)	+100	(450)	+100	(300)	
C	−150	(500)	−100	(300)	+150	(500)	+100	(300)	
D	−200	(450)	0	(400)	+50	(400)	+150	(350)	
E	−175	(475)	−75	(325)	+125	(475)	+125	(325)	
F	−50	(600)	−150	(250)	+150	(500)	+50	(250)	
G	−125	(525)	−125	(275)	+125	(475)	+125	(325)	
H									

Part Two

Now we start the second part, in which we will check in a more direct way your ideas about justice and redistribution. There are no 'right' or 'wrong' answers. It is important for us that you do not change anything in the previous pages.

5) Do you think that the government has to pay an equal subsidy to all people with the same genetic characteristics, i.e. people with the same innate inclination to become ill?
yes ☐ go to question 9
no ☐ go to question 6

6) Medical expenses are not only caused by the illness of individuals, but also by their lifestyle which they can choose to a certain extent themselves. Do you think that people who take the same decisions concerning their lifestyle should bear the same amount of medical expenses?
yes ☐ go to question 14
no ☐ go to question 7

7) Look at your answer to question 1. Which reasoning have you followed to come to your decision?

....

go then to question 8

277

8) Look at your answer to question 2. Which reasoning have you followed to come to your decision?

....

    go then to question 18

9) Look at your answer to question 1. Have you chosen row B or C?
yes ☐   go to question 11
no ☐   go to question 10

10) If you have not chosen row B or C in question 1, this means that you have given either Chris and John or Tim and Tom a different subsidy although they have the same genetic constitution. Are you now inclined to change your answer on question 1?
yes ☐   new choice = . . .   go then to question 11
no ☐   why not? . . .

    go then to question 11

11) Look at your answer to question 2. Have you chosen row B, F or G?
yes ☐   go to question 13
no ☐   go to question 12

12) If you have not chosen B, F or G in question 2, this means that you have given either Bart and Bert or Hans and Henk a different subsidy although they have the same genetic constitution. Are you now inclined to change your answer?
yes ☐   new choice = . . .   go then to question 13
no ☐   why not? . . .

    go then to question 13

13) Medical expenses are not only caused by the illness of individuals, but also by their lifestyle, which they can choose to a certain extent themselves. Do you think that people who take the same decisions concerning their lifestyle should bear the same amount of medical expenses?
yes ☐   go to question 14
no ☐   go to question 18

14) Look at your answer to question 1. Have you chosen row C, F or G?
yes ☐   go to question 16
no ☐   go to question 15

15) If you have not chosen row C, F or G in question 1, this means that according to your intuition either John and Tom or Chris and Tim have to bear a different amount of the medical expenses, although they have the same lifestyle. Are you now inclined to change your answer on question 1?

yes ☐   new choice = . . .   go then to question 16
no ☐   why not? . . .

go then to question 16

16) Look at your answer to question 2. Have you chosen row A, C or E?
yes ☐   go to question 18
no ☐   go to question 17

17) If you have not chosen A, C or E in question 2, this means that according to your intuition either both Bart and Hans or both Bert and Henk have to bear a different amount of the medical expenses, although they have the same lifestyle. Are you now inclined to change your answer on question 2?

yes ☐   new choice = . . .   go then to question 18
no ☐   why not? . . .

go then to question 18

18) Do you think that the government should treat people with the same innate talents in the same way, i.e. that they pay the same taxes or receive the same subsidy?
yes ☐   go to question 22
no ☐   go to question 19

19) Do you think that people who perform the same effort can claim an equal income?
yes ☐   go to question 27
no ☐   go to question 20

20) Look at your answer to question 3. Which reasoning have you followed to come to your decision?

....

go then to question 21

21) Look at your answer to question 4. Which reasoning have you followed to come to your decision?

....

go then to question 31

279

22) Look at your answer to question 3. Have you chosen row B, C or G?
yes ☐   go to question 24
no ☐   go to question 23

23) If you have not chosen row B, C or G in question 3, this means that according to your intuition either Babette and Barbara or Ann and Anna have to pay different taxes (or receive a different subsidy), although they have the same innate talents. Are you now inclined to change your answer on question 3?
yes ☐   new choice = . . .   go then to question 24
no ☐   why not? . . .

go then to question 24

24) Look at your answer to question 4. Have you chosen row B or G?
yes ☐   go to question 26
no ☐   go to question 25

25) If you have not chosen row B or G in question 4, this means that according to your intuition either Paul and Peter or Jan and Karel have to pay different taxes (or receive a different subsidy), although they have the same innate talents. Are you now inclined to change your answer on question 4?
yes ☐   new choice = . . .   go then to question 26
no ☐   why not? . . .

go then to question 26

26) Do you think that people who perform the same effort can claim an equal income?
yes ☐   go to question 27
no ☐   go to question 31

27) Look at your answer to question 3. Have you chosen row A or B?
yes ☐   go to question 29
no ☐   go to question 28

28) If you have not chosen A or B in question 3, this means that according to your intuition either Barbara and Ann or Babette and Anna receive a different income, although they perform the same effort. Are you now inclined to change your answer to question 3?
yes ☐   new choice = . . .   go then to question 29
no ☐   why not? . . .

go then to question 29

29) Look at your answer to question 4. Have you chosen row A, C or E?

    yes ☐   go to question 31

    no ☐   go to question 30

30) If you have not chosen A, C or E in question 4, this means that according to your intuition either Paul and Jan or Peter and Karel receive a different income, although they perform the same effort. Are you now inclined to change your answer to question 4?

    yes ☐   new choice = . . .   go then to question 31

    no ☐   why not? . . .

        go then to question 31

31) Thank you for your co-operation!

20

COMMENTS ON 'THE EMPIRICAL ACCEPTANCE OF COMPENSATION AXIOMS'

Walter Bossert

There is now a growing body of literature that deals with the question of how *responsibility* should be taken into account in the design of redistribution policies based on principles of justice and fairness. So far, most of the contributions to this debate have been theoretical in nature and have provided discussions of the ethical foundations of selective redistribution mechanisms. The purpose of a selective redistribution mechanism is, in this context, to correct for individual characteristics that are deemed *irrelevant* (such as characteristics for which an agent cannot be held responsible) while preserving the effects of *relevant* characteristics (characteristics that can be controlled by the agent). Thus, the objective is to compensate for disparities that are caused by factors outside the agents' control and, at the same time, preserve differences that come about through the influence of factors for which the agents can be held responsible. Different value judgements that express specific notions of justice or fairness in this context are often formulated as *axioms* – properties that are considered desirable for a selective redistribution mechanism.

Schokkaert and Devooght's paper complements some of these theoretical studies by examining empirical aspects of this issue. In particular, the primary purpose of the paper is to investigate whether the respondents of a questionnaire study share the view that certain properties of redistribution mechanisms that have been introduced in the literature are desirable. As is usually the case in studies of that nature, the subjects are selected in a way that is supposed to guarantee that they have not been exposed to scholarly debates on the issue in question before – the intention is to get the responses of representatives of the general non-expert public. This methodology has been used in other areas as well. For example, there are studies that examine the acceptance of distributional principles in the absence of responsibility considerations in the theory of income inequality measurement (see Schokkaert and Devooght's paper for references). The experimental study carried out by Schokkaert and Devooght is well-documented, and the authors explain their methodology very well in the paper. Therefore, rather than going into details concerning this particular study, I will focus my comments on a discussion of what can be learned from such empirical studies in normative economics and ethics in general, and how they fit into the research programme under consideration.

Let me first summarize what I think those experimental studies cannot be expected to achieve. One possible interpretation of the results of those questionnaire studies that is sometimes put forward is to view them as 'tests' of the plausibility of the ethical value judgements underlying the properties that the subjects in the experiments are asked to (directly or indirectly) express opinions about. If a majority of respondents do not agree with a given ethical value judgement (formulated, for instance, in the form of a property that is deemed desirable for a redistribution mechanism), it is sometimes concluded that this constitutes a weakness of the notion of justice expressed by this axiom. Similarly, if there is broad support for a principle among the respondents of the survey, this is taken as an argument in favour of the principle in question.

The above interpretation rests, in my opinion, on a rather weak conceptual foundation. We cannot expect to settle ethical issues in a satisfactory manner by having a 'vote' among uninformed individuals. Rather, the arguments that are used for and against the principle in question have to be examined carefully. The mere observation that a large number of respondents without much knowledge of the issue under consideration reject a moral principle provides no reason to abandon the principle. A valid argument against an ethical principle would have to be based on a thorough assessment of the arguments that are being put forward in favour of the principle. By the same token, being widely accepted among the subjects without providing convincing arguments in favour of adopting a principle is not a sufficient reason to declare the principle in question a 'good' one. Essential ingredients of a debate over normative issues are critical reflection and thorough assessment of the arguments being used. Though there may, of course, still be abundant room for disagreement and, in the end, decisions may very well be made by putting the matter to a vote, it could hardly be considered reasonable to have this vote without first examining and discussing the arguments for and against. Therefore, empirical studies that assess the extent to which ethical principles are accepted among an uninformed group of respondents will not allow us to evaluate the value of the principle itself: merely counting the number of favourable and non-favourable responses tells us nothing about the arguments that were (explicitly or implicitly) used by respondents in arriving at their conclusions.

On the other hand, there undoubtedly is a need to go beyond a discussion of the theoretical aspects of matters regarding social justice, such as selective redistribution. Ultimately, the principles of justice that are being studied and advocated on the basis of their ethical merits are intended to be put into practice. It is a common observation that even principles which can be supported by strong ethical arguments can take a rather long time to be implemented by policy makers because of a lack of public support. This observation is what makes empirical studies important complements to theoretical considerations. Even though, in the long run, it is desirable to settle debates on issues regarding social justice in terms of an informed discussion and on the basis of the validity of the arguments that can be presented, it is important to realize that this process takes place over (possibly a long period of) time, and that compromises have to be sought in the short run. The acceptability of redistributive policies among the general public is an important criterion when it comes to establishing what are the policies that may be implementable. Thoughtful experimental studies such as the one carried out by Schokkaert and Devooght play an important role in identifying the compromises that are feasible in the sense that one can expect them to have sufficient public support. This is what I consider the main contribution of these studies in general, and in the case of the paper by Schokkaert and Devooght, the authors have succeeded in providing a very valuable addition to the relevant literature.

Let me conclude with a suggestion for further research. I think much could be learned from complementing the experimental studies involving uninformed individuals with studies that examine to what extent individuals can be persuaded by arguments that are provided in favour of ethical principles. This may give us a better idea of what can actually be achieved if a public debate takes place, rather than restricting attention to what is immediately acceptable even without any discussion. I appreciate that the intention of choosing non-expert individuals is to get answers that are not influenced by prior 'conditioning' but, on the other hand, this approach may underestimate the potential acceptance of ethical principles. If more information in the form of solid arguments were provided, the respondents might look more favorably upon many principles that they would reject if asked to make a less informed judgement.

SUBJECT INDEX

NAME INDEX